'*Up from the Mission* is among the most ___
I have read in recent years … Pearson's analysis is blisteringly
compelling' —WALEED ALY, *The Sunday Age*

'Pearson is a master of the essay as a literary form … [*Up from the
Mission*] is a serious contribution to Australian letters'
—PETER SUTTON, *The Monthly*

'Noel Pearson is the best political and social essayist in the country'
—MICHAEL GAWENDA, *Crikey*

'Noel Pearson is, I suspect, an historic figure … *Up from the Mission*
is the most engaging book on Australian politics I have read since
Mark Latham's diaries' —MARTIN FLANAGAN, *The Age*

'A powerhouse of a book' —JON ALTMAN, *Australian Book Review*

'Noel Pearson is the most influential intellectual in Australia'
—JOHN HIRST, *The Australian Literary Review*

'An exciting, even electrifying, read' —EVE VINCENT, *New Matilda*

'Compelling and convincing … Recommended to every Australian'
—IAN NICHOLS, *West Weekend*

'[Pearson] explores uncomfortable social and indigenous issues,
offering solutions where many people opt for despair or apathy
… Illuminating' —BLANCHE CLARK, *The Herald Sun*

'[*Up from the Mission*] not only displays the lawyer and advocate's
incisive thinking … but also an ability to write elegantly, with
clarity, and with controlled passion' —ROSEMARY SORENSEN,
The Australian

UP FROM THE MISSION

NOEL PEARSON

UP FROM THE MISSION

SELECTED WRITINGS

Published by Black Inc.
an imprint of Schwartz Media Pty Ltd
Level 5, 289 Flinders Lane
Melbourne Victoria 3000 Australia
email: enquiries@blackincbooks.com
http://www.blackincbooks.com

The National Library of Australia Cataloguing-in-Publication entry:

Pearson, Noel, 1965-

Up from the mission : selected writings / Noel Pearson.

ISBN: 9781863954280 (pbk.)

Includes index.

Aboriginal Australians--Government relations.
Public welfare--Australia. Leadership. Radicalism.
Australia--Politics and government.

323.119915

Book design: Thomas Deverall
Edited by Jan Arvid Götesson
Typeset by J&M Typesetting Pty Ltd
Index by Michael Ramsden

Printed in Australia by McPherson's Printing Group

CONTENTS

For my late parents, Glen and Ivy Pearson

INTRODUCTION

In the dying months of his prime ministership in 2007, I initiated a conversation with John Howard about Australia's great leaders and how one might rank them. Inspired by Dick Morris's account, in his book *Behind the Oval Office,* of the ranking system for the presidents of the United States he had devised with Bill Clinton, I proposed that Australia had never had an indisputable first-tier leader. Such leaders are forged in extraordinary circumstances ('people who do great things in great times'), such as national liberation, war and catastrophe. While Australian prime ministers had certainly acquitted themselves well through such periods in the nation's history, none was in the same league as Washington, Jefferson, Lincoln, Wilson or FDR.

I proposed Curtin to be a third-tier leader. My second-tier Australian leaders were Menzies, Hawke, Keating and Howard; whether they ranked as 2(a) or 2(b), I left as a matter for debate. The then prime minister made two responses. Firstly, he would add Deakin to my list. Secondly, he rated Hawke most highly among his Labor opponents: winning and holding power was surely a prerequisite of great leadership.

It was a rare opportunity to speak with a serving prime minister about his place in history. I came to form close relationships with two of the most diametrically opposed of our national leaders: Keating and Howard. Over time my perspective on Howard changed from visceral antipathy in the first years of his prime ministership to an abiding respect, which was neither grudging nor unqualified. His long-serving chief of staff, Arthur Sinodinos, said something to me about Howard that I could understand: his boss was someone for whom his respect grew the longer he worked for him. The longer I worked with Howard, the more he grew in my estimation.

Howard would surely not agree with my assessment of Keating. If one were permitted to take into account the pre-prime ministerial record of Australia's great leaders, then the case for Paul Keating as our sole first-tier leadership contender is compelling. His record as treasurer, the situation faced by the nation in 1983, the tectonic shifts he brought about in the economy, the relentless championing of these reforms, both through Cabinet and to the Australian electorate in an extraordinary partnership with a popular and populist prime minister, are only discernible in retrospect. Keating had the intellectual analysis. He had imagination. He had an agenda. He had style.

These attributes were necessary, but not sufficient. Keating also had the political skills – particularly at close quarters – that enabled him alternately to persuade, intellectually dominate, seduce and bludgeon the people whose support he needed to achieve his aims. The personal grasp of power, not just in the political domain but also in his capacity to command the machinery of government, was his forte. Many leaders become the nominal leaders of their governments, but few actually *govern*. Howard and Keating seem to me to be leaders who governed the machinery: they were not just titular heads of the Leviathan of power. And Keating had the oratory (*ex tempore* he is still without peer, chiefly because of his love of words, sharpened by many years spent hammering them into swords at the anvils of political argument).

The thing about Keating's thirteen years is that he didn't just have a reform agenda; he turned the agenda into *reality*. This is the true measure of leadership: not just the assumption of power, but the use of it.

I believed during Keating's prime ministership that the foundations of my people's freedom were being laid down through a fair compromise between our original ownership of the land and the colonists' irreversible accumulation of rights.

The recognition of Indigenous Australians' place in the nation became part of Keating's agenda through a series of events culminating in the High Court's *Mabo* judgment in 1992. It is testament to Keating's greatness that Indigenous policy during his prime ministership was not merely reactive. Almost certainly, the Labor Party under any other leader would have aimed to manage this policy area pragmatically, which inevitably was fraught with electoral danger. I believe that the highest ideals on Earth are realised when leaders strive to secure them through close attention to reality. I know no better example of this than Paul Keating's leadership for Indigenous justice.

Not that Keating embarked on his political career with the idealistic ambition to free the Aborigines, any more than Lincoln set out to emancipate the slaves. Great leadership emerges when leaders of sufficient calibre contend with conflicts between opposing interests in the complexity of the real world. Some leaders achieve their lasting legacy under the compulsion of external forces as much as internal imperatives.

John Howard had the potential to become a great Australian leader. Of course, after the Coalition's victory in 1996, I thought everything was lost. But following Kim Beazley's failure to take his opportunities in the 1998 election, I started to reassess the situation.

First, I admitted that the Left had never faced up to Indigenous social disintegration and the question of Indigenous responsibility. Aboriginal disadvantage was attributed to the effects of dispossession and discrimination. This explanation was, of course, partially correct, particularly when it came to the historical antecedents of contemporary social and economic problems. However, a historical understanding of dispossession and racism was not the central insight needed to turn the disaster around. This explanation of our problems did not necessarily produce solutions.

The second process of reassessment that was forced on me by the conservative ascendancy was the realisation that Indigenous people couldn't rely on one side of politics alone – the Left – to reach a fair settlement. Here I learnt most from the late Ron Castan QC AM, with whom I shared the belief that *Mabo* needed to be followed by a formal and lasting settlement between Indigenous and non-indigenous Australians. The starting point for any consideration of such a settlement must be this: it requires a majority of voters in a majority of the states to amend the Australian Constitution. That is, it requires the support of 80 to 90 per cent of the Australian people. In order to have any chance of securing this level of support, the proposal will need bipartisan political support – and furthermore, in the case of an amendment concerning Indigenous peoples, it will have to be championed by the conservative political parties if it is to have any chance of success. And not only championed by the conservative parties – a Liberal leader in the mould of Howard, who can carry the rural as well as the urban conservative constituency, will also be needed. I realised that if it were not going to be the present-day Howard, a Howard of the future would be needed to champion such a settlement.

It was clear to me that Howard had been truly pained by his failures in the matter of reconciliation, both at the symbolic level – he was famously rejected by the Indigenous audience who turned their backs on him at the Reconciliation Convention in Melbourne in 1997 – and in terms of practical achievement. He had once nominated water and salinity issues and Aboriginal disadvantage as the two most important areas where his government – and previous governments – had failed to make any progress.

My respect for Howard grew over the years, but not because I thought his government's Indigenous policies were outstanding. The conservatives' policies were often misguided and inept, and I was bitterly opposed to the Howard government's native title policies, which remain the most important source of Indigenous Australians' distrust of the conservatives. But no government will deliver salvation for us – we must take our rightful place in our own country through a more complicated and arduous process than the forces of good finally winning government and passing legislation that restores to us our lost heritage.

I saw Howard's potential to lead the nation to the necessary syntheses of Indigenous rights and responsibilities, and of the symbolic and practical in Indigenous affairs. Many Indigenous Australians cannot follow me here. But I believed Howard would be able to rise to the challenge of providing leadership on reconciliation and thereby transcend the traditional position of the conservatives.

In the lead-up to the 2007 election, in a letter to the prime minister, I put forward a three-part program by which Howard might change Australia fundamentally but prudently, so that the country moved:

1. From symbolic and practical reconciliation to the recognition of Indigenous people within a reconciled, indivisible nation;
2. From a repudiational republic (which is Australia's current default direction) to an affirmational republic; and
3. From a welfare state to an opportunity state.

I told him that the conservatives' position on reconciliation was to some extent an understandable reaction to the repudiation of Australia's British heritage and the blanket condemnation of the history of European settlement. However, I also argued that the government's practical reconciliation policies were inadequate. They would not solve the social and economic problems and would not achieve reconciliation; his government was too unwilling to recognise the importance of culture and identity to Indigenous Australians.

Successful reconciliation, I pointed out, is a prerequisite for the development of a confident Australian identity. Australia is built on two foundation stones: one is the Indigenous heritage; the other, laid on top of that, is the British heritage. The great Australian migration success story was built on these twin foundations.

I suggested that there are not just two options for Australia's constitutional future: the existing situation or a repudiational republic. In reality there are three models: in the middle is the *affirmational* republic. In such a republic, it will be declared unequivocally that the head of state is an Australian, but there will be no need to repudiate continuing ties with the Crown or with Britain. The affirmational republic, I suggested, is the optimal constitutional framework for a reconciled Australia. It would satisfy a large majority of Australians – moderate republicans and conservatives – and it would allow proper recognition of Indigenous Australians' special place as the First Australians.

The third idea I discussed with Howard – moving from a welfare state to an 'opportunity state' – is an extension to the Australian mainstream of the ideas we have developed in Cape York to combat poverty. Poverty, we believe, is a four-sided problem, involving four basic needs: an income, education for children, health care and shelter – the family home.

The problem is that the welfare state has come to treat poverty as an endlessly faceted problem. A vast panoply of secondary programs has been developed. Australia needs to put the focus back on what is primary, namely the bread-and-butter issues of family functioning: income, health, education and housing. If disadvantaged families live in safe and ordered neighbourhoods and have their four primary needs secured, they will have the old working-class uplift formula back together again. The Australian opportunity state – Howard corrected this formulation by referring to an 'opportunity society' rather than a state – must guarantee these four basic needs. Our welfare reforms in Cape York are a pioneering attempt to show how government and society can support individuals and families by providing them with opportunity, rather than delivering them passive welfare.

While prime minister, John Howard moved on the first of my propositions and committed to one of my suggestions for constitutional change: to recognise Indigenous people's special status in the preamble to the Constitution. (My second suggested constitutional amendment was that the Commonwealth be given jurisdiction to make laws 'with respect to the cultural, social and economic development of Aboriginal and Torres Strait Islander peoples and the achievement of reconciliation between Indigenous and non-indigenous Australians'.) Howard's commitment to symbolic recognition has been dismissed as meaningless by his detractors, but I believe that it is a lasting gain that Australia's most conservative leader put this on the agenda.

By and large, however, my hope that Howard would be able to move Australia towards a resolution of the tensions caused by Indigenous dispossession was unfulfilled. I believe an opportunity was lost for dialogue between Indigenous leaders and Howard during the second half of his tenure. A window in history opened in the lead-up to and in the wake of the 2004 election, which a more coherent and hard-headed Indigenous leadership would have seized.

*

Upon reading this collection of my texts, the reader will see that my 2007 advice to Howard is a distillation of the questions that have preoccupied me all my adult life. The first few pieces sketch my people's existence under the so-called protection of Queensland's discriminatory *Aborigines Act*. The theme of *Fighting Old Enemies* is the struggle against Australia's unutterably shameful legacy of oppression – foremost the denial of our ownership of our land.

However, my doubts that the radical consensus on Indigenous issues was correct are obvious already in my first published text, *Peoples of the North: Anthropology and Tradition* (which was then publicly attributed to my co-author and mentor from my hometown, the late Mervyn Gibson), from 1987. From 1999 onwards, I challenged the Left's inability to understand that self-determination is not only a question of Indigenous rights – it is also the right to take responsibility.

The fourth section, *The Quest for a Radical Centre*, roughly coincides with the last five or so years, when we have started to implement policies designed to move our communities away from the passive welfare economy in Cape York Peninsula. Most of my writings have been about policy detail in the areas of substance abuse, welfare reform, employment, housing, education and so on. Almost all of those texts have been left out of this book, to avoid burdening the reader with detail. The tilt towards commentary and theory in this selection thus partly obscures the fact that my main occupation in the last decade has been working with my colleagues in Cape York to get legislation through, get funding for programs and implement reforms.

I believe this is what sets my home region apart from other Indigenous regions in Australia: we precipitate state and Commonwealth legislation that otherwise would not exist. We have not just been commentators, we have not just been reacting to government policy. We have driven reform arguments and sought to frame legislation.

The reform agenda in Cape York could not have been developed without an intense engagement with Australia's and Queensland's political leadership. The thing about Cape York that most alienates many Indigenous leaders is our determination to engage at the highest level of political responsibility. But I don't think Indigenous Australia has any choice. I will never forget Paul Keating's words from 1993, when his negotiations with Indigenous leaders had broken down on what the media dubbed 'Black Friday'. His pointed stab at the heart of our weakness was as follows:

I am not sure whether Indigenous leaders can ever psychologically make the change to decide to come into a process, be part of it and take the burden of responsibility which goes with it. That is, whether they believe they can ever summon the authority of their own community to negotiate … on their behalf.

My assessment is that many Indigenous leaders continue to choose the strategy – if it can be called such – of perpetual commentary and opposition, rather than trying to get governments to do what they want them to do. The political scientist Patrick Sullivan once observed that the great political card held by Indigenous people is the power to say 'No'. The ability to withhold consent can indeed be a source of power, but it has become virtually the only item in what is a thin repertoire. Whatever our mistakes in Cape York Peninsula, we have long refused just to say 'No' while governments walk straight over the top of us.

Freedom for our people will not come as a result of progressive governments giving us our rights back or enacting 'social justice'. We will be free when we take back our right to take responsibility.

Noel Pearson

THE MISSION

FOREBEARS

Speech to the National Reconciliation Conference

It was astounding to me when I went to university in the 1980s to read a doctoral thesis by an anthropologist who had come to my mission in the early 1960s and interviewed my aunts and grandfathers and people whom I grew up with and loved, who asked her: 'Is there any foundation to the suggestion that perhaps we as a people are somehow the missing link between humanity and the ape kingdom?'

It was, for me, testament to the fact that the notion of Aboriginal inhumanity was indeed embedded in popular belief, particularly in regional Australia. That legacy lives on. There is still in the Australian community a lingering suspicion about that inhumanity.

But we have made a great deal of progress, and that progress started to steamroll after 1967. It took ten years to convince the Australian community to vote overwhelmingly to include Indigenous people in the Commonwealth.

And of course, the subsequent struggles at Wave Hill, the Tent Embassy, Noonkanbah and the 1982 Commonwealth Games, and the struggle by Eddie Mabo, gathered pace. And we made progress, the like of which our founding fathers, William Cooper, Jack Ferguson and Jack Patten, perhaps had the imagination to believe was possible, but which they could never have believed would happen easily and would happen in time.

Let me tell you about my personal views on citizenship. Like many Indigenous people in this country, I am equivocal about my Australian citizenship. I don't think I have embraced my Australian citizenship; let me express some of the reasons why I harbour this equivocation.

My great-grandfather Arrimi was a Kuku Warra man, whose people were almost entirely annihilated in the wake of the Cooktown to Palmer River goldrush from the 1870s. This was one of the bloodiest episodes in the colonial occupation of this continent. He eventually died, a fringe-dweller on the outskirts of Cooktown, during the Second World War. My father and grandfather told me that he spent all of his adult life evading the police. They wanted to take him to Palm Island or to Yarrabah or to Cherbourg. They wanted him to be part of the history of stolen generations, and he utterly and absolutely refused to submit to this European law.

So his identity was entirely the traditional identity of the Kuku Warra people prior to the British acquisition of sovereignty over this country. For him, whatever had legally and symbolically happened in 1788 in Sydney Cove had no relevance to his identity and to his person.

My grandfather Ngulunhthul, also known as Charlie, was taken away as a ten-year-old to the Cape Bedford Lutheran Mission at the turn of the century. And his identity gathered a layer that his father didn't have. That layer was the identity of a mission Aborigine in a new community of children who were the victims of a diaspora spreading from Winton in central Queensland to the tip of the Cape York Peninsula.

The mission community was a gathering of young strangers that developed an identity of its own. So my grandfather took on a new mission identity and a new Aboriginal identity; he became a Guugu Yimithirr-speaking Aborigine and adopted the language and culture of the people onto whose land he was relocated. And he became a stockman.

My father was also a stockman, and he also grew up in the Hope Valley Lutheran Mission and inherited the identity of my grandfather. I have to say that in all of the years I spent with them, I could never really say how they felt about being Queenslanders and about being Australians. I never heard from them any rejection of those layers of identity, but I expect that it did not mean all that much to them.

Indeed, if they felt connected to anything outside the mission, it was to the church community to which they belonged: the wider Lutheran church in which they shared faith.

For my part, I spent only two years as a constitutional alien before the 1967 referendum was passed. And I inherited the identity of my father and grandfather. I also inherited their equivocal feelings about our place beyond the mission.

I went down, harbouring this equivocation, to a Lutheran secondary school in Brisbane. I suppose the thing that most tipped me towards being enthusiastic about being a Queenslander, and then about being an Australian, was seeing successful Aboriginal sportsmen. And nobody filled me with pride so much as the Ella brothers. It started to make sense to me why being an Australian might not be such a bad thing. I don't know whether this was ever their intention, but that was the result.

1997

FAMILY

Though my mission home on the eastern Cape York Peninsula, where I grew up in the late '60s and '70s, was materially poor, I was aware from an early age that my family and community were in fact the source of great wealth. Even while I read, by the light of a kerosene lamp in our small fibro house, the only available literature – the Holy Bible, books about Martin Luther and tracts prosecuting his cause (which was of course now the cause of my community, my father's cause and indeed my own) – I knew I had it good. Even though all there was to eat on most days was green tripe, fresh out of the bowels of bullocks my father slaughtered for the local butcher shop, or a thin soup of fat, onions and bones with small strips of meat and gristle, which we would gnaw desperately out of the crevices, I thought I had the best life as a kid.

When we went for visits to the hospital in the white town of Cooktown on the back of the mission truck, we would observe the unofficial apartheid and follow my mother and the other women down to the park next to the café, where we could have lunch away from the main street. The contempt and paternalism of the whites and the deference and humiliation of adult people who happened to be black – at the mission to some degree, but more so in the world outside – disturbed my young soul. But I took it as the natural order of the world outside my home.

The world outside my home was a daunting place, promising episodes of shame and humiliation. One of my brothers had explicitly warned me about it before I went away to college. People at home told joking stories about their experiences amongst the whitefellas, and though they laughed about it now, these incidents were obviously not so funny at the time; the laughter was a way of dealing with the pain and anger that would otherwise have crippled people.

I was most unhappy as a child when people I knew and loved, my friends and relations, were made to feel humiliated in their relations with white people or ashamed of their material poverty.

But despite their material impoverishment, the 500 or so people in the mission with whom I grew up – today, the population is close to 1000 – had families and a community. They had golden things and I think they often knew it.

Growing up in a tight-knit community of extended families, dealing with upheavals and fights from time to time, enduring the gossip and sharing a history enabled me to see families in action, and to see how community worked.

I have been both an active participant and an observer of my community for all of my life. If you come from Hope Vale Mission you talk about Hope Vale Mission, you analyse the people and the politics of Hope Vale Mission, you complain and swear bitterly about Hope Vale people, you laugh about and mock Hope Vale people – as they say, you run them down to the lowest and you lift them up to the highest. Wherever two or three are gathered together in Hope Vale's name, there will be endless hours of gossip, the most trivial but far from mundane political intrigue, despair and hope.

My hometown taught me one thing about families: there is no ideal model. Families have their own traditions that vary widely and wildly, and are particular to the people involved. Some families are essentially serious. Others are notoriously comic. Some produce rodeo rough-riding showoffs, meathead bullies when they're drunk but with sentimental hearts nevertheless. Some families are quiet, others loud and brash. Some patient, others not so. They all carry a genetic and social history.

I can see in a young Rosendale or a young Jacko or a young Darken the character of a deceased grandfather I knew when I was a kid or about whom I have heard. When you live in a community like this, you can see the Old People, long dead, living in their descendants.

2000

OLD MAN URWUNHTHIN

I was six years old when this tall American who everybody said was 'half Chinaman' or 'half Filipino' came to stay in our back street at Hope Vale. He was staying at Old Man Billy Muunduu's place, two doors away from our house. He was learning Guugu, our language.

When I went over to my *yumurr* Mary McIvor's house every day, to play cards or marbles under the mango tree, to listen to Amy's Charley Pride records and to pretend to look for *wuugul*, lice, on Mary's head, I wondered why this white couple next door chose to live amongst all the blackfellas, instead of with the European staff and school teachers at the top side of the mission.

Like the rest of us, they were using an outside bathroom with no hot water, the outhouse toilet, and they were eating black people's damper and *mayi*, food, all the time – what was the matter with them? Maybe they were the hippies the elders at church and Sunday school were warning us about.

The tall American, I later learned, was the eminent linguist John Haviland, who in time wrote a rigorous and comprehensive description of Guugu Yimithirr. John became formidable in his grasp of 'true Guugu Yimithirr' – as my old friend Urwunhthin would later say, *'alu uwu mindiir'*.

When I was a kid I knew Old Man Urwunhthin as Roger Hart, father of Janice and Bernard and that mob. He was one of the many people who formed the social universe of my childhood at Hope Vale. I didn't see him much during the 1970s when he was out working in the cane fields at Mossman, but I knew who he was and he would have been able to tell that I was Glen Pearson's son, Charlie's grandson and old Arrimi's great-grandson. It's like this when you live at Hope Vale. He would have known more about me than I did.

I grew up thinking that Roger Hart was just another mission man who spoke Guugu Yimithirr and was removed to the Cape Bedford mission as a child, same as my grandfather Charlie. When I began to tape some oral histories with older people for my honours thesis at the history department at the University of Sydney in late 1985 and 1986, I was surprised to be told by my father that I should go and talk to Roger Hart, who spoke his own language. I had known from an early age that Roger's country was Gambiilmugu, northern neighbours of my great-grandfather's country, Bagaarrmugu at Jeannie River. But I knew nothing about a Gambiilmugu language. And it was still spoken?

I only knew people at Hope Vale who spoke Guugu Yimithirr and my mother's language, Kuku Yalanji. A couple of old people used to speak some Lamalama languages, but I had not heard of the Barrow Point language being spoken by anyone in the mission.

I went to see Old Man Roger and there began our friendship. It started on the verandah of the old people's home in the company of another newly found mate of mine, and Roger's childhood friend and relation from Cape Melville, the late Bob Flinders. It turned out that a number of old people, including Bob, the late Leo Rosendale and Lindsay Nipper, could speak snippets of Roger's language. I decided to learn Roger's language so I could converse with him.

Athirr wulu, alcohol, and *mathiirmul*, brainless, were early additions to my vocabulary. Roger appreciated my desire to learn, and we soon had our own secret language in which to observe and mock those around us.

Sitting with the old men on the verandah, looking down at the village, watching the mission life, I would spend hours and days yarning. About language, about history at the mission, about history before the mission, about customs, about hunting, about birds and animals and plants. About the weather. About the past and about the present. About the future. About Christianity and the church. About politics. About land rights.

Roger and I would spend days under his mango tree talking. I was lucky to find this friendship, because it came at a time when identity and history and land rights were uppermost in my thoughts. My long hours and days and weeks of talking with Roger and Bob and the other old people turned into years, during which time Roger and I mourned the steady passing of our friends.

Urwunhthin, Roger Hart, had a desire to record the traditions of his people of Iipwulin, Barrow Point. The arrival of John Haviland – who learned Roger's language as well as Guugu Yimithirr – made this possible. The book John and Roger have written, *Old Man Fog and the Last Aborigines of Barrow Point*, is the best evocation we have of life in the wake of the devastation wrought by the violent invasion of the Cooktown hinterland after the Palmer River gold rush. That is, of life on the fringes, outside of the mission.

This history covers the period from the turn of the century to the Second World War. Remnant Aboriginal groups lived an itinerant traditional life where they could, caught between the frontier cattlemen, miners and fishermen, who inhumanely exploited them, and the government and missionaries, who wanted to take the children away from their families and to bring this camp life to an end. The government and missions eventually succeeded and a handful of lonely old people ended their days on the reserve at the edge of Cooktown.

My great-grandfather Arrimi, who appears in Roger's story, inhabited my childhood dreams. He was an outlaw bushman who evaded the police and could only surreptitiously bring *mayi*, food, to my father at Cape Bedford Mission. I often wondered how he and the people who still lived a bush life managed to survive. Roger's book tells me something about this life.

Roger's story tells of the last days of the bush people. In many respects life in these circumstances – occasional work for whites, hunting and travelling around the countryside – sounds like it might have had possibilities. If only they could have been free. If only they had some land for themselves. If only the whites weren't so inhumane and there was no exploitation. Maybe they could have kept their families and remained on their country.

If there is much sadness and loss in Roger's story about the removal of the people from their homeland and his eventual loneliness as the last survivor of the mob born in the bush, the land claim that Roger and his family and other Yiithuwarra people would eventually win before the Queensland Land Tribunal in the early 1990s tells a hopeful story of reunion. The Gambiilmugu people are alive and well, and they have a future. Roger, through his diligent accumulation of knowledge and through the patient recording of this knowledge, as well as that of other old people like the brothers Bob and Johnny Flinders, made it possible for his descendants to reclaim Iipwulin under the land rights opportunities that have arisen in the twilight of his life.

As well as having a strong memory and sharp mind, Roger is the most gracious and generous of men. My affection, which blossomed instantly, remains steadfast for *athunbi anggatha*, my friend, from Iipwulin.

1998

PEOPLES OF THE NORTH: ANTHROPOLOGY AND TRADITION

Written with Mervyn Gibson, who presented it to the Australian and New Zealand Association for the Advancement of Science

It appears that the present-day Aboriginal situation is one of hopelessness and despair. There is every indication that there will be no positive trend towards the achievement of economic, social, and political self-determination. In fact, it seems that social and cultural disintegration continues to escalate despite successive attempts by countless white and black policy makers, reformers and bureaucrats, and despite the passage of 200 years.

Australian Aborigines are proportionately the most over-represented race in any criminal justice system in the world. The legal system in Australia is at a loss to deal with this problem, and the Australian Law Reform Commission has acknowledged that the problems Aborigines face in the legal system are immense and remain unresolved. In a recent paper Justice Michael Kirby said, 'Any fair Australian will have a sense of disquiet, and even shame, at the way the Australian legal system has operated in relation to the Aboriginal ... it represents a cruel assertion of power, sometimes deliberate, sometimes mindless, resulting in the destruction of Aboriginal culture, unparalleled rates of criminal conviction and imprisonment and massive deprivation of property and land.'

In a country that has one of the highest standards of living in the world for the majority of the population, most Aborigines live in circumstances well below the poverty line. To use the usual indicators such as the provision of housing, the state of health, life expectancy, infant mortality and the availability of social services and amenities, Aborigines are worse off than people in Third World countries. This is so despite massive expenditure since 1967 by both state and federal agencies in the areas of Aboriginal health, housing, education and employment. Aborigines continue to die from diseases that have long since been eradicated from the white population. There is chronic dependency on government welfare – but the figures still show massive unemployment, poor health, low school retention rates and low representation in the higher levels of the white education system.

The segregation of Aborigines from mainstream Australian society continues, despite assimilation policies that have attempted to encourage them to be part of that society. Even in 1987, many black and white people assume that Aborigines must head in the direction of assimilation in order to deal with their problems.

However, black people today are feeling increasingly alienated from white society, and their dissatisfaction grows every day. It seems to me that we are searching for a place in mainstream Australian society that doesn't exist. We want Aborigines to live like us in an urban environment, but we don't want them to be closely associated with us. Australians want Aborigines to be employed, but they won't provide employment, or they expect Aborigines to remain in servile and unskilled jobs. Despite increased access to white education and white institutions, there are still considerable barriers, which has led Aborigines not to consider education in white society socially valuable.

So far I have described the failure of Aborigines to adapt to a white way of life. Does this mean that they have successfully retained the values and achievements of their own way of life?

The present situation clearly shows that Aborigines have not been entirely successful in retaining their culture. Cultural loss and disintegration continue at an alarming rate. For example, children from the Hope Vale Aboriginal community know significantly less about the language and traditions of their parents than did children a generation ago. It is somewhat morally disturbing that a program to preserve culture is implemented in a white-oriented institution which represents the very same ideas that have contributed to cultural disintegration in the first place.

Further to this, cultural fragmentation and dispossession remain devastating factors in the breakdown of Aboriginal society. Aborigines are not only rejecting education in non-Aboriginal terms, but they are also either rejecting black cultural education or are simply failing in their responsibility to maintain it.

This paper is the product of my own personal consideration of anthropology and Aboriginal society. Having studied anthropology and archaeology at the University of Queensland, I took a year off my studies to return to the Aboriginal community at Hope Vale. In my work as a projects officer in the community, I had the opportunity to observe my own society, equipped with the ideas that my years of study had given me. My practical experience there, considering the community's social problems and talking to community members, has led me to believe that there is a vast disparity between the science of anthropology and its ideas about Aboriginal society, especially with regard to their social problems, and Aboriginal society itself.

Anthropologists and other white people who have set themselves up as 'experts' on Aboriginal society, such as missionaries and government officials, have contributed to the creation and perpetuation of the myths that now shackle Aboriginal society. This paper argues that Aboriginal society has internalised these myths, and that these myths enable sections of the Aboriginal community to justify social exploitation. In this paper I have chosen to dwell on the problem of alcohol among Aboriginal people.

Alcohol has become such a problem for Aboriginal people because, under 'the myth', it has become an expression of identity and culture for them. For black people, to drink alcohol is to be an Aborigine. Social relationships are expressed through the consumption of alcohol. This paper is concerned with the question of whether the social phenomenon of alcohol among Aborigines is the expression of true culture and identity, or whether it is a distortion and an exploitation of that culture and identity. This paper argues that Aboriginal society is caught in the stranglehold of distorted mythic traditions.

For example: Jack collects his pay cheque or social-security cheque and spends most of it providing alcohol for himself and his cousins. His wife is unable to purchase enough food for their children until the next cheque, and therefore the children are hungry and his wife has to borrow food from a neighbour to feed them. Because Jack regularly appropriates the family income in this way, it is highly unlikely that his wife will ever repay what she is given. What was once a relationship of equal cadging between her family and the neighbours becomes unequal. What was once dependency by Jack's wife and the children based on necessity becomes dependence by Jack based on social exploitation and parasitism.

Why is such exploitation and parasitism allowed to continue? It is allowed to continue because the myth has convinced the members of the society that it is part and parcel of Aboriginal culture and tradition. Exploitation and social parasitism has been given such currency in Aboriginal society that the myth has to a large extent turned into reality. To return to our example: Jack justifies his appropriation of the family income for the purposes of buying alcohol for his cousins as a true expression of cultural identity and as a fulfilment of cultural and kinship obligations. For Jack, consuming alcohol in the way that he does is all about reinforcing kinship and cultural ties. During the course of consuming the alcohol, Jack can be heard explaining his kinship ties to his fellows. As any observer of Aboriginal alcohol consumption will testify, it is a ritual of reinforcing and observing so-called cultural ties and obligations. In fact this is a myth. It is a gross denial and distortion of true Aboriginal tradition.

Either consciously or unconsciously, Jack believes that he is being a true Aborigine in sharing his cheque with his cousins, who may have shared their cheques with him previously. He fails to realise that true Aboriginal tradition requires him to observe all his kinship obligations, especially those towards his wife, children and parents, not just those involving alcohol. Jack has become a social parasite who uses Aboriginal tradition to justify what is in essence selfish exploitation based on an individual physical desire for alcohol. It will be evident that the kinship and cultural obligations that Jack is willing to acknowledge are those that can be centred around alcohol.

He will neglect all of his other obligations. The myth that tradition is expressed during the consumption of alcohol by the group has gained tremendous currency in the Aboriginal community, and it has followed that any denial of the myth amounts to a denial of tradition. For example, when in an Aboriginal drinking group a request for money is refused by Jimmy, the person requesting the money will stress his relationship with Jimmy and, if necessary, create a relationship, no matter how fanciful and artificial it might be, and stress the obligations that arise from that relationship. In this way, kinship ties, either real or imaginary, are manipulated for self-serving and exploitative purposes. In the event that Jimmy still refuses, the person may then challenge his allegiance to kin, his respect for cultural ties and indeed his very Aboriginality. As any person conversant with Aboriginal drinking practices will testify, the question: 'Are you denying me?' is used quite often against people who dare to go against the myth, as if to say: 'Are you denying your Aboriginality? Who do you think you are? Do you think you're white?' In fact, people who fail to conform to the myth – in other words, those who refuse to succumb to the exploitation and parasitism inherent in the myth – are threatened with social alienation. The person who rejects the myth will be told how, in time of need, there will be no-one to provide for him, since he has neglected to fulfill his obligations under the myth.

The consequence of the operation of such myths is that alcoholism and social irresponsibility are associated with Aboriginal identity. Heath, hygiene and care about nutrition and economic welfare are associated with a white identity. There is this assumption amongst Aborigines that achievement and social responsibility are the preserve of white people. A lady from my community, upon seeing the food my wife had prepared for our family, once commented, 'Hey, you live like white people!' This comment was directed at the fact, not that the food was European, but that it was sufficient to our needs. Financially the lady was no worse off than our family, and yet in her mind, sufficient provision of food was not an Aboriginal characteristic. The same lady's finances were mostly committed to or appropriated for alcohol, vehicles and horse racing.

The myth is probably the greatest problem facing Aboriginal society. It is a monumental problem to overcome, because Aboriginal people need to acknowledge the deformities that have developed in their traditions and in their ideas about cultural identity. They also need to point out the distinction between true and distorted traditions to people whose view of Aboriginal culture comes from within the confines of the myth.

This is not to say that all of Aboriginal society has succumbed to the myth. There are sections of the Aboriginal community who have upheld the idea that social responsibility means more than the observance of obligations involving alcohol or any other essentially selfish activity.

Observing the history of the Hope Vale Aboriginal community from the period following dispossession after the arrival of Europeans at Cooktown in 1873, one can see how an Aboriginal community was formed from diverse and disparate backgrounds. The members of the mission at Cape Bedford were torn from their families and their lands, from their traditions and their people, and yet they were successful in forming a unified community. The young children who entered the mission under the *Protection Act* were assimilated into Guugu Yimithirr culture, and specifically a Christian Guugu Yimithirr culture. The mission was a successful community with members who observed true Aboriginal social responsibility, and their leaders resisted any adoption of the alcohol and gambling lifestyles that other Aboriginal communities had adopted. In fact, when the Cape Bedford mission people were removed to the Aboriginal settlement of Woorabinda during the Second World War, there was a blatantly apparent difference in the social ethics of the two communities. Only a handful of the young men from Cape Bedford adopted alcohol and virtually no-one took part in gambling, which was entrenched among the Woorabinda people. The power of the social ethic against gambling among the mission people can be seen in the fact that gambling has failed to flourish at Hope Vale, where other social problems have arisen. The Cape Bedford leaders utterly rejected the myth.

The recent history of the community shows that social problems have escalated tremendously. There is widespread economic and social breakdown, and alcohol appears to be destroying the traditions that were proudly established by the mission people over the course of the community's 100-year history. The last fifteen to twenty years have seen the decline, not of what the missionaries had achieved among the people, but rather the decline of what the people had themselves achieved in the face of dispossession and colonisation.

The myth has been adopted by sections of the community. Twenty years ago there was widespread resistance to the introduction of social ethics from other communities by the younger folk, especially the men. Families were unwilling to allow people to engage in an alcoholic lifestyle or to live off them. Now that resistance has broken down to a large extent. Hope Vale people are now more and more amenable to the operation of the myth in their society.

The ideas that form the myth are those that have been internalised from the white view of black people. Anthropologists, through their advice to policy makers and in their contribution to the public perception of Aborigines, have contributed to the construction of the myth, which has been used to justify some of the most outrageous things.

It is time to stop portraying gambling in Aboriginal society as some kind of traditional redistribution of wealth. It is time to stop interpreting alcoholism as some kind of helpless result of cultural clash. Rather we should be seeing it for what it is. That is: the deliberate distortion of tradition for the sake of fulfilling an individual physical desire for alcohol. It is time to stop portraying the contemporary Hope Vale alcoholic as a passive victim of colonisation. Rather we must consider how he has actively created his own problems.

My generation at Hope Vale cannot honestly point to colonisation and dispossession as the immediate causes of our social problems. The generations before us are an example of how the maintenance of true Aboriginal traditions within the context of adaptation to a Christian mission produced a successful community. Rather, our social problems stem from our inability to recognise how members of our community, and indeed how we ourselves, are using 'tradition' and 'culture' and 'kinship' to exploit our own society.

If anthropology is to serve any purpose for Aboriginal people, surely it must be to help recognise these problems. Anthropology has contributed to the construction and the maintenance of the myths under which Aborigines labour; surely now it must engage in their destruction.

1987

FIGHTING OLD ENEMIES

MABO: TOWARDS RESPECTING EQUALITY AND DIFFERENCE

Boyer Lecture

The Boyer Lectures of the eminent Australian anthropologist Professor William Stanner entitled *After the Dreaming* hold their own amongst this country's finest writings on matters black and white.

Stanner wrote one year after the 1967 referendum which, amongst other things, finally incorporated into the Commonwealth the Indigenous people of this country. In this lecture I propose to reflect on some aspects of Stanner's lectures, whilst tracing some of the developments of the past two decades, leading to the watershed decision of the High Court of Australia on 3 June 1992 on the question of native title to the Murray Islands in the case brought by the late Eddie Mabo and others.

I stood but a child of tender years when Professor Stanner spoke hopefully about our entry with a vengeance into the country's history. To tell the story of that time and the changes which have happened since and the changes which, like Stanner, we still await, it is appropriate first to tell of the man who commandeered Aboriginal policy in the state of Queensland for more than two decades.

In 1989, on a bright Sunday morning, Joh Bjelke-Petersen stood at the front of the old church at Hope Vale, surveying the long wide street, framed by mango trees and frangipannis, as barking dogs idly chased horses in the background.

Earlier, the former state premier, whose once-authoritarian aspect had by now waned considerably, had regaled the congregation of black faces in the weatherboard church with stories. Stories of how they had transformed dense woodland into paddocks and rows of tin shacks and wide streets named after German missionaries now long departed. How they had built this glorious church from the timber that had stood on the paddocks where cattle now grazed. He had returned to the mission to commemorate a community milestone: it was forty years since the Guugu Yimithirr had returned from seven years' exile in central Queensland. The mission, which had been established in 1886, was closed down during the Second World War, and the people removed when the resident German missionary was interned in 1942.

After the church service, a journalist asked the former premier about land tenure for the people of the community. With perhaps accidental candour, he replied that the land had always belonged to the Guugu Yimithirr. It was just that the government had been looking after it for them. And now they had handed the land back to its rightful owners.

It was a startling admission from one who had an international reputation for denying Aboriginal human rights in the state of Queensland and had steadfastly opposed the notion that Indigenous people had certain inherent, traditional rights to their homelands. His government could scarcely bring itself to mention the word 'traditional' without suffering acute political nausea.

In the early years of government policy, when it was said we lived 'under the Act', Aborigines could be treated unequally because of their alleged backwardness. This belief in innate difference and inequality underpinned a policy of assimilation: by a process of training, civilising and indeed breeding out their backwardness, the blacks could lose their difference and become like everyone else. They could come out into the mainstream society as people exempted from the Act and finally equal. The churches would assist in this endeavour, and to that end no church body broke more sweat than the Hope Vale Lutheran Mission Board under Bjelke-Petersen's ten-year chairmanship.

My parents watched their contemporaries pack up their young families, leave the mission and go south to live near Lutheran congregations, to milk cows, pick peanuts, cut cane and work on highways, just like poor whites did. I don't recall wishing that my family had also gone south, but I do recall the strange tolerance that my father and the older people showed those who administered the paternalistic regime under which we lived on the mission: the missionaries and the managers. This was explicable by their over-riding devotion to the church, and by their fierce sense of the mission's history and of the community's survival through times of extreme tribulation, hardship, loss and dislocation. Like those born before us and those who would follow, our collective psyche was dominated by the Moses-like figure of Georg Heinrich Schwarz of Neuendettelsau, who had died six years before I was born.

Old Missionary Schwarz had first landed at Cape Bedford in 1887, by which time the Guugu Yimithirr people had been reduced to a demoralised, fringe-dwelling existence by the establishment of Cooktown. Many of their number had by now been exterminated; their bones lined the bloodstained tracks to the Palmer River goldfields. There was gratitude for Schwarz's lifelong efforts to provide shelter from the colonial storm whose waves had almost completely swamped the Guugu Yimithirr, drowning many of the descendants of those who had first met James Cook at the Endeavour River in 1770. Who among those who saw the sails disappear northwards after the crew of the *Endeavour* had finished repairing their vessel would have thought that four generations later, the captain's descendants would return with such vengeance, with a fever for gold and for land, leaving demoralised strugglers begging, sneaking and apologising for an existence in their own country?

Given the church's role in the secular administration of the mission, and the fact that the government was now headed by Bjelke-Petersen, a church friend, indeed a mission friend during the years of my early youth, the older people forgave and suffered government paternalism in much the same way that they had suffered the paternalism of Old Missionary Schwarz.

But there was increasing disquiet among the younger people about the government- and church-sanctioned policy of inequality justified by difference. Why were people prohibited from buying motor vehicles, why should they have to seek permission from the manager to leave the reserve, why did the money they earned have to be kept and managed by the mission, why could not the community have title to its land in its own hands?

The increasing awareness that the Queensland government's policies concerning Aboriginal people breached fundamental human rights, and that our mission friend was a leading and vehement opponent of Aboriginal rights, brought on a significant identity crisis for the community. This crisis led to a realisation that paternalism within the family might be a natural, affectionate relationship, but when it involved adults of different races it was undeniably racist, and arose from a fundamental assumption of inferiority and superiority. The government and the church had assumed our innate inferiority and their own superiority. Like many paternal relationships put asunder, the bitterness of this realisation was painful.

As with the memory of the old missionary, the pain was most acutely felt by those who had watched their parents and grandparents endure a system that treated them as state wards, as incapable and undeserving of equality and dignity. In the young hearts of those who contemplated this history, indignation burned, and their indignation resonated with the memories and secret, long-suppressed feelings of those who had endured the old system. There arose a movement for change and a demand for equality.

During the Brisbane Commonwealth Games in 1982, Aboriginal protests focused international attention on Queensland's record on human rights generally and land rights in particular and signalled a change in the direction of the National Party government's policies on Aboriginal affairs. The infamous *Aborigines Act* was repealed and new, less draconian legislation governing communities was introduced. Together with legislation granting a form of land title to Aboriginal reserves under an instrument called a Deed of Grant in Trust, this heralded a new era during which the government strove to address the long-standing and widespread criticism of its discriminatory laws.

Rather than sanctioning difference and inequality, the new policies emphasised equality and sameness. Aboriginal people were no longer to be distinct from the rest of the Queensland community; they were equal, and this meant that they must not be allowed to be different. Aborigines were to be considered merely dark-skinned Queenslanders.

Formal equality was now largely a fact. The government's policies were therefore difficult to reproach. The response was always that it now treated Aborigines like any other Queenslanders.

Of course, the respect in which Aborigines were most similar to their fellow Queenslanders was that they had no special claim or right to their traditional homelands. Non-Aboriginal Queenslanders had no such inherent rights: all rights to land in the state were granted by the Crown and there was neither any legal nor moral claim on behalf of Indigenous people to what they claimed were their lands.

Therefore, whilst a substantial policy change occurred in the 1980s, from inequality and difference to equality and sameness, both policies were discriminatory and were premised on a vehement denial of the notion of traditional rights to land. Professor Stanner had confronted the myth of waste and desert lands and said that if Crown title were paraded by, every Aboriginal child would say, like the child in the fairy tale, 'But the emperor is naked ...'; but in Queensland, the government continued to insist that the emperor was decently attired. Thus the Bjelke-Petersen government moved at a night sitting of the parliament to pass the *Queensland Coast Islands Declaratory Act 1985*. This Act purported to retrospectively extinguish any native title that might have existed in the Murray Islands. If valid, the legislation would bring to an end the court action brought by Eddie Mabo and others three years before.

That action had challenged the Deed of Grant in Trust system by disputing the Crown's power to grant title to people who claimed they already held a pre-existing title to their homelands. Before dealing further with the question of pre-existing title and the outcome of what is the most important and controversial decision of the High Court of Australia, I would like to survey briefly the developments which unfolded at the national level following the 1967 referendum and Stanner's hopes for a final breaking of the Great Australian Silence and for recognition of Aboriginal land rights.

Prior to his Boyer Lectures, Professor Stanner had been to Yirrkala on the Gove Peninsula, consulting the Aboriginal people in relation to bauxite mining leases granted to the Nabalco corporation. He spoke in his lecture about the people's anxiety about the proposed development, and the strong feelings they expressed about their homelands and what lay ahead. In 1968, the Yirrkala people launched an action in the Supreme Court of the Northern Territory against the mining company, claiming that they held a communal native title, recognised by Australian common law, to their traditional lands. Professor Stanner gave expert evidence for the plaintiffs.

In a 1971 decision now known as the Gove land rights case, Justice Blackburn of the Northern Territory Supreme Court found that there was a traditional system in place in the claimed lands, which he described as 'a government of laws and not of men'. Nevertheless, his judgment denied that native title was part of Australian common law, and he confirmed the assumed doctrine of *terra nullius*: before 1788, Australia had been an empty land without owners.

However, the negative finding in the Gove case, combined with increasing political agitation by Aboriginal people in the early 1970s, gave rise to a political imperative to address land rights. If Aboriginal people possessed no inherent rights to land as a matter of law, then a moral onus fell upon parliament to grant them rights to land. Such Aboriginal 'rights' to land would emanate from the same source as the land tenure held by non-Aboriginal Australians; that is, by virtue of Crown grants. The Indigenous people possessed no inherent or pre-existing legal rights to land.

The Woodward Commission, established by the Whitlam Labor government, eventually led to the enactment of the *Northern Territory Land Rights Act 1976*. Other parliaments were slower and less willing to act and, despite having the constitutional ability to create similar statutory regimes for the states, the Commonwealth was only willing to act in relation to the territories, principally the Northern Territory. Statutory land rights schemes were eventually established in South Australia, New South Wales and Queensland with varied, and mostly unsatisfactory, results; it is true to say that each subsequent measure was less inspired than the last.

The recommendations of the Seaman Inquiry for a statutory scheme in Western Australia were not taken up by the state Labor government, which succumbed to an intense opposition campaign from the mining lobby. This campaign also saw the Commonwealth's attempt to establish a national land rights scheme come to grief because of a failure of political will. Tasmania has refused to enact even the most modest of measures.

What has resulted is a patchwork of legislative regimes that have made provision for some areas of the country and no provision in respect of others. Moves in the mid 1980s at the federal level to introduce a national land rights model failed to fulfil the need for a national provision. The wellspring of goodwill which erupted after the Gove case had petered out to a trickle by the time Michael Mansell made his assessment in 1989 that no more would we see land rights legislation in this country. The question, so far as the materialistic Australians of the 1980s were concerned, had been more or less addressed and, if not addressed, then at least attempted. In confirmation of Mansell's assessment, in 1991 the Queensland Labor government introduced the *Aboriginal Land Act*, which restricted native title claims to land that had been expressly made available by the government. This was a much more conservative approach than the ALP had promised before the 1990 election, and the party subsequently adjusted its land rights policy platform downwards to match its legislation. The outcome determined the policy.

It therefore appeared by 1991 that there would be no more political or social impetus for any national movement on land rights. At this point, Mansell quite correctly asked whether our better prospects might lie outside of the nation rather than within it.

The constitutional mandate over Aboriginal affairs which the 1967 referendum gave the Commonwealth has been infrequently exercised. The states have too often been left to repeat the long history of neglect and denial that gave rise to the need for constitutional change in the first place. One of the few occasions on which the Commonwealth assumed responsibility for Aboriginal affairs was the Whitlam Labor government's enactment of legislation outlawing Queensland's discriminatory laws. And of course, the most significant exercise of the race power came in the last days of that government with the enactment of the *Racial Discrimination Act* in October 1975.

This Act has proved to be pivotal in the protection of native title as established in the *Mabo* cases. The High Court found in 1992 that although, under Australian common law, the British Crown had acquired sovereignty over the country, this did not extinguish the beneficial title of the Indigenous inhabitants. This decision has revolutionised the nation's understanding of its land laws and indeed its history.

Certain historical truths are difficult for some to accept, given that history is so important to contemporary political ideology. Certain prescriptions taste like too many bitter pills to many Australians, who have lamented, grieved and felt betrayed by the Court's decision. There are black Australians, too, who will feel betrayed by the Court's decision, who will feel short-changed by history and white law. But for many Australians, both black and white, *Mabo* represents an opportunity to achieve a greater national resolution of the question of Aboriginal land rights, and to improve relations between the new and old of this land; *Mabo* represents a first step in a new direction which might yield the changes necessary for Indigenous people to be genuinely repossessed of their inheritance.

Mabo is an attempt by the colonialist legal system to accommodate Aboriginal land rights. It is by no means the most perfect accommodation between rights under Aboriginal law and the white legal system. But, from all assessments, it is close to the best accommodation achievable within the Australian legal system. It stands creditably against similar accommodations in Canada, the United States and New Zealand. The significance of the decision is that it recognises Aboriginal law and custom as a source of law for the first time in 204 years of colonial settlement. For the most part, however, Aboriginal law remains unrecognised. *Mabo* sets the stage for an interaction which has never before been possible.

Colonial law has been a reality in Australia since 1788. Colonial law is part of our Indigenous reality here in Australia: it determines our ability to exercise our law, enjoy our rights and maintain our identities. But Aboriginal law is also a reality, and we are unanimous in our resolve that it continue to be so. With *Mabo*, the colonial system is saying: yes, we do recognise Aboriginal law in certain circumstances relating to land, but our law also says that there has been legal extinguishment of Aboriginal title in many circumstances. As to the balance of Aboriginal law, well, the colonial law is saying: it has no reality, insofar as we are concerned and insofar as we are prepared to act.

No matter the illegitimacy of the imposition of colonial law, no matter how revisionist and how artificial and pragmatic the High Court's recognition of Indigenous law in the Murray Island case might be said to be – it is nevertheless the prevailing reality. If this is the situation – that Aboriginal law has restricted recognition and there is little prospect for an extension of that recognition through agitation of the common law – what strategies can we pursue to make Aboriginal law have consequence for our colonial condition?

First of all, we need a new political ideology for Indigenous political strategy. For the most part, the Aboriginal political system occupies a sphere quite distinct from the white political system. Indigenous political activity and philosophy tend to spin in an orbit that does not have much relevance to, or impact upon, the dominant sphere in which many of the critical developments take place.

Uncle Tom and Malcolm X represent the two extreme characterisations of racial politics in the United States, where the pan-African American struggle has provided an image of how black politics ought to be understood. At one end of the spectrum is the sell-out, at the other the radical activist. These characterisations are largely white constructs. The colonists have defined the way in which our struggle is to be understood – they, the media, the wider colonial society, define our struggles as moderate or radical, conservative or activist, to suit themselves, and we have internalised these characterisations and made them our own.

In Australia, early black leaders seized upon the politics of liberating victims that had defined the black struggle against segregation in America. Later, the emergence of radical activism forced Australians to change how they viewed the victims, but it did not always change the position from which the victims spoke – they were still defined as a powerless and oppressed minority. The language of victim politics positioned the rest of Australia as guilty perpetrators. This is an uncomfortable position, and not one which will sustain a political cause. The Australian body politic will salve its conscience for only so long before it reacts with an indignant backlash – the 'we can't be blamed for what happened' response.

Such conscience-salving is to be particularly observed in the ready agreement of those most vehemently opposed to land rights who nevertheless concede the need to address the shameful health, sanitation, educational, employment and housing conditions of black Australians. Rather than land rights, this view urges conscience-salving through the pursuit of what Stanner called 'hobby horses': particular measures targeting specific problems. In 1968, many of the statistics were deteriorating rather than improving, which makes Stanner's questioning of this approach relevant to 1993. Of those who pursued these pet projects he said: 'They are all in part right and therefore dangerous. If all these particular measures, with perhaps fifty or a hundred other, were carried out everywhere, simultaneously, and on a sufficient scale, possibly there would be a general advance ... But who shall mobilise and command this regiment of one-eyed hobby horses? And keep them in column?'

For the Indigenous quarter, our changing political circumstances require us to re-evaluate our political strategies. People aren't moderates or conservatives on the one hand, and radicals and extremists on the other. Rather, actions and strategies should be seen as moderate or radical. The test of a strategy's credibility is not whether it is radical or conservative, but whether it is smart or dumb, and whether it enhances or jeopardises the rights and interests of one's people.

The politics of victimhood asserts that unless the dominant state accepts us on our own terms, any complicity, any dealing, constitutes an unacceptable relinquishment of our power. For a long time, the only political currency Aboriginal people could use was their refusal to be involved. Now that the non-Aboriginal legal system has offered something in the way of rights, however narrow, to refuse to engage in the game and to fail to appreciate the rules and its limitations – even if we still wish to disrupt the game – no longer seems smart. The challenge is to negotiate the expansion of those rights without losing ground and without damaging the chances of future advances in a struggle which has incrementally advanced and whose destination is still far away.

1993

THE CONCEPT OF NATIVE TITLE

Of all of the miserable cargo that ever left the shores of England for the Antipodes, there are three things that I celebrate as amongst the finest imports: that sublime game of cricket, Earl Grey's tea and the common law of England.

It may well now be politically heretical for me to say so, but I was afflicted with a young lawyer's infatuation with the amazing grace of the common law well before the decision in *Mabo and Others v. The State of Queensland*. Needless to say, the judgment of the High Court of Australia of 3 June 1992 reinforced my enthusiasm for the capacity of the common law – its capacity for logic and justice and balance and change.

Excited by what Professor Richard Bartlett described, accurately if somewhat inelegantly, as the 'pragmatic compromise' of *Mabo* – a compromise between the fact of the original right of the Indigenous peoples to their homelands, and the historical accumulation of rights by the colonists – I am of course acutely aware that not all of the development of the common law of native title in Australia will give our side joy.

But rather than surrendering, as Mr Justice French did in his decision on the Waanyi peoples' application for determination of native title, to the notion that it will be up to parliament to correct the 'moral shortcomings' of the common law, I am a great believer in the imperative for those charged with developing the common law to redouble our efforts when injustice looms. This imperative remains as long as, to paraphrase His Honour Justice Brennan (as he then was) in *Mabo*, the skeleton of the common law, which gives it its internal logic and consistency, is not fractured.

I am concerned about the future development of the common law of native title in Australia. Having long agonised over the jurisprudence, I have attempted to grapple with a fundamental question: what is the concept of native title? Despite the fact that native title is long established all over the common law world, and particularly in North America, my reading of the cases and articles on the subject, particularly the Canadian jurisprudence, leaves me convinced that the correct answer to this basic question still eludes us. Our inability to articulate clearly the concept of native title has implications for our understanding of its recognition, its extinguishment and its content.

Tonight, I am going to attempt to articulate some arguments about the concept of native title that have been swirling around in my head ever since I read rapturously that judgment of 3 June 1992. I will now set out a summary of my contentions about the concept of native title.

Summary of contentions
1. Native title is neither a common law nor an Aboriginal law title, but represents the recognition by the common law of title under Aboriginal law.
2. 'Extinguishment' must therefore be understood as extinguishment of recognition.
3. Extinguishment of recognition of native title occurs where the foundation of title in Aboriginal law and custom has been washed away as a matter of fact. There can be no revival of recognition in this event. This is extinguishment amounting to extinction.
4. Extinguishment of recognition of native title also occurs where there is an interest inconsistent with the continued enjoyment of Aboriginal title. Aboriginal title remains unrecognised by the common law so long as the inconsistent interest remains.
5. Given the recognition concept of native title and the notion of extinguishment of recognition, it follows that where there is partial inconsistency between an interest and the continued enjoyment of native title, then there is a partial extinguishment of

recognition of native title. Where the inconsistency is removed, recognition is again possible.

6. The *sui generis* nature of native title is a consequence of the interaction between two systems of law – the common law recognising Aboriginal law with the consequence that Aboriginal title is recognised. Native title has two aspects. Firstly, native title concerns the relationship between the native title holders and the rest of the world. This relationship can be described by the common law, because it is inherent to the occupation of land by human societies and identical to the kind of dominion that people of all societies assert over land. As His Honour Justice Brennan said in that great and succinct phrase in *Mabo*: 'land is susceptible of ownership.' The common law describes this aspect of native title in terms of possession. In relation to the Meriam peoples, the High Court described it as a right to 'possession, occupation, enjoyment and use' of land as against the whole world. Secondly, native title deals with relations between the native title holders, which must be ascertained by reference to Aboriginal law and custom.

7. Understood in this way, the concept of possessory title or, as Professor McNeil and His Honour Justice Toohey described it, 'common law Aboriginal title', is an aspect of native title and not a separate concept.

8. These two aspects of native title determine its content. Where there are questions about the rights of the native title holders in relation to one another, then they must be settled by reference to Aboriginal law and custom. Where there are questions concerning the rights of native title holders in relation to those outside of the Aboriginal system of law and custom, then they must be determined by the common law.

9. We need to recognise the clear articulation by His Honour Justice Brennan in *Mabo* that the right of the individual is carved out of the communal right. The usufructuary right is carved out of the communal proprietary title.

10. Where native title is to be established, the task of the common law courts is to assume the existence of a full proprietary title and then

to identify those valid acts of the Crown which have qualified that title by regulation or by partial extinguishment of recognition by the creation of an inconsistent interest. The notion that the content of the native title is solely to be determined by reference to the rights established under Aboriginal law and custom is misconceived.

A recognition concept

Fundamentally I proceed from the notion that native title is a 'recognition concept'. The High Court told us in *Mabo* that native title is not a common law title but is instead a title recognised by the common law. What they failed to tell us, and what we have failed to appreciate, is that neither is native title an Aboriginal law title. Because patently, Aboriginal law will recognise title where the common law will not. Native title is therefore the space between the two systems of law, where there is recognition. Native title is, for want of a better word, the recognition space between the common law and the Aboriginal law, which is now afforded recognition in particular circumstances.

Adopting this concept allows us to see two systems of law running in relation to land. This is a matter of fact. No matter what the common law might say about the existence of native title in respect of land that is subject to an inconsistent grant, the fact is that Aboriginal law still allocates entitlement to those traditionally connected with the land. The extinguishment of native title should therefore be understood as extinguishment of *recognition* of Aboriginal title. The extinguishment of recognition does not result in the extinguishment of Aboriginal title in relation to the land. It survives as a social reality under Aboriginal law. It is fictive to assume that Aboriginal law is extinguished where the common law is unable to recognise it.

The common law as a matter of justice recognises Aboriginal law in certain circumstances. In *Mabo*, the High Court constructed inconsistency as the test by which to determine whether the common law can recognise Aboriginal title. Where there is an interest inconsistent with the continued enjoyment of native title by the native title holders, then the High Court's schema in *Mabo* will not allow recognition. Where there is no inconsistency, the native title is recognised. The concept of inconsistency, which exclusive possession implies, is a keystone of the High Court's construct of what is practical and just in terms of recognising accumulated historical interests while accommodating belated recognition of original title.

Native title and extinguishment

Appreciating native title as a recognition concept challenges the assumption that we have all laboured under since *Mabo*, but which is not a necessary consequence of *Mabo*: that extinguishment is somehow a fatal and irreversible event. According to this assumption, if an obscure past action by the Crown can be found to be inconsistent with the continued enjoyment of native title, then native title will be extinguished no matter the actual facts on the ground and the subsequent history of the land concerned. In my view, lawyers and judges have been too quick to assume that a so-called extinguishment event is fatal to the recognition of Aboriginal entitlement to land.

Because native title is a recognition concept, its extinguishment should be understood as being 'extinguishment of recognition'. This raises the question of whether the common law will endorse the notion of revival of recognition.

His Honour Justice Brennan said in *Mabo*:

> when the tide of history has washed away any real acknowledgment of traditional law and any real observance of traditional custom, the foundation of native title has disappeared. A native title which has ceased with the abandoning of laws and customs based on tradition cannot be revived for contemporary recognition ... Once traditional native title expires the Crown's radical title expands to a full beneficial title ...

In ruling out revival, this passage has led to the assumption that extinguishment is always a fatal and permanent event. But note that His Honour has correctly confined this conclusion to situations where Aboriginal law and custom have washed away. The passage does not refer to circumstances where recognition has been extinguished as a matter of law in response to an inconsistent interest, and does not rule out the revival of recognition should this inconsistent interest be removed.

Understood in this way, His Honour's conclusion can only be correct: when the law and custom expires or the Aboriginal people themselves expire, then clearly there can be no revival. But what if the law and custom are still running in relation to the land, the traditional connection is being maintained, and the inconsistent interest is lifted?

For present purposes, there are at least two ways in which native title can be extinguished, as set out in *Mabo*: firstly by the legislature or executive expressing a clear intention to extinguish title, chiefly by making an inconsistent grant, and secondly by the abandonment or loss of the traditional connection with the land (which implies the loss of law and custom or the extinction of the people). Either of these will result in the extinguishment of recognition of native title.

Where the traditional connection with the land is lost (by the abandonment of traditional laws and customs or the extinction of the people) then the native title expires and cannot be revived for contemporary recognition. This is as His Honour expressed it. Where the traditional connection is maintained and the Crown or the legislature shows a clear and plain intention to revive recognition of a native title that has previously been subject to an inconsistent grant, then we have revival of native title.

How is the Crown's intention to revive recognition of native title to be established? To quote His Honour:

> the exercise of a power to [revive recognition of] native title must reveal a clear and plain intention to do so, whether the action be taken by the Legislature or the Executive …

and

> The [revival of recognition] of native title does not depend on the actual intention of the Governor in Council (who may not have adverted to the rights and interests of the indigenous inhabitants or their descendants) but on the effect which it has on the right to enjoy native title …

The situation in *Waanyi* affords an excellent illustration of the logic of this approach to extinguishment. The common law recognised native title to the land in 1788. Subsequently the land was made subject to an inconsistent grant, namely a pastoral lease, and there was extinguishment of recognition (accepting for these purposes the Full Federal Court's conclusion in the *Waanyi* case that a pastoral lease is an inconsistent grant). Then the inconsistent grant was lifted and a camping and water reserve was put in place, which was consistent with the continued enjoyment of native title. Therefore there was revival of recognition, because the effect of the creation of the reserve was to permit again the enjoyment of native title by the Aborigines.

This approach to the recognition and extinguishment of native title has important implications for whether the common law of native title in Australia is going to be just and fair. There are many lands today (particularly in national parks, public-purpose reserves, Aboriginal reserves and vacant Crown lands) which were previously subject to tenures (leasehold and freehold) that may have been inconsistent with native title according to the High Court's test in *Mabo*, but where the inconsistency has now been removed. A common law scheme which sees technical legal events as fatal extinguishing events, even where Aboriginal traditional connection with the land is being maintained, would be a perverse law, and inconsistent with the *Mabo* compromise.

1996

AFTER *MABO*

Lionel Murphy Memorial Lecture

In 1981 Percy Neal, then the chairman of Yarrabah Aboriginal Council in North Queensland, was sentenced to a prison term of two months with hard labour for expectorating at the white store manager of that particular Aboriginal reserve. At his hearing the magistrate rebuked Mr Neal as follows:

> Violence is something in recent times which has crept into Aboriginal communities. I blame your type for this growing hatred of black against white ... As a magistrate I visit [many] communities, and I can say unequivocally that the majority of genuine Aboriginals do not condone this behaviour and are not desirous in any shape or form of having changes made. They live a happy life, and it is only the likes of yourself who push this attitude of the hatred of white authority, that upset the harmonious running of these communities.

On appeal, the Queensland Court of Criminal Appeal increased Neal's sentence to six months without granting him right of appeal. The High Court subsequently quashed the Queensland court's extension of the sentence, but was divided as to whether an appeal should have been granted. Chief Justice Gibbs and Justice Wilson declined to interfere with the Queensland court's decision. Justices Brennan and Murphy dissented.

In his now famous judgment, Justice Lionel Murphy suggested that the magistrate had been influenced in his judgment by his political views and by racism, and that Mr Neal's reputation as a 'stirrer' had obviously contributed to the severity of the sentence:

> In its supervision of the criminal justice system of a State, the Court of Criminal Appeal has a duty to see that racism is not allowed to operate within the judicial system.
>
> Many of the great religious and political figures of history have been agitators, and human progress owes much to the efforts of these and the many who are unknown ... Without them, in our incomplete state, there would be no advance toward civilisation. Mr Neal is entitled to be an agitator.

Murphy contended that a person should not be penalised for attempting to change social conditions which he or she found to be unjust. In a foreword to a collection of essays with Justice Murphy as their subject, Michael Kirby reflected in 1987 that:

> Given the right person and opportune conditions, a determined reformer can use the institutions of Australian society to effect change for the better. He or she can do so in an entirely constitutional way. The reformer in Australia needs no resort to guns ... The institutions for change are there beckoning. They can be found in Parliament, in the bureaucracy, in the Cabinet room, in the courts, in the trade union movement, in the media and in society's countless groups.

This is an inspiring thought, tempered only by Kirby's observation that the enemies of reform are 'mainly inertia, complacency, greed and selfishness'. Inertia, complacency, greed and selfishness are no mean enemies with which to reckon. That the leaders of reform in Australia have struggled, sometimes successfully, with these forces is to their credit. But that the struggle can be hard and terribly protracted is demonstrated by the grinding pace at which Aboriginal land rights reform has limped onto Australia's national agenda, and by the inordinate amount of blood and sweat that have, over the years, been wrung from the most determined social reformers. Justice Murphy had the power to do more than spit in the face of authority but even he, like Mr Neal, suffered a fate common to agitators and was later dragged through the courts. Gough Whitlam was removed from office, John Koowarta's hopes of regaining his land were dashed by the spiteful acts of Bjelke-Petersen and Eddie Mabo died, after ten years of struggle, on the eve of triumph. Perhaps the institutions for change do not quite beckon!

It was many years before an Australian government of courage and vision came to tackle inertia, complacency, greed and selfishness head on. The opportunities were there in 1972 to use, as Kirby has suggested, 'the institutions of Australian society to effect change for the better'. A diary of the initiatives taken during the first days of the Whitlam government reads like the chronicle of a social revolution.

Mabo is a consequence of this revolution. The Whitlam government, with Lionel Murphy as attorney-general, took international human-rights standards and applied them to Indigenous peoples in Australia. First, Murphy introduced federal laws outlawing Queensland's discriminatory laws applying to Aboriginal reserves and their inmates. These discriminatory laws prompted the great resentment and resistance of Mr Neal and countless others who fought against Queensland's long-standing system of discrimination and denial of human rights.

Furthermore, in the final days of the Whitlam government, the *Racial Discrimination Act* was made law, implementing Australia's obligations under the International Convention on the Elimination of All Forms of Racial Discrimination. The internationalist approach taken by Murphy and Whitlam to domestic human rights was the subject of a constitutional challenge in the watershed case of *Koowarta v. Bjelke-Petersen*.

I had the great privilege of working with John Koowarta in 1991 on the Queensland land rights campaign. A decade earlier, Koowarta had been prevented from purchasing a pastoral lease in Cape York Peninsula by the Bjelke-Petersen government, which then had a policy of preventing Aboriginal groups from buying land on the open market. The judgment of the High Court in the *Koowarta* case in 1981 established one of the most important principles under our constitution. That is, that the Commonwealth has the power and indeed the obligation to implement international law in Australia, and particularly to guarantee such fundamental human rights as the right to be free from racial discrimination. In 1981, Koowarta was unable to benefit from this judgment, Bjelke-Petersen having made the land in question a national park. Ten years later, with a state Labor government now in office, Koowarta fared no better in the land rights campaign of 1991. He died soon after, still dispossessed of his traditional lands.

The *Racial Discrimination Act* also proved to be critical to the survival of the *Mabo* litigation in 1988, when the High Court invalidated a Queensland law enacted in 1985 which purported to retrospectively extinguish native title in the Murray Islands and therefore to terminate the *Mabo* action. Strangely enough, three weeks ago the Goss Labor government passed a law which seeks to pre-empt a question that is central to proceedings currently before the federal court in the *Wik* litigation. The Queensland law seeks to declare that native title is extinguished on pastoral leases, a declaration which the federal parliament explicitly left for determination by the courts. This action by the Goss government and the processes by which this law was introduced are in substance no different from what Bjelke-Petersen did by sheer jackboot political force in 1985. I observed at the time that the Bjelke-Petersen handbook on unprincipled government had apparently been left lying around the Queensland parliament house after the Nationals were routed in December 1989.

For a party that has led social reform in this country since the 1970s, it appears that the Labor Party's central challenge is how it can hold power and exercise it in the most responsible and principled way. The Queensland experience, after five years of the Goss government, suggests that there are only two choices for Labor governments: pragmatic and hard-nosed politicking aimed at retaining power, or idealistic and careless prosecution of principle. The poll-driven apparatchik versus the coffee-shop revolutionary. I will later argue that the choice is not one or the other, not left or right. Principled pragmatism or, to put it another way, pragmatic idealism, must surely be the guiding strategy of those from the hungry side of politics.

This might be an appropriate point at which to seek the guidance of history. In his official history of the New South Wales Labor Party, Graham Freudenberg has suggested that:

> the Australian Labor Party remains the authentic expression of Australianism. More than any other political party in the world, the Australian Labor Party reflects and represents the character of the nation which produced it.

Freudenberg's claim is in a Labor Party tradition of seeking historical validity for its right to represent Australians and to shape Australia's future. It is in the context of this tradition that members of the Labor Party speak of 'keeping the faith', and it is in this context I would like to examine Freudenberg's claim. Does the Australian Labor Party reflect and represent the character of the nation which produced it?

The legal and administrative structures of Australian society are necessarily Anglo-Celtic in origin. But no-one would now seriously contend, as the historian W.K. Hancock once did, that the Australian people are a 'product of the blending of all the stocks and regional types which exist within the British Isles'. One of the declared objectives of the New South Wales branch at the Interstate Conference of the Australian Labor Party in 1905 was the:

> cultivation of an Australian sentiment, based upon the maintenance
> of racial purity and the development in Australia of an enlightened
> and self-reliant community.

The inextricable links between the ideals of Australian nationalism and racist policy are here explicit, and Freudenberg asserts that the promotion of racist policy was critical to any hope of electoral success for the Labor Party. In attempting to explain Labor's adoption, in 1895, of a policy of national exclusion of 'alien and inferior races' he asserts that:

> What must be clearly understood, however unpalatable it may be
> in 1991, is that in the 1890s, radical idealism and racial purity were
> entirely compatible and usually spoke in the same voice. Liberal and

progressive thought everywhere was profoundly influenced by the idea of social evolution, a development, or as we would see it now, a corruption of Darwinian theory. Radical ideas about progress and nationalism reinforced each other. Just as nationalism could too easily degenerate into chauvinism, the idea of evolutionary progress could easily merge into open racism.

The currency of such sentiments was apparent as late as 1978, when the author Marjorie Barnard exclaimed: 'That the population was not brindled from the outset was the bright side of misfortune.'

Gordon Childe, scholar and civil libertarian, was private secretary to the Labor leader John Storey from 1919 to 1921. In *How Labor Governs*, Childe maintained that the watchword of a 'White Australia' had been adopted by the Labor Party for 'purely economic reasons' as a means of sustaining Anglo-Celtic Australian employment and living standards (an aim with which I am sure this audience is familiar).

It took some time for the party to emerge from the petty preoccupations of jingoistic nationalism to the broader international perspective that has characterised some of its greater undertakings. And while courageous reformers such as Gough Whitlam and Lionel Murphy often rejected the Australian Labor Party's narrow jingoistic tradition in favour of an internationalist perspective, the tradition is a hard one to live down. The White Australia policy is an inescapable aspect of Australia's and the Labor Party's legacy.

That the internationalism of socialist theory did not overturn the ignorance of racism in the tumultuous beginnings of the Australian Labor Party is certainly true, but I would also argue that Freudenberg exaggerates somewhat the naturalness of the degeneration of evolutionary theory into racist attitudes. To the contrary, I would assert that it is essential to recognise this type of development as conditional on there being vested interests in such views. No necessary link exists between evolutionary theory and racism. The link, I would argue, is between imperialism, colonialism and the national psychological need for an apologetic. Once developed, this apologetic gathered the momentum to permeate every aspect of this nation's identity, but it remains a rationalisation for greed. Professor Henry Reynolds' histories, in particular *Frontier*, tell clearly the history of colonial racism in Australia.

Perhaps, as Freudenberg asserts, the Labor Party exemplifies Australianness, but such a claim is not unproblematic. By this I do not imply that any other Australian political party has been less racist, simply that this is an aspect of Labor Party history which must be confronted rather than explained away in terms of the context of the times. Contextualisation is all very well, but justification of such retrograde attitudes is not.

On 2 December 1972, Whitlam described his task as being not merely to reverse the government policies of two decades but 'to change Australian attitudes, deeply entrenched over two generations'. Racism, he charged, was the basis for most of the foreign policy of the Menzies era. It was relatively easy to change the policy, but more difficult to change the attitudes of the Australian people.

Time will tell whether this assertion is valid, but it is my view that it is the leadership of Paul Keating in the past three years that has most decisively confronted the inherent racism of the Australian community to which Whitlam referred. I am astounded by the palpable changes in Australian attitudes since the start of the 1990s. Those who never have to deal with racism in all of its institutional and social manifestations from day to day may not so clearly appreciate the change that unequivocal and principled leadership has forced. The High Court's imprimatur in *Mabo* established the context for this major change in Australian attitudes toward Aboriginal people particularly and race generally. This has been the prosecution of principled pragmatism at its best.

The battle is not yet won, and sustained leadership at the national level will be needed for some time to come. If there is disappointment, it is in the failure of leadership at the state level. Rather than confronting and educating a conservative electorate, the Queensland Labor leadership has reflected community attitudes. I also regret that change has not swept the conservative side of politics; it appears that the Liberal Party in particular has regressed from its previously principled policies on race, Indigenous rights and social equity. I fear therefore that the gains that have materialised, and those which are still emerging, may be lost. However, I hold steadfastly to the view that for the great bulk of ordinary Australians, Aboriginal-affairs policy is now and will increasingly be a barometer for political decency. In the 1990s, a party's approach to Aboriginal affairs will be considered reflective of its standing on social justice generally. In other words: 'If they do us in, they'll do you in too.'

Gordon Childe described how the Australian Labor Party began as both a social-democratic party and a union party. Those attracted to the party by sentimental bonds included democrats and nationalists; by economic interests, small farmers, settlers, prospectors, mining proprietors and small shopkeepers; by self-interest, the Catholic Church and some business interests, including the liquor trade. Childe attributed what he deemed to be the failure of the party to maintain its idealism to its contamination by forces outside the urban proletariat. 'The Labor Party,' he complained, 'starting with a band of inspired Socialists, degenerated into a vast machine for capturing political power, but did not know how to use that power when attained except for the profit of individuals ... Such is the history of all Labor organizations in Australia, and that not because they are Australian, but because they are Labor.' These are the words of a disillusioned idealist. Freudenberg has countered that what Childe 'saw as degeneration was the Labor Party's capacity for change and renewal'.

Though the Labor Party today professes (admittedly with diminished enthusiasm) its commitment to the international democratic socialist movement, it might be a mistake to separate the true party, perceived in Marxist terms by Childe, from those elements of the community who were attracted to it for various other reasons. The party is arguably far better explained if one accepts the real diversity of its origins.

With all respect to Childe, I would argue that the history of the Labor Party has not necessarily been one of degeneration. It has been, and should continue to be, a necessarily complex and diverse history of dialogue between the pragmatic and the idealistic.

The failure of the colony of New Australia, founded in Paraguay by William Lane in 1893, is portrayed by Freudenberg as symbolising the failure of idealism:

The idealists, writing on a clean new page, defying the imperatives of established society and its institutions, had failed. The pragmatists, working within these flawed institutions and accepting the reality of human nature, remained at home to try their hand.

And yet, as Stuart McIntyre pointed out at the ALP National Conference this year, true believers do need beliefs.

Whatever It Takes, Graham Richardson's rollicking and unabashed insight into Labor's accumulation and exercise of power in the last decade, necessarily raised questions about how the Labor Party should preserve principle while pursuing the imperatives of political pragmatism. For all his unapologetic frankness about Machiavellian procedure, Richardson's cynical concept of mateship belies a commitment to actual reform for the national good. His achievements in the environment portfolio will stand as one of the great ministerial contributions of Labor government in this country. For all his bald larrikinism, I suspect that his commitment to the 'fair go' runs deeper than a good Machiavellian would care to admit.

Richardson, however, is inarticulate in defining the social good. So where should we look for some articulation of the ALP's ideals? We could look to an 1891 address by James McGowen, former secretary and president of the Boilermakers' Union, in which he professed that:

> the whole object of the Labor Party is for democratic legislation in the interests of the people. We believe almost to a man in these lines of the English writer Landor: 'Every Government should provide for every subject the means of living honestly and at ease'.

The importance of a philosophical basis was recognised by Whitlam, who emphasised the development of a practical program of reform, one which would meet the real needs of Australian people, within the existing Constitution. Whitlam coined the phrase 'positive equality' to describe his philosophy, which departed from radical socialism in its pragmatic support for the private sector as the mainstay of a national economy, concentrating on the provision of services rather than the levelling of individual wealth.

Of course, for our true beliefs we also need to look within and to search our national soul. Reconciliation requires recognising the need to reform chauvinistic and apathetic public attitudes as much as institutions and laws. In doing this, what do we appeal to? The 'fair go' tradition, as Vincent Lingiari did in 1966? It still has charm as a principle and relevance as a national ideology. Do we see the 'fair go' tradition at work in the enormous electoral support for the 1967 referendum? Or perhaps in the 1965 battle by the North Australian Workers' Union for equal wages for Aboriginal stockworkers?

Of Justice Lionel Murphy's faith in the democratic process and of his dogged pursuit of justice, Michael Kirby has written:

> What was it in his make up that sustained his optimism when all of the constitutional, institutional, parliamentary, bureaucratic and social pressures pushed him in the opposite direction: to inertia, to inactivity, to accept the status quo? ... Some fellow Celts would doubtless say that one answer was genetic: a kind of turbulent larrikinism that tends to be a feature of many of the descendants from that rain-swept island off the coast of Britain. Others would say experience ... when he gained office he wanted to do good and noble things and to do them quickly because he realised, only too well, the dominance in Australia of the forces of inaction.

The paradigms are beginning to shift. The silence is breaking. Mainstream journalists, politicians and academics now dare to examine some of Australia's most sacred national shibboleths with clear rather than misty eyes.

*

The process of national reconciliation being undertaken by the Council for Aboriginal Reconciliation must eventually lead to some document of reconciliation which is guaranteed by our Constitution. Such a document must have bipartisan and overwhelming support from the Australian community. I believe that this country will eventually embrace such an instrument as part of our national legal apparatus.

We must review our institutional and constitutional structure so that Indigenous peoples, and indeed all non-Anglo-Celtic people, are included as founding citizens of a new order. This new order must affirm the positive core of our democratic inheritance, whilst setting out an agenda for an Australia in which *terra nullius* and *homo nullius* are artefacts of the past and no longer an intrinsic part of our national culture.

We must now seriously consider the need for a bill of human rights for our country. The rights of minorities against the tyranny of the majority, and indeed a constitutional right to equality, must be guaranteed by such a bill. This is critical to maintaining national cohesion in the future. Australia must implement international law over and above notions of states' rights and regional parochialism. There must be fidelity to international human-rights and environmental-protection standards.

Our inevitable movement towards a republic is the central vehicle for institutional and constitutional renovation. It must be a mature review, which affirms the positive aspects of our achievements and institutions, and which also builds a new un-colonial foundation for a country where all peoples can share a place. Both the environment and Aboriginal affairs must become primarily Commonwealth responsibilities, and a direct relationship must be developed between Aboriginal people and the Commonwealth.

Finally, with all of the other things that we expect to export to Asia in the future, we can export values through our achievements, advice, diplomacy and, most importantly, our example. We can provide an example of a society that is reconciled with its indigenous peoples, has abandoned colonialism, is a strong, cohesive democracy and is capable of celebrating difference, guaranteeing equality and respecting human rights.

In a policy speech delivered before the 1972 federal election, Gough Whitlam highlighted the inevitable relationship between Australia's foreign affairs and its policy toward Aboriginal people:

Let us never forget this: Australia's real test as far as the rest of the world and particularly our region is concerned is the role we create for our own Aborigines. In this sense, and it is a very real sense, the Aborigines are our true link with our region. More than any foreign aid program, more than any international obligation which we meet or forfeit, more than any part we may play on any treaty of agreement or alliance, Australia's treatment of her Aboriginal people will be the thing upon which the rest of the world will judge Australia and Australians ...

I am confident enough to suggest that this prescription might be enlarged. Rather than continuing to perceive ourselves defensively as a nation succumbing to international judgment, Australia in the future should seek to fulfil its potential to be an international example of a responsible and just modern democracy. The example and the moral force of reconciliation founded on justice may well be the most important contribution that Indigenous and non-indigenous Australians will make to the Asia-Pacific.

Both black and white Australians have struggled for two centuries for that elusive ideal: a moral community in the Antipodes. Eddie Mabo stands as the latest figure in that substantial if uncelebrated line of agitators, which includes the late Lionel Murphy. Mabo was an agitator, a pragmatic idealist. Someone who dared to dream of the ideal of Indigenous justice whilst pursuing this ideal with such contagious zeal that the ideal became reality. The by-then putrid foundation stones of our country were torn out in a fundamental legal renovation, and replaced with a new cornerstone – a cornerstone hewn over ten years by a motley group of black activists and white lawyers, agitators the lot of them.

Two hundred years of clinging to *terra nullius* as a moral and legal foundation for nationhood left this country torn by irreconcilable contradictions. For the invisible had become visible. Those doomed to extinction had survived. Those willed to disappear through assimilation had refused to abandon their cultures, their families and their identities.

Now that the symbolic and institutional founding stones have been suggested after *Mabo*, we must very clearly appreciate that substantive justice must now follow. The symbols have got to be filled out.

Reconciliation must mean more than good feelings; it must be premised on actual justice. Social justice must become a reality for the people who still walk the streets, who still sleep under the bridges, who still have little prospect of living past their fifth decade, who are still the most likely to be in Australian criminal custody and who continue to be amongst the most wretched of the Earth. After *Mabo*, we surely have the best opportunity to change these things.

1994

FOR ALL OF US (BUT NOT FOR THEM): *MABO* AND THE 1996 FEDERAL ELECTION

Speech to the Sydney Institute

If I do one thing here this evening, let me at least invest in you the depth of my conviction that on 2 March 1996, Australians will make the most important decision in this country's modern political history, as to our future as a nation and as to the kind of country we want in the new millennium. More than at any time in the past, the national atmosphere is pregnant with possibilities unrealised and potentials yet to be fulfilled. The air is heavy with promise.

As Australians we can continue to develop, becoming an inclusive nation founded on unity in diversity – or we can go back to the Australia of old. We can head towards 2000 with optimism about our problems and challenges and a commitment to work hard to make things better. Or we can be pessimistic and cynical about the gains we have made and we can allow our resolve to be questioned. We can go backwards.

Concerning the fundamental question of our national culture and identity and the relationship between the old and new of this continent, we as a country simply cannot afford to turn back. We now have the foundations upon which we can begin to build truly great things. The cornerstone that *Mabo* laid for us will withstand the most blistering cynicism that our national critics can muster.

Mabo is the correct foundation for our future, no matter the frustrations we will all experience and despite the impatience, anger, arguments, misgivings and faithlessness that might afflict us from time to time. It is the correct foundation, because without a foundation of truth no national structure can endure. If we forsake *Mabo* we will be bereft of our one chance at national coherence: an opportunity to come to terms with the past, take its prescriptions in the present and map out a future.

Tonight I want to talk about *Mabo* and native title in the context of the 1996 election campaign. The spirit of *Mabo* has hovered silently but persistently over this campaign from the outset. It has, in different ways, informed the leadership philosophies of both contenders, Paul Keating and John Howard, and has played no small part in determining the respective political strategies of the Australian Labor Party and the Liberal–National Coalition.

Now, it is necessary to admit that I have come to a painful conclusion about the philosophy and strategy behind the Liberal Party's campaign to assume government in this country. The decision to discuss my views has not been made lightly. There is also no doubt in my mind that there are countless candidates and members of the party who have neither given thought to nor participated in the development of what amounts to a grotesque but familiar political strategy, a strategy which exploits racism for political gain.

My thesis here tonight only by coincidence takes up the observations of Gerard Henderson in his excellent article in today's *Sydney Morning Herald* about racism and the federal campaign. I was unaware of Gerard's article and I am sure he was unaware of the focus of my presentation here tonight.

Let me begin my analysis by saying that it is a political fact, borne out by the polls, that Aboriginal affairs are not an electoral priority and that there is a substantial reservoir of resentment and prejudice in some sections of the Australian community regarding Aborigines. *Mabo* and native title encapsulate 'the Aboriginal Problem' in the Australian subconscious. In campaign terms, *Mabo*, native title and Aboriginal people are difficult issues to be positive about, given that there is a sizeable proportion of the population who still cling to obscurantist outlooks.

Because of the political problems that *Mabo* presented, there were a few people in the parliamentary Labor Party who were not convinced that it should have been honoured in the way it was. Bob McMullan frankly articulated the political problem that *Mabo* represented for a pragmatic party anxious to stay in office when he said recently on the *Four Corners* program:

> Mabo wasn't ever seen as a vote winner for the government. It was just seen as being right. I think all of us were nervous nellies. I don't know about Paul but I was very excited by what we were doing as an important bit of agenda setting for Australia into the twenty-first century. But was I apprehensive about the public response to it, whether it would be seen to be workable and whether it would be accepted? Yes, I was very apprehensive.

There is still in Australia a sinister undercurrent of xenophobia and ignorance that informs a virulent racism. This subterranean ugliness rears its head from time to time, but with the country's maturation, explicit racism is increasingly regarded as unacceptable and indecent. What Russ Hinze and Joh Bjelke-Petersen used to say with impunity every other week when I was a kid in Queensland is today rightly considered offensive and indecent.

But has racism yet properly become un-Australian?

In its strategic prosecution of the 1996 campaign, the Liberal Party has brought this question to the fore. In the drive for political office, the Liberals have allowed themselves to besmirch their proud record on race and multiculturalism for the sake of expedience. The subtle irony of the slogan for the 1996 Liberal campaign struck me with a visceral force: *For All of Us*. After living for at least three febrile years with a desperate belief that we as a country were about to cross the Rubicon, if only, if only, if only … now I knew that the Liberal campaign was going to destroy the national promise because they so much want to destroy their political opponents.

This morning Gerard Henderson referred, in addition to the 'de-wogging' statements of National Party candidate Bob Burgess and the 'slanty-eyed ideologues' of Bob Katter, to two incredible incidents involving two National Party backbenchers. The member for Queanbeyan,

Peter Cochran, and the member for Parkes, Michael Cobb, separately alluded to rumours that Aborigines from Redfern were going to be relocated to these electorates to make way for the Olympics.

The Liberal Party candidate for Oxley, Pauline Hanson, who was subsequently forced to quit, was quoted by the *Courier Mail* on Thursday, 15 February:

> She said Aborigines could 'walk into a job' in the police force, received lenient court sentences, had better chances of getting housing and business loans and were the main instigators of crime and violence.
>
> 'I'm not racist but I'm asking for equality ... what I believe is racism is starting in this country because the government is looking after the Aborigines too much. Uni places have been set aside for them and if you are an Aborigine you get into the police force automatically while anyone else has to study and work for two years.'

Mr Howard was reported to be disgusted by her comments. However, Pauline Hanson has expressed the very sentiment that the Liberals' campaign slogan, *For All of Us*, is trying to exploit. By alleging government favouritism and special treatment, unscrupulous people are generating racist sentiment and criticism of government largesse to minorities. Why has Andrew Robb chosen *For All of Us* as the Liberals' campaign slogan? It is because on a subliminal level, they are seeking to exploit the very sentiment that Pauline Hanson has articulated.

Mabo and the *Native Title Act* set the context for the Liberals' clever slogan and there is no other issue with which Paul Keating is more identified than Aboriginal reconciliation. Few dispute his commitment to it; he has mentioned it at every turn, and sought to lead the nation at every opportunity. This has been despite complaints from within his own party about 'too much *Mabo*' and despite the sheer difficulty of standing up consistently in this policy area. So the subliminal message is: Keating has only been governing for the Abos, who get everything free ...

The idea that there are minorities – and Aborigines are the unmentioned exemplars – who are living it up while we in Middle Australia remain unrepresented by the government presses some buttons. It presses buttons with decent Australians at a subliminal level, because they don't necessarily follow through the nasty logic of the propaganda. These Australians would be appalled if the logic was put to them in an explicit way, as Pauline Hanson's comments have done. The Liberals' slogan works, however, through more subtle implication.

Talk about American-style electioneering propaganda! The message is so subtly crafted that it sickened me from the moment I saw it, and yet it is very difficult to expose. People need it explained clearly before they can see how it works. The clever and sinister thing about the slogan is that it can be used on different groups to focus resentment and prejudice against other groups.

If your beef is with environmentalists: then John Howard will govern *For All of Us*.

If you hate the unions: then John Howard will govern *For All of Us*.

If you want Asians out: then John Howard will govern *For All of Us*.

If you don't like the great Jewish conspiracy: then John Howard will govern *For All of Us*.

If you don't like the femo-nazis: then John Howard will govern *For All of Us*.

If you are sick of the wog multiculturalists: then John Howard will govern *For All of Us*.

If you don't like Abos who are getting free cars and houses and jobs: well, John Howard will govern *For All of Us*.

Goebbels would have been proud.

What the Liberals have failed to understand is that leadership for all of us requires government to rise to the challenge of bringing the people on the margins onboard. People such as Aborigines. People out on the fringes. No-one else has come close to the inclusive leadership that Paul Keating has provided. By bringing Aboriginal people into the national mainstream and providing the foundation for reconciliation and inclusion, he has shown the requisite leadership and has indeed governed for all of us. When he spoke about 'one nation', he sought to bring the people on the margins into the national fold. The Liberals' racist and divisive campaign slogan is a scary foreshadowing of an uninclusive government for Middle Australia.

However, along with Paul Keating and contrary to the Liberal Party, I believe that Middle Australia really believes in a nation that includes the people on the margins. They will be revolted by political campaigning that seeks to focus resentment on people at the margins for political purposes. Despite the electoral difficulties, there has never been a greater need for a leader who is not afraid to show inclusive leadership. I have consistently supported Keating's leadership in Aboriginal affairs and his championing of *Mabo* and Aboriginal reconciliation. Let me explain why.

Because he believes in one nation and in bringing people on the margins into the mainstream;

Because his vision is not about guilt about the past but about optimism for the future;

Because he believes in the decency of Australians and our unbending commitment to a fair go for all;

Because it is not about being a bleeding heart, it's about doing something practical and decent;

Because it is not about being obsessive, it's about doing what needs to be done;

Because it is about Aboriginal people taking responsibility for their own lives and showing leadership in their own communities, so that the egregious problems can be worked out in partnership with government and not by government alone;

Because Keating believes (as I and many Australians do) that with leadership we can lead the world in forging a reconciliation based on justice and inclusion and on coming to terms with the truths of the past and a belief in the possibilities of the future;

Because this is a good thing for Indigenous people as well as for the nation.

John Howard has expressed disgust at Pauline Hanson's explicit articulation of the subliminal campaign. So John Howard has a publicly decent position, while he allows Andrew Robb to run the nasty subliminal line. In the same way, Howard has expressed disgust at the Nationals' Katter and Burgess, while he takes the benefit of their bigotry. So John Howard has a publicly decent position, while the Nationals exploit the racist vote. It is almost as if the Liberals are saying to the Nationals:

'We'll collect the votes of Middle Australia, and you guys go and round up the votes from the racists – in fact incite them – and then we'll add them together.'

As a young Australian with a very keen sense of excitement about our country and what we can achieve, let me say that despite the tremendous challenges and the daunting problems we face, I have a brimming optimism about our prospects. Australia is a good country, but we have the capacity to be better. But if you think that opportunity and success and achievement are just going to fall into our laps while we sit on our hands, you're wrong. If you think that we're going to have a great and prosperous nation without some pain and uncertainty, then you're wrong. The potential that is inherent in all of us, and which is our national inheritance, will only be fulfilled with faith in each other, goodwill, perseverance and an unequivocal leadership.

I don't believe that the Australian Labor Party is necessarily the natural party of government in Australia, nor that the country should be saddled with its perpetual leadership. I believe that the Liberal Party under Malcolm Fraser in fact espoused inclusive government. It was the party that unequivocally rejected racism and championed the concept of a multicultural Australia. Fred Chaney, Ian Viner and Peter E. Baume were my political heroes. There are young people in the present Liberal Party, such as Christopher Pyne and Ian Campbell, who hold great promise for a party which is in a grievous ideological decline. Their time should come for government in the new millennium.

But for the ALP to lose office because of Paul Keating's stand on inclusive leadership and *Mabo* would be to our eternal discredit. *Mabo* should not necessarily be a reason for John Howard not to win the election, but it should never be a reason for Paul Keating to lose it. Ultimately, for the nation, what is more important than who wins the election is whether, in the process, in their drive for power, they have damaged the country by projecting resentment and prejudice against minority groups.

1996

SHIFTING GROUND INDEED

Speech to the ACT Council of Social Services

Last week, tributes flowed in the wake of the resignation of Andrew Robb, mastermind behind the Howard landslide of 1996, as federal director of the Liberal Party. That Robb devised and ran a brilliant strategy based on an acute understanding of the psychology of the nation is not disputed. Robb knew which were the hot buttons and how to press them. He engineered an electoral victory using state-of-the-art polling and communication techniques borrowed from the Republican Party in the United States.

For my part, however, I still harbour grave reservations about the ruthlessness of the strategies Robb employed to get John Howard the prize that had for so long eluded the conservatives. The Hanson phenomenon is the cat that Andrew Robb let out of the bag during the 1996 election campaign. And he knows it.

This was the campaign in which the Great Mainstream of Australia rose up against those who for so long had kept its people outcast and dispossessed. The Great Mainstream of Australia conquered all before it at that March poll. The Great Mainstream then embarked on a relentless crusade against the appalling state of Aboriginal privilege. The wrath of the Great Mainstream was then visited on immigrants, who had for too long been luxuriating in our dole queues. The Great Mainstream freed itself from the bondage of political correctness. The Great Mainstream tore off the black armbands that the former prime minister had foisted upon it. Free at last. Free at last. Thank God

Almighty we were free at last. And of course, the Great Mainstream was returned to its rightful place in the firmament with the delivery of the new government's first budget. Or so we were told.

Since Pauline Hanson gave her maiden speech, there has been a lot of public analysis of the politics of blame that was, for me, the true undercurrent of the election. It underpinned not just Hanson's own resounding success in the former Labor stronghold of Oxley, but also the national Coalition landslide. The recent release of her book *The Truth* (some chapters of which, I would wager, she had not read before she was interviewed about it) has generated more analysis of the circumstances in our society that have given rise to the so-called Hanson phenomenon.

The historical context for the political and economic changes that have led to Pauline Hanson is of course best captured in the title of Paul Kelly's seminal account of the Hawke–Keating era's place in Australian history: *The End of Certainty*. In the *Australian* last weekend Kelly wrote that:

> Hanson symbolises an alienation within part of the community caused by a conjunction of forces – globalisation, economic restructuring and social changes – where people need scapegoats to explain their frustration.

This analysis is now familiar to us. However, most of this kind of discussion is focused on Pauline Hanson. But did Hanson deliberately identify these hot buttons in the community as part of a calculated political strategy? The analysts avoid this question. My own view is that she did not. Although she is now very much aware of how scapegoat-herding works for her politically, I do not believe that this was the case when she started. Given her lack of analytical and political sophistication, I believe that Hanson's identification of these hot buttons was the instinctive manifestation of primal and inarticulate grief. Her message resonated because she actually believed in the correctness of her complaints, and these complaints were patently shared by many other people in similar circumstances to her own. This is why I am not inclined to support the notion that Pauline Hanson is evil. The ideas she espouses, the feelings she is cultivating and the controversy she is revelling in are certainly ugly and repugnant, but my feelings for her are more of pity than of anger. I do not believe she knows what she is doing; she is caught in a tragic redneck celebrity vortex from which she does not want to escape.

I am not so concerned with Pauline Hanson. I am concerned with those who know the truth, who are not ignorant of the facts of Aboriginal disadvantage, Asian immigration and so on, but who nevertheless deliberately scapegoat minorities in the same way as Hanson. There has been almost no analytical focus on the other beneficiaries of the politics of blame: John Howard's Coalition. Not during the 1996 campaign or in its aftermath. Only when the prime minister gave that incredible speech which implied that the Pauline Hanson issue was an issue of free speech was there any focus on the government's role in the subtle and sometimes not-so-subtle cultivation and exploitation of the politics of blame.

Only Malcolm MacGregor in the *Australian Financial Review* had the insight and the courage to analyse the strategic exploitation of feelings of resentment and alienation by politicians and apparatchiks more seasoned and more cynical than Pauline Hanson. Read MacGregor's coverage of the campaign and its aftermath. It is all there. It was brutally honest and foretold of the Australia we have endured over the past twelve months. Most of the other social and political commentators were either oblivious to the realpolitik or unwilling to acknowledge its real dynamics, both before and after the election.

In an address to the Sydney Institute in the third week of the campaign, I delivered my own interpretation of the psychology underlying the Coalition's campaign. You will appreciate that I burned more bridges with that speech than a prudent man, feeling the good ship *Paul* sinking inevitably into the unforgiving depths, would have done. In retrospect I have to say that my views have not changed much. The 1996 election was a very different one for Australia. I don't know if we have ever before had a national election, at least in the modern era, in which the victorious party traded on the mainstream's resentment of other sections of the community. It left many of us asking: for whom had Paul Keating's Labor government governed, if not for us?

The Liberal Party's slogan implied a righteous sense of deprivation and neglect in Middle Australia. Many uncertainties, frustrations, unfulfilled expectations and dashed ambitions could easily be attributed to government indulgence of minorities and 'special-interest groups'. (Of course, we in Middle Australia don't count the numerous business, professional, recreational, religious and community groups that we are members of as 'special-interest groups'.)

Andrew Robb's 1996 campaign was very clever. He made the usual pet scapegoats – most obviously Aborigines, Asians and unions – Paul Keating's running mates, in much the same way as the Republicans had made the black prisoner Willie Horton Michael Dukakis's running mate in his failed 1988 presidential bid. *Mabo* and Asia had so coloured Keating's leadership over the previous term, they were like albatrosses around Labor's political neck. This is not to say that Labor was not on the way out for a host of other reasons, but Keating's vulnerability on these fronts was ruthlessly exploited by Andrew Robb.

It was a watershed election because it seems to me to have been the first time we have employed wedge politics in Australia. Although elections in the Northern Territory have routinely generated and exploited white paranoia and racism in relation to Aboriginal people and land rights for a long time, I cannot think of a national election in which Aboriginal affairs, and particularly questions of Aboriginal privilege and comparative white disadvantage, have featured at all. It was a big part of the undercurrent of the last campaign – particularly in regional Australia – and if you accept my view, this was done deliberately. Remember that John Howard's senior adviser, Grahame Morris, is a veteran of Northern Territory campaigns by the Country Liberal Party. Remember also Alan Ramsey's post-election analysis of how the most severe regional swings against Labor were in seats with visible Aboriginal populations.

Pauline Hanson, Bob Burgess and Bob Katter were instances when the putrid sewage broke the surface and became visible. They were instances when the dog-whistle could be heard at normal frequency. Their contributions, however, were not unhelpful to the overall strategy. Remember the point in the campaign when Bob Katter complained that only Aborigines and the rich could afford to send their children to boarding school? The most telling thing was John Howard's response. Whilst he continued to maintain that he abhorred racism, Howard said that what Bob Katter was saying was true: Aboriginal children did receive benefits that were not available to other country kids. Of course this was an untruth. The Labor government had already lifted the assets test cut-off for Austudy for country children to about three-quarters of a million dollars as part of its drought response, and this socialism was thanks to lobbying by National Party backbenchers such as Bob Katter. Furthermore, Department of Employment, Education and Training statistics showed that whilst there were about 3000 Aboriginal students on maximum assistance under Abstudy, there were about 11,000 non-Aboriginal students on the maximum assistance under Austudy. So through untruth, John Howard was able to give his subtle imprimatur to Katter's allegation of black privilege and white disadvantage. And Howard's response penetrated.

I think that USA-style wedge politics are now with us to stay. They are likely to become a part of election campaigning in our country in the future. The conservatives have realised that they can drive a wedge between sections of the community who would not otherwise have voted for them. The projection of blame onto minorities has worked very well for them.

Let me make two final points in relation to this. Firstly, when I realised what the conservatives were doing and how successfully they were doing it, I resigned myself to accepting that this kind of ruthlessness is to be expected during elections. The drive for power can obliterate all principle and decency. I put myself in Canberra mode and said to myself: they woulda been mugs not to use it. The second point, however, is that I also hoped that, having been so ruthless in seizing power, upon gaining government they would change tack. Conscious of the damage their ruthless button-pushing may have inflicted on society, I actually expected the new government to pause and seek to heal the very wounds they had so vigorously agitated. After all, the business of government is not the business of elections.

But even this benign hypocrisy was beyond them. Andrew Robb

was onto too good a thing. He could not resist pressing those hot buttons that had yielded such great success in the election. The Pauline Hanson bandwagon was too good to miss. So from day one of the new government we saw a sustained orgy of divisiveness and meanness about immigration, Aborigines and dole bludgers.

Robb wanted to turn the phenomenon that he had observed well before the election, and which he had successfully capitalised on during it, into a fundamental cultural shift in the Australian community. He wanted the government to be seen to be tough on the scapegoats, and to follow public opinion to the letter, whilst at the same time talking about 'government for all of us'. The public good was presented as a matter of charity – not of equality or right. The blacks and the Asians and the unionists and the dole bludgers had to resume their place on the margins of society, where they could be the recipients of a kind of frugal and ascetic charity.

Robb wanted to turn ephemeral madness into a permanent psychosis. To this end, the Howard government has been a slavish devotee of data, which Liberal Party headquarters produces using techniques learned from American politics. This was most bizarrely expressed in the prime minister's constant claim that he 'understands' whatever ignorant or offensive attitude, prejudice or anger has registered in the polls or arisen in public debate. Listen, it's not nice to bash Asians, but I can understand why some sections of the community might feel that they are entitled to. Listen, I can understand that some sections of the community feel that Aborigines have been wasting taxpayers' money. To 'understand' a problem allows you to avoid taking a position on it; it allows you to be understood to be legitimising certain views without claiming them as your own.

The cultural shift which Robb set out to achieve, so that Howard's battlers could remain Howard's battlers, is what, in my view, has fuelled the racism and social division that so concern Australians today. When I look at Hanson and her so-called followers, I can't help thinking that sections of our society are willing themselves – defiantly – to ignorance. If you live at Kingaroy or Gatton, it is as if reason and enlightenment do not count. This phenomenon of an obdurate citizenry for whom ideology founded on ignorance and prejudice becomes as immovable and righteous as religion is the product of manipulation. Woe betide us when the mainstream political machines feel they need this citizenry and must woo and indeed exploit its voters.

1997

THE *WIK* DECISION AND HOWARD'S TEN-POINT PLAN *

It was with a degree of political trepidation that I met Prime Minister John Howard earlier this year to discuss the Cape York Land Use Agreement and the implications of the *Wik* decision. I had told the National Press Club last year that I believed Howard fundamentally disagreed with the High Court's original *Mabo* decision. This he indignantly denied. Privately, the prime minister holds the mistaken view that the Indigenous leadership is 'Labor to the bootstraps'.

During last year's federal election campaign, I expressed the view that the Coalition's concept of government *For All of Us* was in fact an exclusivist, if clever, slogan for mainstream Australia. It tapped into a rich vein in the Australian community after long years of a growing sense of economic malaise and social insecurity. The Pauline Hanson phenomenon manifested what the Coalition election strategists had understood long before the last federal poll: that, among other things, a 'backlash' was in the offing.

Given this background, I went to the meeting half-wondering whether I would have to undergo some ritual denunciation of former

---

*   In 1992, in the *Mabo* judgment, the High Court found that the common law recognised native title in certain circumstances. In the following year, the federal parliament enacted the *Native Title Act*. Together, *Mabo* and the *Native Title Act* made clear that native title is completely and irreversibly extinguished on freehold land. However, they did not establish whether native title is extinguished on pastoral leases and other Crown-derived titles. In 1996, in the *Wik* judgment, the High Court found that pastoral leases do not afford exclusive possession to the leaseholder, and

Labor prime minister Paul Keating and all his works and ways in front of the Queen's portrait in the prime ministerial foyer. If Howard was convinced of anything about Aboriginal policy it was this: that Keating got it wrong and there needed to be a decisive break with the policies developed under Labor.

My view is that Keating laid the foundation for Indigenous inclusion in the Australian nation by seizing the opportunity *Mabo* presented to begin to get everything else right. From the smouldering ruins of previous Indigenous economic and social policy initiatives, Keating had carved out a place for Indigenous people in the national future. The fringe dwellers could finally see a place for themselves in their own country.

I suspect Howard is not convinced of this. Whereas Keating pulled together the various philosophical threads that must anchor Indigenous policy if we are to get it right, his successor is extremely sceptical. I expect Howard believes that the country was held hostage by a native title delirium induced by the café-society cultural elite. His comments about the 'black armband view of history' and the convulsions in Indigenous affairs in the first six months of his government indicate how deeply held are his views on our colonial history and the position of Indigenous people in Australian society. I think they also indicate a vehement and, indeed, personal disagreement with his predecessor on the subject.

When the Coalition took office, I expressed the hope that it would recognise the essential correctness of the emerging national policy direction. This hope has not been fulfilled, but it has by no means been entirely lost. I often wonder whether the residual political enmity between these two longstanding political foes clouds Howard's assessment of his predecessor's leadership on Indigenous policy. Given his

---

that native title and Crown titles such as pastoral leases can coexist. In the event of inconsistency, the Crown-derived title prevails. After *Wik*, the Howard government introduced legislation known as the ten-point plan, with the expressed aim of delivering certainty to pastoralists, miners and other leaseholders. The ten-point plan, even after amendment in the Senate, significantly diminished the Indigenous right to negotiate and, in many instances, extinguished native title. This legislation was passed in 1998 as the *Native Title Amendment Act*.

own ascetic style, I suspect Howard believes that there was too much euphoria and not enough practical outcomes from *Mabo*.

One could never have reasonably expected the Coalition simply to carry over the policies of the past. The failures in Indigenous health, employment and social policies after thirteen years of Labor were egregious and needed a new energy. But the causes of such failures lie as much in the denial of adequate resources to address Indigenous disadvantage as they do in the will of the Indigenous community to help provide solutions. That is why Aboriginal Affairs Minister John Herron's refreshing emphasis on empowerment has to be seen as a critical part of the formula.

Like other societies, Indigenous society can and will advance only when we realise that rights and responsibilities are sides of the same coin. Howard has long held a vision of One Australia, for which he believes he was unfairly maligned in the past. But Keating also spoke of One Nation. Pat Dodson and his colleagues on the Council for Aboriginal Reconciliation, who will host a milestone national conference in May, also speak of a united nation. The differences within this apparent consensus relate to the relative emphasis placed on diversity. Indigenous peoples, as well as the numerous ethnic communities in our country, have a desire to maintain diversity and to celebrate our differences as well as those things that we share as Australians. They reject assimilation. On the other hand, there is a strong view in the Howard government that the emphasis on diversity has been at the expense of unity and that the 'multi-culti', to use Robert Hughes's phrase, is a barely disguised Labor outpost. Despite the origins of multicultural policy in the Fraser government, it is for these reasons heading for the political-correctness dustbin.

But my own view is that those things that separate and those things that unite us are also two sides of the same coin. The disaster of assimilation and the sheer resilience of our various identities – and the fact that humans have layered identities and do not simply fall within one box or another – have surely taught us that diversity is essential to unity. Is there really such a gaping philosophical divide between Howard's approach to rights and responsibilities and diversity and unity and that of Keating? I don't know. But I hope that, since the

Whitlam government, Australia has been developing a bipartisan consensus founded on justice and equality for Indigenous people, and not just on convenience and apathy.

In the wake of the *Wik* decision, however, and knowing too well the political imperatives facing Howard, from the moment he expressed 'disappointment' in the High Court's decision I believed there was no hope of a fair outcome for Indigenous people. There are strong, if not overwhelming, reasons why the prime minister will likely fail to deliver justice to those who were supposed to be the beneficiaries of *Wik*, even though he may wish to.

Howard has met Indigenous representatives to discuss proposals for the resolution of native title issues on a number of occasions. There is clearly some reserve and suspicion in these relations. However, he has been straightforward in his view that *Wik* was unexpected and overturned long-held understandings. He seems to be sincere in his determination to deliver justice for both sides – if he can, he says – but we have been left in no doubt that he also believes that there is a question of justice for pastoralists. Few on our side would deny that there is an imperative for justice for both parties – pastoral and Indigenous. However, Howard's constant reiteration of the need for certainty for pastoralists and his selectively political interpretation of the *Native Title Act* cause some palpitations on our side.

If there is not trust in the present process, there is at least a commitment from the Indigenous leaders who have been working in Canberra over the past two months and from the government's *Wik* task force to try to find fair solutions. The bureaucrats clearly have the prime minister's imprimatur to work closely with Indigenous representatives. Obviously the same thing is taking place with the miners and farmers.

The pressing policy and legislative challenge is this: if Aboriginal people agree that the existing rights of leaseholders should be confirmed, what exactly are these 'existing rights'? Under some legislation, such as the *Northern Territory Pastoral Lands Act*, the rights of pastoralists can easily be ascertained. Under the *Queensland Land Act*, the rights under leases are less clear. There is a need for clarification. The fact that many leases include certain rights to undertake agriculture as well as pastoral activities adds to the complication.

There is also a need to ensure that leaseholders have continued access to natural resources in order to carry out their rights under their leases. Many of these issues – such as access to water and the ability to construct fencing and other improvements – are, according to legal advice to Indigenous organisations, not disputed.

To the extent that these issues are under question, there is a preparedness to clarify the situation. But not all of the questions about native title can be answered with legislation. We could not hope to produce legislation which comprehensively delineates the common law concept of native title. What we can aim for is to produce legislation which provides pastoralists with the utmost certainty in relation to their understanding of, and the exercise of, their legal rights under their leases. There also should be certain and efficient processes for miners who will need to deal with native titleholders.

There is much that can be done to secure these objectives and to make the *Native Title Act* work better. The problem has been that those who are troubled by the 'workability' of the legislation have chosen what they think is the most efficient path to certainty: simply extinguish native title so that you don't have to deal with it. This has a superficial attraction to the hardliners in the National Farmers' Federation, the United Graziers' Association and some quarters of the National Party. But, given the constitutional problems involved in this approach and the fact that we cannot retreat from the High Court's prescription that we should share the country, there will be no certainty in extinguishment.

If Keating had been prime minister when the *Wik* judgment was delivered, he, too, would have wanted to avoid the political problems and challenges posed by the decision. While the *Native Title Act* did not set out to extinguish native title in valid pastoral leases, the Keating government believed that the High Court would find in favour of extinguishment. However, both the Keating and Howard governments understood that there was always a chance the Court would find in favour of co-existence.

The prime minister has to deal with the fact that the High Court has so ruled. Co-existence in pastoral country is inescapable. Given the fact that conservative politics is in the ascendant in Canberra, and given the high passions on all sides and the fact that the opinion polls show that resentment towards and ignorance about Indigenous people and their rights are rampant in the community, it seems strange to me that Howard represents our best chance of securing a fair outcome for all of us.

29 March 1997

*

The Queensland National Party has a 'compromise' proposal on *Wik*: native title should be extinguished on pastoral leases. The state government would then give leaseholders whatever increased title they wanted – perpetual leases or freehold for a pittance.

What would Aborigines get? They would get freehold title to vacant Crown land. Sounds fair, some might think. In fact, the Nationals are trying to pull a huge scam so brazen it could only have come from political cowboys. There is almost no vacant Crown land in Queensland. Queensland has less vacant Crown land than any other state or territory. On a map of state land tenures, you cannot see the areas of vacant Crown land with the naked eye. About 57 per cent of Cape York Peninsula is covered by pastoral leases, with vacant Crown land limited to about 0.7 per cent.

If there is so little vacant land on Cape York, imagine what there is elsewhere in the state. Small blocks of vacant Crown land are known to exist on salt flats, small uninhabitable islands and small blocks on the outskirts of towns near sewage ponds and rubbish dumps. To find vacant Crown land in Queensland is truly a needle-in-a-haystack exercise. Almost the entire state is covered by freehold and leasehold tenures and Crown reserves.

So what exactly is the National Party offering Aborigines? Zero. Beads and mirrors have been replaced by smoke and mirrors. And yet we have Senator Bill O'Chee running around the countryside trying to beat up support for this scam. Not since former New South Wales chief magistrate Murray Farquhar tried one on the Philippines gold-bullion reserve has there been a more egregious try-on than this.

It won't happen because it can't happen. Native title over pastoral leases cannot be extinguished without generating even more uncertainty and conflict. It would make the present confusion pale in comparison. The economic cost to the country would be horrendous. Not only would the requirement under the Constitution to pay just terms make the present national deficit look like the least of our economic problems, but the lost opportunities for development of land and resources for tourism, mining and primary production would be of even greater cost. Who is going to invest in the country while countless legal challenges to extinguishment are still running? And what will the necessary legal discrimination (which would be the unavoidable consequence of extinguishment) mean for Australia's international reputation? What will it mean for our human-rights record and treaty obligations? What will it mean for the Olympics, the new millennium and the centenary of Federation? What will it mean for our souls? One mob left eternally to account for their infidelity to their own rule of law and for racial discrimination; another mob left with everlasting hatred burning in their hearts.

These are not scenarios we can afford to countenance as an economy, as a democracy and as a people. Sharing the country and respecting its Indigenous heritage while respecting the moral and legal entitlement of Aborigines is our destiny. This is what white Australians must accept. The High Court also put forward principles which recognise the accumulated and continuing moral and legal entitlements of those who have come to this country since 1788. This is what black Australians must accept.

If the National Farmers' Federation was led by rational and sensible leaders in this present trauma, Indigenous representatives would want to work with them toward two objectives. The first would be to ensure that co-existence did not cause economic detriment to pastoral leaseholders. While native title will provide an economic base for Aborigines to finally climb out of the welfare trap in the long term, this cost cannot be borne by pastoralists. There is more than enough economic hardship in rural Australia and we have to ensure that our co-existence scheme does not add to this burden.

Pastoralists might have to do things differently. They might have to develop a new regard for Indigenous cultural issues. They might have to plan for the management of heritage, as they are increasingly expected to in relation to the environment. They should develop relationships with Indigenous groups. They might want to jointly advance developments for mutual benefit. But any requirements on leaseholders should not place them at any commercial disadvantage that they did not suffer before the *Wik* judgment.

The second objective is to ensure there is appropriate flexibility for leaseholders to undertake their diverse production activities and to utilise new techniques. Crown leases have historically been crafted to ensure that land use and development is appropriate and sensible given the soils, climatic and vegetation conditions of the land. The disasters that wholesale land clearing and overstocking have wreaked on Australian rangelands are well-known. The national embrace of Landcare – championed by that historic alliance between Rick Farley, then of the National Farmers' Federation, and Phillip Toyne, then of the Australian Conservation Foundation – is testament to the importance of lease management in the future. In securing opportunities for leaseholders to diversify, we must observe the precautionary principles that our less-than-proud history of land degradation has taught us. Leaseholders cannot expect to radically change land use from, say, growing sorghum for cattle feed to growing cotton, without dealing with native title implications. Such radical changes to land use must be appropriately assessed.

These are critical policy issues, and the co-existence scheme must seek to strike the right balance between the reasonable expectation of leaseholders to develop the land and to diversify, and the Aborigines' ability to enjoy their native title rights and interests. It is a pity we are unable to work closely with representatives of the rural sector on devising a co-existence scheme which achieves the right balance. But you simply cannot negotiate with another party whose sole contribution from across the table is this: we want to extinguish your rights.

In the 1980s, the National Farmers' Federation provided much of the intellectual leadership on national economic reforms. The NFF developed Landcare. In 1993, it played the most constructive role on *Mabo*. All of these achievements were contrary to the instincts of the

National Party and were pursued by the NFF despite the politicians. In 1997, we have an NFF leadership that cannot distinguish itself from the National Party, and this has made the search for the best co-existence scheme very difficult. But this has not dimmed my conviction that a fair solution for Aborigines must also be fair for leaseholders.

12 April 1997

*

There is a world of difference between 'amendment' of legislation and 'repeal and replacement' of legislation. Prime Minister John Howard's 300-page *Native Title Amendment Bill*, tabled in the House of Representatives last Thursday, is not amending legislation. It represents a total rewrite of the original 1993 Act that Aboriginal leaders negotiated with federal parliament and destroys a number of the cornerstone principles that were settled then. This massive bill puts the lie to Howard's promise before the 1996 federal election that his government would only address the 'workability' of the Act and not extinguish native title. Howard's bill must, at all costs, be stopped from passing federal parliament without a number of fundamental changes and omissions.

The consequences for the future of the country should such vile proposals become the law of the land are too depressing to contemplate. We have to maintain a belief that justice will prevail in the debate and Australians of goodwill everywhere will need to work hard to ensure that it does.

Does my rejection of the Howard bill mean that I am opposed to amendments to the *Native Title Act*? No, it does not. Changes clearly need to be made – but Howard has gone completely overboard with his bill. Does my urging of senators to oppose this bill in its current form mean that I don't support the right of pastoralists and miners to pursue economic development? No, it does not. Again, there are useful changes that can and should be made to the *Native Title Act*. But why has Howard followed Senator Nick Minchin's extreme ideological advice and gone beyond providing security to farmers and miners to destroying the security of native title holders?

The *Courier-Mail*'s editorial last Friday suggested that 'there will be losers' from the forthcoming debate. I disagree. Australians should clearly understand that the issues at the heart of this debate do not necessitate losers. If we are sensible and fair about this, there need not be any losers.

We can have legislation which confirms the rights of leaseholders, so that they can carry on their business. As the High Court judges said in the *Wik* case, the leaseholder's rights already prevail over any native title rights. We can have legislation which ensures that the right to negotiate on mining works smoothly and efficiently – without taking away rights from Aborigines. We can have legislation which removes overlapping and multiple claims by Aboriginal groups (which has been a major problem with the Act) so that the native title process can work with greater certainty. This will require changes to the threshold test for claims but, again, Howard's proposals go way overboard on this crucial issue. We can have legislation which urges parties to come to negotiated agreements at the local and regional (and even statewide) level rather than promoting litigation in the federal court, which represents a crippling and unnecessary cost in most cases.

A win-win outcome requires us to make sensible and balanced amendments to the *Native Title Act* without destroying its foundation principles. We cannot achieve this with 300 pages of new law, based on new principles that take, take, take from the Aboriginal side and give, give, give to the other stakeholders. I am afraid this debate is going to become shrill, and the opinion leaders and editorialists will come to lazy conclusions, because they just want the issues to be settled and to go away. They will start to prescribe their own versions of 'pragmatic balance' and 'fair and realistic' outcomes (Aborigines will just have to take the hit), without taking responsibility as Australians to properly comprehend the issues.

The chief difficulty the nation will have as we embark again on this debate is the prime minister's unabashed propensity to misrepresent the truth about key issues. Howard has shown clearly that there will be no leadership from him in the native title debate. He has marked himself as the champion of the mining corporations, the millionaire land barons, the state and territory governments. He has shown that he is prepared to stoop to every kind of cheap distortion and misrepresentation of the truth – including waving coloured maps of Australia on national television – to convince people he is doing the fair and right thing. He is not, and he will be opposed utterly.

9 September 1997

THE COALITION GOVERNMENT, *MABO* AND *WIK*

Speech to the Australian Jewish Democratic Society

I suppose in some ways I want to apologise for some intemperate remarks that I made during the course of the 1996 federal election, when I alleged that the Coalition government's campaign *For All of Us* was not an inclusive campaign, that it was in fact a campaign prompting division in Australian society.

I made those intemperate remarks during the course of an address to the Sydney Institute in the middle of the campaign, and the wrong theory I had at that time was based on my gut analysis of the various strategies of the major contenders in that election.

I'd always feared, particularly since 1993, that the prominence of *Mabo* and native title as an issue in Australian politics and society, and the high profile given to the concept of reconciliation by the former federal government, would inevitably lead to a backlash. I thought that whenever there were expressions of racism against Aboriginal people, the situation had to be too good, when you had the national leader, no less, consistently defending reconciliation and advocating Indigenous land rights at every turn. Because it's obvious to everybody who has been involved in Aboriginal politics, being such a small and detested minority in a community such as this, that it is very difficult to get people to understand and to feel positive about Aboriginal issues. Aboriginal affairs and Aboriginal people are not readily marketable in the business of politics.

So for very good reason, politicians are reticent about coming out and identifying themselves with Indigenous issues and Indigenous people. So I always thought that the prominence given to native title, *Mabo*, reconciliation and so on during those salad days in the three years from 1993 to 1996 might one day come to an end. I was fearful about the continuing controversy surrounding native title after the *Native Title Act* was put in place in 1993. And I was in fact speculating as to whether it might be in our better interests for the issue to assume a lower profile.

During the course of 1994 and 1995 I learnt from polling conducted by the Council for Aboriginal Reconciliation and by the Australian Labor Party that there was a solid core of opposition to *Mabo* and to native title, particularly amongst the so-called battlers of the country. But there was hope, at least in the Labor ranks, that opposition was dissipating and that *Mabo* might even become a political positive. I think I allowed myself to believe, as did a lot of people, that *Mabo* had, by the end of 1995, finally come to be seen as an act of political decency. Native title had become a barometer of political decency in Australian society. And I relaxed into feeling that there was no way a political party could enter into an election making *Mabo* a negative issue without paying some political cost.

Mabo didn't become an explicit issue in the 1996 election campaign. On the surface, the federal Coalition merely committed itself to amending the native title legislation to make it 'more workable'. There was no substantive debate about the issue of native title in that election.

But I have to tell you that when I saw, on the first day of the campaign, the slogan of the Liberal Party – *For All of Us* – I was struck with a visceral force because it immediately hit me with its implicit strategy. I understood from the minute I saw that slogan that it invited a question: If John Howard was going to be for all of us, for whom were the other mob? If this was going to be the government for all of us, for whom had Paul Keating been governing?

Well, Paul Keating had been governing, in the subliminal and subterranean imagination of Australia, for the *Mabo* crowd, the APEC crowd, the multicultural crowd and any minority or fringe-interest group you happened to resent: anyone you wanted to hold accountable for your own sense of economic, social and psychological malaise.

So I gave this lunatic speech to the Sydney Institute in the middle of the campaign, outlining my analysis of the psychological strategy underlining the federal campaign by the Liberals. I said that this was the cleverest campaign slogan that could ever have been thought up by smart political operators who had their fingers on the pulse of economic and social malaise – the sense out there in Middle Australia that people weren't getting it as good as they were entitled to. That somehow the Paxtons out there were ruining our economic opportunities. That somehow these undefined groups were living it up at the Labor trough at our expense.

So poor Middle Australia, the Great Mainstream of Australia (who hasn't heard those terms consistently over the last year and a half?) had lived through thirteen long years of neglect and misery at the hands of an uncaring federal government. And my analysis was that the *For All of Us* slogan invited people to project an undefined resentment. It invited voters to believe that somehow other people were to blame for our condition.

Those of us who were outraged at John Howard's refusal to answer Pauline Hanson during the last two years should not be outraged. We should understand that John Howard came before Pauline Hanson. John Howard did things deliberately, whereas Pauline Hanson did things instinctively. John Howard knew the truth about Aboriginal disadvantage, about the fact that Aboriginal people just don't get free homes and free cars and free loans. He knows all those facts. In Pauline Hanson's defence, a lot of the ignorant things she professes she actually believes. But the same cannot be said of our prime minister. The first press conference that John Howard gave as prime minister of this country was to announce an enquiry into corruption at ATSIC. There was then, of course, a sustained abuse of Aboriginal organisations and Aboriginal people, as though the money spent on Aboriginal affairs was at the core of our economic malaise in this country.

Let me talk about Howard's ten-point plan and true liberalism.

Essentially, the *Native Title Amendment Bill* should be called the *Compensation for the Extinguishment of Native Title Act*, because we have 400 pages of new amendments that basically authorise the extinguishment of native title and of course the payment of compensation. For the federal government to say that it is at least providing compensation is no concession whatsoever. Everybody is already entitled to compensation under the Constitution. We did not need John Howard's version of courage and leadership in order to be entitled to compensation. Governments cannot escape paying compensation under our existing Constitution. So it is no answer to Aboriginal people to say that fiscal compensation is available. Throughout the country, I constantly hear Aboriginal elders saying that we're not interested in the money; we want our land.

John Howard's plan is complex – every 'i' dotted, every 't' crossed – to allow state and territory governments to extinguish native title. It really is (although I'm not sure this is the right audience to which to say this) a piece of Pontius Pilate legislation. John Howard will say, 'I'm not extinguishing native title. I'm just going to allow the state and territory governments to extinguish.' And that's what the whole scheme is all about.

He will be able to run up and down every Australian hill and dale and say, 'I'm not extinguishing. I'm just allowing Rob Borbidge to extinguish.' This is going to be a very difficult argument for us to counter. Because if the *Native Title Act* of 1993 served any purpose, it served the purpose of restraining the state and territory governments from just arbitrarily extinguishing native title, as Richard Court attempted to do in 1993.

You see how easily we forget that the Court government of Western Australia passed legislation in 1993 that wiped out native title across the entire state in one fell swoop. If Court's legislation had been constitutionally valid, there would be not one square inch of native title in the whole state of Western Australia. Thankfully the High Court struck down that legislation as unconstitutional. But protection against that kind of predatory and arbitrary and racially discriminatory deprivation of property by state and territory governments was provided by the *Native Title Act*, and that protection is now under grave threat.

The Indigenous position, if it can be summarised, is this. We don't want the money; we want to share our land. That is the essence of the Aboriginal submission in relation to pastoral leases. We don't want to be paid to have our title killed (and such a payment would be very large for Australian taxpayers). We don't want to be paid for extinguishment of our title. We just want to be able to share our land under the prescription laid out by the High Court.

I had a very depressing evening last night in Sydney, and please don't tell the people I was with about this. But I was in a room full of Liberal Party supporters and I attempted to urge them to consider three principles of true liberalism that we can't deny in this current debate.

Firstly, the fundamental and central importance of the rule of law. How can liberals renounce a decision that emanates from the rule of law? There should be no stronger defenders of the benefits and protections – not just the prohibitions and the punishments – of the rule of law, and of the extension of those benefits to Aboriginal people as citizens and as subjects of the rule of law. So how is it that liberals are not standing up for the rule of law when Aboriginal people are concerned?

Secondly, property rights. There should be no stauncher defenders of property rights than true liberals. But when it concerns Aboriginal people, the benefits of the rule of law and the benefits of true liberalism are not extended.

Thirdly, arbitrary deprivation of rights by governments. Ron Castan, Bryan Keon-Cohen and Eddie Mabo struggled for ten years with their famous court case. In 1985, three years into it, the Bjelke-Petersen government arbitrarily passed a law called the *Queensland Coast Islands Declaratory Act*, in the middle of the night, which retrospectively extinguished native title on Murray Island. The law basically said that if the State of Queensland had not extinguished or had not intended to extinguish native title in 1879, it intended to do so now.

That was an arbitrary deprivation of property. No report in the newspaper next day. No political movement of outrage in the community. Not a single voice raised against that arbitrary deprivation of property rights by the government. And it fell upon the legal team and upon Eddie Mabo to go to the High Court to say that this Bjelke-Petersen law was unlawful and unconstitutional. And they eventually succeeded in striking down that law. And once they struck that law down they were able to continue with their litigation until they achieved success in 1992. The arbitrary deprivation of property rights is something that true liberals ought to be concerned about.

The debate over the coming weeks will be a desperate debate, and it is fundamentally important that we preserve the High Court's decision in *Mabo*. Unfortunately, however, the biggest problem we're going to have is the prime minister's lies. I say this advisedly. He went out to Longreach three months ago and told the farmers out there – and you've all seen the grabs on the television – 'You're not going to lose your land. I won't let them.' As if the decisions in *Mabo* or *Wik* allowed Aboriginal people to take over pastoral leases from the leaseholders. There has never been any prospect of anyone losing their title to land, but this fear is held by enormous sections of the rural community. The fear is totally unfounded. But we have our national leader telling the people of Longreach, 'I won't let them take your land.' Instead of saying, 'Well, in fact the High Court decision means that if anything, you should share the land with the traditional owners.'

Another lie: on the *7.30 Report* on ABC television last Thursday, the prime minster said that Aboriginal people could end up having a right of veto over 78 per cent of the country under the *Native Title Act*. The *Native Title Act* provides the right to negotiate, the right to discuss and the right to make agreements for six months. If you can't reach an agreement about a mining proposal then there is arbitration. The arbitrator can rule against the Aboriginal people, and if the arbitrator rules in favour of them, the minister can override the arbitrator. There is no veto. The only people I know who have a comprehensive veto over mining in this country are Western Australian farmers. There is no way under Western Australian law that you can mine on farming land without the consent of the landowner. There is no ministerial power to grant leases or mining access in the absence of consent by the landowners. But Western Australian wheat farmers are the only beneficiaries of a right of veto. As I've explained, under the *Native Title Act*, the Aboriginal right to negotiate is a fairly weak right.

So for the prime minister to be waving around a map of Australia, saying that Aboriginal people are going to have a right of veto over 78 per cent of the country, shows exactly the kind of difficulty we're going to have in the forthcoming debate. The person who is supposed to be in the middle is in fact out there on the extreme fringe.

The other lie that will be peddled, and which is so fundamentally wrong, is the lie about the pendulum: 'It's swung too far in favour of the black fellas. I've got to bring it back here to the centre.' The High Court spelt out a three-point compromise, and that is where the pendulum should properly sit. That is balance. That is the fair centre. Because it requires both sides to abandon their fantasies. One side must abandon the fantasy of *terra nullius*; the other side must abandon the fantasy that somehow the whitefellas are all going to go away. The High Court has already located the fair centre for the pendulum.

And yet we have a prime minister who has commissioned 400 pages of pendulum fixing. Four hundred pages which, in an honest analysis, annihilate our position. In my assessment of the bill tabled last Thursday, I have attempted to be as unemotional and rational as I could possibly be – and I have to say that it totally annihilates our position. The published legislation is worse than the legislation that was tabled in June. It's no longer a ten-point plan. It's a thirty-point plan. It covers issues that were never mentioned in the original ten-point plan. It deals with extinguishment of native title in Crown reserves, which has nothing to do with the *Wik* decision. There's hardly going to be any native title left if this legislation goes through.

Finally, let me say that no other group should better understand the tactics about which I have talked tonight. No other group knows how hard it is. No other group knows what it's like to be hated by more people than have ever met your people. So I look forward to your support in the coming months.

1997

TALKING TO THE RIGHT

Speech to the Castan Centre for Human Rights Law

It was late in the long campaign against the ten-point plan and many Indigenous leaders who had been involved in the politics of the *Native Title Act* in 1993 were absent from Canberra in the crucial weeks and days before the passage of the Howard government's legislation in response to the *Wik* decision. I arrived in Canberra picking up ominous indications that the independent senator Brian Harradine would make a deal with the government to pass the legislation. Earlier we thought we had won the day when the delegation of *Wik* people, led by Richard Ah Mat, the chair of the Cape York Land Council, together with other Indigenous leaders, had persuaded the senator to oppose the government's bill. When I heard the news back in Cape York Peninsula and saw the images of Senator Harradine dancing with the Wik people on the lawns of Parliament House, I was ecstatic. I had no problem with the failure of the bill leading to the much-feared double-dissolution 'race election'. But then Harradine recommended negotiations with the government.

The afternoon I arrived in Parliament House, I was walking down the corridors with Ah Mat and Terry O'Shane from the North Queensland Land Council when we bumped into Senator Harradine. He informed us, no doubt thinking that it was the very news we wanted to hear, that he had made, or was very close to making, a deal with the government for the passage of the bill. We were dismayed. The game was over and the ten-point plan was heading for the statute books with some ameliorations extracted by Harradine. The concessions secured by Harradine did not make an unjust bill just, and the Senator was responsible for allowing a fundamental tilt of the pendulum away from the native title rights of Indigenous people, which continues to this day.

Faced with the inevitability of the passage of the bill that evening in the Senate, I decided on a last desperate strategy. Invited to appear on the *7.30 Report*, I decided to endorse the passage of the bill and to give the impression that Harradine had won huge gains for Indigenous people. My hope was to incite the lunatics from the far Right of the Coalition – Senators Bill O'Chee, Ross Lightfoot *et al.* – so that they would reject the bill. The metaphor that was in my mind was that it was like trying to push some livestock into a pen. I thought a sudden scare just as the stock were at the mouth of the pen would have two possible consequences: there was a chance they would take fright and run off down the paddock; or they would run straight through the gate and into the pen. I was prepared to take the risk in the hope that we could snatch victory from the jaws of defeat – jaws which Harradine had sprung open, supposedly for our own good, to save us from a race election. The ABC's Barry Cassidy knew what I was trying to do but Kerry O'Brien did not, and when I did the interview with Kerry he was bewildered by my support for the passage of the bill.

Alas, my gamble did not work. It quickly became clear that my stunt had not influenced anybody. The Coalition senators knew they had secured victory for the Australians they felt they represented – and they dutifully voted in unison to pass the ten-point plan a week later. All I had achieved was that I had defused the whole debate. The Senate vote clearly having become a formality, federal politics moved on to the next issue on the very next day.

Let me now turn to another story going back to 1997 and 1998, when the ten-point plan and the government's commitment to secure 'bucketloads of extinguishment' consumed the nation.

Ron Castan, QC had long spoken to me about the need to move the momentum created by *Mabo* from the plane of litigation and the courts to the plane of a larger political and economic settlement. Ron had warned that reliance upon the law alone was not sufficient. The furore that arose in the wake of the High Court's *Wik* decision in December 1996 underlined Ron's view, and the bitter debates that raged during 1997 underlined the need for an alternative solution.

At the same time, the notorious former leader of the Country Labor Party in the Northern Territory, Ian Tuxworth, and his colleague (who had become a good friend to us in far northern Queensland) Jim Petrich, commenced a discussion on the far Right of rural Australian politics, questioning whether the ten-point plan would deliver the kind of resolutions that were needed, particularly in the relationship between traditional owners, pastoralists and resource developers. They doubted the workability of any imposed legislative regime.

Ron, Ian and Jim decided to bring together the parties that were furthest apart from each other in the national debates that had raged about *Wik* and the ten-point plan. Ron brought together key Indigenous leaders from the land councils, and Tuxworth and Petrich brought together key leaders from the National Party and farmers' representatives. They secured Michael Costello, a former diplomat and then CEO of the Australian Securities Exchange, as the facilitator. He would help the two sides to see if we could find common ground.

We did. And this common ground was set out in a number of principles, which were set out in a draft Heads of Agreement. The preamble to these Heads of Agreement began as follows:

> For tens of thousands of years the Aboriginal people settled and owned this land. They were part of it in a unique and primary way. For the Aboriginal people, the land was the essence of their culture, and their culture was the essence of their being. To deny their ownership of the land is therefore to deny their very existence. It is for this reason that of all the wrongs done to the Aboriginal people over the centuries since European settlement, none has been more profound than the assertion of the doctrine that this land had been owned by no-one before 1788.
>
> The confirmation by the High Court that the concept *terra nullius* was a myth and that the Aboriginal ownership of land was reality was a defining moment in the nation's history ...

The document went on to say:

> In order to give effect to these principles of recognition; security and certainty; a stake in the country; and empowerment; we have agreed to seek a resolution of native title and related issues by negotiation in accordance with the following framework:
>
> Recognition of prior settlement and ownership by Aboriginal people.
>
> Recognition of valid Crown titles, such as freehold and leasehold, and agreement on the necessity for a fair procedure to ensure any necessary validation of post-1993 grants of title.
>
> Existing Aboriginal land including Aboriginal Reserves be recognised and placed under appropriate title as soon as practicable.
>
> Acknowledgement of Aboriginal interests in national parks, and development of principles for appropriate Aboriginal involvement in their management and development.
>
> Recognition that native title can only have continuing effect where that native title is consistent in whole or in part with a validly granted Crown title. Native title therefore has no effect, for example, where a valid freehold or exclusive leasehold title exists, but native title has full effect over unalienated Crown land.
>
> Common law has recognised that native title can co-exist with a pastoral lease, but only to the extent that it does not interfere with the rights of the leaseholder under that lease.
>
> We agree to separate economic rights on pastoral leases from non-economic (or cultural) rights held or claimed by Aboriginal people.
>
> We therefore agree on the following principles for co-existence:
>
> We agree to separate the provision of compensation for the relinquishment of economic rights from the provision of resources to address the 'citizenship' entitlements of Aboriginal people in health, education, housing and welfare. The first is based on justice for economic rights foregone. The second is based on the strict needs of Aboriginal people as Australian citizens.
>
> We therefore agree:
>
> (a) That in compensation for the relinquishment of economic rights an annual payment will be made to Aboriginal people for the

following [x] years. The amount of this annual payment will be [either ($x) or (calculated according to an agreed formula, for example annual mineral production or GDP]

The payment will be made in such a way that it provides a long term capital base for all Aboriginal Australians through which they can participate more fully in the economic development and prosperity of the broader economy, and can sustain their culture

(b) That 'citizenship' entitlements will be properly funded and administered through arrangements to be agreed.

It is agreed that fairer and more efficient procedures for native title claims need to be devised as soon as practicable to ensure that legitimate claimants are treated fairly and that the uncertainties of multiple or frivolous claims are avoided.

We agree that a document of reconciliation in the form of a domestic treaty between the First Australians and the Commonwealth and State/Territory Parliaments on behalf of the Australian people, is the desired goal of the reconciliation process.

We recognise that the settlement will be one between citizens of the one, united Australia and that our futures are inescapably intertwined and we are, at a fundamental level, one people.

The outcome of negotiations under this framework should be incorporated in a Treaty and put to a referendum in the centenary year of Federation. We believe this is necessary to confirm there is overwhelming support of the Australian people for the outcome, and to provide certainty against any potential legal challenge or change of legislation.

We also believe it will provide a great opportunity for the Australian people to show that we are able to move forward as a nation united, where all Australians can live their culture, achieve respect and realise their aspirations.

These principles, referring to the establishment of a 'long-term capital base' for Indigenous Australians culminating in a 'document of reconciliation in the form of a domestic Treaty' to be put to a referendum, were the product of an informal dialogue between key Indigenous leaders and key leaders from the regional and rural Right of Australian politics. These were the people whom I described as coming from 'just this side of One Nation'.

Having identified the basis for common ground between rural and Indigenous interests, the next challenge was to see if the same principles could gain the support of the miners. Ron and I met with the then chair of the Minerals Council in Brisbane, but the miners were banking on the ten-point plan to deliver certainty and workability for them. Similarly, representatives from the teams that had developed these Heads of Agreement briefed members of the government and the opposition in Canberra, but without the miners there was little prospect of the federal government changing course. So what was at the time called the Bennelong Process – not be confused with the Bennelong Society – was put aside, and the parliamentary process of the ten-point plan continued.

Ron Castan taught me a critical lesson in 1998. He illuminated what I have since called the '80 or 90 per cent strategy' of Indigenous advocacy, as opposed to the '51 per cent strategy' with which I was previously familiar. I used to say to him, 'You look after the law, Ron, I'll look after the politics.' But it was Ron who would get me to see that there is more common ground between Indigenous people and people from the Right of Australian politics and society than conventional political wisdom would have it. Firstly, people from the rural and regional Right of Australia have many interests in common with Indigenous people. Secondly, they have an understanding of the issues and problems Indigenous people face. Thirdly, they have many genuine friendships and relationships with Indigenous people. They may be unsentimental or inelegant in their demeanour, but many of the people to whom I am referring are fundamentally decent and goodwilled. I came to understand that many of the Right's objections to Aboriginal aspirations were rooted in their identification of these aspirations with leftist moralising. I came to see how the presentation of Indigenous issues, as opposed to their substance, disproportionately determined the responses of both sides of Australian politics and society.

To make certain changes in Australia, particularly when you need to win a referendum, you need the support of a large majority: hence the '80 or 90 per cent strategy'. Only sometimes – for instance, when the Labor government, because it held power, was able to pass the *Land Rights Act* – can you rely on achieving change with a bare majority ('the 51 per cent' approach). The only way to get wide support for Indigenous Australians' aspirations is to first get support from the most conservative people among decent Australians. If you first get the support of the Left, it will became a Left-versus-Right issue.

Who would have thought that you could get leading figures from the far Right of Australian politics endorsing a set of principles that included the establishment of a long-term capital base for Indigenous people and a treaty to be put to a referendum? The Bennelong Process allowed both sides, for a brief time, to survey common ground with clear eyes.

2004

LAND IS SUSCEPTIBLE OF OWNERSHIP

In its recent decisions in *Commonwealth v. Yarmirr*[1], *Western Australia v. Ward*[2] and *Members of the Yorta Yorta Aboriginal Community v. Victoria*[3], the High Court has misinterpreted the definition of native title under the *Native Title Act 1993–1998 (Cth)*[4] and fundamentally misapplied the common law. Before turning to these two allegations, I will first set out the historic meaning of the High Court's decision in *Mabo v. Queensland (No. 2)*.[5]

The three principles of native title
On 3 June 1992, the High Court finally illuminated the true legal history of the British colonisation of Australia. Properly understood, the law of the colonisers recognised a native entitlement to land from the time that sovereignty was first acquired. The High Court confirmed that the common law of England, carried upon the shoulders of the colonists and falling upon Australian soil, included the doctrine of recognition of native title.[6]

At the moment of sovereignty, as subjects of the British Crown, in occupation of their traditional homelands and entitled to the protection of the new law, the Indigenous peoples became under British law the owners of the entire continent. Native title existed wherever Aboriginal people held traditional connections with their homelands. The High Court told us that their dispossession of those titles occurred over the next 204 years through a process of 'parcel by parcel' extinguishment. This legal truth about the foundations of the country was obscured for two centuries, and that obfuscation resulted in the dispossession and removal and suffering and death of numerous Aboriginal peoples.

In 1992, the High Court had to contend with two compelling realities. The first was the fact of original occupation and possession of Australia by its Indigenous peoples and the recognition of this by the imported common law. The second was that the recognition and protection of these original rights to the land did not occur until 204 years after sovereign acquisition, and the colonists and their descendants had acquired many titles and privileges over the course of the intervening two centuries. How were these two facts to be reconciled?

In my view, the Mason and then Brennan courts articulated three basic principles which set out a reconciliation of these two realities, and which should have formed the architecture for the final settlement of the longstanding and unresolved question of Indigenous land justice.

The first principle was that non-indigenous Australians could not now be disturbed in the enjoyment of the rights and titles they had accumulated, notwithstanding the circumstances by which they came to possess them. So the first principle of native title law in this country should be known to all Australians – though it is not – as the 'white land rights' principle: the lands of the non-indigenes, including the lands alienated by the Crown for its own use, are indefeasible, and cannot now be disturbed by any claim to native title.

The second principle was that, seeing as the whole country was once subject to native title, whatever lands were left unalienated after 204 years were the entitlement of its traditional owners; and that in all fairness, title should be declared for their benefit forthwith.[7] In other words, the Indigenous people were entitled to whatever lands were left over. The remnant lands after two centuries were not substantial, the largest areas being in the desert and remote parts of the country.

The third principle, which was articulated in *Wik Peoples v. Queensland*[8] in 1996, was that there were some larger tenures, such as pastoral leases and national parks, where the Crown title could co-exist with native title, and in that co-existence the Crown-derived title prevailed over native title in the event of inconsistency.[9]

These three principles, if properly understood, and if faithfully followed, potentially laid the foundations for a just settlement of the historic grievance about land justice which lay unresolved between the old and new Australians.

Alas, it has not turned out this way. The High Court's judgment in the *Yorta Yorta* case in December 2002 put the lie to my interpretation of native title. The three principles of native title law are not that non-indigenous parties get to keep all that they have accumulated, that Indigenous people get what is left over and that they share some larger categories of land titles with the granted titles prevailing over the native title. Rather the three principles of native title are that non-indigenous parties not only get to keep all that they have accumulated, but Indigenous people only get a fraction of what is left over and get only a subservient title co-existing with Crown titles (which always prevail over any native title). To claim this title, they must surmount the most unreasonable and unyielding barriers of proof – and they must prove that they meet white Australia's cultural and legal preju-dices about what constitute 'real Aborigines'. To the Australian courts charged with the responsibility of administering the historic compro-mise set out in *Mabo,* the Yorta Yorta peoples were not sufficiently Aboriginal to get one square metre of what was left over after the whites had taken all that they wanted.

What is not understood about native title claims after *Mabo (No. 2),* and certainly after the *Native Title Act,* is that it is simply not possible for non-indigenous parties to lose any legal rights or title as a conse-quence of a native title finding. These land claims are not true litiga-tions in the sense that either party may suffer loss as an outcome. Non-indigenous parties to land claims can never lose any of their rights or titles, because these are indefeasible under the common law – and if they were ever invalid, the *Native Title Act* has now cured any invalidities.[10] The only party that can truly lose in a native title claim is the Indigenous claimant. The non-indigenous parties – including the Crown – have nothing to lose, other than an argument to the effect that the Indigenous people have no entitlement.

And yet not only is there political and social resistance to Indige-nous people's claims for leftover land, but there are now also significant judicial and legal impediments to the working out of this belated and meagre land justice. The travesty of the current native title system in

Australia, and the reason why the process is not delivering justice in line with the principles that *Mabo (No. 2)* set out, lies in the fact that non-indigenous parties are allowed to oppose claims for native title even though they have no rights or interests that are vulnerable as a result of a native title finding.[11] These third parties are in an extraordinary position: all of their rights and interests are guaranteed by the common law and by validating legislation, and the attorney-general pays for their legal costs. They thus have nothing to lose by refusing to consent to native title determinations. The native title legislation was founded on the assumption that most claims could be settled by mediation and negotiation. But if you can never ultimately lose, and the attorney-general is paying your legal costs, you can resist native title until the cows come home. What's more, parliaments and the judicial system will assume that you are a vulnerable party in the native title claims process, without understanding the clear truth: that non-indigenous Australians are secure in their entitlements and can never lose a vested right, or even an expectation of a right, thanks to the broadening of the definition of 'past acts'[12] in legislation.

The country forgets that in April 1993, when Indigenous leaders met with Prime Minister Paul Keating to discuss impending legislation responding to *Mabo (No. 2)*, it was the Indigenous leaders who proposed support for legislation validating non-indigenous titles that were uncertain as a consequence of the operation of the *Racial Discrimination Act*. To the extent that non-indigenous rights were uncertain after *Mabo (No. 2)*, it was Indigenous people who proposed the validation of these uncertain titles.[13] This was a gracious concession on our part in 1993. This act of graciousness on the part of Aboriginal people turned out to be a fatal mistake. Industry and state governments, rather than being gracious, essentially took this position: not only do we want our own rights and titles to be secure, but we will also resist any claims for remnant native title as well.

The present High Court does not know what it is doing with the responsibility its predecessors assumed with *Mabo*. They have rendered a great disservice to Indigenous Australians and to our past and future as a nation. For in their flawed and discriminatory conceptualisation of native title, and in their egregious misinterpretation of fundamental provisions of the *Native Title Act,* they are destroying the opportunity for native title to finally settle the outstanding question of Indigenous land justice in Australia.

Let me now turn to the two allegations I alluded to in the beginning. The first concerns the misinterpretation of section 223(1) of the *Native Title Act*, namely, the very definition of native title.

The misinterpretation of the Native Title Act section 223(1)
Section 223(1) reads:

> The expression *native title* or *native title rights and interests* means the communal, group or individual rights and interests of Aboriginal peoples or Torres Strait Islanders in relation to land or waters, where:
> (a) the rights and interests are possessed under the traditional laws acknowledged, and the traditional customs observed, by the Aboriginal peoples or Torres Strait Islanders; and
> (b) the Aboriginal peoples or Torres Strait Islanders, by those laws and customs, have a connection with the land or waters; and
> (c) the rights and interests are recognised by the common law of Australia.

In my respectful view, the Court's decisions in *Yarmirr, Ward* and now *Yorta Yorta* have yielded a complete misinterpretation of a fundamental provision of the *Native Title Act*.[14] I am in respectful agreement with the judgment of His Honour Justice McHugh in *Yorta Yorta* in relation to s 223(1).[15] This definition was intended to make clear that native title was whatever the common law of Australia decided it was. Paragraphs (a) and (b) of s 223(1) were intended to faithfully reflect the key requirements of the common law as set out in the judgment of Justice Brennan in *Mabo (No. 2)*. They were not intended to supplant or in any way amend or supersede the definition of native title at common law.

And yet the Court has basically taken the view that the *Native Title Act* has somehow 'transmogrified'[16] the common law meaning of native title; that the starting point – and ending point – for the definition of native title is legislation that was intended to protect, not define, the title. As a result, in *Ward* and *Yorta Yorta*, the entire discussion of native title is treated as an exercise in statutory interpretation rather than an articulation of the common law. Important questions concerning the concept and nature of native title, its content, extinguishment and proof are dealt with, without any reference to the large body of common law of which Australian native title forms a part.

Even a circumspect party to the Australian native title story since *Mabo (No. 2)* such as Justice French, the first president of the National Native Title Tribunal, makes clear that the High Court's interpretation of s 223(1) defied reasonable understandings and expectations:

> Most recently, in *Members of the Yorta Yorta Aboriginal Community v. Victoria* ... the High Court again emphasised the statutory definition of native title as defining the criteria that had to be satisfied before a determination could be made. To that extent the Court appears to have moved away from the original concept of the Act as a vehicle for the development of the common law of native title.[17]

His Honour went on to say:

> The way it [the High Court in *Yorta Yorta*] applies the words of s 223(1) paragraphs (a) and (b) of the Act to the determination of native title rights and interests may have transformed the Act from a vessel for the development of the common law into a cage for its confinement.[18]

The judgments in *Ward* and *Yorta Yorta* run to hundreds of pages. And all of these pages of discussion concern statutory interpretation – rather than any discussion of cases. A search of the cases cited in these judgments reveals that hardly any cases are canvassed in support of the Court's conclusions on the state of Australian law. Astoundingly, there is absolutely no reference in either of these Australian cases to what is the seminal Canadian decision on native title, and in my view the most important decision on the subject since the High Court's decision in *Mabo (No. 2)*, namely the decision of the Supreme Court of Canada in *Delgamuukw v. British Columbia*,[19] which was substantially informed by the Australian High Court's decision. Given that *Delgamuukw* dealt with the very questions that were at issue in *Ward* and *Yorta Yorta*, it is startling that no reference[20] is made to it in Australian law.

Indeed *Mabo (No. 2)* itself is only referred to for its place in the chronology of native title in Australian law, rather than for the purposes of discussing its articulation of the common law. In their joint judgment in *Yorta Yorta* at paragraph 70, Chief Justice Gleeson and Justices Gummow and Hayne almost dismiss the relevance of *Mabo (No. 2)* to the meaning of native title:

> The legal principles which the primary judge considered were to be applied to the facts found were principles which he correctly identified as being found in the *Native Title Act*'s definition of native title. It is true to say that his Honour said that this definition of native title was 'consistent with' language in the reasons in *Mabo (No. 2)* and that it was, in his Honour's view, necessary to understand the context in which the statutory definition was developed by reference to what was said in that case. *It may be that undue emphasis was given in the reasons to what was said in* Mabo (No. 2), *at the expense of recognising the principal, indeed determinative, place that should be given to the* Native Title Act (emphasis added).

Let me repeat this astounding last sentence: 'It may be that that undue emphasis was given in the reasons to what was said in *Mabo (No. 2)*, at the expense of recognising the principal, indeed determinative, place that should be given to the *Native Title Act*.'

The majority explain their approach to section 223(1) as follows:[21]

> To speak of the 'common law requirements' of native title is to invite fundamental error. Native title is not a creature of the common law, whether the Imperial common law as that existed at the time of sovereignty and first settlement, or the Australian common law as it exists today. Native title, for present purposes, is what is defined and described in s. 223(1) of the *Native Title Act. Mabo (No. 2)* decided that certain rights and interests relating to land, and rooted in traditional law and custom, survived the Crown's acquisition of sovereignty and radical title in Australia. It was this native title that was

then 'recognised, and protected'[22] in accordance with the *Native Title Act* and which, thereafter, was not able to be extinguished contrary to that Act[23].

The *Native Title Act*, when read as a whole, does not seek to create some new species of right or interest in relation to land or waters which it then calls native title. Rather, the Act has as one of its main objects[24] 'to provide for the recognition and protection of native title', which is to say those rights and interests in relation to land or waters with which the Act deals, but which are rights and interests finding their origin in traditional law and custom, not the Act. It follows that the reference in par (c) of s. 223(1) to the rights or interests being recognised by the common law of Australia cannot be understood as a form of drafting by incorporation, by which some pre-existing body of the common law of Australia defining the rights or interests known as native title is brought into the Act. To understand par (c) as a drafting device of that kind would be to treat native title as owing its origins to the common law when it does not. And to speak of there being common law elements for the establishment of native title is to commit the same error. It is, therefore, wrong to read par (c) of the definition of native title as requiring reference to any such body of common law, for there is none to which reference could be made.

In *Yarmirr* (2001) 208 CLR 1, 39, Chief Justice Gleeson and Justices Gaudron, Gummow and Hayne had said that whilst the *Native Title Act* should be the starting point of any inquiry, it should be understood as 'supplementing the rights and interest of native title holders under the common law of Australia'. Later in *Ward* (2002) 191 ALR 1, 16, Chief Justice Gleeson and Justices Gaudron, Gummow and Hayne moved the emphasis decisively towards the legislation:

No doubt account may be taken of what was decided and what was said in [*Mabo (No. 2)*] when considering the meaning and effect of the NTA. This especially is so when it is recognised that paras (a) and (b) of s 223(1) plainly are based on what was said by Brennan J in *Mabo (No. 2)*. It is, however, of the very first importance to recognise two critical points: that s 11(1) of the *NTA* provides that native title is not able to be extinguished contrary to the *NTA* and *that the claims that gave rise to the present appeals are claims made under the NTA for rights that are defined in that statute* (emphasis added).

And later:

Yet again it must be emphasised that *it is to the terms of the NTA that primary regard must be had, and not the decision in Mabo (No. 2) or Wik.* The only present relevance of those decisions is for whatever light they cast on the *NTA* (emphasis added).

In my respectful view, the High Court has decided that it will draw a line between the Australian law on native title after the enactment of the *Native Title Act* and the body of North American and British colonial case law which has dealt with native title over the past two centuries, and which informed and underpinned the decision in *Mabo (No. 2).*

This case law, upon which Justice Brennan and other members of the Court drew in their judgments in *Mabo (No. 2)* concerning colonies in the subcontinent and West Africa, the United States and Canada – as well as cases concerning Wales and Ireland – has been conveniently disposed of. Rather than developing the fledgling Australian law by grappling with this considerable body of law, with which – as *Mabo (No. 2)* showed – there are more areas of common principle than there are differences, the High Court has taken the easy road of interpreting and developing native title under the rubric of statutory interpretation.

This leaves Australian pronouncements on important questions and principles of native title open to bare assertion, as the body of the common law dealing with native title is rendered irrelevant because the legislation is treated as having superseded the common law. That this is what has happened is readily evidenced by a perusal of the cases cited in *Ward* and *Yorta Yorta.*

The High Court has not so much given 'reasons' for completely ignoring the common law on native title (called 'Aboriginal title' in Canada) as expressed bald assumptions. Probably the worst example of judicial dereliction on the part of Justice Kirby is his decision in *Fejo v. Northern Territory*, in which he legitimised the High Court's abandonment of the body of common law of native title. He dismissed the relevance of case law in North America in other former colonies of the Crown with a specious generalisation:

> care must be exercised in the use of judicial authorities of other former colonies and territories of the Crown because of the peculiarities which exist in each of them arising out of historical and constitutional developments, the organisation of the indigenous peoples concerned and applicable geographical or social considerations ...[25]

This assumption underlies the approach taken by all of the members of the High Court to overseas precedents. It was patently a reflection of their reluctance to contend with principles in the native title law of these other jurisdictions that might challenge their more simplistic approach to native title. Rather than grappling with the overseas case law and setting out rigorous arguments for distinguishing Australian law from these precedents, it was easier to dismiss the case law's relevance with sweeping generalisations.

Earlier, I quoted a passage from the judgment of Chief Justice Gleeson and Justices Gummow and Hayne in which they dismissed the view that there were 'common law requirements' or 'common law elements' to the establishment and proof of native title, concluding that 'it is, therefore, wrong to read paragraph (c) of the definition of native title as requiring reference to any such body of common law, for there is none to which reference could be made.'

This is a completely unfortunate argument; it would be scholastic if it were not so patently disingenuous. True, native title is not an institution of the common law; it is a title recognised by the common law. No, native title is not a common law title in the sense that, say, a fee simple is. But there is a body of common law which discusses the recognition, proof, content and extinguishment of native title. This body of law is considerable, and it has been developed in numerous decisions of the Privy Council, the United States Supreme Court, the Supreme Court of Canada and in courts throughout the common law world. It is to this

body of law that paragraph (c) of section 223(1) of the *Native Title Act* –
if it had been properly interpreted – refers. *Mabo (No. 2)* forms the cornerstone of the Australian branch of this body of law. It is a nonsense
for the High Court to disavow the existence of this body of law, which
deals with the recognition, proof, enforcement and extinguishment of
native title.

This approach is in stark contrast to the judgments in *Mabo (No. 2)*,
which drew heavily on other common law jurisdictions (and indeed,
Justice Brennan had specifically rejected as discriminatory[26] the notion
that what Justice Kirby calls 'the organisation of the indigenous peoples concerned' should ever be a factor in determining whether their
rights to land would be respected by the common law). During the
course of argument in *Ward*, Justice Gummow said that the applicabil-
ity of the Canadian law in the Australian context was 'an important
question'.[27] It was a question that remained unanswered in all of the
judgments in that case, and indeed in the subsequent *Yorta Yorta* case.
If the Court has not been derelict in its duty to the Indigenous peoples
of Australia in failing to give sound reasons for refusing to grapple
with overseas precedents that are at odds with its preferred views, it
has certainly made its task easier by relying upon the legislation rather
than engaging with two centuries of precedent developed throughout
the English common law world.

If the Court's interpretation of s 223(1) of the *Native Title Act* is
accepted as correct, then the parliaments that passed the 1993 legislation and the amendments of 1998 were under grave misapprehension
as to what they had done. The enactment of native title legislation in
the wake of the High Court's 1992 decision in *Mabo (No. 2)* was the
subject of an intense national political and legislative debate during
1993, in which Aboriginal advocates participated vigorously. What
were we defending, and what did we think we had achieved with the
Commonwealth government under Prime Minister Paul Keating? We
thought, and I am sure all members of parliament and all Australians
who followed the proceedings thought, that the whole exercise was
about preserving the rights declared under the common law of Australia. In other words, we thought that the *Mabo* decision, and the
rights and interests that flowed from that decision, were being recog-

nised and protected by the Commonwealth legislation. So we thought that the *Native Title Act* preserved the *Mabo* decision. We thought that under the new legislation, all native title claims would be adjudicated according to principles of *Mabo* and the body of common law of which *Mabo* forms a part. Indeed, Indigenous leaders and Prime Minister Paul Keating had assumed that the legislation simply protected native title from hostile extinguishment. We believed that what was being protected by the legislation was the common law right.[28]

It is not enough to respond that it is a misnomer to talk of native title as a 'common law right'.[29] Native title is not a common law title, but it is a title recognised by the common law.[30] The point about the common law and native title was well made by Justice McHugh in *Yorta Yorta* when he reviewed the statements made in parliament in respect of section 223:

> Given the decisions in *Yarmirr*[31] and *Ward*, the [position of Chief Justice Gleeson and Justices Gummow and Hayne in their *Yorta Yorta* judgment] concerning the construction of the Act must be accepted as correct.
>
> However, I remain unconvinced that the construction that this Court has placed on s. 223 accords with what the Parliament intended. In *Yarmirr*, I cited statements from the Ministers in charge of the Act when it was enacted in 1993 and when it was amended in 1997. They showed that the Parliament believed that, under the *Native Title Act*, the content of native title would depend on the developing common law. Thus, Senator Evans told the Senate in 1993:[32]
>
>> We are not attempting to define with precision the extent and incidence of native title. That will be a matter still for case by case determination through tribunal processes and so on. *The crucial element of the common law is the fact that native title as such, as a proprietary right capable of being recognised and enjoyed, and excluding other competing forms of proprietary claim, is recognised as part of the common law of the country.* (emphasis added)

Similarly, Senator Minchin told the Senate in 1997:[33]

I repeat that our [A]ct preserves the fact of common law; who holds native title, what it consists of, is entirely a matter for the courts of Australia. *It is a common law right.* (emphasis added)

Section 12 of the *Native Title Act 1993* also made it clear that the content of native title under that Act was to be determined in accordance with the developing common law. Section 12 provided:

Subject to this Act, the common law of Australia in respect of native title has, after 30 June 1993, the force of a law of the Commonwealth.

In *Western Australia v. The Commonwealth (Native Title Act Case)*,[34] however, this Court held that s 12 was invalid. As Justice McHugh explained in the *Yorta Yorta* case in 2002:

In the *Native Title Act Case*, six justices of the Court said: 'If s. 12 be construed as an attempt to make the common law a law of the Commonwealth, it is invalid either because it purports to confer legislative power on the courts or because the enactment of the common law relating to native title finds no constitutional support in s. 51(xxvi) or (xxiv).'

Section 12 has now been removed from the statute book. But its enactment in the 1993 Act shows that the *Parliament intended native title to be determined by the common law principles laid down in Mabo v Queensland (No. 2)*,[35] *particularly those formulated by Brennan J in his judgment in that case. When s. 223(1)(c) of the 1993 Act referred to the rights and interests 'recognised by the common law of Australia', it was, in my view, referring to the principles expounded by Brennan J in Mabo (No.2).*

But this Court has now given the concept of 'recognition' a narrower scope than I think the Parliament intended, and this Court's interpretation of s. 223 must now be accepted as settling the law. As a result, the majority judges in the Full Court erred when they approached the case in the manner that they did. (emphasis added)

Justice McHugh's understanding of section 223(1) is the same as my understanding. This was also Prime Minister Keating and Senator

Gareth Evans's understanding in 1993. It was Prime Minister John Howard and Senator Nick Minchin's understanding in 1998. The High Court's interpretation is at odds with the intention of parliament, both during the Keating government[36] and at the time the *Native Title Amendment Act* was passed by the Howard government in 1998.[37] Both parliaments understood that their respective laws were preserving the common law rights articulated in the *Mabo* decision.

Amazingly, despite Justice McHugh's clear acknowledgment that his colleagues' interpretation of section 223 was 'narrower' than parliament had intended, he capitulated to this narrower interpretation and was prepared to accept it as settled law. This in itself is instructive; it is indicative of the Court's abandonment of Indigenous Australians, who might have expected more diligence. Justice McHugh was dealing here with a profound question of fundamental property rights of Australian citizens. All citizens are entitled to a rigorous application of the rules of law when they bring their claims before the courts. It is hard to imagine any other area of law in which a judge would so lightly abandon his or her conviction about an interpretation of a statutory provision which is pivotal not just to the case at hand, but to all future cases.

Since Justice McHugh was prepared to accept this incorrect interpretation of the *Native Title Act* to the detriment of Indigenous interests, the Yorta Yorta Aboriginal Community's claim for the recognition of their remnant native title was not dealt with according to law. Their claim was considered and rejected according to the definition of native title set out in section 223(1) of the *Native Title Act*. It was not considered in accordance with the common law of Australia.

The Yorta Yorta went to the courts to claim their rights under common law. They went to claim rights emanating from the same source as those claimed by the Meriam people of the Murray Islands who had successfully established their title in *Mabo (No. 2)*. Instead, their claim was considered under the terms of a statutory definition – interpreted in a way that parliament never intended. In my view, the claim of the Yorta Yorta under the common law of Australia and under the terms of the *Mabo* decision has yet to be properly adjudicated.

During the 1993 arguments about native title legislation, the Indigenous parties were concerned that the common law rights articulated in *Mabo (No. 2)* be protected. We were vigilant against any attempt to replace or transform the common law rights with any form of statutory creature. Our understanding of section 223(1) was consistent with that of the Commonwealth; namely, that it was intended to be a faithful reflection of the common law – no more and no less. Now that the High Court has contradicted this position, it would seem to me that the most urgently needed reform of Australian native title law is to amend the definition of native title to make clear that it means whatever the common law of Australia says that it means. Given the gross misinterpretation of section 223(1) by the High Court, this provision in the *Native Title Act* must be amended before any further cases are determined. Section 223 must be amended to reflect the original intentions of the parliament in 1993 and 1998: that is, that all native titles would be proved in accordance with the High Court's decision in *Mabo (No. 2)* and the body of common law which surrounds that decision.

Section 223(1) should be amended to read:

'native title' and 'native title rights and interests' are those rights and interests which are recognised by the common law of Australia.

Without such an amendment, the whole basis on which the *Native Title Act* was enacted – to recognise and protect native title – is destroyed forever.

Native title should be illuminated, not by bare assertion in respect of statutory provisions enacted to protect native title from extinguishment, but by what Justice MacLachlin, as she then was, described in that elegant phrase in *R v. Van der Peet*[38], quoted by Justice Gummow in *Wik*,[39] as 'the time-honoured methodology of the common law'.[40]

The misapplication of the common law
Let me now turn to the second allegation concerning the misapplication of the common law in relation to the concept of native title.

Prior to *Mabo (No. 2)*, it was unclear what effect the acquisition of sovereignty by the Crown would have on the position of the Indigenous occupants of land made subject to the change in sovereignty. It is clear that it was open to the Crown to acquire not only the radical title to the territory occupied by Indigenous inhabitants, but it could also expropriate the beneficial title to the land. The Crown could thereby dispossess the Indigenous inhabitants of their title. Under the Act of State doctrine, this expropriation needed to occur at the time of the acquisition of sovereignty.

Following annexation, however, if the Crown had not expropriated the private title of the Indigenous inhabitants, it could not do so subsequently except through legislation. This is because the Indigenous peoples would have become British citizens and would therefore be entitled to the protection of the imported common law that had now become the law of the land. Any seizure of the indigenes' land after annexation would have amounted to the commission of an unlawful Act of State on the part of the Crown against its own citizens. This was prohibited by the law, and the Crown had no authority to expropriate land except through legislation.

This statement of the law concerning Acts of State is uncontroversial. The question that was controversial before *Mabo (No. 2)* was whether the survival of Aboriginal land rights following a change in sovereignty required a positive act of recognition of the original indigenous title by the Crown, or whether there was a presumption of continuity of indigenous title. The authorities preceding *Mabo* fell into two categories, which Canadian Professor Kent McNeil, in his landmark work *Common Law Aboriginal Title*,[41] labelled the 'doctrine of recognition'[42] and the 'doctrine of continuity'.[43]

In *Mabo (No. 2)*, in the absence of any positive act of recognition of indigenous title on the part of the Crown in the settlement of its Australian colonies, if the High Court had followed those cases that subscribed to the 'doctrine of recognition' there would now be no native title in Australia. Instead, the High Court ruled, consistently with rulings across the common law world, that the 'doctrine of continuity' represented the correct position in Australian law.

Again, the correctness of the application of the 'doctrine of continuity' is now also uncontroversial. It is settled law in Australia[44] and Canada and all of the leading cases in both of these jurisdictions are founded upon the acceptance of continuity.

Mabo (No. 2) and the *Native Title Act Case*[45] confirmed that the Acts of State establishing the colonies of Australia did not extinguish the rights of the indigenous inhabitants. But now that we know that the rights of the indigenous inhabitants of land at the time of the acquisition of sovereignty, in the absence of any express abrogation, are presumed to continue under the new sovereign and the new legal order, there is a further unresolved question, which the courts have not asked. The question is this: *what* is it that continues after the change of sovereignty?

In his seminal treatise *Common Law Aboriginal Title*, McNeil applied the English law on possession to the position of indigenous inhabitants at the time the British Crown acquired sovereignty.[46] He concluded that the fact of indigenous occupation of land gave rise to the right to possession.[47] Professor McNeil's treatise is the most rigorous examination of the application of English common law on possession to the situation of indigenous peoples. He concluded, and the one judge who discussed this thesis in *Mabo (No. 2)*, Justice Toohey, accepted, that indigenous people would be entitled to a so-called possessory title to land.[48] Both Professor McNeil and Justice Toohey assumed that possessory title and native title – what Professor McNeil called 'customary title' and his Honour called 'traditional title' – were separate concepts, and separate bases of claim to land by indigenous people.[49]

In my respectful view, this assumption was in error. Rather than possessory title being separate from native or customary title to land, my view is that the common law on possession *applies to native title*. The principles concerning occupation and possession apply to native title. Indeed, if we return to the foundational cases on native title in the common law world – namely the decisions of the United States Supreme Court under Chief Justice Marshall in the early decades of the nineteenth century, *Johnson v. McIntosh*,[50] *Worcester v. Georgia*[51] and *Mitchell v. United States*[52] – we find that recognition of Native American title was founded on the fact of their occupation of land, not in a primary sense on their traditional laws and customs. Sure, the Native American Indians lived on their land in accordance with their traditional laws and customs, which determined entitlement between them and governed their internal affairs – but the protection afforded them by the common law arose from the fact of their occupation of their homelands. After a very careful analysis of the early American cases, Kent McNeil concluded as follows:

> The Crown (and hence the States or the United States, as the case might be) ... acquired the 'naked fee', which it could grant, subject always to the Indian right of occupancy ... That right, it seems, is generally the same throughout the United States: *it depends not on the particular customs or laws of individual tribes* (the general existence of which has none the less been acknowledged) ... *but on their actual occupation of lands* from what has occasionally been said to be 'time immemorial' ...[53]

The core misconception centres on our understanding of what happened at the time of sovereignty when the rights of the indigenous inhabitants to their homelands continued under the doctrine of continuity. What continues after annexation? The rights and interests established under traditional laws and customs, or the right to occupy and possess the land under authority of, and in accordance with, the traditional laws and customs of the indigenous people?

It has been assumed throughout the Australian discussion[54] of native title, and through some of the Canadian discussion[55] up to *Delgamuukw* – including by Professor McNeil[56] – that it is the rights and interests established under traditional laws and customs that continue. In my respectful view, the correct answer is that it is *the right to occupy and possess the land* under the authority of, and in accordance with, the traditional laws and customs of the indigenous people that survives annexation. The distinction is subtle, but crucial.

This distinction underlines the fact that the foundation of native title is possession arising from occupation – not the details of traditional laws and customs. These laws and customs determine who is entitled to the possession, and they govern the internal allocation of rights, interests and responsibilities amongst members of the native community – but they do not determine the content of the community's title, which is possession. Possession being what Justice Toohey described as a 'conclusion of law' arising from the fact of occupation.[57]

Instead, our Australian law has misconceived native title by focusing on the traditional laws and customs of the indigenous people. The end result – evident from the High Court's decision in *Yorta Yorta* – is that in order to establish native title today, Indigenous claimants are forced to prove the details of their traditional laws and customs at the time of sovereignty, when the English common law of possession would only require that claimants prove occupancy. An horrendous burden of proof has been placed upon native claimants, purely through this misconception of title arising from the misapplication of the common law.

This explication that communal native title is a right to possession arising from the occupation of land by the predecessor native community at the time of sovereignty also explains the content of the title which arises from occupation. The content of communal native title is the title which occupation affords, namely possession. Properly understood, communal native titles across the continent are not determined by what his Honour Justice Gummow described in *Yanner v. Eaton* as the 'idiosyncratic' laws and customs of the particular native community.[58] These idiosyncratic laws and customs do determine those native title rights and interests that are variously described as 'pendant upon',[59] 'parasitic upon',[60] 'privileges of'[61] or 'carved out of'[62] the communal title. But the idiosyncratic laws and customs of the community are only relevant in the following ways:

- they identify which Indigenous people are entitled to the right to occupation of the land, and they govern the descent of this entitlement through the generations (that is, they identify *entitlement*);
- they identify *the territory* to which the indigenous people are entitled; and
- they govern the *internal allocation of rights, interests and responsibilities* amongst members of the indigenous community and *regulate* how members of the community exercise these.

But the title of the community as a whole, as against the world at large, is a mundane possession. The communal native title of the indigenous community is founded upon their occupation of land. This is what Justice Toohey meant when he said in *Mabo (No. 2)* that:[63]

> It is presence amounting to occupancy which is the foundation of the title and which attracts protection, and it is that which must be proved to establish title ... Thus traditional title is rooted in physical presence.[64]

Following 1788, all communal native titles in the acquired colonies were the same. They all amounted to a uniform possession. If there is variation between communal native titles today it is because they have suffered some form of specific derogation by valid act of the legislature or Crown – not because they were originally diverse and determined by idiosyncratic laws and customs.[65]

Pendant native title rights and interests should be understood as constituting any right or interest to which possession gives rise as regulated by traditional law and custom, and of course today, subject to any valid derogation or regulation by valid act of the legislature or Crown. Traditional laws and customs regulate the exercise of any and all of the rights and interests that flow from possession. This is where evidence of traditional law and custom is relevant.

However, in the Australian law as it now stands, it is assumed that native titles are entirely constituted by reference to traditional laws and customs adduced as a matter of proof. The High Court made this assumption about 'what continues' following annexation without grappling with the host of Canadian authorities who emphasise occupation at the time of sovereignty as the foundation of native title – not the least the leading case of *Delgamuukw*,[66] brought down by the Supreme Court of Canada in 1997. They proceeded with their assumption without grappling with what our own court has said in *Mabo (No. 2)* about the role that occupation plays in the foundation of native title. The assumption that what continues after annexation are the rights and interests established by traditional law and custom, rather than the right to occupy land by authority of, and in accordance with, one's traditional laws and customs, has had profound implications for how the Court conceptualises native title and, ultimately, how it deals with its proof. This is why the High Court's error in relation to this issue was so prejudicial to its handling of the *Yorta Yorta* appeal.

There are two further sources for the misconception that native titles are entirely constituted by reference to traditional laws and customs. Firstly, the term 'native title' is subject to a confusing conflation – it is used indiscriminately to mean both communal native title and the rights and interests that are carved out of the communal title.[67] But there is a critical difference between the communal title and the pendant rights and interests. Mr Yanner's entitlement to hunt crocodiles is a right which is carved out of the communal title of his people. The right to hunt crocodiles is an incident of possession, and the traditional laws and customs of the Gangalida people regulate Mr Yanner's exercise of his rights under the communal tenure. But the Gangalida people's communal title is based on their occupation and possession of the land, which under English common law entitles them to land title. Their particular customs and traditions are irrelevant when it comes to establishing their right to communal title.

The problem is that the judicial and academic discussion of native title switches (often unconsciously) between the discussion of native title in its communal sense, and its pendant rights and interests sense, thereby causing conceptual confusion. The principles which apply to these two senses of native title are different, and these differences are critical. This is why the oft-quoted statement of Justice Brennan in *Mabo (No. 2)* is the source of so much confusion. He said:

> Native title has its origin in and is given its content by the traditional laws acknowledged by and the traditional customs observed by the indigenous inhabitants of a territory. The nature and incidents of native title must be ascertained as a matter of fact by reference to those laws and customs.[68]

This statement is correct in relation to the native title rights and interests that are carved out of the communal title. But it is apt to mislead in relation to the description of communal native title.[69] After all, the title of the Meriam people in *Mabo (No. 2)* amounted to 'possession, occupation, use and enjoyment', 'as against the world' – concepts known to the common law and not comprising the details of Meriam law and custom.[70] It is elsewhere in his judgment that Justice Brennan articulated the approach to understanding the nature of communal native title when he said:

> If it be necessary to categorise an interest in land as proprietary in order that it survive a change in sovereignty, the interest possessed by a community that is in exclusive possession of land falls into that category. Whether or not land is owned by individual members of a community, a community which asserts and asserts effectively that none but its members has any right to occupy or use the land has an interest in the land that must be proprietary in nature: there is no other proprietor ... The ownership of land within a territory in the exclusive occupation of a people must be vested in that people: land is susceptible of ownership and there are no other owners.[71]

His Honour went on to describe the relationship between the communal title and the pendant rights and interests when he referred to *Milirrpum v. Nabalco Pty Ltd:*[72]

> The fact that individual members of the community, like the individual plaintiff Aborigines in *Milirrpum,* enjoy only usufructuary rights that are not proprietary in nature is no impediment to the recognition of a proprietary community title. Indeed, it is not possible to admit traditional usufructuary rights without admitting a traditional proprietary community title.[73]

There is a second source of misconception, and this is the failure to recognise that the term 'title'[74] has two senses that are related but distinct, one referring to the manner by which a right to real property is acquired and the other referring to the right itself. That is, the first sense concerns 'entitling conditions' and the second concerns 'rights'. The two senses correspond with conditions and consequences respectively; the one causal, the other resultant.

In the term 'native title', the common law and Aboriginal law play different roles. Aboriginal law determines *who* is entitled to the rights recognised by the common law arising from the occupation of land at the time of sovereignty (and indeed Aboriginal law recognises the descent of these rights to any contemporary claimant community). The form of the title is possession, which flows from occupation. The entitling condition is the occupation of land under authority of Aboriginal law and custom. The right afforded by the common law is possession. Rather than appreciating that 'native title' incorporates the common law and Aboriginal law in these two different senses, the prevalent assumption is that native title is constituted by Aboriginal law alone.

Conclusions

I will conclude by amending Professor McNeil's compelling thesis on possessory title in two respects. Firstly, as I have already said, in my respectful view, Professor McNeil was incorrect to assume that possessory title is a separate basis of claim to that of customary law or native title. Rather, the law on possession applies to the law on native title. In my view, this position is already confirmed by the Supreme Court of Canada in its decision in *Delgamuukw*. Then Chief Justice Lamer said:

> prior occupation, however, is relevant in two different ways, both of which illustrate the sui generis nature of aboriginal title. The first *is the physical fact of occupation, which derives from the common law principle that occupation is proof of possession in law:* see Kent McNeil, 'Common Law Aboriginal Title.'[75]

and:

> *Under common law, the act of occupation or possession is sufficient to ground aboriginal title* and it is not necessary to prove that the land was a distinctive or integral part of the aboriginal society before the arrival of Europeans.[76]

and:

> However the aboriginal perspective must be taken into account alongside the perspective of the common law. *Professor McNeil has convincingly argued that at common law, the fact of physical occupation is proof*

of possession at law, which in turn will ground title to the land: Common Law Aboriginal Title.[77] (emphasis added)

So there we have it: the application of the English common law principles concerning possession to the law on native title.

The second respect in which I would amend Professor McNeil's thesis concerns the question of the form of title to which possessory title gives rise. Professor McNeil argued that the indigenous occupants of land, holding possession, would be entitled to a fee simple on the basis of a presumed lost grant.[78] That is, the common law would apply in much the same way as it would to any possessor who could not show an actual grant from the Crown (in England, the presumed lost grant applied to a great many titles). At least one commentator has baulked at piling fiction upon fiction.[79] In my respectful view, it is unnecessary to conclude that possessory title amounts to a fee simple on the fiction of a lost grant. Rather, the title should be seen for what it truly is: it is a *sui generis* form of possession. It is *sui generis* in that it is an allodial possession and does not have its origin in the tenurial system, and secondly, it is subject to derogation by valid exercise of sovereign power.

By way of conclusion, let me revisit Lord Sumner's famous statement in *Re Southern Rhodesia*, where his Lordship described a now outdated approach to the recognition of native title by reference to where claimant peoples stood in relation to some 'Darwinian' scale of social organisation. The passage is as follows:

> The estimation of the rights of aboriginal tribes is always inherently difficult. Some tribes are so low in the scale of social organisation that their usages and conceptions of rights and duties are not to be reconciled with the institutions or the legal ideas of civilised society. Such a gulf cannot be bridged. It would be idle to impute to such people some shadow of the rights known to our law and then to transmute it into the substance of transferable rights of property as we know them.[80]

Justice Brennan said in *Mabo (No. 2)* that this kind of approach 'depended on a discriminatory denigration of indigenous inhabitants, their social organisation and customs', and he concluded that 'it is imperative in today's world that the common law should neither be nor be seen to be frozen in an age of racial discrimination'.[81]

The danger into which the Australian law on native title has fallen is that whilst the discriminatory approach inherent in *Re Southern Rhodesia* has been rejected in respect of whether indigenous rights in a settled colony survive annexation – no matter how peculiar the social organisation and customs of the people concerned might be – in relation to the question that follows, namely *what* rights survive annexation, the prejudice of *Re Southern Rhodesia* is revived and indigenous social organisation and customs are used to accord to Indigenous occupants of land a lesser form of possession than would be accorded to any other occupant by the common law.

Why should the Indigenous conception of land ownership be any less comprehensive than that of landholders in the English legal tradition? It can only be through miscomprehension, and the difficulties of the courts' fact-finding process, that courts can say that Indigenous people owned the land in any sense less than possession. The courts justify this discrimination on the grounds that these minimal rights are what the traditional laws and customs of the people have disclosed as a matter of fact. But what people – of any social and cultural organisation – would conceive of their occupation and possession of land as being anything less than what the holder of a fee simple would conceive of? As against the world, the conception of possession of the Englishman, the Trobriand Islanders, the nomadic peoples cited by Justice Brennan in the *Western Sahara* case, and indeed the Aboriginal peoples of Australia, is a universal conception. This is what Justice Brennan meant when he said in his classic statement in *Mabo* that 'land is susceptible of ownership, and there are no other owners'.

It matters not what the nature of the indigenous social and cultural organisation may be. It matters not what arcane and idiosyncratic laws and customs may govern the indigenous people's internal allocation of rights, interests and responsibilities amongst their members. It matters not whether it is an English lord slaughtering innocent fowls on his estate, or an Australian Aborigine standing on one leg in the sunset in his father's ancient homeland – *the title is the same*. The common law is only concerned to presume possession in those who are in occupation.

And the content of this possession is not determined by the nature of the occupation, and certainly not by the laws and customs of the occupants. The form of the title is the one form of title always afforded by occupation: namely, possession.

But this is not how the Australian courts have approached native title. They have recast the prejudice expressed in *Re Southern Rhodesia* so that prejudice against social and cultural organisation is used to justify Indigenous Australians being accorded a *lesser* form of ownership than would be accorded by the common law to someone who was in wrongful occupation, such as that of an adverse possessor.

Indeed, the content of the title of an adverse possessor is not limited to what she can prove by reference to laws, customs and social organisation. Rather, she is accorded possession because she is in factual occupation of the land. Yet, the title of the Indigenous occupant is limited by proof of whatever traditional laws and customs may be adduced to a court, no matter how arcane they might be. The common law only required that Indigenous claimants prove occupation at the time of sovereignty, but *Yorta Yorta* now requires them to prove the details of the traditional laws and customs that existed more than two centuries ago.

This situation is not good. It is pregnant with the prospect that the opportunity which *Mabo (No. 2)* represented for the settlement of land grievances will ultimately be unfulfilled. In my view, this situation can only be fixed if the definition of 'native title' in section 223(1) of the *Native Title Act* is restored to its original intention by parliament, and if the explication of native title be undertaken by the Australian courts in accordance with 'the time-honoured methodology of the common law'. This is the least that Indigenous peoples with faith in the common law heritage of this country should be able to expect from the country's parliament and High Court.

2003

NOTES

1   (2001) 208 CLR 1 ('*Yarmirr*').
2   (2002) 191 ALR 1 ('*Ward*').
3   (2002) 194 ALR 538 ('*Yorta Yorta*').
4   '*Native Title Act*'
5   (1992) 175 CLR 1 ('*Mabo No. 2*').
6   Ibid, 58 (Brennan J), 109 (Deane and Gaudron JJ), 182 (Toohey J).
7   Ibid, 70 (Brennan J).
8   (1996) 187 CLR 1 ('*Wik*').
9   See, e.g. ibid, 249 (Kirby J).
10   See *Native Title Act* div 2, div 2A, div 2AA.
11   More than 500 parties joined the *Yorta Yorta* litigation alleging that they had interests that were affected by the claim. See further, Wayne Atkinson, '"Not One Iota" of Land Justice: Reflections on the *Yorta Yorta* Native Title Claim 1994–2001' (2001), *Indigenous Law Bulletin*, 19, 21–2.
12   *Native Title Act 1993–1998*: s 228.
13   The document handed to the prime minister was called the 'Aboriginal Peace Plan'. An account of this document and this meeting between Indigenous leaders and the prime minister is set out in Mick Dodson, Aboriginal and Torres Strait Islander Social Justice Commission, *First Report*, 1993. Dodson wrote:
     'The Aboriginal Peace Plan contained eight principles, including:
     •   protecting native title interest by requiring the titleholders to consent to any future dealings in native title land,
     •   expanding the basis of claims to include people who cannot claim traditional connection to land,
     •   ensuring future claims for native title could be made more simply,
     •   establishing a process for settlement of future claims.
     In return, the Aboriginal Peace Plan proposed to accept the validation of interests granted over native title land which may have been invalid because of the *Racial Discrimination Act*. The validation proposal said that compensation should be negotiated, not decided upon by government.'
14   See Noel Pearson, 'The High Court's Abandonment of "The Time-Honoured Methodology of the Common Law" in Its Interpretation of Native Title in *Mirriuwung Gajerrong* and *Yorta Yorta*', Sir Ninian Stephen Annual Lecture 2003, University of Newcastle, 17 March 2003 (www.capeyorkpartnerships.com).
15   *Yorta Yorta* (2002) 194 ALR 538, 571–3 (McHugh J).
16   Whilst the judgments in *Yarmirr, Ward* and *Yorta Yorta* do not refer to the common law rights in *Mabo (No. 2)* being 'transmogrified' by the *Native Title Act,* this seems to be the assumption on the part of all justices other than McHugh J and perhaps Callinan J. This underlying assumption was articulated most explicitly by Kirby J during the course of argument in *Ward* (High Court Transcripts, P59/2000, 6 March 2001):

KIRBY J: You seem to be starting your submissions with the common law. You are going back to *Mabo* and to what Justice Brennan said and so on.

MR BARKER: Yes, I am, Your Honour.

KIRBY J: Is not the starting point now, the river having moved on, the statute, because the people in parliament have, as it were, taken another step? Recognition by the common law is one element in what parliament has provided, *but the starting point now is surely the Act of the federal parliament* (emphasis added).

And later:

KIRBY J: ... At least on one view, the passage of the *Native Title Act transmogrified* the common law entitlements. It is an Act valid on the face of it, it has been enacted under the powers that are given by the Constitution to the federal parliament. It talks of 'title', and it provides for the recognition of native title as defined – that is in section 10 – it provides for limits on extinguishment in section 11, and, at least in my view at the moment, *foraging around amongst what members of this court said before the federal parliament within its constitutional power provided for native title, its recognition and limits on its extinguishment, is just misconceived. It is starting at the wrong place.*

We have title, we have native title, but we have it under an Act of the federal parliament, the validity of which is not challenged, and at least orthodox approaches would suggest that you then look into the Act with the benefit of the past, but not controlled by the past. You are giving meaning to what the federal parliament, within its constitutional power, has provided. It has talked of 'title' and therefore *you have to give content to an Act, not forage around amongst the predecessor provisions of the common law* (emphasis added).

17 Justice Robert French, 'A Moment of Change – Personal Reflections on the National Native Title Tribunal 1994–1998', (2003) 27 *Melbourne University Law Review,* 488, 520. See also Maureen Tehan, 'A Hope Disillusioned, an Opportunity Lost? Reflections on Common Law Native Title and Ten Years of the *Native Title Act*', (2003) 27 *Melbourne University Law Review,* 523, 558–64.

18 Op. cit., French, 521.

19 (1997) 3 SCR 1010 ('*Delgamuukw*').

20 The only reference, in *Western Australia v. Ward* (2002) 191 ALR 1 at 34, 36 and 177 is to Lambert J's judgment in the British Columbia Court of Appeal's decision in *Delgamuukw v. British Columbia* (1993) 104 DLR (4th) 470. There is no reference in any of the cases to the Supreme Court's decision in *Delgamuukw.*

21 Paragraphs 75–6.

22 *Native Title Act* 1993 (Cth), s 10.

23 Ibid, s 11(1).

24 Ibid, s 3 (a).

25 (1998) 187 CLR 721 at paragraph 101 ('*Fejo*').

26 *Mabo (No. 2)* (1992) 175 CLR 1, 41–2 (Brennan J).

27 High Court transcripts, P59/2000, 6 March 2001:

> BARKER: Yes. There is no doubt, Your Honour, that *Delgamuukw* sets up a contrary proposition, that Justice Lee strongly relied on it and we, indeed, strongly rely on it here. *We do not accept that on any proper reading of Delgamuukw the constitutional provisions infect the reasoning in a way that makes it inapplicable in the Australian common law.*
>
> GUMMOW J: *That is an important question,* I guess.
>
> MR BARKER: It is an important question, and I would like to come back to that as well, if I could (emphasis added).

28 See, for example, Commonwealth, *Parliamentary Debates*, House of Representatives, 16 November 1993, 2877–83 (Paul Keating, Prime Minister); Commonwealth, *Parliamentary Debates*, House of Representatives, 9 March 1998, 781–8 (Daryl Williams, Attorney-General).

29 Op. cit., *Yorta Yorta* at paragraphs 75–6.

30 Op. cit., *Mabo (No. 2)* F.C. 92/014, Brennan J said as follows at paragraph 65:

> Native title, though recognised by the common law, is not an institution of the common law and is not alienable by the common law.

And also at paragraph 68:

> native title, being recognised by the common law (though not as a common law tenure) …

31 *Commonwealth v. Yarmirr* (2001) 75 ALJR 1582.

32 Australia, Senate, *Parliamentary Debates* (Hansard), 16 December 1993 at 5097.

33 Australia, Senate, *Parliamentary Debates* (Hansard), 2 December 1997 at 10171.

34 (1995) 183 CLR 373 at 486–7.

35 (1992) 175 CLR 1.

36 The *Explanatory Memorandum* to the *Native Title Bill 1993*, Part A at page 1 stated as follows:

> The Commonwealth's major purpose in enacting this legislation is to recognise and protect native title (see clauses 3 and 9). Native title is defined as the rights and interests that are possessed under the traditional laws and customs of Aboriginal peoples and Torres Strait Islanders in land and waters and that are recognized by the common law (clause 208). *The Commonwealth has sought to adopt the common law definition.* (my emphasis)

The *Explanatory Memorandum* to the *Native Title Bill 1993*, Part B at page 76 stated as follows:

> Subclause (1) of the definition uses terms similar to those used by the High Court of Australia in *Mabo* in defining native title. This definition is not a codification of the common law.

37 The *Explanatory Memorandum* to the *Native Title Amendment Bill 1997* stated as follows at paragraph 3.7:

The Commonwealth Parliament's major purpose in enacting the NTA was to recognise and protect native title (see sections 3 and 10). *The NTA adopted the common law definition of 'native title' as being the rights and interests possessed under the traditional laws and customs of Aboriginal peoples and Torres Strait Islanders in land and waters, and recognized by the common law* (section 223). The decision in *Mabo (No. 2)* referred only to native *land* title, but the NTA did not preclude the possibility that native title rights and interests may also exist in relation to *waters*, including offshore waters. This remains an unresolved issue. (my emphasis)

38 [1996] 2 SCR 507 ('*Van der Peet*').

39 *Wik* (1996) 187 CLR 1.

40 Op. cit., *Van der Peet*, 377.

41 Kent McNeil, *Common Law Aboriginal Title*, Clarendon Press, Oxford, 1989.

42 *Vajesingji Joravarsingji v. Sec. Of State for India* (1924) LR 51 IA 357, *Sec. of State for India v. Kamachee Boye Sahaba* (1859) 7 Moo. IA 476, *Cook v. Sprigg* [1899] AC 572, *Sec. of State for India v. Bai Rajbai* (1915) LR 42 IA 229.

43 *Re Southern Rhodesia* [1919] AC 211, *Amodu Tijani v. Secretary, Southern Nigeria* [1921] 2 AC 399, *Bakare Ajakaiye v. Lieutenant-Governor, Southern Provinces* [1929] AC 679, *Case of Tanistry* (1608) Davis 28, *Witrong v. Blany* (1674) 3 Keb. 401.

44 *Mabo (No. 2)* Toohey J, p. 182.

45 *Western Australia v. Commonwealth ('Native Title Act Case')* (1995) 183 CLR 373.

46 Op. cit., McNeil (1989). See also Kent McNeil, 'A Question of Title: Has the Common Law been Misapplied to Dispossess the Aboriginals' (1990), 16 *Monash University Law Review*, 91.

47 Op. cit., McNeil (1989), 205–8.

48 *Mabo (No. 2)* (1992) 175 CLR 1, 207–13 (Toohey J).

49 Op. cit., McNeil (1989), 195, 300, 241; *Mabo (No. 2)* (1992) 175 CLR 1, 178 (Toohey J).

50 21 US 543 (1823).

51 31 US 515 (1832).

52 34 US 711 (1835).

53 Op. cit., McNeil 1989, 255 (emphasis added).

54 See *Mabo (No. 2)* (1992) 175 CLR 1, 58–9 (Brennan J); 88 (Deane and Gaudron JJ).

55 See *Mabo (No. 2)* (1992) 175 CLR 1, 58–9 (Brennan J); 88 (Deane and Gaudron JJ).

56 See op. cit., McNeil (1989), chapter 6. Following the British Columbia Court of Appeal's decision in *Delgamuukw* and before the Supreme Court's decision on the appeal, McNeil analysed the judgments of the Court of Appeal in 'The Meaning of Aboriginal Title' in Michael Asch

(ed.) *Aboriginal and Treaty Rights in Canada,* UBC Press, 1997, 135 at 137 and commented on the source of Aboriginal title as follows: 'The courts seem to be vacillating between two possible sources of Aboriginal title – Aboriginal occupation and Aboriginal laws – without pronouncing in favour of one or the other.'

It was this search for a single answer to the question of 'what is the *source* of native or Aboriginal title?' – which is the subject of much of the circular commentary on native title over the years – that led to the misconception which this paper is directed at. It is not a question of *choosing* between Aboriginal occupation or Aboriginal laws as the source of indigenous title – both are relevant, because indigenous title is sourced in *the occupation of land by indigenous peoples under the authority of their Aboriginal laws and customs.* Aboriginal law determines:

(i) *who* is entitled to the communal possession which the common law recognises as arising from the fact of occupation of the land by a native community and

(ii) the *allocation of rights, interests and responsibilities* that are 'carved out of' of the communal possession, within the community of title-holders

Aboriginal law also contributes evidence of:

(i) the *territory* to which the native community is entitled to possession

(ii) the *descent* of this entitlement to possession from the predecessor native community that held the title at the time of annexation, to the successor native community which holds the contemporary entitlement

For a summary of my views on this matter, see Noel Pearson, 'Principles of Communal Native Title' (2000) 5 *Indigenous Law Bulletin* 4.

57 *Mabo (No. 2)* (1992) 175 CLR 1, 207 (Toohey J).

58 (1999) 201 CLR 351, 384 (Gummow J) ('*Yanner*').

59 *Western Australia v. Ward* (2000) 170 ALR 159 at paragraphs 96 and 106, per Beaumont and von Doussa JJ.

60 Op. cit., *Delgamuukw,* per Lamer CJ at 241.

61 *Yanner v. Eaton* (1999) HCA 53, per Gummow J at paragraph 74:
The exercise of rights, or incidents, of an indigenous community's native title, by sub-groups and individuals within that community, is best described as the exercise of privileges of native title. The right, or incident, to hunt may be a component of the native title of a numerous community but the exercise by individuals of the privilege to hunt may be defined by the idiosyncratic laws and customs of that community.

62 Op. cit., *Mabo (No. 2),* per Brennan J at paragraph 69:
'... where an indigenous people (including a clan or group), as a community, are in possession or are entitled to possession of land under a proprietary native title, their possession may be protected or their entitlement to possession may be enforced by a representative action brought on behalf of the people or by a sub-group or individual who sues to protect

or enforce rights or interests which are dependent on the communal native title. Those rights and interests are, so to speak, carved out of the communal native title. A sub-group or individual asserting a native title dependent on a communal native title has a sufficient interest to sue to enforce or protect the communal title ...'

63 P. 186

64 Given that this reference to 'physical presence' has been often misquoted and misrepresented, it should be made clear that Toohey J is here talking about physical presence on land *at the time of annexation,* not necessarily at any time afterwards or in the present. The important issue is that it is because an indigenous community is in physical occupation of land at the time of annexation – when the common law arrives – that the common law recognises their communal native title. In the words of Lamer CJC in *Delgamuukw v. British Columbia ('Delgamuukw')* (1997) 153 DLR 192 at paragraph 145, it is at the time of annexation that the native title 'crystallized':

'*...aboriginal title arises out of prior occupation of the land by aboriginal peoples and out of the relationship between the common law and pre-existing systems of aboriginal law.* Aboriginal title is a burden on the Crown's underlying title. However, the Crown did not gain this title until it asserted sovereignty over the land in question. Because it does not make sense to speak of a burden on the underlying title before that title existed, aboriginal title *crystallized* at the time sovereignty was asserted. Second, aboriginal title does not raise the problem of distinguishing between distinctive, integral aboriginal practices, customs and traditions and those influenced or introduced by European contact. *Under common law, the act of occupation or possession is sufficient to ground aboriginal title* and it is not necessary to prove that the land was a distinctive or integral part of the aboriginal society before the arrival of Europeans ...' (my emphasis).

Whether physical presence is required to prove continuity of title after annexation and in the context of a contemporary claim is entirely another question (which will not be dealt with here). The point about the title 'crystallizing' at the time of annexation is very important, because it underlines the fact that *a title* comes into existence at this time. It is no longer an Aboriginal law title. It is a title constituting the recognition by the common law of the fact of occupation of land by an indigenous community under authority of and in accordance with their traditional laws and customs. This recognition is essentially *a conclusion of law* based upon *the fact of occupation of land* under traditional law and custom. The conclusion of the common law is that the indigenous occupation gives rise to a presumption of possession. This is why the courts have often referred to a 'presumptive' native title: see Deane and Gaudron JJ in *Mabo (No. 2)* at paragraphs 31, 36, 38, 42 ('the doctrine of presumptive common law native title, which has long been recognised by the common law, is applicable to a settled British colony ...') and 69. The presumption is a legal presumption founded on the fact that people are in occupation of

land when the Crown acquires sovereignty and makes these people subject to its sovereignty – and entitled to recognition under the common
law.

65 With respect, I believe it is the failure to grasp this point which leads
McNeil to error in his interpretation of *Wik,* to which I make reference in
note 55 below.

66 *Supra* note 24 above.

67 S 223(1) of the *Native Title Act* conflates the two forms of title by including in the same definition 'native title' and 'native title rights and interests', expressions which are said to 'mean the communal, group or
individual rights and interests of Aboriginal peoples or Torres Strait
Islanders in relation to land or waters'.

68 *Mabo (No. 2)* (1992) 175 CLR 1, 58.

69 In a 1997 article, 'Aboriginal Title and Aboriginal Rights: What's the
Connection?' (1997) 36 *Alberta Law Review* 117, 138–42, Kent McNeil set
out the most coherent understanding of Brennan J's judgment in *Mabo
(No. 2)* – which corrected the prevailing misinterpretation in the Australian judicial and academic commentary. Despite the availability of this
excellent analysis, it has been completely ignored – both by the judgments
and by the submissions put forward by practitioners representing native
claimants in Australia. It is not possible in the space of this paper to set
out my allegation that McNeil was however in error in his analysis of *Wik*
at 142–3.

70 Op. cit., *Mabo (No. 2)* (1992) 175 CLR 1, 76 (Brennan J).

71 Ibid 51 (Brennan J).

72 (1972–3) ALR 65 ('*Milirrpum*').

73 *Mabo (No. 2)* (1992) 175 CLR 1, 51 (Brennan J).

74 This explanation follows McNeil, op. cit., 10. McNeil discusses the term
'title' as part of his introduction to possession and title to land in English
law. He did not, as I have now done, apply this explication of the term
'title' to native title, or customary law title as he called it. The question of
the meaning of 'native title' was fruitlessly discussed in argument before
Ward (High Court Transcripts, P59/2000, 6 March 2001).

75 *Delgamuukw* (1997) 3 SCR 1010, 1082 [114] (emphasis added).

76 Ibid 1098 (145) (emphasis added).

77 Ibid 1110–1 (149) (emphasis added).

78 Op. cit., McNeil 1989, 208, 242–3.

79 Brendan Edgeworth, 'Tenure, Allodialism and Indigenous Rights at
Common Law: English, United States and Australian Land Law Compared after *Mabo v. Queensland*' (1994) 23 *Anglo-American Law Review,*
397.

80 Op. cit., 233–4.

81 *Mabo (No. 2)* (1992) 175 CLR 1, 41–2 (Brennan J).

A MIGHTY MORAL VICTORY

Just when the whitefellas were getting relaxed and comfortable about native title, Justice Murray Wilcox of the Federal Court has dropped a bombshell right in the centre of Perth, a metropolis that governs the most booming natural-resources economy in the world.

Australians have never experienced as much wealth as exists today, and the China-driven resources boom has meant that the Labor politicians who govern Western Australia preside over unprecedented mountains of revenue. The whitefellas have never had it so good.

Of course, contrary to the evening news images of backyards filmed from helicopters, the ruling in *Noongar* is not a legal bombshell, because it does not extend the law on native title beyond what had already been decided by the High Court of Australia. It is not even a political bombshell. The political arguments were well canvassed before the Keating government passed the *Native Title Act* in 1993, following the High Court's landmark decision in the *Mabo* case in 1992. And for good measure, we had another two bitter years of political argument when the Howard government passed its ten-point plan amendments to the *Native Title Act* in 1998, following the High Court's second landmark decision in the 1996 *Wik* case. The arguments about the law and politics of native title have been near exhausted in Australia.

The bombshell in *Noongar* is moral and psychological. Just when the whitefellas had come to regard native title benignly, as largely a symbolic form of title that would be found only in the remote and desert parts of central and northern Australia, the Noongar people establish native title over the city that was established on their traditional homelands. The Noongar are shadow-dwellers in their own country; these urban-dwelling blackfellas were not supposed to get native title.

The Federal Court decision will not result in one square centimetre of land held by the whitefellas being lost. In fact, the Noongar specifically did not claim any freehold or leasehold land, on which everybody knows native title is extinguished. Indeed, they did not claim any land affected by other tenure that extinguishes native title. Backyards were safe after *Mabo*. They are still safe after *Noongar*.

The effect of the Wilcox ruling is that the Noongar are entitled to whatever lands are left over in Perth. The stark reality is that not much will be left after 177 years: the Noongar will eventually recover only the remnants of their original estates. But what is left will be valuable. Most observers will see the value of the land as real estate in a booming city. The Noongar will no doubt see its economic value as well, but for them the value of the land is that it is their cultural hearth.

The Noongar can also be expected to be entitled to substantial compensation for the extinguishment of their native title as a result of land dealings following the *Racial Discrimination Act* of 1975. Payment of compensation was provided for in the *Native Title Act*, but the sheer expense and difficulty involved in seeking compensation has meant that no compensation has been paid to a native title group. The compensation bill since the *Native Title Act* was passed in 1993 has been zero. The Noongar will be the first group to receive compensation for the loss of native title.

The ruling will also affect the capacity of local and state governments to deal with Crown lands that they assumed were no longer affected by native title. These lands must now be understood to have an owner: the Noongar. There will be procedural and other provisions that governments will have to abide by.

How did this extraordinary result come about? In 1993 I was a member of the team of Indigenous negotiators, led by Lowitja O'Donoghue and Mick Dodson, who negotiated the terms of the *Native Title Act* with then prime minister Paul Keating. We were derided by our detractors among the blackfellas as 'the Magnificent Seven'. The team included a young Aranda man from central Australia,

Darryl Pearce. Pearce largely disappeared from public view, but in 2000 he became director of what is now the Southwest Aboriginal Land and Sea Council, based in Perth. This would have been one of the hardest jobs in native title anywhere in the country.

The south-western corner of Australia was a Balkanised mess of competing and overlapping native title claims. It's the kind of mess that we see far too often across the continent, with every two-bit lawyer hooked up with their own client, whose main aim seems to be to crush the claims of Indigenous rivals rather than properly seeking native title. This madness fulfilled Dodson's prescient 1993 take on Bob Hawke's famous pledge: 'By the year 2000, no Aboriginal child will be without their own lawyer!'

Into this cauldron Pearce, the outsider, dared to intervene. And through his energy and, no doubt, that of the Noongar elders, by 2003 all six native title claims that had been lodged in the south-west were consolidated into one united claim. Pearce said at the time: 'The aim of the single Noongar claim is to break out of the old way of thinking on native title and help finally resolve one of the most complex and difficult issues facing the West Australian community. The aim of the single Noongar claim is to secure negotiated native title outcomes for Noongars. No-one wins if we continue to travel down the rocky road of litigation and conflict.' Alas, the overtures made by Pearce and the Noongar to state and local governments to settle the claims by negotiation were ultimately rejected, and the claim proceeded to a hearing in the Federal Court in 2005.

Justice Wilcox has ruled on the question of traditional connection to the claimed lands and has found in favour of the Noongar. He has not ruled on a second question: in what lands does native title still survive? The answer to this second question will be complex and expensive, and can be dealt with only through negotiation. Each and every tenure that is not clearly an extinguishing tenure must be looked at. The Western Australian government must now respond to the original Noongar invitation to negotiate a comprehensive settlement.

Wilcox has ruled on connection, which is a question of fact. Appeal courts rely on trial judges and are reluctant to disturb findings of fact. The path of appeal and further litigation is expensive and irresponsible.

It is also morally reprehensible. It is not surprising that a Labor government in Western Australia has pledged to appeal the Wilcox decision. After all, it was a Labor government, that of Brian Burke, that scuttled the national land rights legislation proposed by the Hawke government in the 1980s. Had a national scheme for land rights been implemented by the federal parliament back then, it would have been unlikely that the High Court would have needed to rule on native title.

Both Kim Beazley and John Howard support the Western Australian government's decision to appeal. Howard's aspiration to limit the extent of native title to a minimum is at least consistent with his well-known convictions. Beazley was a minister in the government that enacted the *Native Title Act* in 1993 under the leadership of Keating and Gareth Evans. Beazley's position on Noongar is a measure of the man: he has no convictions.

2006

CHALLENGING OLD FRIENDS

HOPE VALE LOST

On a recent Friday night I walked out onto the lawn of my mother's house in my hometown. It was after 2 a.m. and though my family lives a kilometre away, I could hear loud music booming from several stereos in various parts of what I would have called a village in my youth, but which more accurately answers to the description of an outback ghetto today. The music emanated from houses known as party houses, where numbers of men and women congregate to binge drink, share marijuana, often out of what are called bucket bongs, laughing, shouting, singing and dancing and seeking sexual partners – consensual and otherwise.

By midnight the bonhomie of the early evening descends into tension, as various bingers develop dark moods, vent anger, resentment and suspicions at those to whom they earlier professed love. Arguments and fights ensue, over the smallest slights and often over ownership of and access to the dwindling supplies of alcohol. While parties rage at a number of notorious locations throughout the town, with hosts boosting their stereos with specially bought amplifiers, often placed at windows facing outwards as if for the benefit of the rest of the inmates of this sad place, it is hard to maintain the fiction that this place is a community, because it has become a hellhole. For many the hell outside their concrete-block homes is shut out with the aid of whirring fans and air-conditioners, which help to drown out the noise, including the screams.

This Friday night was the third night in a row of parties. They began on Wednesday evening following the receipt of Family Tax

Benefit payments, continued at a lower gear over the next day and got back into top gear on Thursday night following the receipt of CDEP work-for-the-dole payments. This continues during the next day. The number of people missing from work has led almost every community to declare Friday the unofficial start of the weekend. School attendance collapses on Friday, from already low levels earlier in the week. This has led to many proposals from educators over the years to reduce the school week in Cape York Peninsula to four days, as if that would be a solution.

As I drove around the streets at 3 a.m., I passed by drunks stumbling from one party house to another. I passed groups of young teenage girls walking around or sitting on the kerbside. For too many of them, sexual activity begins young at Hope Vale, very young. Who knows the circumstances of their first experience, but the incidences of abuse that come to light are only the tip of the iceberg of sexual assault, unlawful intercourse with minors and incest.

The self-destructive promiscuity of young people in the communities of Cape York Peninsula is not only the product of their individual tragic histories, but is also the product of the sick norms that now prevail. That older men should be able to have sexual relations with the young girls I passed in the street in exchange for alcohol, marijuana or esteem is water off the moral backs of our people. Young men may jump through windows to rendezvous with their paramours, but they are as likely to do so to interfere with women and children, and this has nearly become socially normal. That young teenagers should set up as couples and have children before they even know how to look after themselves is now commonplace.

My hometown looks and feels like a ghetto. The mango trees, frangipannis and old wooden church still evoke the mission of my early youth, but the fibro and weatherboard cottages built by the hands of our own local carpenters have all been replaced by welfare housing, increasingly built by outside contractors. The uniform rows of kit homes and Besser Block houses are of course much more expensive and have better amenities (at least at first, because they do not last for long), but they look squalid. The once lovingly tended gardens with topiary, gardenias and fruit trees are scarce today, and plastic bags, VB cans, old motor cars and general rubbish spill out of the homes and onto the streets.

With the eyes of someone who returns to his hometown for holidays and occasional weekends, I marvel that the people who live here do not see the shit in front of their eyes. Despite vastly improved levels of funding and infrastructure, the place is a mess compared to the village of my childhood. I drove past the place where my parents brought up our family in a small fibro cottage with no hot water and a pit toilet out the back. We got electricity when I was in Year 4 but I did not see television until I went to college. Now they have Austar and adults carelessly expose children and young people to their pornographic videos and DVDs.

Earlier in the afternoon at the roundabout I had seen the shocking site of a beautiful puppy that had been run over by a vehicle; it was lying in a pool of blood on the bitumen. As we say in the language of this place, *Ngathu wawu baathi*, my soul cried, for this lost life. People were walking up the street past where this puppy lay. In my nocturnal drive I passed the puppy in the same place. The binge drinking will continue to daybreak, and on through Saturday. Bingers pass out and catch some sleep before waking again to resume the fray. The parties change gear during the course of the four days as participants come and go, supplies run out and fresh supplies are brought in from Cooktown. The beauty of electronic banking is that welfare and CDEP income is dropped into keycard accounts automatically, and Centrelink will assist recipients to stagger payments to members of a household. So Jimmy can get his on Wednesday and Sally can get hers on Friday. There is money for drinking and drugs over a longer stretch of the week. Centrelink's intention with these flexible payment plans, of course, is to assist people to manage their income in order to purchase food and pay their bills, but the reality is that it makes more money available for binge drinking over a longer period of time.

As I drive down to the beach early on Saturday morning I see the young children emerging out of the houses, as if from a war zone. Yes, there are children and young girls in the homes of the hosts of the binge-drinking parties. How they fare through these weekly episodes depends on whether their parents, who are often inebriated, are able to keep an eye on their welfare; the chances that molesters are amongst the party people are very high. Older children may run off and stay with sober relatives, particularly grandparents, but what happens to the ones left behind? Some of the young people sitting on the kerbside at 3 a.m. are simply scared to go back home.

On Sunday things will be quiet. 'They run out of grog', people explain to me. The town will be mostly quiet for the next two or – if you are lucky – three days. The bureaucrats from Peter Beattie's government will do their business with the people and organisations of Hope Vale in the sane part of the week. If they spend their time at the shire-council offices and at the school and the hospital, they can miss what is happening down the street. Certainly the communities of Cape York Peninsula during the quiet days can give the impression of being pleasant, if untidy, 'communities'. You can excuse the rubbish and the ubiquitous high barbed-wire fences and iron cages that have to be constructed around almost every public facility, because after all, this is an Aboriginal community.

But the public servants and politicians only visit for the day; they never sleep in the town. They never have anything other than the official conversations down in the administration offices, so they too easily form the view that 'this place is not too bad'. They tell themselves that 'we just need to co-ordinate the programs', and that 'we have a demand reduction plan' for the alcohol problem. The underbelly of these so-called communities is not intriguing – it is not like something from a David Lynch movie. It is Hobbesian. And all of this takes place week-in, week-out.

Last year, Hope Vale's mayor, Greg McLean, invited a delegation of children from the local primary school to present their views to a large roundtable of assembled bureaucrats and community leaders, black and white. In plain English the children pleaded that they wanted the drinking and violence in their community to stop.

As I drove through my hometown on the Sunday evening on my way back to Cairns, I saw the dead puppy still in the street. I thought about the distance between being inured to the fate of a puppy that didn't see a car coming, and being inured to the fate of our own children.

2006

OUR RIGHT TO TAKE RESPONSIBILITY

If we are to survive as a people, we have to get passive welfare out of Aboriginal governance in Cape York Peninsula. We have to get rid of the passive welfare mentality that has taken over our people

The right to self-determination is ultimately the right to take responsibility. Our traditional economy was a real economy and demanded responsibility (you don't work, you starve). The whitefella market economy is real (you don't work, you don't get paid).

After we became citizens with equal rights and equal pay, we lost our place in the real economy. What is the exception among whitefellas – almost complete dependence on cash handouts from the government – is the rule for us. There is no responsibility and reciprocity built into our present artificial economy, which is based on passive welfare (money for nothing).

Passive welfare has undermined Aboriginal law – our traditional values and relationships. When you look at the culture of Aboriginal binge drinking you can see how passive welfare has corrupted Aboriginal values of responsibility and sharing, and changed them into exploitation and manipulation. The obligation to share has become the obligation to buy grog when your cheque arrives, and the obligation of the non-drinkers to surrender their money to the drinkers. Our traditional value of responsibility has become the responsibility of the non-drinkers to feed the drinkers and their children when the money is gone.

Passive welfare and grog and drugs are finally tearing our society apart. We were dispossessed and discriminated against before we were included in the welfare state, but our law – based on trust, respect and mutual help – was better honoured during those times of hardship and guardianship than it is today. Our struggle for rights is not over and must continue – but we must also struggle to restore our traditional values of responsibility. We have to be as forthright and unequivocal about our responsibilities as we are about our rights – otherwise, our society will fall apart while we are still fighting for our rights. We do not have a right to passive welfare. Indeed, we can no longer accept it. We have a right to a real economy; we have a right to build a real economy.

Aboriginal society in Cape York Peninsula

Our society today is clearly unsuccessful. It is a sad but clear fact that Aboriginal society in Cape York Peninsula today is not a successful society. There are numerous indications that our communities are severely dysfunctional.

These are just some of the signs that our society is not functioning successfully:

- Our people die twenty years earlier, on average, than other Australians;
- Our health is by far the worst of any group in the Australian community;
- Our people suffer from diseases that other Australians simply do not have;
- Our children do not participate in the education system anywhere near as successfully as other Australian children;
- We are over-represented in the juvenile justice system, in the criminal justice system and the jails;
- There is more violence amongst our people than in other communities in Australia.

We need to face up to this reality. The kind of society we inhabit today and the lifestyles our people lead are ridden with problems. Whilst other communities and groups in Australia, and indeed across the planet, suffer from many of these same problems, the degree to which our Aboriginal society suffers from these problems is extraordinary.

We should not romanticise the way things were in the past. Life was certainly not easy for our people in the years before citizenship. Nevertheless, it is also obvious that in a number of important ways our situation has deteriorated over the past thirty years. Probably the clearest indication of this is the decline in life expectancy. Perversely, this social deterioration occurred despite the vast improvement in the material circumstances of our communities that resulted from the transfer of resources that came in the wake of our citizenship and the recognition of our material poverty by the state since 1970.

There are Third World societies which are materially far worse off, but which appear much more successful than Aboriginal society in Cape York. Those societies are not gripped by such despair and helplessness as our people are. Access to material goods and cash is not itself a guarantee of success. Anastasia Shkilnyk, in *A Poison Stronger Than Love*, her account of the Grassy Narrows community of Ontario, describes an indigenous group in Canada, a First World country which, like Australia, can afford welfare provisions for its indigenous peoples. Shkilnyk pointed out that this community's situation was more parlous than more materially deprived societies. She wrote:

> I could never escape the feeling that I had been parachuted into a void – a drab and lifeless place in which the vital spark of life had gone out. It wasn't just the poverty of the place, the isolation, or even the lack of a decent bed that depressed me. I had seen worse material deprivation when I was working in squatter settlements around Santiago, Chile. And I had been in worse physical surroundings while working in war-devastated Ismailia on the project for the reconstruction of the Suez Canal. What struck me about Grassy Narrows was the numbness in the human spirit. There was an indifference, a listlessness, a total passivity that I could neither understand nor seem to do any thing about. I had never seen such hopelessness anywhere in the Third World.

Shkilnyk here describes our future. Whilst no communities in Cape York Peninsula have deteriorated as badly as the Grassy Narrows community described by Shkilnyk, Cape York communities are increasingly exhibiting the very symptoms she observed there.

Despite the fact that ours is one of the most dysfunctional societies on the planet, none of the current discourse on the subject gives me any satisfaction that the underlying issues have been grasped, let alone confidence that the right measures are being taken to change this situation.

Facing the social and cultural pathology of grog

We all know that the problem of grog in Cape York Peninsula is of an incredible dimension. Yes, it is true that diet, smoking and stress are other key factors in our atrocious health situation and increasingly early death – but the relationship between grog and all of these other 'lifestyle' problems is obvious. For younger people in the Peninsula, the problem of drugs is as bad as grog. Drug dependency and petrol sniffing amongst the young were unknown in Cape York Peninsula not too long ago. Drugs are now rife and communities are reporting outbreaks of petrol sniffing.

We need to see clearly what is involved in Aboriginal binge drinking. When you look at a drinking circle you see people who are socialising around grog. Social and cultural relationships between the drinkers are expressed, reinforced and reiterated whilst people are engaged in drinking. Everyone involved in the drinking is obliged to contribute resources – money – for the purchase of grog. Everyone is obliged to share the money and the grog.

These social and cultural obligations are invoked at every turn by members of the drinking circle. These invocations are very heavy indeed and they most often draw upon real obligations and relationships under Aboriginal laws and customs. What, when people are not drinking but hunting, is a cultural obligation to share food with countrymen, is turned into a cultural obligation to share grog. In fact your fellow drinkers will challenge your Aboriginal identity in order to establish your obligation to contribute money to buy grog: 'Come on, don't be flash! We not whitefellas! You–me black people!'

When you look at the obligations which are set up around the drinking circle, you see the drinkers under reciprocal obligations to contribute to buying the grog. When I have money, it's my turn to shout. When your money comes, it's your turn to shout. Outside of this drinking circle are the women and the children and old people and the non-drinkers. The resources of these non-drinkers are used to feed the families – including those who have spent most or all of their money on grog – when they are hungry. But more than that, these non-drinkers are placed under tremendous social and cultural pressure to contribute resources to the drinking circle for buying grog. So the drinking circle becomes a hole into which the family's resources are sucked. Wives and girlfriends, parents and grandparents, are placed under tremendous pressure – social and cultural and ultimately through physical violence – to contribute to this pathological behaviour. Whilst the relationships between drinkers are reciprocal ('We share our grog because you-me brothers – one mob'), the relationship between drinkers and non-drinkers is not reciprocal. The drinkers take, the non-drinkers are forced to give.

Looking back, in the 1970s it was mainly the men who formed these drinking circles. The children, the youth, the women, the old people, stood outside of these circles but were affected by their behaviour and forced to supply resources to the drinkers. Then in the 1980s, you started to see younger women despair and join the drinking circles. And now it is the old people – yes, mainly the women – who are keeping the society fed, and who have an anxiety for the future of these children and their community. Who want to change things.

How is it that our society has been so corrupted?

The manipulation and corruption of Aboriginal values and relationships
Whilst we understand that colonial society has taken a toll on the structures and principles of our society in Cape York Peninsula, there is no discourse among our people about how we can reconcile what remains of our traditional culture with the development of a successful society. When we recognise elements of our traditional social arrangements and values in our current arrangements, we assume that they are right and should be maintained because traditional society was successful. But there are problems with this assumption. By simply assuming that everything that we think of as 'Aboriginal' or 'traditional' is good, we fail to analyse the deformities that these arrangements and values have undergone. Clearly the traditional obligation to share resources has been corrupted.

It was during discussions with Mervyn Gibson from the Hope Vale community that I came to understand the social and cultural manipulation and distortion that is involved in Aboriginal drinking. When you grow up in a family, a community and a society in which the society's values and relationships are daily being exploited by pathological behaviour – to such an extent that this becomes the social norm – you tend not to see that we are being badly manipulated by the drinkers. But you realise that it is manipulation – not culture, not tradition, not identity, but manipulation – when you look at how other obligations and relationships are ignored or abused. What about the obligation towards children? Why are all of the family's resources going to fulfil so-called obligations to cousins and uncles for drinking, when the children have nothing to eat? What about the old people, what about our obligation to look after them? How is it that they end up with the total responsibility to look after all of us?

What about our social and cultural relationships with other people, people outside of the drinking circle? What about their needs? What about our obligations to them? What about these values? If you talk about identity, what kind of Aboriginal are you if you are not caring for your children and your old people? The culture of Aboriginal drinking ignores these questions. Indeed, drinking circles are seen as essential Aboriginal behaviour – by the drinkers themselves, and by those (black and white) who see Aboriginal drinkers as pitiful victims, and thereby perpetuate and sanction the corruption of Aboriginal values and relationships.

It is well known to us that Aboriginal drinking results in the breaking of Aboriginal law. Relationships under Aboriginal law and custom are daily corrupted by drinking. Wrong people socialise together. Inappropriate behaviours ensue. So rather than drinking being a true expression of Aboriginal social and cultural values and relationships, it is a blatant corruption of them.

Those who are caught in the misery of social and cultural corruption –
and those who deliberately perpetuate it
Of course, most Aboriginal people we know in the Peninsula – our cousins, our friends, our uncles, our brothers – who are involved in the

pathologies of drinking and gambling are caught in an economic and social system not of their choosing. The suction hole of these drinking and gambling coteries, and all of the social and cultural pressure that they bring to bear on people, are almost impossible to resist. This is not a matter of blame. People are caught in an economic and social system that precipitated this misery. But it is a matter of responsibility. Our people as individuals must face their responsibility for the state of our society – for respecting and upholding our true values and relationships, our own laws and customs.

Whilst the great majority of our people are unconsciously involved in a system which involves exploitation and manipulation, there are those, black and white, who cynically exploit this pathology. These are the white publicans and canteen owners, the air-charter companies, the taxi companies, the store owners who cash cheques for profit, who sell methylated spirits to known alcoholics. These are the black and white sly-grog sellers who charge $50 for a flagon or $200 for a carton of beer. These are the people who sell drugs to our children, and get them to deal on their behalf.

Often the people who are involved in, say, selling sly grog are themselves not heavy drinkers. Perfectly sober people will exploit this pathology, and sly grog is a highly profitable business. These are the parasites feeding on the misery of our people. And we allow them to. It is a testament to the degree to which our values and our Aboriginal law have been overborne that we tolerate this exploitation in the midst of our own society.

The unravelling of Aboriginal law

The High Court's ruling in the *Mabo* case has now recognised Aboriginal laws and customs as part of the legal system applicable to Aboriginal society and Aboriginal lands. This is a fundamentally important step in the right direction.

Central to the recovery and empowerment of Aboriginal society will be the restoration of Aboriginal values and Aboriginal relationships, which have their roots in our traditional society. Even as our traditional society was ruptured by colonial invasion and our people underwent an ugly colonial history, we survived. At least in a spiritual sense our ancestors prevailed over this colonial bastardry and inhumanity. Our ancestors struggled to keep our society alive against an onslaught which even the colonists believed would end in our extinction as a people.

And the thing that we retained – even if we lost our lands and our economy and our rights, and even if our families were torn apart – was our law: our Aboriginal values and relationships. From the bush to the country towns to the working suburbs, these values and relationships make us a rich people. They have shielded our people against loneliness and provided sustenance during desperately mean times. They still do. But when we look at our society in Cape York and the nature of our problems, it is these very values and relationships that are now unravelling before our eyes. It is passive welfare that has caused this social dissolution. Dependence on passive welfare is our most urgent problem.

The passive welfare paradigm
Passive welfare has several aspects, which together constitute what I will call 'the passive welfare paradigm'.

Firstly, passive welfare is an irrational, 'gammon' economic relationship, where transactions between the provider and the recipient are not based on reciprocity. The principle in this relationship is 'money for nothing' or 'help for nothing'. Essentially it is charity. Unlike commercial transactions, no mechanisms promote rational and constructive behaviour, either on the hand of the recipient or on the hand of the provider, which is usually the government. As Immanuel Kant wrote in *The Conflict of the Faculties* in 1798: 'Welfare, however, has no principle, neither for him who receives it, nor for him who distributes it, one will place it here and another there.'

Secondly, welfare is a method of governance. Welfare involves a superior power having all of the rights and all of the responsibilities to make decisions and take actions on behalf of relatively powerless people. People on the ground are seen as passive recipients, clients or customers. They are provided 'services', essentially on a plate, by far superior people (white and black) with greater expertise and knowledge. Those with power will jealously and steadfastly work to keep it.

Invariably, all initiative and resources are concentrated in the hands of the people who are supposed to save and serve the hapless and the helpless. As a method of governance, welfare is increasingly becoming a means of managing marginalised groups at minimal cost without even maintaining the fiction that a lasting solution to their problems is sought.

Thirdly, welfare is a mentality. It is a mentality that accepts the principles underlying the economic relationship and the method of governance described above. This mentality is internalised and perpetuated by recipients, who see themselves as victimised or incapable and in need of assistance without reciprocation. This mentality says that it is their right to have assistance without reciprocation. But this mentality is also held by people in power (white and black). The bureaucracy views people on the ground as incapable – and therefore, instead of simply providing resources and facilitating decision-making and action at the ground level (especially concerning social programs), it hoards power.

Following are some of the problems with passive welfare:

- It is a poor substitute for participation in the real economy, psychologically, socially and economically. Welfare is never enough to live properly on. Rather than providing the opportunity for a proper place in the wider economy and society, passive welfare confines the recipient to her or his stagnant environment;
- It pacifies recipients rather than invigorating them into social, political and economic action to secure a better deal for themselves and their children;
- It reproduces these same problems in following generations.

Many of the passive welfare programs are in fact aimed at overcoming the very problems which passive welfare created in the first place. The problems caused by passive welfare give rise to a whole set of other problems, so more passive welfare is administered to try to alleviate the original problems that it caused. And so on.

The welfare paradigm has been particularly destructive in the governance of Aboriginal society. The passive welfare mentality results in:

- Our people thinking that the solutions to our problems lie outside of ourselves. We think that 'somebody else' will address the problems, be it the government, white people or other Aboriginal people – but not ourselves;
- Our people failing to take responsibility for ourselves as individuals, for our families and for our communities;
- The promotion of a victim mentality amongst our people;
- The expectation that assistance will be provided to people without us doing anything in return;
- The devaluation of resources that are important and which should be properly valued and used to develop our communities. Passive welfare cheapens money. Welfare money does not have the same value as personally earned money.

These effects of passive welfare are well known.

The nature of passive welfare and its relationship to our social breakdown
The nature of passive welfare (which today is nearly our sole material resource) explains our social crisis. It explains why, even as our material condition improved over recent decades, our social condition deteriorated. Passive welfare has come to be the dominant influence on the relationships, values and attitudes of our society in Cape York Peninsula. This influence soon came to be directly at odds with our traditional relationships, values and attitudes – our Aboriginal law – which our ancestors had hitherto managed to keep alive, and which gave structure and strength to our families and communities in the face of ill treatment by the wider society. Invariably the outcome of the ongoing conflicts between our traditions and the economic base of our society is that our traditions succumb and are eroded daily. Indeed, we are now at a stage where many of the traditions we purport to follow are too often merely self-deceptions (that we care for each other, that we respect our elders, that we value our culture and traditions) and the 'traditions' which we do follow are in fact distortions conditioned by the pathological social situation which passive welfare has reduced us to: that we sit around in a drinking circle because we are Aboriginal; that you are trying to be a flash whitefella if you are not giving your brother money for grog.

The resources of passive welfare are fundamentally irrational. Whereas the dollar earned through a commercial or labour transaction has a rationale, the dollar given as a matter of course has none. Everyone in a passive welfare economy is susceptible to irrational (mis)appropriation and (mis)expenditure of money, because that is the very nature of the money. Money acquired without principle is expended without principle.

When people have only one means of existence, the nature of that income obviously influences their whole outlook. The irrational basis of our economy has inclined us to wasteful, aimless behaviour. Like other people who can't see any connection between their actions and their circumstances, we waste our money, our time, our lives. We neglect our material possessions, our education, our social and economic development. We do not seize opportunities that arise. There always comes another day and another cheque. No-one feels the need to use a sum of money for a meaningful investment, or to use a day to build something that will last.

The worst consequence of this lack of meaning and purpose is that it has compounded the effects of dispossession and trauma by making us susceptible to an epidemic of grog and drug abuse. This epidemic now has its own momentum and in turn makes it inevitable that our scarce resources increasingly finance irrational and destructive behaviour. We must now deal with both passive welfare dependence and substance abuse simultaneously, as these two problems feed off one another and undermine all efforts toward social recovery. I will leave for another paper a discussion of our most serious social ill: our grog and other drug addictions. It is enough to say that the notion underlying most discussion about substance abuse, the theory that substance abuse is only a symptom of underlying social and psychological problems, is wrong: addiction is a condition in its own right, not a symptom.

Passive welfare alone would not have caused our social disaster. But the combination of passive welfare dependence and the grog and drug epidemic will, if not checked, cause the final breakdown of our traditional social relationships and values. Grog and drug abuse coupled with an outlook determined by a passive welfare economy is a fatal combination. The intrinsic force in the grog and drug epidemic is now stronger than the force of our traditional social norms and values. People motivated by their addiction to grog or drugs now regard and treat other people in our society in the same way as they regard the passive welfare money: these people (wives, girlfriends, parents, grandparents, children, relatives) are not valued and respected. They will always be there and the addicted do not have to take any responsibility for them. These people are simply a source of resources (money, shelter, food, comfort and care), and they are treated accordingly.

The economic is the social

Those who are concerned about the social problems in Cape York Peninsula need to have a clear understanding of our economic history, because the relationship between economic circumstances and social problems is critical. There has been too much of a separation of the social from the economic when we consider our problems. The fact is, every economic relationship is also necessarily a social relationship, and underlying many of our social problems are these economic relationships and issues. The relationship between government and the community, and between government and the individual, is perpetuated and recreated in all of the internal relationships of our society. The principles upon which money circulates within the community carry with them all of the inherent values of the original passive welfare.

Whilst there is general nominal acceptance of the interrelationship between economic issues and social problems, in practice economic issues have been relegated to the 'too hard basket' and attention has been focused on behavioural problems such as domestic violence or health problems. But we cannot defer tackling the fundamental issue of the economic basis of our society.

Real economies and the gammon economy of passive welfare

In order to understand the contended relationship between our social problems and passive welfare, we need to analyse our history. In particular, we must understand the difference between 'real' economies and what I have called the gammon economy of passive welfare, and we must understand our experience of these different economic systems throughout our history.

In real economies, there is a correspondence between what we consume and what we produce. There might be an exchange of goods and services between our economy and other economies, but the good things we enjoy we have earned through our work. Broadly, there are three kinds of real economies that we know of in Cape York Peninsula:

The *traditional subsistence economy* was very much a real economy. If you didn't work, you starved. No *minha* or *minya* came to our ancestors' camp ready to eat.

In the mission days we lived partly in what I call the institutional *modern subsistence economy*: growing our own food, raising cattle and so on, whilst also undertaking traditional hunting and gathering and moving between the mission and work in the outside market economy. This was a real economy. If you didn't work, you starved.

The whitefella *market economy* is a real economy. If you don't work, you don't get paid.

Then there is the gammon economy of passive welfare, which is artificially created by government on gammon principles. By gammon principles, I mean that it is not based on any real transaction. Personal sustenance is received as a matter of course, with the recipient not being required to work or to provide anything in return. This kind of passive sustenance was not available in our traditional subsistence economy (staying alive in the old days was hard work) or in the old mission subsistence economy. It is, however, available under the principles of the welfare system.

The real economy of traditional subsistence

Hunting, fishing and gathering have been practised within our communities in Cape York Peninsula all through our modern history. Facilitated by modern equipment, traditional subsistence activities continue to contribute a significant proportion of the food consumed by the people of Cape York Peninsula and are therefore very important. There are two very valuable aspects to the exploitation of our traditional resources: the high quality of the food improves our health, and the traditional subsistence activities revive the social values of responsibility and reciprocity, which have been eroded by our passive welfare dependency.

The real economy of modern subsistence

During the 'protection' phase of our colonial experience, our grand-parents were removed to missions, which were isolated from the mainstream society and economy. The state established an elaborate system to regulate relations with the outside mainstream economy, the stated intention being to avoid the gross exploitation of Aboriginal people as sexual and labour slaves. Where work permits allowed Aboriginal people to work for white employers, the state sanctioned a system of unequal pay and poor conditions. Aboriginal workers were not free to manage the wages they earned. The state managed all income via the administration of missions and government settlements.

Within the missions and settlements of Cape York Peninsula, the authorities and their inmates developed a subsistence economy. State assistance to the missions in this period was minimal. The economy of these institutions was a modern form of subsistence in which community ventures in the fishing industry, cattle and various agricultural experiments were supplemented by a mixture of traditional foods, the raising of domestic animals and the maintenance of food gardens.

Aboriginal workers moved between the subsistence economy of the institution and the outside mainstream economy according to the availability of work and the dictates of the authorities. Needless to say, life was hard and work was imperative to survival. This modern subsistence economy was real.

The real economy of the market

The real market economy of the colonists affected Aboriginal people wherever colonial society was established. Whilst groups of Aboriginal people continued to cling to their traditional economy, and it remains today a component of the Indigenous livelihood in Cape York Peninsula, the colonial intrusion necessarily engulfed Aboriginal society and economy as well. During the frontier phase, Aboriginal people were dragged into the colonial economy for purposes of exploitation, which was only partially ameliorated during the protection phase when the state, in collaboration with the Christian churches, created the isolated institutions of the Aboriginal reserves, and a modern form of subsistence economy was developed in these institutions.

Aboriginal people have therefore participated in the market economy for most of Australia's colonial history, and we have done so at the lowest end of the scale. Engagement in the market economy was often degrading and involved tragic exploitation. But our ancestors managed to survive a long colonial history, doing whatever work was available. This was the only option available to people before welfare. They had to work under bad conditions or starve.

The gammon welfare economy

The great tragedy of recent Aboriginal history was the Australian failure – when discrimination against Aboriginal people became untenable and citizenship was finally recognised in 1967 – to remove the discrimination that our people suffered in the mainstream economy, *and keep us there.* Instead, Australia's idea of the great benefits of removing discrimination and granting us citizenship was to take our people out of the real economy and dump us into passive welfare. The Aboriginal peoples of Cape York Peninsula are now firmly embedded in the passive welfare economy. Perhaps less than 5 per cent of the economy of Peninsula communities is the result of Aboriginal people's involvement in the market economy. Employment at the Cape Flattery silica mine and the Weipa bauxite mine, the small-scale manufacture of arts and crafts and native seed collecting for mining rehabilitation provide the few examples of Aboriginal engagement in the market economy. Most of the economic activity, including the operation of community enterprises, occurs within the passive welfare economy and is reliant upon government transfers. The passive welfare economy is totally dependent upon government funding; without it, the economy would collapse.

A recent feature of our economy is that the recognition of our native title rights may be followed by monetary compensation for the exploitation of natural resources on our land. Though some employment has been created for us as a result of this exploitation, there is a great danger that compensatory income will not be the beginning of an economy very different from our passive welfare dependence, since the destructive welfare paradigm is so firmly established and since our involvement in and knowledge of the market economy is currently so limited.

We share many problems with rural Australia generally, such as the decline of rural industries and the lack of infrastructure. When these difficulties are compounded by our social disintegration, our lack of resources and education, and by the low expectations the larger community has of us, it is difficult to see how a real market economy could replace this passive welfare economy.

Welfare dependency is the result of colonial history

European colonisation took away the self-sufficiency of Aboriginal society. The land and its resources were appropriated during the colonial period. The means for our people to sustain our traditional society were taken from our ancestors. The Aboriginal economy was fundamentally disrupted by colonisation. In a short time, options for Aboriginal people were reduced to:

- Trying to survive by moving between the traditional economy where possible and working in the white economy (this itinerant existence became increasingly difficult and, in time, impossible);
- Begging for scraps on the fringes of the white economy and being exploited as prostitutes and slaves (and therefore soon dying out);
- Being removed from white society and its slave economy to missions and government settlements;
- Finding a more stable situation in the white economy, usually as exploited labour at the lowest end of the economy (for instance in the cattle industry or as domestic labourers).

The reduction of Aboriginal people to fringe-dwelling beggars whose only economic option was charity from whites was a prescription for genocide. For there was no charity. Aboriginal society survived where it was isolated from the white economy, on settlements where people could endeavour to provide for themselves with the assistance of missionaries and 'protectors' by creating an institutional subsistence economy, or where they could find some more stable place at the lower end of the white economy. This lower end of the white economy amounted to an informal system of slave labour. However, the Aboriginal participation in this economy, though the circumstances were harsh and cruel, was not on the basis of passive welfare or charity.

This situation persisted until the late 1960s. The Aboriginal people of Cape York Peninsula moved between the institutional economy of the settlements and the real economy. Therefore men resident on the missions had to leave the settlements to seek work in the pastoral, agricultural, mining and fishing industries. Up until the 1970s, the Aboriginal people of Cape York Peninsula participated in the real economy at its meanest level.

The welfare take-over since the 1970s
Social welfare as provided by government since the 1970s produced a revolutionary change in the Aboriginal economy of Cape York Peninsula. Aboriginal people withdrew from participation in the real economy. People came back home to work nominally in the institutional economy of the mission – an economy which was becoming more and more dependent on government funding. The impact of the equal wage decision on Aboriginal labour in the cattle industry was decisive. People lost their place in the pastoral industry and were forced into the increasingly welfare-based economy of the settlements.

The assumption of responsibility for Aboriginal affairs by the federal parliament after the 1967 referendum and the recognition of the rights of citizenship of Aboriginal people resulted in an increase in welfare provisioning by the Commonwealth government. The people and communities of Cape York Peninsula are now almost completely dependent on passive welfare. Most income is from government payments to individuals and to Aboriginal organisations. The economy of the communities is artificially sustained by government funds. This funding also creates the few job opportunities that are available in the communities.

Our confrontation with racism through history
I have suggested that the nature of the passive welfare economy is reflected in our social relationships, but our social problems are most often interpreted as the legacy of our colonisation. In discussions of our historical legacy there are three general themes that arise: racism, dispossession and trauma. These are said to explain our position in Australian society and are seen as the origin of the problems this paper is seeking to confront.

Our recent history can be seen as a sequence of phases, character-ised by the different roles played by dispossession, trauma and dis-crimination at different times. Initially, we were for a brief period simply formally dispossessed. Dispossession followed the initial judg-ment that we were inherently less capable to use this land for the good of ourselves and for humanity.

A phase of traumatic confrontation necessarily followed as that judgment was acted upon, since we were in fact inextricably linked to our land. The destruction of our traditional society through frontier wars, murder, sexual enslavement and abduction was compounded by the spread of diseases against which we had little resistance.

Official discrimination was then the dominant aspect of the third phase of our confrontation with racism, the recent period after the breakdown of traditional society when we became a 'protected' peo-ple. The survivors of the traumatic confrontations were suppressed as an underclass, unable to claim their traditional homelands and work-ing for almost nothing. Whilst discrimination had been present from the moment of colonial intrusion, it was during this protection phase that institutionalised discrimination became the dominant aspect of racism. An enormous legal and bureaucratic apparatus was developed in order to manage the remnants of the beaten peoples. This system regulated the smallest movements and events in our lives and we were still being traumatised, but more often through administrative deci-sions, for example in relation to the removal of children, and less so by violent assaults.

Today, during the current phase of our confrontation with racism, official discrimination has been abolished, though there has been a return to official discrimination in recent years, the Commonwealth parliament's amendments to the *Native Title Act* being the most blatant. Dispossession is still in place. Traumatic decimation of our people and disruption of our culture and families are the dominant factors in our collective psychology, and trauma is daily recreated in our dysfunctional communities. Whether today's unofficial discrimination is just a regret-table residue of past official discrimination or fulfils the same function of holding us down is a matter for dispute. But it is there.

Racism: an impediment but not a disability

In the light of our experience, it is understandable that racism is offered as the main explanation for our present situation. One of the strong but unstated reasons why we justify passive welfare amongst able-bodied Aboriginal people, in spite of the obvious harmful effects on our society, is that we consider racism a disability.

Make no mistake, racism is a terrible burden. It attacks the spirit. It attacks self-esteem and the soul in ways that those who are not subjected to it would have not an inkling of. Racism is a major handicap: it results in Aboriginal people not having access to opportunities, in not recognising opportunities when they arise, and in not being able to seize and hold onto opportunities when they recognise them. Australians concerned about the position of Aboriginal people in this country should not underestimate the decisive role that racism plays in the well-being of Aboriginal individuals and society. Australians need to stop kidding themselves that 'racism isn't all that bad – black people should just get over it and get on with it'. If you are black in this country, you start life with a great and crushing burden. Most non-Aboriginal Australians do not appreciate how crushing this racism has been and continues to be. They do not understand how destructive it is. Only if they could take on the identity of an Aboriginal person for a while would they gain some understanding of the central role racism plays in the oppression of Aboriginal people as individuals and as a community.

In addition to this direct experience of racism, we sense that we are excluded from the domains of real power, political and economic. I understand only too keenly the paralysing effect of this burden. But my argument in this paper is that, though racism looms so large that it is tempting to characterise it as a disability, we should not and must not treat it as such. The minute we treat racism as a disability, we concede its power over our lives and over our future. As bad as racism is, we cannot allow it to reduce us to being treated – and seeing ourselves – as if we are not fully capable people in our own right. Though our people have it harder than others in society because of racism, we must not succumb to the racism that is latent in the welfare paradigm – the idea that though we seem to be fully able-bodied people, we need to be treated by the state as if we are not.

Trauma: personal and inherited

Trauma is an especially difficult issue to come to terms with because its personal manifestations can be incapacitating. The many Aboriginal people with personal traumas caused by separation of family members and by abuse and violence are often truly incapacitated. Of course, even where many of the current perpetrators are Aboriginal, such trauma has ultimately been caused by the racist degradation of our people into a dysfunctional underclass. It is true, however, that economic recovery will contribute to recovery from trauma. Conversely, being immersed in passive welfare dependency will not alleviate trauma; indeed, this situation surely exacerbates and perpetuates the problems. It passes trauma on to the next generation.

In acknowledging the need for trauma to be specifically addressed, I would urge people to draw a distinction between that trauma which is personal and immediate and which may incapacitate individuals or families, and that trauma which is inherited and more remote, and which renders people *susceptible* to problems, but does not leave them incapacitated. Prevailing discussions of trauma in Aboriginal society unhelpfully conflate these two kinds of trauma.

Personal trauma needs to be recognised and attended to. Inherited trauma needs to be recognised, but it is also imperative that we recognise that economic and social empowerment is ultimately the best – and arguably the only – cure. It is by re-establishing our families and communities in the wake of social disaster and dislocation that we put trauma behind us – just as our grandparents did after they were torn away from their families and their lives in the bush and 'removed' to the mission as young children. The danger with ideological fixation on inherited trauma is that we promote a culture of victimhood, rather than a determination to get back on our feet as a people. We must never let the true history of our people be forgotten or obscured, but we must avoid creating an ideology that turns history into a personal disability for able-bodied members of our community.

The economic effects of dispossession

There is a good reason why we need to concentrate on the economy: because it is a structural issue that we can actually do something about.

Racism and our passive welfare dependency are the key structural problems which afflict the Aboriginal people of Cape York Peninsula, and they explain our predicament as a people in Australia today.

Racism is a structural obstacle that is unlikely to recede in the near future. For the Aboriginal people of Cape York Peninsula who seek to interact with the wider Australian society, racism in Australia will continue to constitute a social and personal burden. This paper is not aimed at setting out a strategy to attack and change the structural problem of racism.

It is time we analysed our condition as a people without being defeated and paralysed by racism. This is not to say we should forget about racism, or pretend that it doesn't exist. Rather, we, as Aboriginal people, must understand and keep in mind the pervasive role racism plays in the oppression and dysfunction of our society; but we must concentrate our efforts on the concrete economic and social structures that we can change, instead of dwelling on those things that don't seem to change no matter what we do.

By addressing the concrete social and economic circumstances of our passive welfare dependency, we can find the power necessary to prevail against racism. If we overcome the structural debilitation of our welfare condition, our people will be empowered to deal with racism, and indeed to resist letting racism degrade us and inhibit our development as individuals and as communities.

Understanding our current social problems

It is a misconception that the social problems suffered by our people in Cape York Peninsula today have been with us since our traditional society was ruptured by European colonisation. This is not the case at all. Anybody who knows the history of our communities knows that the kind of social problems that afflict our society today – and their severity and extent – were not always with us.

The abuse and neglect of children today does not resemble the situation in the Peninsula communities of the 1960s and earlier. The numbers of people in prison and juvenile institutions today are unprecedented: these are statistics that started to emerge in the 1970s. There was not one Hope Vale person in prison in the early 1970s. At any time today, a dozen Hope Vale people are either in prison, or would be in prison without diversionary measures. The same dramatic differences apply to the other communities in the Peninsula. Alcohol abuse in Peninsula communities became the huge problem that it now is only in these same recent decades. And these problems have bred new problems. Petrol sniffing amongst children and youth was unknown in Cape York Peninsula until recently. The bashing of old people for money for grog was inconceivable in earlier times.

Even if there is a range of reasons why these social problems have emerged in the last three decades of the century, it is significant that the emergence of these problems coincides with the period when passive welfare became the economic basis of our society. And yet it is generally not acknowledged that the nature and extent of our social crisis is of recent origin, just like the crisis of the Grassy Narrows people, which had no precedent in their life on the old reserve prior to their forced relocation, the destruction of their subsistence trapping economy and the introduction of passive welfare. And our entire policy proceeds from this ignorance. This ignorance is hugely problematic for at least three reasons.

Firstly, it obscures the fact that our society was once functional – not just back in the long distant pre-colonial past, but only a bit more than three decades ago. We have ourselves internalised this official forgetfulness and we therefore lose hope.

Secondly, the assumption of the service deliverers is that our social problems are *endemic to Aboriginal society*. They proceed with their programs as though we were subhuman.

The third problem is that ignoring the historical development of our problems reinforces further misconceptions about their source; namely, the erroneous assumption that our social problems are the legacy of racism, dispossession and trauma and that our chronic welfare dependency is the end result of these social problems. If this is true, our passive welfare dependency is ultimately caused by racism, dispossession and trauma. But this generally accepted causal chain – racism, dispossession and trauma create social problems, which create passive welfare dependency – is wrong. Both steps in the reasoning are wrong. Firstly, prior to the 1970s, even though racism was state-sanctioned, dispossession had been well effected and trauma was still fresh and ongoing in our society, we did not have the kind or degree of social problems we see today. Secondly, our social problems didn't come before our passive welfare dependence – rather, our social problems arose out of the economic condition of passive welfare dependence.

Of course, racism, dispossession and trauma are the ultimate explanations for our precarious situation as a people. But the point is: they do not explain our recent, rapid and almost total social breakdown. And most importantly: if we build our ideology and base our plan of action on our justified bitterness about what has happened to us, we won't be able to claim our place in the modern economy, because our current social dysfunction is caused by the artificial economy of our communities and by the corrupting nature of passive welfare.

We have allowed Aboriginal policy to forget that our parents, grandparents and great-grandparents struggled mightily to preserve our families and communities – our society, our laws and values – against great and sustained attack, and we survived. Whatever our material deprivations, whatever our poverty, we had a strong, if bruised, society.

Our social degeneration in fact accompanied the vast improvement in our material condition from our earlier poverty over the past thirty years. We are socially poorer today despite vastly improved material circumstances. It should not be necessary for me to say that, in this analysis, I am not urging poverty as a solution to our social predicament. I argue that poverty needs to be overcome via the development of real economies, and that we should use our welfare resources to develop an economic foundation for our society that is based on real economic principles. Anti-poverty programs based on passive welfare have only produced 'opulent disasters', and this is now surely plain to see.

Strategic conditions
The failure on the part of the political Left to take up issues of responsibility in public-policy debate no doubt was and is informed by tactical considerations. Aboriginal policy debate has been similarly hamstrung by such considerations. Whatever misgivings we might have had about welfare provisioning by government over the years, these were and are

often set aside for tactical and ideological reasons. However, those of us concerned about the predicament of marginalised people in society need to consider the wisdom of such tactics, because our people suffer daily from the absence of responsibility in the way we approach Aboriginal policy.

It may be argued that frank and balanced discussion of our problems, and especially of the central problem of passive welfare dependence in our society, may reinforce negative stereotypes of our people. Indeed, our failure to speak about many of our problems is frequently because of our concerns about reinforcing prejudices in the wider society.

These are legitimate considerations. However, given the serious and ongoing threat that passive welfare represents to Aboriginal society in Cape York Peninsula, we need to consider what is more important: confronting our problems or worrying about the reinforcement of stereotypes. There are a number of reasons why the 'stereotype' argument, whilst it should be acknowledged, should not be decisive.

Firstly, it is doubtful that those who hold prejudiced views of Aboriginal people will amend their views whatever happens: these people regret Aboriginal success as vehemently as they decry Aboriginal failure. Secondly, whilst it is important to maintain public support and empathy for the cause of Aboriginal rights, the calamitous problems of our people on the ground will not be alleviated by public perceptions or public relations. Goodwill and understanding from the wider community is important, but it will not solve the problems that we are talking about here. Indeed, if we confront these problems by ourselves, the mealy-mouthed stereotypes of those with ill-will will not matter much.

Thirdly, there is no use denying problems and causes that are patently obvious to outsiders. Our failure to make progress in the recovery of Aboriginal society from the effects of colonialism is well known, and we cannot solve these problems until we face the issues head on. As long as we fail to deal with the facts of failure and the reasons for them, our excuse-making will be seen for what it is. When we refuse to confront the truth about our problems head on, and when we continue to run ideological arguments, not only do our people internalise these excuses, but we come to believe our own rhetoric. Just when our people need clear direction and honest thinking, we simply spout the company line, which says nothing about personal responsibility.

A few examples of our muddled thinking on Aboriginal policy are discussed below. As we shall see, it is often the consequence of our penchant for ideological straitjackets borrowed from our compatriots of the Left – who seriously need to rethink their approach to these issues for the sake of their own mob as well.

What is the true meaning of self-determination?

Ever since the Whitlam government introduced the language of self-determination into official Aboriginal policy, we have never been in agreement as to its meaning. The Left supported the rhetoric of self-determination (more power to the blackfellas), the Right have been opposed (the blackfellas will break up the nation), but no-one has been clear about what was meant by the policy. We Aboriginal people have not been particularly clear on its meaning either. There is still interminable musing about the 'powers' which self-determination should afford Aboriginal people, but no clear idea, let alone consensus, about what self-determination means.

My own perspective on the meaning of self-determination came from Lars Emil Johansen, the indigenous premier of Greenland, who addressed the Regional Agreements Conference organised by the Cape York Land Council in Cairns in July 1994. He explained: 'Self-determination is the right to take responsibility. Self-determination is hard work.'

This is a critical insight for those concerned with Aboriginal policy, at the highest levels and at the grass roots: in claiming the right to self-determination, we are claiming the right to take responsibility. We need to restore the importance of responsibility in our understanding of our problems and in our understanding of the solutions; if we don't, we are kidding ourselves and our people. The quest for self-determination in fact raises serious questions for us. Do we really want to take responsibility? Do we want to do the hard work of self-determination? Are we sufficiently unified to fulfil our responsibilities? Are we prepared to show leadership and build consensus and overcome division?

Or are we so divided that, if we took on the responsibilities, we would do just as bad a job as the bureaucracy and the whitefellas have?

Rather than deal with these hard and real questions, our concept of self-determination has instead been restricted to the realm of legal and political theory and rhetoric. We talk about the right to self-determination and international law, about concepts of autonomy and sovereignty and so on. Whilst this level of discourse is important, the practical realities of self-determination are being ignored.

These discourses show a fascination with power – that is, the right to power – but they fail to deal with the other aspect of power: responsibility. So we have vigorous rhetoric about our right to autonomy, but we can't even get our medical service and land council to talk to each other, or the legal service is going in one direction and the housing co-operative is heading in completely another. If self-determination is to become meaningful, we have to do the hard grind and make our structures of Indigenous governance unified and coherent.

To whom should we be accountable?

We are equivocal about accountability, and this is related to the question of responsibility. There are some (self-serving) ideological reasons why some of our people resist accountability. Resources intended to benefit our community are seen as 'belonging to the whitefellas'; they have been 'given by the government'. There is a feeling that we need not account for them: 'Anyway, they owe us this, and more.' This attitude to accountability is usually held by leaders who don't particularly care about the situation of their people. But the fact that the resources arrive in the form of passive welfare underpins this abandonment of responsibility.

In fact, there are legitimate historical reasons why the state holds little moral sway over Aboriginal people. Although the state can demand accountability through formal legal mechanisms – audits, financial returns and the like – it enjoys little moral respect. But whatever our view of the moral authority of the state, the important point for us is to see that we need to be accountable to our own people. The moral justification for accountability lies in the fact that these resources belong to our people. For this reason, Aboriginal leaders must take utmost responsibility for their stewardship of scarce and valuable resources.

As offensive as it often is when the bureaucracy demands accountability, the fact is that we must account to our people. We need to turn our view of accountability away from the state and focus it on our people: the young, the old, the vulnerable. The ideological and philosophical shrugging off of accountability – 'it belongs to the government, the government owes us this' – must be banished. We need to see every resource as an entitlement of our people, to whom we are directly accountable.

There are other points to be made about accountability that are relevant to government and to the wider community. It is of little use to see accountability predominantly in terms of bureaucratic process rather than actual progress on the ground. All too often, one sees situations in which the effort and expertise of community organisations are concentrated on fulfilling bureaucratic requirements rather than doing substantive work. So organisations end up with clean audit reports – just like government departments – but the work on the ground has hardly progressed. This lack of progress results in government imposing more and more layers of bureaucracy. Communities are hamstrung by a bureaucracy that sees accountability in a shallow and useless sense. It is no lie to say that Aboriginal affairs is bound by far more red tape and bureaucratic requirements than are necessary. We should instead be focusing on Aboriginal people being accountable to each other for the stewardship of resources and the production of results.

We need to promote the importance of accountability throughout our community. It is not just our community organisations and its leaders who must take responsibility; individuals who receive resources must also understand their accountability to themselves and to their families and community. Our people must stop seeing resources as merely ephemeral. The fact is that these resources must be used to alleviate suffering and build a future. The passive welfare mentality encourages a distorted view of accountability. The remoteness and lack of moral authority of government allows people to focus on the relationship between Aboriginal people and the distant government – rather than between our own people.

Conclusion

I am conscious that many of the ideas set out in this paper appear to go against the grain of the Aboriginal struggle as many people conceive it. My firm view is that we have to be as forthright and unequivocal about our responsibilities as we are about our rights. Otherwise we will finally get all of our rights, and find that our society has fallen apart in the meantime.

Our struggle for our rights is far from over. Nothing I propose in this paper casts any doubt on the correctness of our struggle for rights – including the rights that spring from our unique position as the original people of this country. We must continue to be vigorous in our advocacy of our rights and our fight against discrimination.

But the Aboriginal struggle has to wake up to the fact that our belated citizenship in 1967 gave us two things. First, it gave us land rights and increasing recognition of our human rights; this has been a good thing. Second, it gave us a passive welfare economy; this has been disastrous. And as long as passive welfare is seen as one of the hard-won 'rights' of our belated citizenship, the true meaning of citizenship is obscured.

Yes, we have always said that we don't want welfare as a permanent destination for our people. But we've been living in passive welfare-dependence for three decades now. The social consequences of this condition are devastating, as anyone who understands our communities knows.

Aboriginal and non-Aboriginal communities that have just half a leg in the gammon passive welfare economy and the rest in the real economy do not quite appreciate how devastating full-body immersion in passive welfare-dependence is to communities. Look at the escalating social problems in Cape York Peninsula, for goodness' sake.

Our parents, grandparents and great-grandparents were severely victimised, abused and discriminated against. They suffered more than we have. Yet they survived, not by seeing themselves as victims or by seeing their salvation in whitefella charity or pity, but by struggling. If we make our recovery as a people dependent on what the *wangaarrn-gay* should, and one day might, do for us, we are deluding ourselves.

Pity, goodwill, charity – these are all poor substitutes for our people taking our fair share and our rightful place in the country.

The thing about passive welfare is that its effect on us is more insidious than any other external threats. The injuries and bruises our people suffer at the hands of Australian society are considerable. The wounds are real and damaging, but we can see that racism and dispossession threaten our survival, and that we must fight. But passive welfare seems to us to be an asset, not a threat. Who doesn't want labour-free income? For this reason, the dangers of passive welfare are difficult for us to see and the condition is harder for us to confront and treat. Our society is weakened and destroyed from within, without us even understanding what is happening to us and why.

Having said this, I am also conscious that many of the ideas set out in this paper have been expressed by many of our people before. The truth is that in our guts we have known that passive welfare was no good. The call for responsibility in this paper is not anything that mothers, grandmothers and old people do not say every day to their children and grandchildren – but they have been, more and more, railing against the wind.

2000

ON THE HUMAN RIGHT TO MISERY, MASS INCARCERATION AND EARLY DEATH

Dr Charles Perkins Memorial Oration

Of the contribution that Charles Perkins made to Australian society and history in the late twentieth century, I take his political fearlessness most to heart. It is his example of fearlessness that I aspire to follow tonight, because I believe that Australian policies concerning the life expectancy of Aboriginal people are grievously wrong. The life expectancy deficit of Aboriginal Australians as compared to the wider community will not decrease with our current policies, and is likely to increase. Neither of the political parties contending for office at the forthcoming election has made the changes in thinking that are necessary for Aboriginal people to turn around our social disaster. Both contenders continue to be half right in the policies that they are prepared to advocate. To simplify the policy contrast: the Australian Labor Party will be strong and correct in their policies in favour of the rights of Aboriginal people – particularly land rights and native title – and they will be weak and wrong in relation to the breakdown of responsibility in Aboriginal society occasioned by passive welfare-dependency, substance abuse and our resulting criminal-justice predicaments. The Coalition will better understand the problems of responsibility but will be antipathetic and wrong in relation to the rights of Aboriginal people: they advocate further diminution of the native title property rights of Aboriginal Australians.

I marvel that neither side of this indulgent political divide in Australian politics can see that what is needed is for the rights favoured by the ALP to be added to the responsibilities that are understood by the Coalition. But the major parties will insist on their indulgences despite the fact that the cost of their policy and political failure will be disproportionately borne by the black vulnerable: the children, the women and the elderly.

In my critique of prevalent Aboriginal policies over the past thirty years, I of course do not discredit or disavow the great achievements that have been made in the area of Aboriginal rights and recognition in this period. There have been a great many achievements, not the least in the fight against formal discrimination, a fight towards which Charles Perkins made a decisive contribution. So let me not be misunderstood: the struggle for these rights was heroic and correct and their achievements were great advances for Aboriginal people and for the nation.

The question that we have to confront is this: why has a social breakdown accompanied this advancement in the formal rights of our people? Indeed, this social breakdown afflicts with equal vehemence those Aboriginal peoples who have never been dispossessed of their lands and who retain their classical traditions, cultures and languages.

Let me pose the question in the broader context of the past thirty years and ask why, during this period of Indigenous policy enlightenment and recognition, and despite billions of dollars and much improved housing and infrastructure and government services, there has been a corresponding social deterioration. What is the explanation for this paradoxical result? Maybe we should confront the possibility that the policy analysis and recommendations that have informed the past thirty years of deterioration may have been wrong. Our refusal to confront this possibility is a testament to the degree to which we will insist on our ideological indulgences even when they prevent us from diminishing social suffering.

Why are my people disintegrating, and why are we unable to do anything about it? I will go straight to the core of the matter and talk about addiction and substance abuse. Our worst mistake is that we have not understood the nature of substance abuse. Following the late

Swedish professor Nils Bejerot, I maintain a fundamental objection to the prevailing analysis of substance abuse amongst our people. The prevailing analysis is that substance abuse and addiction are symptoms of underlying social and personal problems. According to the symptom theory, we must help people to deal with the problems that have caused them to become addicted. According to this theory, we must address the 'underlying issues' if we are to abolish substance abuse. The severe substance abuse in Aboriginal communities is said to have been caused by trauma, trans-generational grief, racism, dispossession, unemployment and poverty.

But the symptom theory of substance abuse is wrong. Addiction is a condition in its own right, not a symptom. Substance abuse is a psycho-socially contagious epidemic and not simply an indicator or function of social and personal problems in a community. Five factors are needed for an outbreak of substance abuse: (i) the availability of the substance; (ii) spare time; (iii) money; (iv) the example of others in the immediate environment; and (v) a permissive social ideology. If these five factors are present, substance abuse can spread rapidly among very successful people as well as marginalised people.

Substance abuse originally got a foothold in our communities because many people were bruised by history and likely to break social norms. The grog and drug epidemics could break out because personal background and underlying factors made many people susceptible to trying addictive substances. But when a young person (or an older non-addict) is recruited to the grog and drug coteries today, the decisive factor is the existence of these epidemics themselves, not his or her personal background. And for those who did begin using an addictive substance as an escape from a shattered life and from our history, treating those original causes (if indeed you can do anything about those original causes) will do little. The addiction is in itself a stronger force than any variation in the circumstances of the addict.

There are two insights here that I want to reiterate. First, at this advanced stage of the grog and drug epidemics, it is not a breach of social norms to take up or participate in substance abuse. It follows that we cannot divert young people away from substance abuse. No matter how much money and effort we spend on alternative activities, drug-free activities cannot compete with the more exciting drug-induced experiences for young people's attention, because all hesitation about the appropriateness of an abusive lifestyle is long since gone. Good living conditions and meaningful activities might, under normal circumstances, make non-addicts less susceptible to trying drugs and thus help in preventing outbreaks of substance-abuse epidemics. Diversionary measures can only prevent substance-abuse epidemics, not cure them once they are underway. Second, even under optimal circumstances, life is difficult and full of conflict. No matter what we do, we can never make life so good that an addict voluntarily leaves her or his antisocial lifestyle and joins us in our struggle for a better future. The addict has already shown that he or she loves the effects of the substance abuse more than his or her own land, people, family and children. We cannot convince an addict to quit by offering a materially and socially better life including land rights, infrastructure, work, education, loving care, voluntary rehabilitation and so on. The addict will just use all these material and human resources to facilitate an abusive lifestyle.

We must understand that trauma, dispossession and the rest make our communities susceptible to grog and drug epidemics, but they do not automatically cause abusive behaviour. Of course, having a high number of people in a community who are susceptible to turning to substance abuse is, in an indirect way, a causal factor that might contribute to the outbreak of a substance-abuse epidemic. But, I repeat for the third time, this fact has led to two fatal logical errors in our efforts to understand the current social disaster. Addiction is a condition in its own right and it is just as difficult to do anything about an addiction if you are a socially and economically strong white professional who became addicted through the careless drinking of exquisite wines, as if you are an unemployed member of a decimated and dispossessed Aboriginal tribe. We must understand that an established addiction is a very strong force at the heart of the will of the addict; it exists independently of the historical causes of the first voluntary consumption of the addictive substance. Trying to undo the past and to solve present difficulties such as unemployment has no impact on an active substance abuser's addiction and lifestyle; the addiction and the consumption must be confronted head on, and immediately.

More surprising than our (understandable and excusable) mistaken view that a troubled person's historical legacy maintains their addiction and must be dealt with if the abusive behaviour is to cease is our blindness to the fact that today, history is increasingly irrelevant not only in the treatment of the addiction, but also as an explanation for the first experimentation with addictive substances. It should be obvious to us that trauma and despair do not explain addiction today, because many strong people who have taken responsibility for communities, and many young people who have not been traumatised by history, get sucked into foolish and destructive behaviours. When abusive behaviour is deeply entrenched in our communities it is not the material destitution, the social ills or the historical legacy that fuels the abuse epidemics. The epidemics perpetuate themselves.

And these epidemics cannot be cured with our current policies, which are based on voluntary rehabilitation and clinical care. An addict may be willing to deal with the addiction after many years of abuse, when the social, medical and economic problems become annoying. In fact, this is the usual pattern of people 'giving up grog' in our communities. After a health scare and a 'last warning' from a doctor, a middle-aged drinker will stop drinking. But by this time he or she is likely to have ruined his or her health irreparably, and in any case will already have caused a lot of damage in his or her community – by making life miserable for family and community members, and by recruiting more people to addiction.

This last point is important. It is mainly during the first part of his or her career that an addict spreads the abusive behaviour, not when he or she has become a social invalid. There is a whole literature by Aboriginal people describing how addicts have been helped after decades of alcohol abuse. It is of course good if people manage to stop abusive behaviour; but if our policies are restricted to offering help to addicts, we will get nowhere. We might marginally reduce the prevalence of substance abuse (that is, the number of active abusers), but not the incidence (the number of new cases in a given period of time). If we have no efficient methods of influencing the behaviour of the addicts who are spreading the abuse, and the people who are just about to be recruited, we will not curb the epidemics.

Put it this way: today, people begin abusing grog and drugs in our communities because other people do. And if 'underlying issues' make somebody start drinking or using drugs, the most important 'underlying issue' today is the chaos caused by the grog and drug epidemics. And if trying addictive substances is a symptom of bad or chaotic circumstances, an established addiction is not; changing the circumstances will not cure addiction, and hence it will not stop abusive behaviour.

This analysis is of course a simplification; our history and our exclusion from mainstream society have not become irrelevant factors. But these generalisations are more valid than the symptom theory. Unfortunately, symptom-theory thinking underpins much of what influential Australians say and do.

In Cape York Peninsula, we are developing plans to combat the substance-abuse epidemics. There are two fundamental points that must underpin our strategy. First, the strategy must be aimed at creating an environment in which there is no more unconditional support for irresponsible lifestyles. Second, the strategy must include enforced treatment. We need a cure for the current epidemic, and the absolute intolerance of illicit drugs, the absolute enforcement of social order and mandatory treatment must be central to our strategy.

A great mistake in our previous discussions has been the idea that we should try to 'normalise' drinking when we are confronted with an epidemic. Given the large number of problem drinkers in our community, who really believes that we can incrementally reduce the problem from, say, a problem affecting 80 per cent of the population down towards a 'normal' 10 per cent? Alcoholics cannot 'normalise' or 'control' their drinking; they must rehabilitate and abstain.

This is the most difficult issue. Many people express the view that abstinence is not going to work as a solution; instead, they argue, there must be controlled or moderate drinking. Anybody who thinks for a moment about the problem will acknowledge that the only long-term solution for alcoholics is abstinence. There can be no 'moderate' or 'controlled' drinking for people who have rehabilitated from severe alcohol addiction. And there are too many people in our society who are alcoholics, for whom abstinence is the only choice. How can this be dealt with if our strategy is to 'normalise' drinking? We can't normalise drinking amongst so many alcoholics.

The question is: how should we deal with people who are 'moderate' or 'controlled' drinkers, and with people whose drinking problem may be getting more and more out of control and may develop into alcoholism in time? We need to give further consideration, firstly, to the role of moderate drinkers in the perpetuation of the grog epidemic and, secondly, to the role they could play in a strategy to overcome the problem.

It may be that we need a strategy that is aimed at helping alcoholics to abstain. This need not necessarily involve long-term prohibition. We could think about a period of prohibition. The (as yet undeveloped) idea is that when a community makes a democratic decision to combat grog and drug problems, this needs to be marked by a dramatic commitment to change the current pattern of drinking and supply.

Alcoholic drinkers and moderate drinkers are part of the same social web. I constantly see moderate drinkers participating in the early 'happy' stages of a drinking session – 'I'll have a couple of beers with my cousins' – and then leaving the heavy drinkers to the misery and violence that come later on, in the aggressive, paranoid, depressive stages.

When it comes to illicit drugs, there can be no policy other than complete intolerance, and there must be a law-enforcement capacity to put this policy into effect. This is only a matter of determination and unity. We can make it impossible for the consumers of these drugs to continue if we have the emotional courage to confront our own family members. And it goes without saying that, if we are serious about attacking these problems, it is unthinkable to have anything to do with white people who use illicit drugs, who tolerate such behaviour in their families or who associate with such people. Such people must be removed from our organisations and our communities must make it clear that white people involved with drugs will have to remove themselves from our land.

It is now over ten years since the Royal Commission into Aboriginal Deaths in Custody made its recommendations, yet media reports recently alleged that Aboriginal representation in custody has increased since then, not decreased. Ten years after comprehensive recommendations were made about the over-representation of Aboriginal people in the Australian criminal justice system, that over-representation remains at the same levels and has, according to some reports, increased. Is this fact not completely bizarre? How do we explain this madness? How can a country and a people invest so much deliberation in producing recommendations and policies, and how can governments spend so much money, and achieve no improvement?

It might be said that not enough time has lapsed for the recommendations to work – but it has been ten years. It might be said that governments did not spend enough money – but we know that considerable funds were allocated and expended. It might be said that governments failed to implement the commission's recommendations, and this may well be partly right. Even if it is not completely right, this explanation allows us to continue to accept the madness of increased Indigenous over-representation in custody.

But the strangest thing is that we would rather accept this continued over-representation than confront the possibility that perhaps the very recommendations that have informed the past ten years of stasis may have been wrong – and that maybe we should revisit them before we begin our next ten years of policy. The Royal Commission's most prominent conclusion was that over-representation was the direct consequence of the underlying social, economic and cultural disadvantage suffered by Aboriginal people, and that these underlying issues needed to be overcome because they lead to breaches of the law. I have no objection to this as a broad proposition, but there are factors and then there are factors. My own view is that the most significant causal chain is this: (i) substance abuse and the chaos it causes lead to (ii) violence and other crimes, which lead to (iii) over-representation in custody and in the criminal justice system. This is as plain as day to anyone who knows life in our communities and the monthly court lists – and yet the primary role of alcohol is just one of the many so-called 'underlying issues' that are said to give rise to over-representation. The truth is that alcohol directly causes, exacerbates or prevents the resolution of the other underlying issues. The Royal Commission's failure to confront this truth helps to explain why its recommendations have failed and will continue to fail us.

In conclusion, it behoves all of us who benefited from the campaigns against exclusion and discrimination – campaigns in which the man whose memory we honour here tonight fought on the front lines – to consider whether we can face up to the fact that that our citizenship gave us the right to passive welfare and the right to drink. We were given the dubious human rights to misery, mass incarceration and early death. We must match the achievements in land rights and human rights with a resolve to get on top of our social problems by confronting substance abuse head on and by moving beyond passive welfare with utmost urgency.

2001

THE LIGHT ON THE HILL

Ben Chifley Memorial Lecture

The historical experience of my people in Cape York is different from that of mainstream Australians. I will therefore talk about two histories: the history of your mob and of my own.

Before I do so, let me first say that my historical and social discussion has been assisted by some of the analyses of the early international labour movement. I am therefore thinking about class. I refer to 'class' in Australia because its existence cannot be denied – it is a historical and contemporary fact, even if the term has lost currency, indeed *respectability,* in public discussion today. Indeed, the Australian Labor Party talks no more about class, let alone class struggle. The C-word has departed from the rhetoric of the official Left. This is understandable, but regrettable.

It is understandable because the political philosophy of the Left in Australia has changed and the notion of the struggle between classes is seen as antiquated, divisive and ultimately fruitless given the apparent inevitability of stratification in a free-market society. This notion is after all associated with a political and economic system that is now discredited with the collapse of communism.

However, it is harder to understand the abandonment of class in our intellectual analysis of our society and history. How can we pretend that class does not exist? If the policy prescription – large-scale expropriation of private enterprises – that followed the class analysis of the early international labour movement was wrong, it does not mean that all aspects of the analysis are therefore invalid. Indeed, whenever there is public discussion of the widening social and economic divide in our country we are faced with the fact that there are class cleavages in our society. And yet our policy debate is largely conducted as if class does not exist.

Classes are treated as political constituencies and labelled with evocative and provocative terms such as 'the battlers' and 'the mainstream' and 'the forgotten people' and 'the elites'. The theory of the dynamics and operation of class society, as explained in the analysis of the early international labour movement, has been largely discarded. It does not inform policy.

But I find that I cannot so easily avoid such analysis in seeking to understand the predicament of that lowest underclass of Australians: my mob. For it explains our predicament in a way that the prevailing confusions do not.

Recently, I read the comments of a prominent young Indigenous sportsman who has been speaking out, in his own way, about his views on the oppression of Indigenous people in this country. In a blunt statement this young man said:

> Today's government and society are trying to keep us down, keep us in our little place, and take away our self-esteem, take away our pride … They want to kill us all and they're still trying to kill us all.

Most Indigenous Australians would understand this feeling, even if they would not articulate their sense of oppression in the same way. Most Indigenous Australians know the sense that every time we try to climb we face daggers of impediment, prejudice, difficulty and strife.

My own thinking is that this viewpoint can be explained by understanding the structures of class which operate to keep our people down. There are *structural* reasons why we occupy the lowest and most dismal place in the underclass of Australian society. There are structural reasons why all of our efforts to rise up and to improve our situation are constantly impeded. The concept of race has been co-opted by the mechanisms of class to devastating effect against the interests of black Australians. It means that even among the lower classes the blacks have few friends, because the whites focus their Hansonesque blame and resentment upon the blacks, who are either to be condemned for their hopelessness or envied for what little hope they might have.

From my acknowledgment of the reality of class society you should not infer that I am a proponent of socialist or indeed *any* economic policies. I do not propose, indeed I do not have, any economic policy for the country. My preoccupation is to understand the situation of my people, which necessitates an understanding of class.

But first I want to analyse the present situation of the lower classes of Australia generally, and the historical origins of the present situation.

The two major influences on the lives of your mob have been industrialisation and the emergence of the welfare state. During the stage of the industrialised market economy when the welfare state was developing, the lower classes consisted mainly of a huge, homogeneous industrial army and their dependants. Since they lived and worked under similar conditions and were in close contact with each other, they had both the incentive and the opportunity to organise themselves into trade unions and struggle for common goals. They possessed a bargaining position through collective industrial action.

Many of your great-grandparents and their parents were members of this industrial army, and they got organised to insist on a fair deal for working people and their families.

At the same time, it was in the objective interest of the industrialists to ensure that the working class didn't turn to radical ideologies, and that the workers weren't worn down by the increasing speed and efficiency of industrial production. Health care, primary education, pensions, minimum wages, collective bargaining and unemployment benefits created a socially stable and secure working class, competent to perform increasingly complex industrial work, and able to raise a new generation of workers.

These two factors – the organisation of the workers and the objective interest of the industrialists – produced an era of class co-operation: the welfare state. The support and security systems of the welfare state included the overwhelming majority of the citizens. The welfare ideology predominated in Australia during the long period of bipartisan consensus founded on what Paul Kelly, in his book *The End of Certainty*, called 'the Australian Settlement', established by Prime Minister Alfred Deakin just after Federation and lasting up to the time of the Hawke and Keating governments in the 1980s.

At this point, let me stress two points about the welfare state that developed in Australia from 1900. Firstly, the key institutional foundations of this welfare state were laid down by the *Liberal* leader Alfred Deakin. As well as a commitment to a strong role for government (what Kelly calls state paternalism) it included a fundamental commitment to wage conciliation and arbitration, which became law in 1904. Throughout most of the twentieth century the commitment to a regulated labour market enjoyed bipartisan support in this country. Whatever complaints the non-Labor parties harboured about organised labour, there prevailed a consensus about the necessity and desirability of a system of labour regulation, right up to the government of Prime Minister Malcolm Fraser. It is important to remember this bipartisan consensus about the general shape of the welfare state that was established in the early 1900s.

Secondly, it is also important to remember that the welfare state was the product of class compromise. In other words it arose out of the struggle by organised labour – it was built on the backs of working people who had united through sustained industrial organisation and action in the 1890s. It was not the product of the efforts of people in the universities, in the bureaucracies or even in parliament. Whilst academics, bureaucrats and parliamentarians soon came to benefit greatly from the development of the welfare state – and they became its official theorists and trustees – it is important to keep in mind that the civilising achievement of the welfare state was the product of the compromise between organised labour and industrial capital.

When the Arbitration Bill was introduced into parliament, Deakin spoke of this compromise as 'the People's Peace'. He said:

This bill marks, in my opinion, the beginning of a new phase of civilisation. It begins the establishment of the People's Peace ... which will comprehend necessarily as great a transformation in the features of industrial society as the creation of the King's Peace brought about in civil society ... imperfect as our legal system may be, it is a distinct gain to transfer to the realm of reason and argument those industrial convulsions which have hitherto involved, not only loss of life, liberty, comfort and opportunities of wellbeing.

The social democrats have given three reasons for defending the welfare state. Firstly to counteract social stratification, and especially to set a lower limit to how deep people are allowed to sink. People with average resources and knowledge will not spend enough on education or on their long-term security (for example, on health care and retirement), and they and their children will be caught in a downward spiral, unless they are taxed and these services provided by the state. This is the main mechanism of enforced egalitarianism; it is not achieved by confiscating the resources of the rich and distributing them among the poor, because the rich are simply not rich enough to finance the welfare state, even if all their wealth were expropriated.

Secondly, the welfare state redistributes income over each individual's lifetime. There is some redistribution from rich to poor, but the principle is that you receive approximately what you contribute. Those who work now help to pay for older people's entitlements, and will be similarly assisted by the next generation. In the process, there is some redistribution from rich to poor.

Thirdly, there is popular support for the welfare state because a majority do not want health care and education (the two main areas of the public sector of the economy) to be reduced to commodities on the market. You can then allow competition in other areas of the economy, but health and education are about making everybody an able player in the market. Classical welfare is therefore *reciprocal,* with a larger or smaller element of wealth redistribution.

But now the circumstances that gave rise to the welfare state have changed. The modern economy of the developed countries, including our own, is no longer based to the same extent on industrial production by a homogeneous army of workers. The bulk of the gross domestic product is now generated by a middle class whose stocks in trade are symbols and information, and by some highly qualified workers. These qualified people have a bargaining position in the labour market because of their individual competence, whereas traditional workers are interchangeable and depend on organisation and solidarity in their negotiations with employers. A large part of the former industrial army is descending into service jobs, menial work and unemployment. Many of their children become irrelevant to economic growth instead of becoming productive workers like their parents and grandparents.

New growth sectors of the economy of course absorb many people who can't make a living in the older sectors. Also, income stratification is now in many countries being permitted to increase. Employment is created at the cost of an increase in income stratification. But even if mass unemployment is avoided, the current economic revolution will have a profound effect on our society: it will bring about the end of collectivism.

The lower classes in developed countries have lost much of their political influence because of the shrinking and disorganisation of the only powerful group among them, the working class proper. The shift in the economy away from manufacturing, and economic globalisation, which makes it possible to shift production to the enormous unregulated labour markets outside the classical welfare states, have deprived industrial workers in the developed countries of their powerful position. They are no longer the sole suppliers of labour. The lower classes are therefore now unable to defend the welfare state. Nor is there any longer any political or economic reason for the influential strata of society to support the preservation of the welfare state.

Those who have important functions in the new economy will be employed on individual contracts, and will be able to find individual solutions for their education, health care, retirement and so on, while the majority of the lower classes will face uncertainty. And the welfare state will increasingly be presented as an impediment to economic growth.

In Australia, the effects of this revolution have been alleviated by compromises between the traditional Australian social system and the economic internationalisation of the Hawke–Keating years. These successive Labor prime ministers presided over this transition in the Australian economy, and they sought to introduce reform without destroying the commitment to the welfare state. Labor eventually lost the 1996 election, but the electorate's earlier endorsement of this compromise to a large extent forced the Coalition parties to be more cautious about dismantling the welfare state, notwithstanding their preferences.

But the story does not end here. The welfare state will continue to face pressure to retreat. As I have said, it will increasingly be presented as an impediment to economic growth. You do not need me to tell you this.

When I consider the history of your people, I am struck by the ironies. Few Australians today appreciate their history. They do not realise that the certainties they yearn for were guaranteed throughout the twentieth century by the welfare state, to which the great majority of Australians were committed. They do not realise that this civilising achievement was founded on the efforts of organised labour. Few people appreciate the critical role that the organised labour movement played in spreading opportunity and underwriting the relatively egalitarian society which so many Australians yearn for today. Instead, organised labour has been diminished in popular esteem. It has come to be demonised, and whilst working people have a proud story to tell – a story of nation-building no less – this is not understood by Australians today.

The second irony concerns the sacrifices that working people and the organised labour movement made during the painful transition period our country experienced from 1983 – and the complete lack of acknowledgment of this in the historical understanding of the Australian community. Wage restraint underpinned the reform processes pursued under prime ministers Hawke and Keating. If these reforms were essential and have underpinned the current economic performance of our country, what credit did the working people get for the responsibilities they shouldered for the sake of the national economic interest? The irony is that rather than taking the credit for the outcomes of the economic reform process (when incomes declined and profit shares surged), the organised labour movement came to be seen as retarding economic performance, and the call for labour market 'flexibility' never abated. Indeed, the pressure mounted and continues today. Organised labour was left between a rock and hard place: responsible for economic reform, but unable to claim the credit. Many workers must have wondered whether the sacrifices had been worth making.

That is the origin and the present predicament of the Australian welfare state, upon which your people have relied for generations and whose future is of critical significance to the prospects of your children.

The predicament of my mob is that not only do we face the same uncertainty as all lower-class Australians, we haven't even benefited from the existence of the welfare state. The welfare state has meant security and opportunity for many of your mob. It has been enabling. The problem of my people in Cape York Peninsula is that we have only experienced the income support that is paid to the permanently unemployed and marginalised. I call this 'passive welfare' to distinguish it from welfare proper, which involves working taxpayers collectively financing systems aimed at their own and their families' security and development. The immersion of a whole region into dependence on passive welfare is different from the mainstream experience of welfare. What is the exception among whitefellas – almost complete dependence on cash handouts from the government – is the rule for us. Rather than the income-support safety net being a temporary solution (as it was for whitefellas moving between jobs when unemployment support was first devised) this safety net became *a permanent destination* for our people.

The irony of our newly won citizenship in 1967 was that after we became citizens with equal rights and the theoretical right to equal pay, we lost the meagre foothold that we had in the real economy and became almost comprehensively dependent upon passive welfare. So we gained citizenship in one sense but lost it in another sense at the same time. Thirty years later, three decades and two generations of life in the safety net have produced a social disaster.

We should not be surprised that this catastrophe was the consequence of our enrolment in the dependent bottom end of the Australian welfare state. If you put any group of people in a condition of overwhelming reliance on passive welfare, within three decades you will get the same results. Our social problems do not emanate from an innate incapacity on the part of our people. Our social problems are not *endemic*; they have not always been with us. We are not a hopeless or imbecilic people.

Resilience and strong values and relationships were not features only of our pre-colonial classical society (which we understandably hearken back to). Our ancestors actually managed to *retain* these values and relationships despite all of the hardships and assaults of our colonial history. It is a testament to the achievements of our grandparents that these values and relationships secured our survival. Our grandparents struggled heroically to keep us alive as a people, and to rebuild and defend our families in the teeth of sustained and vicious maltreatment by white Australian society.

So when I say that the Indigenous experience of the Australian welfare state has been disastrous, I do not mean that the Australian welfare state is a bad thing. It is just that my people have experienced a marginal aspect of that welfare state: income provisioning for people dispossessed from the real economy. Of course, the welfare state means much more than the passive welfare my people have experienced. As I have said, the Australian welfare state was in fact a great and civilising achievement, which produced many great benefits for the great majority of Australians. It is just that our people have largely not experienced the positive features of mainstream life in the Australian welfare state – public health, education, infrastructure and other benefits which have improved the quality of life of generations of Australians. Of course, some government money has been spent on Aboriginal health and education. But the people of my dysfunctional society have struggled to use these resources for our development. Our life expectancy is decreasing and the younger generation is illiterate. Our relegation to dependence on perpetual passive income has meant that our experience of the welfare state has been negative. Indeed, in the final analysis, it has been completely destructive and tragic.

I ask myself two questions about the Australian welfare state in general and the future of Aboriginal Australia in particular. First, why were the lower classes not prepared for the changes in the economy and for the accompanying political changes, in spite of the fact that the labour movement was a powerful influence for most of the century? The stratification of society is increasing, but the lower classes are becoming less organised and less able to use their numbers to influence the development of society. Second, why are we unable to do anything at all about the disintegration of our Aboriginal communities? Let us admit the fact that we have no analysis, no understanding at all. All we have is confusion dressed up as progressive thinking.

When I have been struggling with these questions, I have gone back to the early thinking about history and society of the nineteenth-century international labour movement. A main idea was that social being determines consciousness; that is, that economic relations in society determine our thinking and our culture, and that our thinking is much less conscious and free than we think it is.

If we allow ourselves to analyse our society in the way I think early social democrats would, I think we would come to the following conclusions. Society is stratified. There is a small group at the top that is influential. There is a middle stratum that possesses intellectual tools and performs qualified work. The third and lowest stratum lacks intellectual tools, and does manual, often repetitive work. The middle stratum consists of two groups with no sharp boundary between them. One group (the 'professionals') performs the qualified work in the production of goods and services. The other (the 'intellectuals') upholds the cultural, political and legal superstructure that has been erected over, and which mirrors, the base of our society, the market economy.

I believe that a main function of our culture today, from fine arts to footy, is to keep people from using their intellectual faculties to formulate effective criticism and analysis while still allowing them to do their work in the economy. In this talk I use the word 'culture' in a wide sense, including not only art and literature but also our social and political thinking. To intellectually format people, but still let them acquire the knowledge and faculties they needed in order to be productive, is a complicated process. Therefore, our culture is complex and difficult to analyse.

Our society and our culture are not a conspiracy. There are no cynics at the top of the pyramid using their power to maintain an unnecessarily unequal society. Stratification is perpetuated because everybody has an interest in not sinking down. People believe what it is in their interest to believe. Influential people believe that a stratified society will always be necessary for economic growth and development. Their subordinates, the intellectuals of the middle stratum who maintain our culture, take their cues from above and produce ideology that supports the conservation of the current state of things, but they are not conscious of the reasons for their actions.

So, the objective function of our culture is to stop people from breaking away from the hierarchy, but at the same time to allow them to develop specialised areas of competence and creativity so that they can participate productively in the economy. Our culture treats people differently depending on which stratum they are born into. Workers need only limited intellectual tools. After a basic education, the culture offered to the lower stratum has the objective function of deterring them from unauthorised intellectual activity. That is, it keeps them from using their language and their knowledge to analyse our society and their position within it.

It is therefore wrong to regard the lower stratum as hopeless yobbos who refuse to participate in a cultural life that would make their lives richer. On the contrary, they are right in rejecting most of our culture, but they throw out the baby – *the useful intellectual tools* – with the bathwater. Most people feel unnecessarily guilty about their lack of interest in culture. They shouldn't. Most of our art, literature, history writing, philosophy, social thinking and so on really *is* as irrelevant as most people think. Not by accident, not because those who made it are useless and isolated from real life, but because it is one of the objective functions of our culture to *deter* most people from acquiring intellectual tools. I think that much of our official culture exists in order to scare the majority of people away from acquiring the habits of critical reading and analytical thinking. Our schools often fail to interest children in reading and social and political analysis, or even convince them that such activities are futile, while students are given the option of taking subjects like Soccer Excellence or Rugby League Excellence or Film Studies, as though these were the qualifications necessary for their futures.

And if people can't be prevented from thinking independently by means of discouragement and strict programming, there is a last net that catches almost everybody who makes it that far. I believe that most of what passes for progressive and radical thinking in our cultural, academic and intellectual life are simply *diversions* to keep rebellious minds occupied and isolated from the social predicament of the lower classes.

The great mistake of the social democrats of all countries has been that they put all their efforts into economic redistribution and have failed to build a movement that could take on the laws of thought. They expected to solve society's problems with some major reforms and with settlements between industrialists and representatives of the working classes. Now that the economy is changing, and the welfare state is being dismantled, the majority of the population are unable to take part in an analytical debate about their own future.

Of course, many people will think it is outrageous when I dismiss much of our contemporary cultural and academic life as just a big confusion-producing mechanism in the service of social stratification. They will reject the idea that culture keeps dissenters occupied and makes it difficult for people to analyse our society. But I have been driven to this desperate conclusion by the fact that our current thinking can't provide any solutions to our problems. And for Aboriginal people, the prevalent analyses are more than confusing; they are destructive.

Aboriginal policy is weighed down by confusion. Many of the conventional ideas and policies in Aboriginal affairs – ideas and policies which are considered to be 'progressive' – in fact are destructive. In thinking about the range of problems we face and in talking with my people, the conviction grows in me that this so-called progressive thinking is compounding our predicament. In fact, when you really analyse the nostrums of progressive policy, you find that they have never helped us to resolve our problems; indeed, they have only made our situation worse.

Take for example the problem of Indigenous imprisonment. Like a broken record, over the past couple of decades we have been told that 2 per cent of the population comprise more than 30 per cent of the prison population. The situation in juvenile institutions across the country is worse. Of course these are incredible statistics. The progressive response to this ridiculous situation has been to provide legal aid to Indigenous people charged with criminal offences. The hope is that providing access to proper legal defence will perhaps reduce unnecessary imprisonment. To this day, however, Aboriginal victims of crime – particularly women – have no support. So while the needs of offenders are addressed, victims and their families remain vulnerable. Furthermore, it is apparent that this progressive response has not worked to reduce our rate of imprisonment. In fact, Aboriginal legal aid is part of the criminal justice *industry*. It is like a sausage machine, and Aboriginal people are processed through it with no real belief that the outrageous statistics will ever be overcome.

The truth is that, at least in the communities that I know in Cape York Peninsula, the real need is for the restoration of social order and the enforcement of law. That is what is needed. You ask the grandmothers and the wives. What happens in communities when offenders are defended as victims? Is it any wonder that a sense soon develops that people should not take responsibility for their actions. Why is all of our progressive thinking ignoring these basic social requirements when it comes to black people? Is it any wonder the statistics have never improved? Would the number of people in prison *decrease* if we restored social order in our communities in Cape York Peninsula? What societies prosper in the absence of social order?

Take another example of progressive thinking compounding misery. The predominant analysis of the huge problem of Indigenous alcoholism is the symptom theory. The symptom theory holds that substance abuse is only a symptom of underlying social and psychological problems. But addiction is a condition in its own right, not merely a symptom. It must therefore be addressed as a problem in itself. Of course, miserable circumstances make people in a community *susceptible* to beginning to use addictive substances. But once an epidemic of substance abuse is established, it becomes independent of the original causes and becomes in itself the main cause of further addiction and abuse. The symptom theory absolves people from their personal responsibility to confront and deal with addiction. Worse, it leaves communities to think that nothing can be done to confront substance abuse because its purported causes – dispossession, racism, trauma and poverty – cannot be resolved in the present.

But again, the solution to substance abuse lies in the restriction of addictive substances and the treatment of addiction as a problem in itself. When I talk to people from Cape York Peninsula about what is to be done about our ridiculous levels of grog consumption (and the violence, stress, poor diet, heart disease, diabetes and mental disturbance that result), no-one actually believes that the progressive prescriptions about 'harm reduction' and 'normalising drinking' will ever work.

A rule of thumb in relation to most of the programs and policies that pose as progressive thinking in Indigenous affairs is that if we did the opposite, we would have a chance of making progress. This is because the subservience of our intellectual culture to the cause of class prejudice and stratification is so profound and universal. What we believe is progress is in fact standing still or even moving backwards.

Much of my thinking will seem to many to indicate that I have merely become conservative. But I propose the *reform* of welfare, not its abolition. Like all of you here tonight I am also concerned for the long-term preservation of our commitment to welfare as a nation. If we do not confront the need for the reform of welfare and seize control of its redefinition, then we will lose it in the longer term.

Australia is at a critical time in the history of the welfare state. Its reform is imperative. It is worth remembering that Paul Keating actually initiated a new approach to welfare with Working Nation. This country now needs to develop *a new consensus* around our commitment to welfare. This consensus needs to be built on the principles of personal and family empowerment and the investment of resources to achieve lasting change. In other words, the reform of welfare must be based on the principle that dependency and passivity are a scourge and must be avoided at all costs. Dependency and passivity kill people and are the surest road to social decline. Australians do not have an inalienable right to dependency; they have an inalienable right to a fair place in the real economy.

There is an alternative definition of welfare reform that will take hold if we do not take the approach I have just outlined. This alternative definition sees welfare reform as a matter of *moral judgment* on the part of those who have security of employment and who 'pay taxes' in relation to people whose dependency is seen as a moral failing. This alternative definition is laced with the idea that welfare reform should be about the punishment of bludgers. According to this view, we are seeking to reform welfare because we are concerned about the sentiments of those who work and who pay taxes; welfare recipients have a moral obligation to these people. This alternative approach to welfare reform may merely be a means to reduce government commitments and decrease taxation of those who already have a place in the economy.

I have departed somewhat from the traditions of this annual lecture in that I have not explained my vision of the Light on the Hill. But in order to have a vision, one needs to have an analysis of one's present situation. I contend that people who consider themselves progressive today are, in objective fact, regressive in their thinking. This is especially and painfully obvious if you know the situation in the Aboriginal communities of this country. Petrol sniffing is in some places now so entrenched that crying infants are silenced with petrol-drenched rags on their faces. In one of our communities in Cape York, in a population of less than 1000 there were three murders in one month a few months ago. And we don't know what to do.

And to be honest, *in its cups*, Ben Chifley's party does not know what to do either now that the economy has changed, its traditional political base is decreasing and class divisions are widening. Too many Australians continue to have uncertain prospects. How can we be so bereft of solutions? These negligent thinkers in the academies and the bureaucracies – the very people who have benefited most from the welfare state – have had a century to anticipate our current predicament. How can we not at least have a clearer understanding of it? Those of us who wish for social progress must realise that there are important insights in the materialist interpretation of our history and our culture. The labour movement, unfortunately, left these insights behind in favour of the confusions that have preoccupied and diverted those academics, bureaucrats and parliamentarians who became the intellectual trustees of the welfare state. These trustees had a responsibility to the interests of working people and their families – a responsibility which they grievously failed to fulfil.

2000

ADDICTION EPIDEMICS

Australian Medical Association Oration

This evening I will extend the discussion of substance abuse I first out-lined in my inaugural Dr Charles Perkins Memorial Oration in 2001. In that lecture I set out an analysis of substance abuse in Aboriginal communities based on the late Swedish professor Nils Bejerot's com-pelling analysis of substance abuse as a psycho-socially contagious epi-demic: that is, substance-abuse problems are a social equivalent to biological epidemics and grow through the recruitment of novices by established users.

Our strategy in Cape York Peninsula will be criticised. Advocates of 'harm reduction' will count us among those who oppose substance abuse solely on moral or ideological grounds without examining its causes. Our opponents will assert that their approach is 'evidence-based' and that substance abuse is a 'health issue'. To overcome this initial resistance, we will need to analyse the claim that substance abuse is a 'health issue', and to explain what we mean when we say that substance abuse is a political question.

Health problems have biological as well as social determinants. Some health problems, such as Alzheimer's disease, are more strongly determined by biological factors than by social, behavioural or politi-cal factors. Only great advances in medical science can help us to reduce such problems significantly.

Other health problems are closely connected to the social and eco-nomic organisation of our society. Social and economic changes have both negative and positive effects on mental and physical health. Many health problems that have a biological cause – some infectious diseases, for example – have been greatly reduced mainly through improvements in living conditions and public services.

Substance abuse does not fit neatly into either category. Substance-abuse problems are closely connected to social conditions. Substance abuse may be insignificant in a poor society, or it may be pervasive; likewise in a developed economy. Differences in the nature and scale of substance-abuse problems between countries and communities are greater than can be explained by biological and economic factors.

There is a strong biological component to addiction once an addiction is established. But a person's exposure to addictive substances and their decision to try an addictive substance in the first place are socially determined. How we deal with these problems is predominantly a social and political question. Public opinion alone can achieve quite a lot; we need not wait for the economic and scientific progress that is necessary to deal with our biological limitations, or for solutions to systemic social and economic problems. The demise of smoking illustrates this principle: within a few decades, social attitudes have changed from near-universal acceptance of smoking to rejection.

It is very unfortunate that the phrase 'health issue' is so prominent in public discussion of addiction and substance abuse. The phrase obscures the importance of political and social factors, and of the choices of individuals, in the development of substance-abuse problems (or in other addictions, such as gambling).

If one conceded that substance abuse should be seen as a health issue, harm minimisation and harm reduction might be logical responses. If something cannot be avoided, its harm must be minimised. Unfortunately, the ideology of 'harm minimisation' (which includes 'supply reduction', 'demand reduction' and 'harm reduction') is the official strategy of Australian governments. Demand reduction and supply reduction (such as stopping heroin from coming into Australia) are uncontroversial, but 'harm reduction' is founded on the following assumptions. First, that we have to accept that we will never eradicate the problem of abuse of legally available and illicit substances. And second that, having accepted the entrenchment and inevitability of substance abuse in society, it is more realistic to deal with the consequences and circumstances of substance abuse than to attempt to prevent it.

The most persuasive argument in favour of harm reduction is that many of the negative consequences of illicit drug use for society and for the users are at least partly due to the fact that the substances are illicit. Advocates of harm reduction also argue that there is no logical justification for our different responses to legal and illicit drugs. The consequences of the abuse of alcohol are very severe, but the use of alcohol is not prohibited. We have an arbitrary situation today in which it is legal to sell alcohol to dysfunctional addicts, but illegal to sell most other drugs.

Harm-reduction policies erode the restrictive social consensus required to curb substance-abuse epidemics. Occasionally, however, we must choose whether to prioritise a campaign against substance abuse or a struggle against biological epidemics. The fight against HIV infection, for instance, may require us to consider taking a harm-minimisation approach to intravenous drug use . Even if we have a basically restrictive substance-abuse policy, urgent health problems may occasionally have to take precedence over our desire to avoid the negative consequences of condoning substance abuse. Adopting some harm-reduction policies is not an acknowledgement that harm reduction is generally correct, and does not amount to any concession to the libertarian push for harm reduction.

The phrase 'evidence-based' is another catch-cry of libertarian opinion in Australia. Politicians naturally search for solutions that 'work', but they need to be aware that 'evidence-based' approaches are not as neutral and objective as the phrase implies. Evidence-based harm reduction implies a particular view of society and a particular political philosophy. It sees the increasing availability of psychoactive substances as unavoidable. Its proponents reject our view that collective social and political action can remove a substance-abuse problem from a community.

I believe that the term 'evidence-based' should be reserved for investigations into health issues in which ideological and cultural factors do not play a decisive role. For example, studies into the causes of a certain kind of cancer and the efficacy of treatments thereof must necessarily be evidence-based. Extending the term to describe medical and social inquiries focusing primarily on human behaviour is by no means illegitimate. However, there is a risk associated with the application of an evidence-based approach in policy areas where cultural and ideological determinants are arguably the most important.

Take, for example, the biggest problem of my home region of Cape York Peninsula: widespread alcohol abuse. What is to be done? A purely evidenced-based approach would, I believe, come dangerously close to a 'lab-rat' view of our communities. By experimenting with the circumstances of the lab rats, it is possible to determine what conditions will minimise the harm the rats do to themselves and to each other. Obviously it would be futile to try to agree with the lab rats as to how harm is going to be prevented, or to expect the lab rats to reach such an agreement amongst themselves.

The situation of a small Cape York Community steeped in grog puts into sharp relief the limitations of evidence-based policy. At the end of the day, only a collective decision to change the culture and the norms of the community can remove the grog abuse. The relatively small number of people involved makes it obvious that change can only happen if individual community members assume agency.

Rejecting harm reduction is not necessarily a conservative policy. In a leftist analysis, the societal effect of addiction is to compound disunity and political paralysis and to make people less able to organise themselves, politically and socially. And Aboriginal people, at the very bottom of a stratified society, can least afford this. The struggle against harm-reduction policies is therefore a political struggle; we are fighting to prevent the establishment of new substance-abuse epidemics, and to curb, by means of restrictions, the damage done by problems endemic to Australian society, such as alcohol and gambling.

Substance-abuse epidemics can be dealt with if a broad coalition of democrats – conservatives, responsible economic liberals, principled social democrats, socialists and whoever is in favour of social order – unites around a consistent, restrictive policy.

I ask mainstream Australians to try to see things from a remote Aboriginal perspective. The urban discussion of 'harm minimisation' is irrelevant to our situation; the harm caused by pervasive addictions cannot be 'managed'. In Cape York Peninsula, alcohol, illicit drugs and gambling are not recreational activities, but miserable sources of disunity, passivity, crime, violence, pain and death. Nor is addiction confined to a marginalised minority: entire communities are affected, with the result that they can make little social or economic progress.

Finally I want to ask: 'What is social policy?' People usually think about the redistribution of wealth and the delivery of government services as the main pillars of social policy. The effects of passive welfare and service delivery have not been good in our region. Those effects have been compounded by the failure of governments (and Indigenous leaders) to realise that there must be a third pillar: social policy must also involve managing the factors that lead to epidemics of addiction and substance abuse.

With the benefit of hindsight, we can see that a lethal trap was set up when Indigenous people were exposed to the combination of passive welfare payments, idleness and access to legal and illicit addictive substances and to gambling. One marvels at the ignorance and lack of foresight that allowed Australian governments and Indigenous and non-indigenous Australians to settle on such a policy after the end of the era of protection and official discrimination. How could we not see that the consequence would be short lives, violence, sexual abuse, illiteracy and cultural dissolution?

And that was not the end. When the problems became undeniable, we together, Indigenous and non-indigenous Australians, started behaving like addicts: we claimed that it was all a symptom of something else. We laid the responsibility on earlier generations and on recent racist policies and, by adopting an analysis that identified a root cause that was wrong, we destroyed all prospects of people uniting to stop the disintegration. Moreover, racism and disadvantage, the root causes we had mistakenly identified, were so intractable that we perhaps had no real hope in our hearts.

We need new hope. Indeed, Aboriginal people in Cape York Peninsula and the Queensland government have shown during recent years that by paying attention to social expectations, governance, the supply of addictive substances, money (including welfare payments) and use of time, we can achieve what the flawed policies of the last century denied us.

2004

AFTER KEATING

Launch of Don Watson's Recollections of a Bleeding Heart

What did it avail working people if they received wage increases in an inflationary economy? If what they gained in the pay packet was doubly lost at the grocery store counter? This was one of Paul Keating's explanations for the fundamental redefinition of what was truly progressive policy in a changing economy. It was the explanation he gave me on the long flight in the government jet to North Queensland. It was the explanation he had given to the Australian people during the hard years of economic reform in the 1980s.

The arguments for economic reform in the interests of the future of Australians, including and especially those to whom Paul Keating felt an abiding obligation and fidelity, those from the wrong side of the tracks, are all laid out here in Don Watson's book. Like Don Watson, I recognise that economic policy is not the exclusive province of so-called 'rational' people, separate from those who are concerned with society and culture. In an engaged democracy, all citizens have a responsibility to concern themselves with the main questions of economic policy, because on them depend the common good. It is a responsibility with which Paul Keating intellectually grappled and which he shouldered more completely than anyone, for the lion's share of two decades. It is a responsibility that is distinct from theory, commentary and reportage – it is the responsibility that must result in policies that bring about real change in a real society and a real economy. It is responsibility at the anvils of political practice, where one does not have the luxury of being the voyeur or the dilettante, where the colours of leadership must be nailed unequivocally to the masts of office. How else would fundamental reform and change be achieved if there was no responsibility and no-one prepared to, or capable of, shouldering it? Especially at such a critical time in economic history?

The arguments in favour of the reforms of the Hawke–Keating years were from the start contrary to the mainstream Australian orthodoxies. And it would be Labor governments that delivered this reform in the teeth of the accumulated comforts and certainties of eight decades of the Deakinite Australian settlement and Ben Chifley's post-war welfare state.

I credit John Howard for his recent acknowledgement of the country's indebtedness to his predecessors for the strengths of the Australian economy in this new century. Might I venture my feeling – a feeling somewhat heightened after reading this book – that it was an act of rare grace in a too-often graceless country.

Before I chloroform you with what are now largely truisms about the story of economic reform in the Hawke–Keating years, let me say that there is only one other person without whom the history made by Paul Keating would not have been possible. Bill Kelty took on the responsibility of leadership – intellectually, and in practice – and it is to me one of the wonders of our woeful lack of comprehension of our history that the role played by Kelty and the organised labour movement in the economic reform story from 1983 goes without acknowledgement. I said this in my Ben Chifley Memorial Lecture two years ago:

When I consider the history of your people, I am struck by the ironies. Few Australians today appreciate their history … Wage restraint underpinned the reform processes pursued under prime ministers Hawke and Keating. If these reforms were essential and have underpinned the current economic performance of our country, what credit did the working people get for the responsibilities that they shouldered for the sake of the national economic interest? The irony is that rather than taking the credit for the outcomes of the economic reform (when incomes declined and profit shares surged) the organ-

ised labour movement came to be seen as retarding economic performance, and the call for labour market 'flexibility' never abated.
Indeed the pressure mounted and continues today. Organised labour
was left between a rock and a hard place: responsible for economic
reform, but unable to claim the credit.

More gracious nations would have recognised the service to the common good rendered by the former secretary of the ACTU. Instead the
true heroes of the economic revolution for a better Australian society
are virtually dustbinned by a complacent nation without memory: the
subject of disrespect, slander and opprobrium.

In economic policy, Paul Keating had fundamentally redefined
what it was to be truly progressive. Not just progressive in posture, but
progressive in substance. Not just progressive in perception and opinion, but progressive in the real sense of making life and the future
prospects of people better.

It would have been politically easier to be progressivist, as opposed
to progressive. Progressivist policy would have left unchallenged the
established nostrums – such as protection, which did not only comfort
battlers but the owners of businesses who had long relied upon it – and
concerned itself with the traditional questions of redistribution rather
than taking responsibility for ensuring that there is a healthy common
weal from which opportunity for all could flow.

Much of the reform challenge had been achieved in Australia long
before theorists and Tony Blair conceptualised 'The Third Way' as the
philosophical framework for social democratic parties embracing
market-oriented policies. Paul Keating had developed and executed
'triangulation' long before Dick Morris articulated it for President
Clinton's comeback strategy in the lead-up to 1996 after their 1994 con-
gressional election disaster.

My point here is to distinguish between progressive and progressivist thinking about the reforms that were needed in our national
economy. The transition to an open and internationalised economy
which the Hawke–Keating governments had superintended was not a
wholesale implementation of the neo-classical policies prescribed by
the think-tanks of the Right – rather there was melioration in favour of

workers' rights to bargain and to rely upon minimal conditions, and the maintenance of universal social provisioning and guarantees.

It is hard for me to see how the compromises between market and society shaped by Paul Keating do not lay down the acceptable parameters of an Australian settlement for this new century. How can there be further labour market deregulation than we now have? Did not the profit share for business rise with the assumption of wage responsibility by workers during the reform years? Do we not now have a low-inflation, growth economy of the kind Paul Keating said we would have? Why must working people continue to shoulder the burdens and responsibilities for our society's unemployment problem – alone?

I turn now to Paul Keating's legacy on Aboriginal policy. In relation to his acknowledgment of the truth of our colonial history, Keating was correct. The Redfern Park speech was and continues to be the seminal moment of expression of European Australian acknowledgment of grievous inhumanity to the Indigenes of this land. The prime minister had spoken on behalf of all Australians and to the extent that he used the rhetorical 'we' in that speech, he had of course not claimed the individual responsibility of Australians for the actions of the past, but rather a collective owning up to the truth of that past and to its legacies in the present. The prime minister had explicitly said that it was not a question of guilt, but one of open hearts. How could this acknowledgment have been better put?

As much as I could never understand the reactions and campaigns on the part of the Right in relation to Paul Keating's Redfern Park speech, I could never understand the subsequent incessant campaign on the part of the Left seeking an apology from John Howard. The truths of the past in relation to the stealing of children and the destruction of families were already the subject of prime ministerial acknowledgment. And that acknowledgment came without prompting and could not have been more sincerely expressed. The pointless campaign for an apology from John Howard, to the extent that it expresses the importance which people attach to reconciliation, is understandable, but to the extent that it is touted as one of the most important questions in Aboriginal policy, it underlines for me the distinction between being progressive and progressivist. Paul Keating's Redfern Park speech was progressive. Seeking an apology from John Howard is progressivist and is not the main game in terms of what is important in Aboriginal policy.

Paul Keating's stand on native title was not just progressive. It was at once liberal in its respect for the law and property rights and in its rejection of racial discrimination, and conservative in its fidelity to the legal traditions and institutions that gave us *Mabo*. The prescriptions of the political Right in this country towards the native title property rights of Indigenous Australians would have horrified Friedrich von Hayek. They proposed the very legislative discrimination and governmental appropriation of property that von Hayek stood firmly and clearly against.

Paul Keating recognised the High Court's decision in *Mabo* as the very 'once in a nation's lifetime' opportunity to make peace between the old and the new Australians. Native title proffered the basis for what he called 'peace' and could be the cornerstone for the settlement of fundamental colonial grievance.

Without Paul Keating's *Native Title Act*, this cornerstone that had been hewn by Eddie Mabo, Ron Castan and their colleagues would have been lost to the nation. The cornerstone would have been turned to dust if protective federal legislation had not been put into place by the Keating government. The *Age* editorial got it right when it said that the *Native Title Act* 'may yet be judged the most profound achievement of Paul Keating's political career'. If it had not been a career of so many achievements I would not hesitate to endorse the view of the *Age*. Let me make only two brief observations about the negotiation and passage of the *Native Title Act*.

Firstly, to Don Watson's description of Gareth Evans' performance in the Senate as a 'tour de force he was born to deliver one day', I say Amen. On his feet for forty-eight of the sixty hours it took for the debate to be had in the Senate, Evans turned in what must count as one of the greatest, if not *the* greatest, performance in Australian legislative history. The sheer complexity of the law, the policy and the politics which Evans commanded was staggering.

Secondly, no leader other than Keating – not then and not in the past – would have had the will, the courage and the fidelity to get the *Native Title Act* through parliament and to keep faith with its Indigenous beneficiaries. Even Evans, someone who had been a supporter of Aboriginal causes since his early days, was one of many people in the Cabinet who would have chosen to drop us. Evans rose to the occasion and made his outstanding contribution because of Paul Keating's leadership.

With the opportunity of *Mabo* having been seized by the federal Labor government it was time for a necessary redefinition of what it is to be socially progressive in Aboriginal affairs. I am convinced that Paul Keating would have understood the necessity of such a redefinition. After all, it was he who told me on the way to my hometown in 1995, when I first talked to him about the need for Aboriginal responsibility to confront our social problems, that 'the starting point must be leadership'. Alas, the 1996 election was lost by Paul Keating and so much more was lost.

The progressivist intellectual middle stratum has played a role in achieving recognition of Aboriginal people's property rights, but I contend that the prejudice, social theories and thinking habits of left-leaning, liberal-minded people make them unable to assist Aboriginal people to deal with the real factors behind our disadvantage. The only answer to the epidemics of substance abuse that devastate our communities is organised intolerance of abusive behaviour. The late Professor Nils Bejerot, whose thinking I tried to introduce in Australia last year, pointed out that historically, substance-abuse epidemics have been successfully cured without much in the way of research and voluntary rehabilitation. What can still save our communities is that a policy based on absolute intolerance of substance abuse and irresponsible behaviour is gaining credibility.

In our current perilous situation, the Left tends to support policies that can only waste more precious time: further research, rehabilitation, harm minimisation, improved service delivery and so on.

Robert Manne wrote last year that:

Pearson's contempt for the sentimentality of the pro-reconciliation liberal Left has grown rapidly in recent times. In my view the indulgence of this irritation is a political mistake. Pearson is in danger of forgetting ... that in their common struggle for the survival of the indigenous peoples against the indifference of the mainstream and the assimilationism of the Right, the support of the good-hearted, bridge-walking middle-class liberal Left remains an asset of inestimable worth.

Though I am a great admirer of Professor Manne – particularly his outstanding defence of the true history of the breaking up of Aboriginal families – I disagree with his political analysis. On the contrary, I would like to take my argument from last year one step further. I contended that the two most important factors maintaining and worsening Aboriginal disadvantage are the substance-abuse epidemics and passive welfare. But the correct analysis of our disadvantage has been delayed by the consensus of the progressive, liberal-minded intellectual middle class. A radical shift in the Left's thinking on Indigenous issues would be the single most beneficial change for Aboriginal people, because the people in the communities who want change cannot effect it if left alone; dysfunction and social disintegration have gone too far. They need support, but it is crucial that this support is based on a new understanding of the real situation.

In recent years there has been a great change in the discussion of Aboriginal affairs. Women have spoken out about what things are really like. Federal Labor has been unable to handle this situation. Labor is confined to passively scrutinising the government's policy. In recent weeks they have pointed to government bungling in Aboriginal education and the large amounts spent on litigation against Indigenous interests that the federal government included in their 'record spending' on 'practical reconciliation'. This is of course good, but I can't discern any tendency to an adequate response from Labor in the face of the current humanitarian crisis.

Because the present shift in the debate that reality imposes on us is in conflict with their prejudice and world outlook, federal Labor seems to have abandoned Aboriginal people and simply ceased trying to develop a credible policy. It is not the case that the government has a raft of innovative policies aimed at helping communities to move beyond passive welfare and to confront substance abuse directly – it does not.

The same energy and insight that Labor had in 1983 when it confronted a sclerotic Australian economy – and the same courage to reform its thinking – is needed in this new century if Labor is going to have any solutions to the social predicaments in our nation, not the least the predicaments of those whose social misery is the most egregious.

Federal Labor has a very hard job ahead of them changing this sorry state of affairs. I suggest they look at Paul Keating's break with old thinking and renewal of Labor economic policy for inspiration.

2002

LAND RIGHTS AND PROGRESSIVE WRONGS

Prime Minister Howard assumes that the common policy ground that exists between us in Cape York Peninsula and himself has come about because there has been a 'change of attitude' on the part of Indigenous leaders.

If he means that we have changed our policy and our thinking about our problems, he is wrong. I first articulated my own views about grog, history and dependency back in 1987, when I wrote a paper with my late friend and mentor Mervyn Gibson. In it we described how addiction had corrupted our culture and our social relationships. Reading again what I wrote as a 22-year-old, I am struck by how little my basic convictions have changed. So, with respect to those from the Right who think they have succeeded in a 'cultural war' over Indigenous policy – the truth is that many Indigenous leaders have always understood that rights and responsibilities must run together and that victimhood will get us nowhere. There is little that I have said about the poison of welfare dependency that had not already been said by the late Charles Perkins.

People in Cape York Peninsula have embarked upon what is seen as a radical departure from the thinking that has failed to avert the Indigenous social disaster. We have taken the discussion about Indigenous responsibility further and started implementing a comprehensive program.

I have not moved to the Right
In this article I outline why I have become convinced that Indigenous

people must move decisively beyond the legacy of the past decades – regardless of some real achievements, such as the recognition of native title.

Until the autumn of 1999, I was known as a native title activist. In general politics, I wouldn't have promoted ideas that departed from Left-liberal Labor-oriented progressive thinking. There is a widespread perception, based on brief or selective media reports, that I have moved to the Right since 1999. However, in my published texts I have defended the welfare state and the organisation of people in trade unions and other political and social movements. My good relationship with many political leaders of the Right must be due to their broad-mindedness, because they have read my texts and know where I stand.

In my daily work, my commitment to Indigenous and lower-class people is unchanged. What changed in the late 1990s was that, from my remote Aboriginal-community perspective, I started to doubt whether many of the official policies of the organisations and parties of the Left, and the left-leaning intellectual culture, serve Indigenous people.

I use the label 'Left' in a wide sense. It includes most of the academic, cultural and media spheres whose members have taken a rights-based and service-delivery-based view of the Indigenous predicament. I also include those with 'moderate' and 'liberally minded' attitudes in the Liberal Party. At the same time, many Labor people cannot be labelled 'Left' in this sense.

An unbridgeable gulf between radical rhetoric and reality

As the Indigenous crisis accelerated, it became apparent that leftist or progressive discourse was unable to deliver solutions or even identify policy areas of strategic importance. Of course, there has been much well-targeted criticism from the Left (for example, observations about the sheer neglect of health services). But even if all of the proposals of the Left had been acted upon, any possible gains would have been swallowed up by an explosion of Indigenous dysfunction, the causes of which the Left was unwilling to discuss.

During the 1990s, I thought that there must be academic expertise that could help do something for our people, do something about the accelerating social breakdown. I approached academics and anthropologists because I felt I didn't have enough theoretical under-standing of the questions about culture, alcohol and so on.

Mervyn Gibson and I wrote the paper in 1987 about broader social issues, about how alcohol had insinuated itself into our culture. The discussion was based on the observation that the Hope Vale mission of my childhood was poor but socially stable. But I put our ideas from 1987 to the side for many years while I worked on native title. During this time the social disintegration accelerated and the gulf between the reality in our communities and the thinking of my supporters and allies – the progressives and small 'l' liberals – became intolerably wide.

My original aim was to influence those to the left of the political divide, but I only roused resentment or bewilderment. (Labor politician Mark Latham was the exception and, indeed, I was inspired by his courageous challenge to the established Labor thinking about social policy.) During the 2001 election campaign, my office received a message from federal Labor saying that it would 'differentiate from Howard's policy by not using the words "welfare dependency" in Labor's election policy but have a very strong position on regional control and other things that … Noel would like'.

I wondered how these politicians were going to make any headway if they couldn't even bring themselves to call one of our two main problems – welfare dependency – by its name. And there was hardly any mention of Indigenous communities' other main problems – violence and substance abuse – in Labor's policy documents.

Of course, the conservative parties had no record of serious interest in my people's development. But they were pragmatically open to dialogue about our immediate problems, in spite of the disputes and differences between them and me.

The big problems were that progressive thinking consisted of a fixed set of ideas and attitudes and that Left-liberal and radical opinion was unable to change in response to evident policy failure among our people.

The Left was unwilling to discuss passive welfare even as we saw the deleterious effects of an entire people being predominantly reliant on handouts. The Left also defended the dogma that substance abuse is a 'health problem' caused by 'underlying issues' even as the majority of Indigenous people were severely affected by the self-perpetuating substance-abuse epidemics.

In relation to substance abuse, harm minimisation dominates leftist thinking in Australia, but this is not necessarily the only possible policy of the Left. In many places (including Australia) and in many historical periods there is and has been popular, progressive resistance to the use of addictive substances. However, it is easy to see why 'self-improvement' as a radical cause is difficult to advance. It is compromised because it was used as a diversion against the early labour movement; non-socialist 'workers' associations' were organised by the bourgeoisie and social misery was attributed to lack of self-discipline and drinking among the lower classes by hypocritical elites.

Back to the roots of leftist thought

When I was thinking about passive welfare and abusive behaviour, it seemed obvious to me that the Australian Left was defending societal and intellectual structures that kept my people down in the underclass. This contradicted the official goal of the Left, which is collective advancement of the lower social strata and the marginalised.

This contradiction led me to think about the classical leftist theory: materialism. Traditionally, the central idea of the Left has been that there is unjustifiable stratification in society and that our culture in a very broad sense (including our political thinking) should be seen in the light of material (economic) relations between people. Existing social structures, ideologies and thinking are traditionally suspected by the Left of supporting unnecessary inequality. According to this leftist thinking, the objective function of a societal institution or idea may be opposed to, or radically different from, its subjective justification. A church that preaches equality can contribute to oppression, for example.

Another feature of this perspective is that injustice is not upheld mainly by brute force or overt monopolisation of assets but by social and intellectual confusion among the lower strata.

From my Indigenous perspective, I applied the classical leftist thinking to the contemporary Left itself and concluded that the Left was perhaps more guilty of maintaining thinking that kept Indigenous people down than the Right. The Right has, of course, in an obvious way been opposed to recognition of our property rights and many other rights. But those elements of our political and social thinking that are the most important immediate impediments for Indigenous people are promoted by the Left. Remember that the official Left is no longer an oppositional force like the nineteenth-century workers' movement, but part of the ruling elite. This explains, if we apply the original leftist perspective, why the official contemporary Left can play a role in oppression.

The Right's opposition to Indigenous people's rights is intellectually easy to handle. But the factor that determines whether Indigenous people will be able to do anything at all is our ability to handle substance abuse, passive welfare, educational failure and the other problems that paralyse our communities. Strength in these policy areas is a prerequisite for the struggle for land and social and economic equality with non-indigenous people, but it is harder to formulate correct thinking about passive welfare and substance abuse than it is to argue for our rights to land and culture. In the social-policy areas, leftist opinion is our main opponent.

The freedom to be irresponsible further weakens the weak
I often return to the problem of addiction because it is the area where 'liberal' attitudes have the gravest consequences for my people. My first paper, the speech I wrote with Mervyn Gibson in 1987, was about alcohol and gambling. Now other abuses are growing threats to my people.

The introduction of new abuses hits the weakest people the hardest and has a paralysing effect on people who are not directly involved in abusive behaviour. That is what the Left calls oppression. If the introduction of new potential social problems is reactionary and oppressive, then some radical and liberally minded people must ask themselves some questions.

First, why has participation in new addictions been seen as a 'radical', socially acceptable thing in many circles? Many left-leaning people have, of course, been opposed to abusive behaviour, but it is a fact that the least charge that can be upheld against the Left is that it has consistently diverted the discussion away from individual responsibility towards theories about the underlying social reasons for people's behaviour.

Labor politician Carmen Lawrence has always been opposed to such madness, but her eyewitness account in her speech about the 1960s and the Whitlam years was accurate: 'A growing number of young radicals dedicated prodigious energy – and large quantities of mind-altering substances – to analysing and re-imaging our society … a new strand of libertarianism, impatient with censorship and anti-drug laws, flourished.'

I am not arguing that leftist and libertarian ideas are solely or even mainly responsible for my home region's descent into addiction-ridden dysfunction; the political Right have done little to prevent the alcohol and gambling industries' exploitation of my people. Unprincipled and inconsistent responses to addictive and destructive behaviours, including gambling, are not confined to the Left. In New South Wales, the Greens want to decriminalise the use of currently illicit drugs but are 'hard on pokies' (presumably because putting coins in a slot is not a popular pastime in the Greens constituency), while the NSW National Party is hard on drugs but soft on poker machines because the party is sensitive to the lobbying of clubs.

In any case, making a distinction between 'hard' and 'soft' drugs is not helpful – the 'recreation' of the liberally minded can become lethal for the disadvantaged. In my land, the mixture of alcohol and cannabis causes violent injury and death, and social and economic breakdown.

Second, why is the Left reluctant to support the grassroots rejection of these behaviours, instead preferring to talk about the 'underlying issues' that 'make' people adopt irresponsible behaviours? Every addict was once a non-addict who would have been more easily persuaded by a political argument about the importance of individual responsibility for the common good – solidarity, in leftist parlance.

It is easy for progressives to point to the United States and claim that the war on drugs as a government policy has failed. However, the struggle against addictive behaviours will not be successful if the policy is carried mainly by conservative opinion and by government; a broad popular coalition is needed. The problem with the Left is that it uses its influence to discourage people from establishing a grassroots consensus against behaviours that, in the long run, will be a burden on ordinary people and especially on the most disadvantaged. For example, the Left opposes workplace drug and alcohol testing by insisting that people must display signs of impairment from drugs before being tested. Such obfuscation – pretending that the struggle against substance abuse, which should be part of working-class solidarity, is a workplace-safety issue – is typical of the official Left.

Of course there is much genuine leftist, egalitarian and democratic thinking in the official Left, resulting in policies that I would probably support if I were politically active outside Indigenous affairs: defence of universally accessible health care, defence of public education along the lines advocated by Canadian author and philosopher John Ralston Saul, and so on.

However, the discussion about whether the 'social solidarity' heritage of the Left is economically viable is separate from my criticism of the socially destructive side of leftist ideology. I argue that leftist thinking also contributes to social tension and inequality, by advocating policies that give rise to the spread of irresponsible lifestyles and dysfunction. Policies that objectively worsen Indigenous economic and social marginalisation and the fragmentation of our society obviously contribute to Indigenous disadvantage and racial tension even if their proponents are card-carrying Lefties. Some leftist policies help to drive wedges between groups of unprivileged people who should be allies – divide the masses, the old labour movement would have said.

The Right has a damning record of marginalising and neglecting us Indigenous people and other groups. However, the current situation is that the Right is interested in exploring policies that perhaps can deal with Indigenous people's core social problems, while the Left is not.

2003

THE QUEST FOR A
RADICAL CENTRE

WHITE GUILT, VICTIMHOOD AND THE QUEST FOR A RADICAL CENTRE

The audacious idea of a Barack Obama presidency emerged when the first-term black senator from Illinois was invited by John Kerry to deliver the keynote address to the 2004 Democratic Convention. From gate-crasher without a pass at the previous convention in Los Angeles four years earlier, Obama's exceptional charisma, navigated by a (politically) precise moral compass, led to the fortuitous invitation from Team Kerry. Good for Obama, maybe not so good for Kerry. It must have been akin to asking a before-he-was-famous Bill Clinton to introduce the paler, less gifted candidate. Like sending Jesus before John the Baptist.

Obama's application for his 2008 candidature is set out in last year's bestseller *The Audacity of Hope*, where he does nothing less than boldly set out his 'thoughts on reclaiming the American dream'. It is an impressive statement of beliefs, characterised by its intelligent analysis, a candour that may not be completely calculated and a carefully calibrated self-deprecation. It is counter-weighed by an understandable, but nevertheless disturbing, absence of doubt about whether the contradictions of America can really be resolved: the over-promise of leadership. Obama attributes the audacity of hope to the salt-of-the-earth characters he parades throughout his book (he uses this device with almost toast-masterish sincerity), but there is no doubt – it is really the audacity of his own ambitions that he has in mind.

My concern with Barack Obama is to ask whether he represents 'the radical centre' of the great dialectical tension in black leadership philosophy in the United States, between the omnipresent legacies of black American leaders Booker T. Washington (1856–1915) and William Edward Burghardt Du Bois (1868–1963). Washington exhorted black Americans to work their way up from the bottom of society. He argued that moral self-improvement, vocational training and securing the trust and co-operation of white Americans and government, rather than confronting discriminatory laws, were the necessary first steps.

Washington fought discrimination behind the scenes, but Du Bois emerged as the public face of black protest. Du Bois argued that higher education and removal of discrimination should be more aggressively pursued, and he offered structural and social explanations for black crime, arguing that crime diminished as blacks' social status improved. The history of the Washington–Du Bois dialectic continues to be the prism through which policies for the alleviation of oppression (what we are given to calling in this country – perhaps euphemistically – 'disadvantage') might best be understood. If Jesse Jackson is Du Bois's heir, and Condoleezza Rice is heir to the Washingtonian tradition, then Obama may be the closest thing there is to a synthesis: the radical centre. Black Americans have been mostly subscribers to the Du Boisian tradition, the tradition in which Dr Martin Luther King Jr stood and Rosa Parks sat: it is the predominant model of black advocacy for uplift. Booker T. Washington's disciples, on the other hand, have been mostly silent, living ordered and industrious lives, valuing education and enterprise, bringing up strong families who desire to take their share of a country built largely on the enslavement of their ancestors.

When the doors of citizenship opened and Jim Crow was outlawed, these families quickly emerged as the nascent black middle class, using their sober sense of individual and family responsibility (and, yes, a keen sense of class) to lower their buckets into the deep opportunities of America. Today they are a minority, but not a small one, and their achievements are far from mean: five chief executives of Fortune 500 companies and two successive secretaries of state of the world's only superpower attest to this.

If Obama (who has said: 'I've never had the option of restricting my loyalties on the basis of race, or measuring my worth on the basis of tribe') does transcend the Du Bois–Washington paradigms, then his capacity to defy the enormous gravitational pull of the Du Bois ortho-doxy probably stems from his unique biography: the son of a white American mother ('to the end of her life [she] would proudly proclaim herself an unreconstructed liberal') and an absent Kenyan father (now both deceased), with an Indonesian sister from her mother's second marriage. Obama is an African-American, but not part of the long history that began with slavery. The stigma associated with the Washingtonian legacy – the allegedly Uncle Tomish belief that American opportunity will reward discipline and responsibility – does not shackle Obama.

My only reservation about the capacity of Obama to transcend the Washington–Du Bois paradigm is that, while his rhetoric sometimes embraces the Washingtonian responsibility thesis, he is by background, education, work experience (a civil-rights lawyer and 'community organiser') and temper a liberal whose starting point is the Du Boisian rights thesis. He moves from Du Bois to Washington, and not the other way around. Are his references to economic power and individual responsibility (and the limits of government) just rhetorical genuflections and not innate conviction?

Let me explain my reservation with reference to Opposition Leader Kevin Rudd's critique of what he describes as the neo-liberal fundamentalism of the Howard government: 'Modern Labor … argues that human beings are both "self-regarding" and "other-regarding". By contrast, modern Liberals … argue that human beings are almost exclusively self-regarding.' Rudd concedes that the self-regarding values of security, liberty and property are necessary for economic growth. He argues that the other-regarding values of equity, solidarity and sustainability must be added in order to make the market economy function effectively, and in order to protect human values such as family life from being crushed by unchecked market forces.

My reservation about this analysis is that it is mainly concerned with those who are not deeply disadvantaged in a cultural and inter-generational way. Kevin Rudd's father was a sharefarmer, and his untimely death brought hardship to his widow and children. But hard work and appreciation of education were passed on to Rudd from his parents. Rudd's ideological manifesto is concerned with the effects of neo-liberal policies on people who may have less bargaining power than the most sought-after professionals, but who are nonetheless firmly integrated into the real economy – not only because they have jobs, but because they are culturally and socially committed to a life of responsibility and work. I welcome the debate Kevin Rudd sought to revitalise about the long-term effects on most working people of neo-liberal policies: what will the effects be on family life, on people's sense of security and purpose, on social cohesion? How great is the risk that families of the lower strata of the real economy will descend into the underclass?

These are real issues, but the important question from an African-American or Aboriginal Australian perspective is: what is the correct analysis of self-regard and other-regard in the context for those already disengaged from the real economy? Disengagement is the problem in Cape York Peninsula and in dysfunctional African-American communities. The moderate Left, as represented by Kevin Rudd, would probably argue that neo-liberal dominance increases the number of disengaged people and the difficulties of returning them to the working mainstream. This may well be true. However, disadvantage can develop and become self-perpetuating, even without neo-liberal government policy. In Australia, Aboriginal disadvantage has become entrenched during decades when social democrats, small 'l' liberals and conservatives influenced policy; many policies for Indigenous Australians have been liberal and progressive.

The insight which informs our work in Cape York Peninsula is that disengagement and disadvantage have self-perpetuating and cultural qualities – problems not covered by Rudd's analysis. These are the problems of the underclass, people who are psychologically and culturally disadvantaged. (Rudd does not spend time thinking about the underclass. In the scramble for the political middle, who does?) His is an analysis of the prospects of the upper 80 or 90 or 95 per cent of society, and how they will fare under social democrat or neo-liberal regimes. If Rudd's analysis were extended to the truly disengaged, his model would probably be interpreted like this: some people are successful and, as well as being self-regarding, they should be other-regarding. And then there are the disadvantaged.

The problem is that it is assumed that the life chances of the disadvantaged depend on the other-regard of the successful – either a precarious dependency in the absence of state institutions, or an institutionalised dependency which my people have come to know as passive welfare. In reality, *what is needed is an increase of self-regard among the disadvantaged*, rather than strengthening their belief that the foundation for their uplift is the welfare state and the other-regard of the successful. This, I think, is a deeply Washingtonian view.

Washington versus Du Bois

Born a slave in Virginia in 1856, Booker T. Washington would ascend via an industrial education to be the first president of the famous Tuskegee Institute (now University) in Alabama. Washington became the most powerful black American in the post-bellum era, connected with philanthropists and industrialists: 5000 common schools would be established as a result of his advocacy. He was consulted by politicians and presidents on black matters, and had a decisive say over appointments to government positions. The 'Tuskegee Machine' was renowned for its powerful influence in black politics. Washington's star rose with his Atlanta Compromise speech at the Cotton States and International Exposition on 18 September 1895. His thesis was that blacks should secure their constitutional rights through their own moral and economic advancement in the booming economy of the South rather than through legal or political channels ('Our greatest danger is that in the great leap from slavery to freedom we may overlook the fact that the masses of us are to live by the productions of our hands'). His central metaphor was both literary and instantly folkloric:

> A ship lost at sea for many days suddenly sighted a friendly vessel. From the mast of the unfortunate vessel was seen a signal, 'Water, water; we die of thirst!' The answer from the friendly vessel at once came back, 'Cast down your bucket where you are.' … The captain of the distressed vessel, at last heeding the injunction, cast down his bucket, and it came up full of fresh, sparkling water from the mouth of the Amazon River. To those of my race who depend on bettering

their condition in a foreign land or who underestimate the importance of cultivating friendly relations with the Southern white man, who is their next-door neighbor, I would say: 'Cast down your bucket where you are' ... Cast it down in agriculture, mechanics, in commerce, in domestic service, and in the professions ...

Although Washington's approach angered some blacks, many approved, including W.E.B. Du Bois, the man who would later became the other important protagonist in the policy conflict. Washington's major achievement, however, was to win over diverse elements of the southern white population, without whose support the economic programs he envisioned and subsequently created would have been impossible. Washington's depreciation of political activism, and his acceptance of social segregation, was the key to the compromise with southern whites.

Du Bois was born free in 1868 in Massachusetts. Aided by family, friends and scholarships, he was able to attend university and ultimately received a doctorate from Harvard. The main feature of Du Bois's academic work, after the completion of his university studies and a short period of teaching, was that he closely studied disadvantaged black neighbourhoods. He was a founder of modern social sciences in the United States, and developed structural explanations for inequality. As he recalled in his autobiography, *A Soliloquy on Viewing My Life from the Last Decade of Its First Century*, he advocated 'ceaseless agitation and insistent demand for equality' and the 'use of force of every sort' to remove racism and discrimination. In 1905, Du Bois solicited help from others for 'organised determination and aggressive action on the part of men who believe in black freedom and growth', and the Niagara Movement was launched from the meeting that took place on the Canadian side of the famous falls. This was subsequently superseded by an organisation formed in association with white liberals, the National Association for the Advancement of Colored People (NAACP).

Du Bois's eloquent and often vitriolic calls for action during his period as editor-in-chief of the NAACP's *Crisis* magazine were politically influential, but he would be frustrated by the lack of progress in removing discrimination in America. He then embarked upon a pan-Africanist crusade against colonialism, believing that the freedom of blacks in America was contingent on the freedom of blacks in Africa. He would die a citizen of Ghana in 1963. Du Bois's biographer, David Levering Lewis, wrote in *The Fight for Equality and the American Century: 1919–1963* that Du Bois 'attempted virtually every possible solution to the problem of twentieth-century racism – scholarship, propaganda, integration, cultural and economic separatism, politics, international communism, expatriation, third world solidarity'.

The Washington–Du Bois conflict is well known. But it is critical to understand how *close* they were, despite their fundamental differences. Du Bois had congratulated Washington on his Atlanta Compromise speech, which set out the accommodationist framework. Early in Du Bois's career, they were engaged in a courtship that included the possibility of Du Bois joining Washington at Tuskegee. In the first cordial decade of their relationship they corresponded on legal strategies, planned conferences and sought ways to use each other to the advantage of each. The history of their relationship tells us that Du Bois understood and appreciated Washington's strategy and did not wholly disapprove. He knew the context and the limitations of black advancement as much as Washington. It is also now much better known that Washington devoted significant time, money and effort to surreptitiously fighting the race system behind the scenes through back-door lobbying, lawsuits and editorials, including financial assistance to Du Bois. Du Bois, meanwhile, was well aware of Washington's private opposition to the Jim Crow system but also of Washington's unwillingness to risk losing his influence through public agitation. Du Bois was a much more balanced and generous commentator and critic of Washington than many others who shared his view that discrimination had to be confronted.

But already in the 1890s Du Bois's relationship with Washington had begun to degenerate, and differences deepened in 1903 when Du Bois wrote *The Souls of Black Folk*, which contained a critical chapter entitled 'Of Booker T. Washington and Others'. When Washington died in November 1915, Du Bois's judgement was harsh: 'In stern justice, we must lay on the soul of this man a heavy responsibility for the consummation of Negro disfranchisement, the decline of the Negro college and public school, and the firmer establishment of color caste in this land.'

Whether or not Du Bois was right in this judgment, the salient question is not what Washington intended his (necessarily) one-sided advocacy to achieve, but what effect it had in practice. If it had the effect Du Bois contended, then this was not just the result of Washington's strategic folly, but also of the inability of the advocates of the other side of the dialectic to produce a strong rights antithesis to Washington's responsibility thesis.

Washington's public conciliatory position brought him, especially in the latter part of his career, into direct conflict with black militants who sought to challenge white America. As the clash between these two approaches intensified, Washington and Du Bois found themselves on opposite sides of a polarised debate, which pitted militancy against conciliation, separatism against assimilation, and a focus on higher education for the 'Talented Tenth' against Washington's preference for trade-school training to equip the other nine-tenths, who he understood must needs work by their hands. It was an irreconcilable dichotomy that would shape the race debate in America for the next century.

I can make no judgment as to this history; there is much evidence to support the modern black despisers of Washington and his faith that the white Americans who welcomed his Atlanta Compromise would open the doors to black participation. White America simply did not deliver on the bargain. There was little black progress until after the Second World War. I only wish to posit some of my own convictions about those aspects of Washington's philosophy that were right when he expressed them and, I believe, are still right today.

In his famous address, Washington spoke two compelling lines, the first of which was: 'It is at the bottom of life we must begin, and not at the top.' For a downtrodden people, Washington's notion of improvement was relevant to every black person ('No race can prosper till it learns that there is as much dignity in tilling a field as in writing a poem ...'). I don't think Washington disagreed that the black community would need its 'Talented Tenth' to succeed. I think what he disagreed with was the deprecation of more humble kinds of learning and achievement. He declared: 'Excellence is to do a common thing in an uncommon way.' The excellent pig-slop dispenser would one day send a child to Harvard. His second compelling line was: 'Nor should we permit our grievances to overshadow our opportunities.' This is a psychological point about how a people might deal with grievances of the past and the present, including the injuries sustained from racism. The best insurance is to become socially and economically strong by capitalising on opportunities.

Destroying the civil-rights promise

Shelby Steele, according to the shallow taxonomy of American political culture, is a black conservative. In his book *White Guilt*, Steele tells how disconcerting it was for someone with his background – the son of civil-rights campaigners, a young Afro-haired wannabe campus radical of the 1960s, fellow traveller with high hopes for Lyndon Johnson's Great Society – to be tagged with this label. That he came to question the post-civil-rights trajectory of black America, and to advance a compelling interpretation of the strange twist in the aftermath of the civil-rights victories – how retching defeat came from the bowels of victory – earned him the most dreaded black classification: Uncle Tom.

But even as Harry Belafonte denounced Colin Powell and Condoleezza Rice as 'White House niggers' in 2002, a critique was growing in black America that challenged the progressive consensus around race which has prevailed since the constitutional foundations of Dr Martin Luther King's dream were finally secured in 1964–65. Shelby Steele is one of the intellectuals leading this critique of the progressive orthodoxy. He raises troubling issues for those who see themselves as the heirs of the radical side of the dichotomy I described above.

Steele opens his book with reflections on the Monica Lewinsky scandal, and President Clinton's infamous denial: 'I did not have sexual relations with that woman.' Steele was surprised when he realised 'not only might [Clinton] survive his entire term but also that his survival … spoke volumes about the moral criterion for holding power in the United States'. If similar behaviour had been made public in the 1950s, it would almost certainly have resulted in the resignation or removal of a president. Steele then asked himself what would have happened if President Clinton had been accused of using the word 'nigger' – as President Eisenhower was rumoured to have done. Would the same relativism protect Clinton? *No way.* In America today, there is no moral relativism about race. No sophisticated public sentiment recasts racism as a 'personal choice' or a 'quirk of character'. Instead, America is unwavering in its stance on racism – Eisenhower's flippant use of the word 'nigger' would almost certainly have destroyed Clinton.

How is it, Steele asks, that the moral preoccupation of America shifted away from personal (sexual) virtue and came to focus on issues of social import? He answers this by drawing attention to the fact that institutions and governments earn and sustain their legitimacy through fidelity to democratic principles. These principles include freedom of the individual, equal rights under the law and equality of opportunity. Freedom, Steele asserts, is what follows from adherence to these principles. It is not a state-imposed vision of the social good, but the absence of an imposed vision, which allows individual choice.

Freedom is eroded or lost, he argues, when societies decide that some social good is so important that it justifies suspending the discipline of democratic principles. America's imposition of white supremacy is the pertinent example: 'White Americans presumed that white supremacy was a self-evident divine right, so freedom's discipline of principles did not apply where non-whites were concerned.' Over time, however, the moral authority of American democracy and its institutions was undermined by this failure. The turning point for America, and what Steele refers to as the 'disciplining' of the country's democratic principles, was the civil-rights movement. This movement established that race could not undermine individual rights. Multiracial democracies demand that race (along with gender, ethnicity, class and sexual orientation) cannot obstruct rights. This was, then, the 'concept of social good that would make democracy truly democratic, and thus legitimate'.

The crux of Steele's thesis comes from looking at the effects of the civil-rights movement on institutions and figures of authority in mainstream America. By the mid-1960s, he argues, following acknowledgment of racial hypocrisy, institutions across America suffered a moral-authority deficit. He recounts an occasion in his youth when he and a gang of black students burst into the office of his college president with a list of demands. Expecting to face resistance, even disciplinary action, Steele describes the experience as revelatory: he realised the college president 'knew that we had a point, [and] that our behaviour was in some way connected to centuries of indisputable injustice. The result was that our outrage at racism simply had far greater moral authority than his outrage over our breach of decorum.' This was one of Steele's first encounters with *white guilt* – the notion that past injustices perpetrated on a group of people absolve subsequent generations of that group of standard responsibilities.

For Steele, white guilt is a product of the vacuum of moral authority that comes from knowing that one's people are associated with racism. Whites – and, he asserts, American institutions – must acknowledge historical racism to atone for it. In acknowledging it, however, they lose moral authority over matters of social justice and become morally – and, one could argue, politically – vulnerable. To overcome this vulnerability, white Americans have embraced a social morality designed to rebuild moral authority by simultaneously acknowledging past racial injustices and separating themselves from those injustices. Steele calls this dissociation.

Where white guilt forces white Americans to acknowledge historical injustices, social morality may absolve them of it, restoring authority and democratic bona fides. With authority restored, power relations may continue as before. Critically, Steele argues, 'social morality is not a dissident point of view urged ... by reformers; it is the establishment morality in America. It defines propriety ... so that even those who harbour racist views must conform to a code of decency that defines those views as shameful.'

But Steele does not limit his analysis to white America. He expands his argument to assess the effects of white guilt on the freedoms – tangible or otherwise – of black Americans. In a critique of the 'black consciousness' which challenged traditional American authority, Steele draws a connection between increasingly militant messages of black power and burgeoning manifestations of white guilt. For a generation of black leaders, racism existed within this context – in a society suffering a lack of moral authority.

The new black leaders (adopting a neo-Marxian structural analysis) redefined racism as systemic and sociological. Racism was larger than individual acts, and defined social and political events and decisions. Because racism, as it was interpreted by militant black leaders, did not manifest on an individual level, the mere absence of an overtly racist act – using the word 'nigger', for example – was not enough to prove that racism was not in operation. Even a hint of racism proved the rule, and the only way to address it was with a systemic solution. So, Steele notes, despite the fact that current generations of black students across America have not suffered the oppression or subjugation of their forefathers, 'much less been beaten by white policemen', they enjoy affirmative action (the systemic redress) with a clear sense of entitlement. Black entitlement and white obligation have become interlocked.

Steele contends that racism became valuable to the people who had suffered it because it 'makes the moral authority of whites and the legitimacy of American institutions contingent on proving a negative: that they are not racist'. The power of white guilt is that it functions in the same way as racism – as a stigma. White Americans and American institutions are stigmatised as racist until they prove otherwise. What began as 'an almost petulant alienation from traditional authority', Steele asserts, has now evolved into a sophisticated manipulation to elicit an increasing sense of obligation. In a perversion of civil-rights-era aspirations, racism is no longer a barrier to individual black Americans, but one of the factors contributing to the assurance of their rights.

Pushing the argument one step further, Steele unpacks the effects of the interplay between black consciousness and white guilt. Black consciousness, he argues, led many black Americans to talk themselves out of the personal freedom won by civil-rights activism, for the sole (and unworthy) purpose of triggering white obligation. In a reactionary drift, race came to be seen as more important than individuality, the primary determinant of a person's ability to advance. One's identity became primarily that of the group (race) rather than that of an individual, one of whose characteristics was colour. In this way, identity played a destructive role in the advancement of black Americans.

Few who live in liberal democracies today would contest the idea that freedom is crucial to a decent life. A related – although perhaps more frequently debated – assertion is that only by being responsible for one's life can one assume agency for it. Agency, Steele believes, is what makes us fully human. With the rise and rise of black consciousness, however, the idea that black Americans must take personal responsibility to get ahead was subverted by the idea that responsibility was a tool of oppression and white America was responsible for black American advancement.

The first step in that argument – that responsibility was a tool of oppression in the age of racism – is not without historical justification. Steele's father, born in the American South in 1900, had 'plenty of responsibility' – the same responsibilities as whites – 'but not much possibility'. He could not join the union, and therefore had to raise a family on a lower wage. Steele calls this a 'crucible', 'an absurd bind that … denies one the opportunities to meet adequately the burden of responsibility one must carry'. 'Thus,' Steele continues, 'a heavy and often futile responsibility was the primary experience of racial oppression … this Sisyphean struggle with responsibility was the condition of oppression itself into which all the other indignities – discrimination intimidation, humiliation – were absorbed.'

When his peers raised their consciousness and embraced the neo-Marxian theories of institutionalised racism, Steele argues they began to think of responsibility as something that made blacks complicit in their own repression. Paradoxically, this historically justified insight started influencing black American ideology at the same time as discrimination and oppression were rapidly and formally being removed from the society.

The realisation that white America had a diminished moral authority to tell black Americans to be responsible led many – black and white – to conclude that white America was *obliged* to demonstrate its reformation by taking on the burden of responsibility for black Americans. White America – as in President Johnson's Great Society and the introduction of affirmative-action policies by the American college system – thus assumed considerable responsibility for improving the socio-economic status of blacks. Underpinning this was the unspoken assumption – rooted in America's history of racial injustice – that it was morally wrong (or unnecessary) for blacks to bear full responsibility for 'their own advancement'.

Having drawn out these ideas, Steele examines how they are connected: the new social morality, underpinned by white guilt, dictated that black Americans, as victims of racial oppression, could not be expected to carry the same responsibilities as others: 'American society no longer had the moral authority to enforce a single standard of responsibility ... [and] no-one – least of all the government – had the moral authority to tell me to be responsible for much of anything.'

The devastating effect of this redistribution of responsibility for black advancement to (white) institutions, however, is to perpetually project blacks as weak and incapable of achieving advancement on their own merit. Nevertheless, white Americans and American institutions promote policies of affirmative action to demonstrate their social morality, and at the same time legitimise their own moral and intellectual authority. No group in human history, Steele asserts, has been lifted into excellence or competitiveness by another. No group has even benefited from the assistance of others without taking responsibility for itself. And herein lies the nub of his thesis: that social justice is not a condition of, but an agent or mechanism for, an equitable world. In other words, it cannot be delivered in the same way as basic services. It cannot be absent one day and present the next. Social justice requires work and collaboration; if it is not accompanied by *individual* efforts to 'get ahead', it is unlikely to generate a better life.

In America, then, social morality has become more important than individual morality, effectively de-linking social justice and individual responsibility in the quest to improve the socio-economic conditions of black Americans. White guilt now underpins a sense of white obligation to lift blacks up, with disastrous effects. In a 1999 essay in *Harper's Magazine*, Steele nailed his argument:

> Right after the '60s civil-rights victories came what I believe to be the greatest miscalculation in black American history. Others had oppressed us, but this was to be the first 'fall' to come by our own hand. We allowed ourselves to see a greater power in America's

liability for our oppression than we saw in ourselves. Thus, we were faithless with ourselves just when we had given ourselves reason to have such faith. We couldn't have made a worse mistake. We have not been the same since.

The Australian paradox after 1967: black rights become white responsibilities

There are compelling parallels between what happened to black Americans after the time of civil-rights movement of 1964–65, and to black Australians from the time of the 1967 referendum, when 90.2 per cent of Australians voted to amend the Constitution to count Aboriginal people in the census and to empower the Commonwealth parliament to make laws in respect of Aboriginal and Torres Strait Islander people.

The American rights guarantees were substantive: they provided freedoms and protections denied to black Americans since the abolition of slavery. So, from the time of their passage, blacks in America could invoke federal law in order to combat discrimination in respect of a wide range of civil rights. The Australian changes did not immediately provide any substantive rights; the Commonwealth parliament was merely empowered to make laws – a power previously the exclusive province of the states. Protection from racial discrimination was not available to black Australians (or anyone else) until the Commonwealth parliament passed the *Racial Discrimination Act* in 1975.

Nonetheless, the symbolic significance of the 1967 referendum, which was the culmination of a concerted ten-year public campaign and redressed the complete exclusion of Australia's Indigenous peoples from the federal compact of 1901, marked the beginning of a new era in Indigenous history and policy. It was a hopeful and positive event, and is still mostly seen as such. Substantive rights and protections for Indigenous Australians were enacted in the years before and after the referendum. Voting rights, where they did not already exist, were granted from 1962, although Queensland lagged until 1965; an attempt to protect Indigenous Queenslanders from discriminatory laws was legislated in 1975, as was protection against racial discrimination; land rights were legislated for the Northern Territory in 1976; legislation establishing the Human Rights Commission was enacted in 1986; and a range of state legislation outlawing discrimination was also promulgated in the 1970s and 1980s. But legislation providing affirmative action and access to educational and other institutions was never introduced in Australia. Affirmative-action programs have only ever occurred as voluntary policy decisions by public or private institutions. There has been no Australian law to compel affirmative action.

It is not these events of the 1960s that I (or Shelby Steele and like-minded supporters of the growing critique in the United States) question. They were seminal achievements; it is their aftermath that requires reconsideration. In the aftermath of the civil-rights victories, the politics of 'victimhood' became the predominant methodology of black advocacy and the reigning paradigm of public-policy thinking. Victimhood relied on a phenomenon within the dominant white societies that had two faces: *white guilt* and *moral vanity*. The rise of victim politics meant that, even as there was increased recognition of black rights in the post-citizenship era, there was also a calamitous erosion of black responsibility.

I have often reflected on the downside of the events surrounding citizenship, at least for the remote communities of northern Australia with which I am familiar – particularly Cape York Peninsula. In the light of the problems with which we are grappling today, I see three factors as decisive contributors to the descent into hell three decades later: equal wages, access to social-security income support and the right to enter pubs and to drink alcohol. These factors appeared to be positive developments designed to address inequities, but their unintended consequences – particularly for Aboriginal men – were negative.

Not all the consequences of these measures were unforeseen: it had been clear to the Commonwealth government in the hearings before the Australian Conciliation and Arbitration Commission that a ruling in favour of equal wages would result in the large-scale removal of Aboriginal stockworkers from the stations of northern Australia. The Commonwealth's solution was to make social security available. The Commission ruled:

> If any problems of native welfare whether of employees or their dependants, arise as a result of this decision, the Commonwealth Government has made clear its intention to deal with them. This is not why we have come to our conclusion but it means we know that any welfare problems which arise will be dealt with by those most competent to deal with them.

The then president of the Commission, Sir Richard Kirby, would later tell his biographer Blanche d'Alpuget that the case would 'be seen as the greatest contribution he and other members of the Commission made to Australian society'.

The story of the past four decades is, of course, more complex than this. There were other factors driving the decline in the pastoral industry. The dismantling of the systems of social and administrative control by governments and missions led to growing social chaos. Even where strong and functional social and cultural norms were maintained by Aboriginal people themselves, their maintenance was broken down by values and standards imported from the wider society and the shutting down of Aboriginal authority through the intrusion of the legal system. Legal-aid services to Aboriginal offenders probably did more to undermine the authority of elders and other local justice mechanisms (in Queensland, the Aboriginal Courts presided over by local justices of the peace) than any other intervention. A workable social order based on moral and cultural authority was forced to comply with legal authority – and ultimately had to defer to the law. This moral and cultural authority, which had provided structure to life in the settlements, withered away.

The decline of religion and the influence of the churches in the communities are also part of this story, including the historically problematic role of the churches in the administrative management of Aboriginal communities. In the case of my hometown, I served on the Hope Vale Aboriginal Community Council when the last vestiges of the Lutheran Church's administrative involvement in the affairs of our people were removed in the late 1980s. We cut these last ties with a relishing sense of historic reckoning. The awful truth is that we threw the baby out with the bathwater: the role of the church in the secular and spiritual life of our community was conflated; both the church and our people should have found a way to move beyond the paternalism of the past without destroying the moral and cultural order that had been such a strong quality of our community. But the transfer of moral responsibility that Shelby Steele identified in the United States also played out here. We now repent a social and moral wreckage.

But these are details. The larger context was the growth of the culture and politics of victimhood, which came to be the accepted basis of the relationship between Aboriginal people and the rest of the country. Prior to reading Shelby Steele's thesis on white guilt – and how the success of civil rights transmogrified into the failure of victim politics – I had been thinking about the various positions Indigenous and non-indigenous Australians take in relation to questions of history and race. There is a dichotomy in popular discussion of racism. It is assumed that people and ideas come from one of two possible sides: those who are racists and those who are not, those who are subject to racism and those who are racists, those who believe that racism is a major social ill and those who do not, and so on.

In Australia, the divide is generally seen as being one between those who believe Australia has a problem with racism, and those who believe that Australia is not a racist country. Since the 1960s, heavily influenced by international norms established by the United Nations, decolonisation in Africa and Asia, and by the civil-rights movement in the United States, Australians from the Left and Right have altered their views on racism for the better. Whilst, historically, racism was widely acceptable across Australian society (the White Australia policy was championed by the Australian Labor Party), political opinion and social values shifted fundamentally towards an understanding that overt racism, at least, was unacceptable.

Today, whilst leading conservatives and liberals (notably former prime minister Malcolm Fraser) are avowed opponents of racism, the polarity between those who consider racism a serious problem and those who do not is generally seen as a Left–Right split. As progressive people predominately come from the Left of the cultural and political divide, the ALP (and the progressive minor parties) are generally regarded as opponents of racism, whilst the Liberal and National parties are considered racist – or at least indifferent to racism. Individuals from both sides often contradict this generalisation.

This dichotomous view of racism is simplistic and misleading. My analysis looks at six positions which Indigenous and non-indigenous Australians take in relation to race and history concerning the country's original peoples. For non-indigenous Australians, there is an arc that goes from denial to moral vanity, to acknowledgment and responsibility. For Aboriginal people, the arc ranges from separatism to victimhood, and to pride and principled defence.

There is a strong tradition of *denial* in Australia. The eminent ethnographer W.E.H. Stanner named this tradition in the country's historiography up to the late 1960s the 'Great Australian Silence'. There is a very large constituency that denies that the treatment of Indigenous people in Australia's colonial history (and up to the present) was as bad as those historians who have contributed to the genre known as 'Aboriginal history' demonstrate. These people deny that racism in Australia against the country's Indigenous peoples is a serious problem. Keith Windschuttle, with his refutation of massacres and violence on the frontiers, and Pauline Hanson, with her galvanising resentment of alleged preferences given to Aboriginal people (and other racial minorities) are just the most egregious examples.

Denial is a strong word. It is only a general characterisation of a variety of views amongst non-indigenous Australians. The spectrum ranges from David Irving-style ideological denialism to those who acknowledge the depredations suffered by Indigenous people through history and the racism in our society, but who minimise its nature and extent ('we shouldn't dwell on the past'). Many join this constituency because of political and cultural affiliations with the political Right. There are two important things to understand about this constituency.

First, most of them are defensive about their own identity and heritage. The accusation that they are racist and that their colonial heritage is a catalogue of shame and immoral villainy – and the suggestion that they should therefore feel guilty – makes them defensive. If race and history are raised in such a sharply accusatory and unbalanced way, people who may otherwise be prepared to acknowledge and take responsibility for the truth end up joining the hard-core ideologues.

There is some truth in the proposition that 'political correctness' has had this effect. There is also truth in the proposition that the political Right has deliberately and wilfully galvanised this defensiveness by mischaracterising the progressive position as being about guilt, rather than what former prime minister Paul Keating referred to as 'open hearts' in his landmark 1992 Redfern speech. This has provided great fodder for the Right in their prosecution of the culture wars.

The denialists also keenly understand how debilitating it is to adopt the mentality and outlook of victimhood. It is easy for them to say that victimhood is worthless, as it grows out of their ideological contempt for interventionist social policy, even when it seeks to ameliorate the impact of the market on the most vulnerable. But this does not make them wrong. Those on the cultural and political Right are more correct than their opponents in recognising the folly of policy that turns people into victims.

The second major constituency in contemporary Australia is morally vain about race and history. Its members largely come from the liberal Left and are morally certain about right and wrong and ready to ascribe blame. For them, issues of race and history are a means of gaining the upper hand over their political and cultural opponents. The primary concern of the morally vain is not the plight of those who suffer racism and oppression, but rather their view of themselves and their belief in their superiority over their opponents. There are two things about this constituency that need to be understood.

First, this constituency contributes most to, and actively supports, the outlook that casts Indigenous people as victims. Its members have no understanding of how destructive, demoralising and demeaning this mentality is. Their most telling catchphrase in rebuke of their opponents, whenever there may be a suggestion made about the personal responsibility of Indigenous people (or indeed the disadvantaged at large), is 'Don't blame the victims'. They provide excuses and justifications for those on whose behalf they advocate. They infantilise Indigenous people by not allowing them to face the consequences of their actions: Indigenous people's status as victims means they require protection from the real world.

Moral vanity is perhaps an unfair characterisation. There is a broad spectrum of views within this group, and many within this constituency have decent motivations. They empathise with the plight of Indigenous people who face racism and other real injuries; they acknowledge what has happened through history and recognise that the present is connected to the past. They understand the hypocrisy of the prescription to forget the past, especially in a country whose most famous lapidary exhortation reads: Lest We Forget. But at some point, empathy and acknowledgment turn into moral superiority, and the relative failures of one's cultural and political opponents become the basis of accusations of insensitivity or racism. At this point, race becomes a useful club with which to beat the Neanderthals from the Right, and accusations of racism serve the cultural and political purposes of the progressive accuser rather than the humanity of those subjected to racism.

Let me offer an example. Consider the phenomenon of 'homeless' Aboriginal people binge drinking in public parks. To combat this, the enforcement of laws to prevent drinking in public places could be combined with controlled management of income support so that accommodation, food and other essentials are provided and cash for alcohol is not. The first of these policies has been tried in Australia; the second has not. If this were proposed, it would be characterised as racist by morally vain progressives and vehemently opposed. Indeed, these people run campaigns on behalf of 'long-grassers' to the effect that the homeless have a 'right to sleep'. Long-grassing is romanticised as some kind of final act of resistance against authority, but patently people do not 'choose' to live like this.

Rather than denial or moral vanity, the optimum position for nonindigenous people to take is that of *acknowledgment* – of the past and its legacy in the present, recognising that racism is not a contrivance, that Indigenous people endure great hurt and confront barriers as a result of racism. Non-indigenous Australians need to take *responsibility* for the fact of racism, and work to answer and counter it.

On the Indigenous side, the extreme position is that of *separatism*. In the United States, black nationalists such as Marcus Garvey actively pursued separatist agendas. The separatist rhetoric and strategy of Malcolm X was real. There has been no such equivalent in Australia, despite rhetorical flourishes and stunts such as the Aboriginal Provisional

Government. Separatist posturing has largely been a tactical device in Australia, not entirely without (tactical) effect; however, separatism has not been the subject of a real and serious strategy, despite a profound sense of alienation experienced by many Indigenous people.

The largest constituency on the Indigenous side subscribes to *victimhood*. Again, this is a strong term which covers a broad spectrum of outlooks. People will object to my interpretation of victimhood because what many of our people regard as radical, separatist and resistance politics, I say is victim politics. Further, what many of our people regard as pride and necessary defensiveness against racism is, I believe, victim politics. Argument arises here because of the dynamic way cultural and political currents change over time: what may have been a truly radical act at one time, such as the Tent Embassy in 1971, degenerates into a sad symbol of defeatist, victim politics, as is plain with the squalid demountables at the Tent Embassy site in 2007.

It is one thing to analyse whether some outlook or action proceeds from a mentality of victimhood, and another to analyse the political or social effectiveness of such an action. I am not denying that the politics of victimhood have (and still) yield returns. They have and do, but at an enormous cost that is sometimes hard to recognise. As Shelby Steele has explained, white guilt is a resource blacks in America and Australia have learned to mine.

I want to talk about two problems with victimhood. The first is that we pay a high price for casting ourselves as victims. Victimhood starts as an outlook or a mentality and becomes an identity. The long-grassers and under-the-bridge dwellers are the most visible, end-stage subscribers to this tragic and self-destructive tactic. It damages our people wherever they are – from the young student who believes that academic achievement at school is 'acting white' to those who tolerate domestic violence because it is 'understandable' given the history of the people concerned. This is a self-defeating and pernicious outlook.

We indigenes of Australia are confused in our cultural understanding of victimisation and victimhood. Yes, individuals and groups in our society are victimised in a variety of ways. But it is a terrible thing to encourage victims to adopt a mentality of victimhood, to see themselves as victims. To adopt this mentality is fatal because it concedes defeat, and it can also literally kill. Victims do not take responsibility for what they eat and drink, for their health and mental wellbeing; their families become dysfunctional and their children are damaged even before they are born. The worst indulgence is to take away the one power victims need to survive, to defy victimisation. To say: 'Yes, I have suffered victimisation – but I'm not giving in by becoming a victim!'

This is the difference between the responses of Rosa Parks and Vincent Lingiari to the racist victimisation they endured and the victim politics cultivated by the post-civil rights and post-citizenship leadership. In organisations like the NAACP and the Federal Council for the Advancement of Aborigines and Torres Strait Islanders, the gap between these two generations was profound.

The second problem with victimhood is that the opportunities it produces are of mixed quality. In education and other areas, the 'soft bigotry of low expectations' tends to determine the quality of the opportunities available to people who are taken to be victims. In America, the hot-button issue is affirmative action. In Steele's view, affirmative action does not help victims to rise out of their victimhood. I will not engage in a discussion of affirmative action here, other than to say that three thoughts are on my mind in relation to it. Firstly, I think Steele is right about the problematic consequences of affirmative action for black Americans: the disincentive effects are serious. Secondly, black Australian participation and achievement is even worse than that of black Americans, we have never had affirmative action, and I am not convinced that all doors open from the outside. Thirdly, if we consider affirmative action for Australia, it should be aimed at breaking class barriers rather than race barriers.

Characterising Indigenous people as victims leads to an emphasis on the need for recognition of rights – human rights and land rights – which are undeniably good things. The rights question is complicated in the Australian context. In America, it focused on recognition of formal equality between blacks and other citizens. In Australia, it is not so simple: Indigenous people possess certain rights that flow from their unique position as the first Australians. Therefore their rights to land, language and other matters necessarily involve different rights to those guaranteed other citizens. Where rights could be granted by political and legislative fiat, there were beneficial developments. But in areas such as health and education, where legislation and the provision of services by the state cannot achieve better outcomes without behavioural change, the behaviour of the victims simply could not be confronted, because victims could not be responsible. This is what Shelby Steele calls blameless poverty, and it characterises many Aboriginal communities today.

So, instead of confronting behaviour – even when the first wave of programs did not work, and indeed produced a set of secondary problems – the welfare-state builders simply increased their commitment to the idea that the victims could be rescued from deep poverty through the co-ordination of service delivery. This is still the dominant response today, even as the failure of passive welfare is apparent. Of course, the leadership that campaigned for the 1967 referendum gave way to what would become the new victim leadership of the 1970s. Thomas Wolfe's perspicacious observations of the radical-chic posturing of morally vain whites, and the 'mau-mauing of the flak-catchers' by angry 'radicals' in America all played out here too, right through the 1970s and '80s. Acquisition of an undergraduate command of some key ideas in international and human-rights law led to the new language of 'sovereignty'. I was once told a hilarious story by the late Charlie Perkins of an Indigenous gathering in a Returned Serviceman's League hall in a country town. The entire morning was spent debating whether a portrait of Her Majesty Queen Elizabeth II should remain gazing down at the proceedings as the owners of the establishment intended it to. Those seeking to make a point about the wrongful usurpation of Indigenous sovereignty by the Crown succeeded in their motion, and the rest of the day was spent looking for another venue because the gathering was immediately ejected from the premises.

In my relatively short experience, I have endured my fair share of fanciful separatist rhetoric, and plenty of inane stunts and speeches, founded on vague and insufficiently grasped theories. As long as some key words and concepts are sprinkled amidst the denunciations, any lunatic can be a leader. I've often had the sense that we are playing delusional games in our own obscure little sandpits. We want our sovereignty recognised by the International Court of Justice, and in the meantime I'm off to the TAB and the pub. During my law studies in Sydney in the late 1980s, I expressed my interest in seeking work with an Indigenous organisation to a white trade unionist who was well acquainted with some key figures of the 1970s Indigenous leadership. I was taken by this kindly man to the separate offices of two of the pioneers of the post-Tent Embassy leadership. They were now 'running things' like Leo and Giovanni, the two rival Prohibition-era mobsters in the Coen brothers' masterpiece *Miller's Crossing*. Nothing came from my introductions. But I vividly remember sitting in the office of one of these characters. He was dressed in a black skivvy and smart sports jacket, smoking a cigarette through an elegant cigarette holder. It could have been a scene out of a 'blaxploitation' film starring Jim Kelly circa 1975.

All of this was victim politics, no matter the radical pretence. It was scratching bark, not digging out the roots. A prideful and principled defence against racism is what we need as a people. Many ordinary Indigenous people possess this dignity and strength. We must make it the dominant outlook of our people.

Peoplehood

There is one respect in which the discussion of Indigenous Australian policy differs from the African-American discussion: the question of Indigenous 'peoplehood'. In this sense the position of Native Americans is more relevant. The African-American struggle is for socio-economic advancement and equality. Steele describes the aspiration to 'advance through education, skill development, and entrepreneurialism combined with an unbending assault on any continuing discrimination'. Steele believes that the main obstacles to African-Americans taking their rightful place have been removed, that 'blacks are no longer oppressed in America', and that the main burdens weighing them down are flawed policies and ideologies.

Steele does not see African-Americans as a minority people. Although some radical African-Americans have advocated separatist policies and argue that they constitute a separate people with national rights, that view is not widely held. Generally, African-American issues are thought of as 'race relations', the goal being to end public programs and practices which recognise African-Americans as a distinct group. Americans to the left of Steele argue that policies which go beyond the abolition of official discrimination and the elimination of overt racism are necessary, but they do not advocate perpetual special measures; rather, they expect such measures to gradually disappear as irrational racial prejudice recedes and equality increases.

The Indigenous Australian struggle is for socio-economic advancement and equality, but it is also about the recognition of status and rights as a people. The goal here is to preserve and win legal recognition of cultural distinctness as well as citizenship. Indigenous Australian political issues are 'peoplehood issues'. It is regrettable that this word is so little used in English-language debate. In his book *Modern Peoplehood*, Berkeley professor John Lie defined peoplehood as follows:

> An inclusionary and involuntary group identity with a putatively shared history and distinct way of life [to which] everyone in the group, regardless of status, gender, or moral worth, belongs ... In addition to common descent – a shared sense of genealogy and geography – contemporary commonality, such as language, religion, culture, or consciousness, characterizes the group. It gropes toward a grouping larger than kinship but smaller than humanity. It is not merely a population – an aggregate, an external attribution, an analytical category – but, rather, a people – a group, an internal conviction, a self-reflexive identity.

The word peoplehood is needed in the analysis of national issues because it unambiguously conveys this concept. We are all familiar with the 'inclusionary and involuntary' identity which Lie describes, but we have no generally accepted word for it. The word 'ethnicity' is sometimes used to cover the hole in our linguistic map, but this word suffers from connoting, in Lie's words, 'external attribution', thanks to its anthropological origins. One can imagine people claiming their rights as 'Yorta Yorta people', but hardly as 'the Yorta Yorta ethnic group'. Nor is 'nationhood' the word we need, because it confuses the issue that needs to be discussed – namely the tension between the current world order of approximately two hundred sovereign states, and the several thousand distinct peoples who have demonstrated their desire for recognition. 'Nationhood' is more or less synonymous with the creation of a sovereign nation-state, and is therefore misleading and unhelpful. The term peoplehood, if it came into common usage, would be perfect. It is self-explanatory and refers to something other than nation-states and formal citizenship. It is also likely to convey two desired connotations: it suggests 'outcome[s] achieved through the efforts of the population itself'; and it suggests a situation that is the 'result of a historical process'.

As a result of a global historical process, diverse populations have developed a 'self-reflexive identity', an 'internal conviction' about the bond that unites them. The notion of peoplehood has evolved and become politically more important. As a consequence of the rise of nationalism, the relationships between peoples forced to co-exist within the borders of sovereign states deteriorated during the nineteenth and twentieth centuries and today are a chief source of some of the world's most intractable conflicts.

I strongly object to the modern tendency to categorise people according to a system of exclusive identities. Nobel Prize-winning economist Amartya Sen has called this 'the illusion of singular identity'. We labour under impoverished conceptions of identity. The identity of a group is assumed to be singular – arising from some salient characteristic. The identity of an individual within an ethnic group is also assumed to be singular – again arising from some salient feature of the group. Instead, Sen argues that we should recognise 'competing affiliations' or 'competing identities'. His choice of words is unfortunate; I have proposed a better metaphor: 'layers of identity'. These layers include identification with cultural and linguistic groups; citizenship; religion; place of birth, upbringing, residency and death; local and regional geographic communities; regional, provincial and national polities; and professional, literary, recreational, philosophical and other sub-cultural groups.

A Rugby Union-following Lutheran Aboriginal with a love for the literature of England shares much with many other Australians that he does not share with his closest kin – but he does share with his kin an identity based on peoplehood. In a pluralist and united world, some layers of identity create strong bonds between people who know each other, while others create bridges between strangers.

Indigenous Australian issues are peoplehood issues. The main difference between the Australian and American situations is that the basis for Australian policy is (or should be) the legitimate claim of Indigenous Australians to recognition as a distinct people with constitutionally recognised rights. The point of this essay is that the black American comparison is nevertheless germane – because race relations are relevant here too.

Unintended consequences

'Unintended consequences' is a concept derived from liberal economics: positively, the consequences of choices made in the marketplace are never certain and cannot be completely anticipated; negatively, unintended consequences are also the inevitable product of state planning. By impeding and superseding decision-making in the market, ambitious rationalist social planners cause unintended consequences by attempting to use the state to plan good societies and good futures for citizens, when they do not have the capacity to do so. When used in this negative sense, the phrase 'unintended consequences' forms part of a liberal critique of statist socialist planning. As Friedrich von Hayek might have said, the road to serfdom is paved with good intentions.

There is also a possible Marxist explanation for such unintended consequences: the forces that dominate society inexorably transform progressive movements into regression. The opaque nature of the ideological and cultural superstructure built on society's material base means that movements that appear to be progressive may turn out to be regressive when the question is asked: 'What is the objective effect of this movement?' Unintended consequences arise when radicals fail to maintain an objective analysis and naïvely trust their subjective view.

It is not necessary to decide which is correct – liberals and Marxists can agree that unintended consequences are a ubiquitous phenomenon in human history. A theoretical explanation is not my principal concern. I indicate the framework only to introduce an analysis about which I have become convinced: that the distance between good and bad policies is most often very fine – they are seldom poles apart. People from both sides of the cultural and political divide usually believe the distance between their own correct policies and their opponents' wrong policies to be substantial. Politics is given to stark caricatures. Intellectual discussion in the service of politics is similarly inclined.

This polarisation leads to problems: a failure to distinguish between a potentially correct policy (for instance, policing relatively minor misdemeanours to restore order to crime-ridden, disadvantaged neighbourhoods) and an obviously incorrect one (police harassment and violence). Typically, the Left opposes zero-tolerance policing, although it would be truly progressive to restore social order to disadvantaged neighbourhoods, and such policing is probably critical to achieving this. So the champions of certain ends end up opposing the means needed to achieve them. I see this time and time again in my consideration of the plight of the disadvantaged people who are my concern, Indigenous Australians.

This polarisation leads to a failure of the left to appreciate the correctness of policies promoted by the Right (and vice versa). The fine difference between the correct and the incorrect policy is too subtle for (and I use the following phrase advisedly) usual public discourse, which only sees stark tensions and bald contradictions. Closer, more intense tensions, which might suggest potential syntheses, are overlooked.

The tensions involved in policy debates about crime in neighbourhoods centre around questions of freedom and social order. Obviously, too much social order undermines freedom. Less obviously, too little social order also undermines freedom. People who live in optimally free and ordered communities often fail to appreciate the fact that a high degree of social order underpins the freedom they enjoy. Libertarians are either blind to, or careless of, the advantages they take from the strong social order provided by invisible social norms; this is why classical libertarians come from privileged classes. (Lower-class libertarianism is, of course, the very definition of social dysfunction.)

Where black people are involved, tensions between racial discrimination and non-discrimination, and between advantage and disadvantage, are also intertwined in the freedom/social-order dialectic. Where the problem in disadvantaged neighbourhoods is high rates of blacks offending, measures aimed at strengthening social order (such as zero-tolerance policing) actually deliver advantage and freedom in the long run. The argument against such measures is that they will result in even greater rates of imprisonment of black people. And indeed, in the short and intermediate term they will. There will be a spike. But if we want black neighbourhoods to enjoy freedom, we need to ask the question: 'What is it about advantaged neighbourhoods that guarantees freedom for their denizens?' The answer is: 'They have social order'. If we don't take the hard policy decisions to increase social order where it is weak because we fear that black involvement in the criminal justice system will increase, then we will never solve the egregious (and, in the case of my home state of Queensland, increasing) over-representation of black people in prison.

The 'radical centre' may be defined as the intense resolution of the tensions between opposing principles (in this example, the principles are freedom and social order) – a resolution that produces the synthesis of optimum policy. The radical centre is not to be found simply by splitting the difference between the stark and weak tensions from either side of popularly conceived discourse, but rather where the dialectical tension is most intense, and the policy positions much closer and more carefully calibrated than most people imagine.

Before I turn to my thoughts on the radical centre in policy and leadership, I should make some final theoretical points. First, it is difficult to analyse and identify the correct (radically centrist) policy because commanding ideologies hold sway and limit people's capacity to abandon wrong policies and search for better ones. But even where the right policies have been identified and adopted, their implementation is susceptible to distortion. The correct policy can easily turn sour because of incompetent implementation: if a police force does not understand that the aim of zero-tolerance policing is to restore social order, and that racism and sharp practice must not be tolerated, the policy will degenerate into abuse and victimisation. Even when optimal policies are competently implemented, one must be mindful of the dynamic nature of social, political and economic currents. A measure that is progressive at one time can produce regressive results later. Policy makers must take account of the fluctuations of history.

The radical centre in policy and leadership

I first considered the role of dialectical tension in creating the radical centre when I thought about leadership. My first official job was on a task force appointed by the Queensland premier Wayne Goss in 1991 – led by his *wunderkind* head of the cabinet office, Kevin Rudd – to develop Aboriginal land-rights legislation. Having been in opposition since time immemorial, the fledgling Labor government dreaded implementing its commitment to introduce land-rights legislation in the most conservative of states. In dramatic circumstances, at a national conference hosted by Premier Goss as part of Justice Tony Fitzgerald's Fraser Island Inquiry, the premier announced the government's intention to develop land-rights legislation. I was there with a delegation of Cape York elders and colleagues; I had begun my own trajectory in pursuit of land rights for the people of Cape York Peninsula by forming the Cape York Land Council the year before.

Kevin Rudd and Wayne Goss eventually produced miserable legislation – an opinion that I still hold sixteen years later. The new law provided for a slightly different form of title to replace that previously granted by the National Party government of Sir Joh Bjelke-Petersen. The practical effect was negligible and did not grant any more land than that already under Aboriginal ownership. Most of these title transfers have still not taken place.

Provision was made for Aboriginal groups to claim lands on the basis of their traditional affiliation or historical association, or economic and social need. Claims could be made before a specially established Land Tribunal. Only national parks and vacant Crown land could be claimed – and of these, only those parcels of land that the executive government had decided to make available. This provision, which Kevin Rudd designed, enabled the government to control what could be claimed, and when. In the sixteen years since this legislation was passed, very few parcels of vacant land were ever gazetted for claim: I know of only one claim that went through the process. Around a dozen national parks were made available – principally in Cape York, but also the Great Sandy Desert National Park in the south-western corner of Queensland – and they were all successfully proven before the Land Tribunal.

I represented the traditional owners in the first claim to the Flinders Islands and Cape Melville national parks in 1993. The claim was successful. However, the Yiithuwarra traditional owners have still not received title to the park. They have no role in its management, and not one of them is employed by any of the plethora of government agencies responsible for the 'natural resource management' of these lands and seas. The managers are all white. Half of the Yiithuwarra who gave evidence in the 1993 claim, including almost all the elders, are now dead. The implementation of the original commitment to hand over title and management of national parks to traditional owners has been in abeyance during the three terms of Premier Peter Beattie's government. The government fears an electoral backlash if it proceeds with the Goss/Rudd scheme.

I recount this story first to make the point that if I had a dollar for every time I heard that phrase 'social justice' fall easily from the lips of a Labor politician in my home state, I would be an extremely wealthy man.

My first experience of the realpolitik of fighting for Aboriginal rights was bitterly hard. The most shameful thing occurred on the day Premier Goss tabled the bill. It contained nothing to distress the miners or the farmers, whose interests were fully accounted for. Then the Anglican Archbishop of Brisbane, Peter Hollingworth, duly came out and gave the government's paltry legislation his extraordinary blessing. It was the premier's language that was shocking. He and his advisers had determined that the best way to sell the new law to an unsympathetic Queensland public was to make it clear he was not giving any free handouts to the blackfellas. The grab on the evening news was to the effect that the provision for the payment of royalties for mining would not allow any Aboriginal 'sheiks' to drive around in Rolls-Royce motorcars. It was appalling. True to his promise, the minor provision for the payment of royalties for mining applying to only one of Queensland's numerous mines – the Cape Flattery silica mines owned by Mitsubishi on the land of the Hope Vale community – has not paid one cent of royalties to the community sixteen years later. I learned a bitter truth through this experience: that Aboriginal people are lepers in the Australian democratic process. I have watched with awe how the progressive lobby turned al-Qa'ida recruit David Hicks into a relentless, irrecusable and finally triumphant national cause – from Taliban terrorist to latter-day Nelson Mandela of Guantanamo Bay. It has (occasionally) been said that it is not the man, it is the principle. There is a much clearer principle involved in the breach of the International Convention on the Elimination of All Forms of Racial Discrimination by the Australian government's *Native Title Act*, but this could not be made a *cause célèbre*. In terms of marketability, it is easier to sell a terrorist than an Australian Aborigine. Australia's democracy is telegenically allergic to blackfellas.

This got me thinking about pragmatism and realism in political leadership. The new breed of Labor apparatchiks running state governments after the disasters of the 1980s were more hard-headed about the imperatives of holding on to power: no more Whitlamesque indulgences, no more socialism. Goss, Rudd and Swan were the new pineapple heads of the Sunshine State. I understood that Aboriginal causes were a political hard-sell. I felt at the time that Premier Goss could have produced more just legislation without cutting his government's throat in the process. I thought about low-level, poll-driven pragmatism versus ideals. Wayne Goss had been part of the Labor-lawyer brigade who had spent time working in Aboriginal legal aid, yet in two electorally handsome terms his government did nothing to improve the lot of Queensland's most abject people.

Later, the albatross of Australia's lepers hung around the neck of Paul Keating's prime ministership in 1996. Never before, and likely never again, would Indigenes be invited in from the woodheap to sit at the main table as they did during those Keating years. This just confirmed the opinion that Aborigines are electoral poison. No more bleeding hearts. No more prime-ministerial insistence that the blackfellas come in from the cold.

We are prisoners of our metaphors: by thinking of realism and idealism as opposite ends of a two-dimensional plane, we see leaders inclining to one side or the other. The naïve and indignant yaw towards ideals and get nowhere, but their souls remain pure. The cold-eyed and impatient pride themselves on their lack of romance and emotional foolishness: pragmatism and a remorseless Kissingeresque grasp of power make winning and survival the main prize every time. Those who harbour ideals but who need to work within the parameters of real power (as opposed to simply cloaking lazy capitulation under the easy mantle of righteous impotence) end up splitting the difference somewhere between ideals and reality. This is called compromise.

I prefer a pyramid metaphor of leadership, with one side being realism and the other idealism, and the quality of leadership dependent on how closely the two sides are brought together. The apex of leadership is the point where the two sides meet.

The highest ideals on Earth are realised when leaders strive to secure them through close attention to reality. Lofty idealism without pragmatism is worthless. What is pragmatism without ideals? At best it is management, but not leadership. It takes insight, skill and creativity, careful calculation as well as bold judgment, prudence as well as risk, perseverance as well as preparedness to alter course, belief as well as humility, and great competence as well as the ability to make good from mistakes to bring ideals closer to reality. One must be hard-headed in order never to let go of ideals.

Idealism and realism in leadership do not constitute a zero-sum game. This is not about securing a false compromise. The best leadership occurs at the point of highest tension between ideals and reality. This is the radical centre. If the idealism is weaker than the realism, then optimum leadership cannot be achieved – and vice versa. The radical centre is achieved when both are strong.

Otherwise, you get the problem of skewing. This occurs when one side of what I will call a classic dialectical struggle is weak and the other is strong. Skewing may be a product of history: the balance of tensions may be optimal at one point, but it can change over time. As we have discussed, even ideal policy is not static; what might be truly progressive policy at one time can become regressive as circumstances change. To refer back to an earlier example, legal aid for Aboriginal offenders has treated wrongdoers as victims and contributed to the undermining of social order within Aboriginal society. Legal aid pointed to the criminal justice system as the principal problem, not the behaviour of Aboriginal people towards their kith and kin. This resulted in a vicious spiral downwards, with even more offenders appearing as the social order broke down.

Skewing occurs not just because the intellectual analysis is faulty or weak, but because of the difficulties involved in resolving conflict between opposing interests in the real world; reality poses great challenges for any leader seeking a better resolution in the radical centre. No leadership is immune from the forces that impel confrontation between reality and ideals. Leaders are buffeted by reality and must contend with it – they cannot avoid it. Leaders' ideals are not just innate qualities: ideals are often forced upon them by events or by the people around them. Some of the greatest leaders achieve their apex having been compelled by external forces.

My example may be predictable: Abraham Lincoln. Like Winston Churchill, he brought together the highest ideals and the hardest realism. Lincoln starts with his first inaugural address ('I have no purpose, directly or indirectly, to interfere with the institution of slavery in the states where it exists. I believe I have no lawful right to do so, and I have no inclination to do so.') and ends up leading the country towards emancipation. The journey is not Lincoln's alone: leaders are not gods. As Doris Kearns Goodwin's perspicuous book *Team of Rivals* reveals, Lincoln's competitors for the Republican nomination (Salmon Chase, William H. Seward and Edward Bates) led him to a better result than he would otherwise have achieved, but his decision to bring his rivals into his cabinet marked the nature of the man's leadership.

There are at least ten classic dialectical tensions in human policy: idealism vs realism, rights vs responsibilities, social order vs liberty, individual vs community, efficiency vs equality, structure vs behaviour, opportunity vs choice, unity vs diversity, nature vs man, and peace vs war. This list traverses an entire universe and history of philosophy, policy and politics, and it is not my purpose to set out a prolonged discussion of each of them here. My contentions are these. First, it is important to correctly identify the fundamental dialectical tensions that define human policy and political struggle. Second, the resolution of each of these tensions lies in their dialectical synthesis, not in the absolute triumph of one side or in a weak compromise. Third, other subsidiary struggles have their origins in these classical conflicts. Fourth, complexity arises because questions of human policy are not confined to the neat categories of a ten-point list. Rather, they involve a number of tensions simultaneously. I have discussed the tension between idealism and realism and between social order and liberty. Economist Arthur Okun described the tension between social and economic goals in capitalist democracies in his classic 1975 essay, *Equality and Efficiency: The Big Trade-off.* As Okun observed, too much equality is inefficient and too much efficiency leads to inequality. Discussion of rights and responsibilities is so ubiquitous as to be almost sterile – but the fact that on this question, two tribes still face each other on either side of an ideological divide demonstrates that, while the radical centre may make common sense analytically, it is uncommon to see it emerge in practice. The predominant view in Australian Indigenous policy, from a progressive and Indigenous perspective, remains that rights are the real imperative and responsibilities are an ideological diversion. Their opponents hold exactly the contrary view. I will return to this when I come to discuss my own contribution to this discourse.

I will leave the last three on the list, but will briefly discuss the tension between opportunity and choice and between structure and behaviour because they are pertinent to this essay. In our reform work in Cape York Peninsula, we have come to greatly appreciate the insight of Nobel Laureate Amartya Sen in *Development as Freedom.* Sen argues that it is not enough to say that individuals have the right to choose their own path; people also require some basic capabilities, such as good health and education, to be able to make real choices. Sen's theory is an important gloss on the powerful principle of individual choice, for without capabilities, choice can be a bare conceit. Although there is disagreement as to how best to achieve universal opportunity, there is a strong consensus in Western democracies that opportunity must accompany choice. Indeed, for much of the twentieth century – before Friedrich Hayek's ideas became popular – even capital-L liberals and capital-C conservatives accepted the importance of universal opportunity. Social democrats look to the state to ensure universal opportunity, but the welfare state has had mixed success.

What I call classical welfare has been undeniably successful, but passive welfare has not only failed to spread opportunity, it has in fact increased the incapacity of certain sections of society.

Sen put an important gloss on choice, and I propose a similar gloss on 'opportunity'. Opportunity must be accompanied by responsibility. Opportunity alone will not produce capability. Rather, individuals, families and communities must fulfil their responsibilities if opportunities are to become real. This was a strong conviction of Booker T. Washington; he believed that his people had to take responsibility so that whenever opportunities came knocking, they would be able to capitalise on them. He deprecated opportunity without responsibility. His support for tying suffrage rights to property ownership – provided that black property-owners could also vote – underscored his tremendous belief that no opportunity or right should accrue without responsibility. Whether it is correct to make rights and opportunities conditional on responsibility, it is nevertheless true that without responsibility, people will lack the capacity to take full advantage of the rights and opportunities available to them.

Finally, the dialectic between structure and behaviour. Shelby Steele points to the malignant effect of theories that underpinned leftist thinking about race from the 1960s onwards. He writes:

> The Marxian emphasis on structures and sub-structures gave the new militant leaders of the time an infinitely larger racism to work with, a systemic and sociological racism that was far more 'determinative' than the simpler immoral racism of Martin Luther King's era.

Steele is dismissive of structural explanations which absolve individuals from personal responsibility and which have made race such a heavy burden and an insuperable barrier to opportunity in America.

He is correct in identifying the baleful and shallow theories on which the New Left constructed a cultural and social folly, but this does not mean that there is not a structural dimension to black problems; they are both behavioural and structural. For example, welfare dependency is clearly a behavioural issue, but it also has a structural explanation; it came about for structural reasons but became a behavioural issue. Taking another example, there is a passive welfare industry within government bureaucracies and non-government 'service delivery' organisations. This industry has an entrenched interest in cultivating and maintaining behavioural dependency by its many clients. Tackling welfare dependency requires not just a behavioural challenge: it is a massive structural and institutional challenge.

The problem with discussing structures is that it can become an excuse for failing to deal with behaviour. People are absolved from responsibility because of the daunting scale of the structural explanation. This is what Steele means when he talks about 'social determinism': structures seem so omnipresent and overwhelming that there is no possibility of human agency and responsibility. Progressivist thinking in this area has failed to distinguish between explanation and policy prescription. It is one thing to have a greater understanding of the structural reasons for certain behavioural problems, but this does not by itself suggest a solution. The problem may have a history, but illuminating this is not itself a solution. We will still need to deal with dysfunction and poverty as we seek to tackle those strucutral dimensions that can be reformed.

Some explanations, such as structural violence in history, are beyond contemporary policy reach in any case: we have to deal with what we face now. Some structural problems, such as racism, may not be amenable to reform, and if we make black progress conditional on its elimination or substantial diminution, we might be waiting until kingdom comes. In other words, we are liable to leave ourselves impotent and defeated in the face of racism, and this is infinitely more tragic if we have imagined the barriers of racism to be greater than they really are.

It is one thing to have a structural analysis, but at the end of the day it is through individual agency that structures can be challenged and reformed. Behaviour is ultimately about agency – first personal and then social. The mistake of the structural analysis of the black predicament in America and Australia is that race has been treated in the same way as class. Race is really only an instrument of class. It is an easy and more convenient marker than others.

Flannel shirts, mullet hairstyles and 'hotted up' cars marked the 'plebs' when I attended private boarding school in Brisbane. 'Rat-tails' and other ghastly markers declared the class identity of their innocent offspring. Race is just more explicit. The privileged college I attended was adjacent to a less privileged high school, and the two main roads from these schools met at a Y-junction that led to the train station and shopping centre. Students from my college – with regulation haircuts, carrying violins and book bags and dressed in hats, ties and blazers – met their nemeses at this junction, in a spirit of mutual contempt. I recall walking down our side of this road one day with some students from my hometown. A group of unruly white kids on the other side of the road, half-dressed in an indeterminate school uniform and long hair, started calling us – who were smartly dressed in blazers and ties – 'Abos' and 'Coons'. After an initial shock, we shouted back 'Plebs' and 'White Trash'. We urged them to 'Get back to Inala', the symbolic home of the lower classes in Brisbane in my youth where, in fact, a large Aboriginal population lived in fibro homes that looked dreadfully similar – but were in fact superior – to our families' fibro homes back at the mission.

I began to learn then that race matters, but it is not destiny. Class matters more, but it also need not be destiny. The most profound debility caused by racism is not the externally inflicted harm, but the internalised acceptance of its power, which can become an excuse. If you want 'black consciousness', it is the consciousness of Bill Cosby, Shelby Steele and John McWhorter that is sorely needed, not the victimhood and false separatism of post-'60s black leadership.

I will finish by setting out some reflections on my experience of driving an agenda of rights and responsibilities in Indigenous policy. By the end of the last millennium, it was not possible to continue in this area without facing up to the gaping responsibility deficit. It was a deficit of which I had long been aware, but the prevailing currents were averse to this particular R-word. Two other Rs – rights and reconciliation – were ruling. I have never doubted the correctness of our claim to rights; I have made a contribution to the struggle for the rights of my people in Cape York Peninsula, and have continued this contribution. Our rights to our traditional lands, to our languages and our cultures, our identities and traditions are a constant part of our work for a better future for our people.

When I decided that we could no longer go on without saying that our people held responsibilities as well as rights, I was not repudiating rights. It was just that all the talk, all the advocacy, all the analysis, all the leadership, and all the policy and politics was about rights. There was no talk about responsibility. So when we talked about child malnutrition, we spoke of the rights of the children and the responsibility of governments, but we didn't talk about the responsibilities of parents. We didn't ask, 'How come children are malnourished?' It can't be because the parents have no money, because in Australia the government provides money to all those who don't have an income. It can't be because there is no food available – there are shops in these communities where the malnourished children live, as well as bush food. There was a widespread refusal even to think about responsibility.

If there had been no practical consequences of our failure to talk about responsibility – and no strong strategic reasons to make a concession to the political Right – then this situation could have continued. But there are practical consequences galore! It is simply not possible to see how any social or economic problem can be solved, or opportunity seized, if we don't first accept responsibility. No progress can be made without filling the gaping deficit.

My view is that the main reason why people have refused (and still refuse) to talk about responsibility is not for strong strategic reasons, but because they actually believe that better health and better education and better housing and better life expectancy and better survival of traditional languages are rights that can be enjoyed if other people – specifically governments, but also the wider society – take the necessary actions to make them materialise. It amounts to this absurdity: my rights depend on you fulfilling your responsibilities to me. Who in world history has ever been saved by anyone in the way we hope whitefellas will save our people?

This absurdity drove my campaign for responsibility and my thesis that we have a right to take responsibility. It is a thesis in which I firmly believe. When it all boils down, the most important right we have is the right to take responsibility for ourselves. The misery we endure and have endured as virtual wards of the state points clearly to the urgent need for our right to take responsibility to be restored to us.

Over the past seven years, our responsibility has led us to tackle the largest immediate problems facing our people: substance abuse and the reform of welfare. We aim to tackle these problems at the level of individual responsibility, because addicts and their addictions, and welfare recipients and their passivity, must be tackled. We also aim to tackle these problems at the structural level: the policy, legislative and administrative structure of the income-support system, and the passive welfare services delivered by governments and non-government organisations. We aim to be radical in our reforms, in that we seek to tackle the root of the problems that we say have caused the responsibility crisis among our people.

We have cut through with our advocacy and our policy analysis. We have contributed to a wider discussion of welfare reform and social disadvantage – problems which are not unique to Indigenous affairs, and certainly not unique to Australia. The responsibility agenda is now ascendant. However, while my own experience of talking with Indigenous people in communities confirms that the responsibility agenda resonates widely, most Indigenous leaders are, at best, silent on it. There is still, I suspect, a yearning for the old paradigm.

The problem is that, with the rise of the responsibility agenda, there has been a corresponding collapse of the rights discourse. While there has been a lot of talk about 'the rights agenda' in Australia over the past decade, there has been no effective leadership, advocacy, policy or strategy. It is not enough to stubbornly keep up the talk. There has to be impact. And in order to have impact, there must be new thinking, new strategies and new tactics. For discourse to penetrate the social and political currents of society, we have to get beyond preaching to the converted and complaining in our in-house forums about the failure of wider forums to take up our cause. Influence is not an equal-opportunity exercise. We have to find new ways to have an impact.

We therefore have an example of 'skewing' in Indigenous policy in Australia. The responsibility agenda is ascending, but the rights agenda has receded. There is at present no effective rights leadership and advocacy. This is not to say there is no competent intellectual analysis of the rights agenda (though I have doubts about the quality of the intellectual ballast supporting it). But there needs to be more than compelling analysis; if we are to find the radical centre, there must also be a capacity to increase the necessary dialectical tension.

Only through synthesis can societies transcend conflicting tensions and take an historic leap forward. My experiences have led me to three conclusions about the prerequisites for such synthesis. First, the political analysis must be right. Shelby Steele has described how faulty analysis can derail promising developments. The twin phenomena of 'white guilt' and a problematically conceived 'black consciousness' prevented the United States from achieving a historical breakthrough that would have benefited all Americans. (I do not subscribe to the quasi-radical analysis that white Americans benefit from the current plight of black Americans.) You have to get the analysis right.

Second, it is not possible for one actor to play several roles in the dialectical process. One person may contribute an overall intellectual analysis, but practical politics and the production of theory are not the same thing. In a socially and economically successful country, there will be competition between rival interests and forces. Some of these represent capitalist principles; others represent communal and socialist ideas; inspired political leaders synthesise these contradictions. It is possible for an individual to have an intellectual appreciation of these different roles but in practice that individual can hardly play all three. Only the primary leaders of a society can 'triangulate', to use the crude terminology of Clinton's adviser Dick Morris. In *Behind the Oval Office*, Morris used the phrase to describe his most effective 'third way' period – from mid-term disaster at the hands of Newt Gingrich's Republican revolution of 1994 to re-election against the odds in 1996. 'Triangulation' involved bringing players from opposing sides to a radical centre on vital issues such as welfare reform. This can only be achieved from the vantage-point of the top of the leadership pyramid. People further down can only advance one side of a dialectical debate.

I and my associates in Cape York Peninsula decided to champion the Indigenous responsibility agenda, because this was then the most under-developed area in the Australian discourse. A side-effect of our decision is that we are seen to represent only the principle of responsibility; in a political and societal sense, we are largely limited to this role, despite our continued work and ongoing practical achievements in securing rights for our people.

This leads to the third and closely related prerequisite for synthesis. A successful synthesis between rights and responsibility will not occur unless the rights agenda is equally strong. Perhaps this was W.E.B. Du Bois's great shortcoming: he had the analysis, but not the capacity to increase the necessary dialectical tension.

Australian Indigenous rights consist of both socio-economic rights (which we share with African-Americans) and rights derived from our distinctive 'peoplehood'. A successful Australian synthesis must reconcile these rights with Indigenous responsibility, and with the interests of non-indigenous Australians. But the Indigenous rights agenda is currently so weak that non-Indigenous Australians seem unaware of the nature of our people's aspirations. This might seem a strange contention almost two decades after the *Mabo* decision on native title, but it is becoming clear that our opponents do not understand our point.

Six words struck me like a bolt of lightning when I read Shelby Steele's book. Reflecting on the decision of boxing authorities to strip Muhammad Ali of his world heavyweight title when he refused to fight in Vietnam, Steel wrote:

> When he said, 'I ain't got no quarrel with the Viet Cong', *even his enemies understood his point* [my emphasis]. Where was the moral authority to ask this black man, raised in segregation, to fulfil his responsibility to the draft by fighting in a war against a poor Asian country?

In Cape York, we recently hosted a senior federal minister so that we could explain our reform plans and seek support for them. The minister was supportive, amiable and intellectually astute. He observed the relevance of our work for his portfolio, and I have no doubt he will support our plans. Indeed, I have no doubt he desires our people to rise up in the world. However, as he left he commended our work but said: 'I just don't understand the Indigenous rights stuff.'

The minister was not expressing conscious enmity or opposition to my people's aspirations. His remark was a symptom of the fact that the Indigenous rights agenda is politically irrelevant. Warren Mundine and I (and many others) are carrying the Indigenous responsibility leadership, but there is no sign of effective carriage of the Indigenous rights leadership. There is also no sign of a primary societal leadership that is interested in finding the radical centre. Tension between rights and responsibilities is therefore impossible, and no synthesis can be achieved.

There is a growing insight in the United States about the nature of their problems – importantly by black intellectuals and leaders – and a successful synthesis of the traditions of Booker T. Washington and W.E.B. Du Bois is likely to emerge. I eagerly await Shelby Steele's forthcoming book on Barack Obama and Steele's views on whether or not Obama has 'the right stuff'.

2007

BARACK OBAMA

Last year, Shelby Steele accepted an invitation to a Cape York Institute conference. Alas, we were dismayed when Steele cancelled his trip. After the announcement of Barack Obama's bid for the Democratic nomination for the American presidency, he accepted a commission to write a book on the candidate and was immediately on a tight time-table. The result, *A Bound Man: Why We're Excited about Barack Obama and Why He Can't Win*, turns out to be a fascinating applica-tion of Steele's theory of post-'60s race relations in America.

Steele's starting point is that a militant ideology, based on griev-ance and a tight cultural and racial unity, has been dominant in black America for forty years. Although the civil-rights movement made the case for ending segregation on the basis of a shared humanity, the politicised post-'60s black movement became an identity movement. This movement, Steele contends, wants black protest to be built into each black person's sense of self, and it 'expects many gestures of affiliation – a liberal politics and Democratic Party affiliation among them'.

In the dominant black political culture, the price for belonging is to give up being fully oneself, to disregard what is universal. Steele bases this assessment on his own experience, which in some respects is similar to Barack Obama's: Steele's mother was white, and he spent his early adulthood working in poor black neighbourhoods. Steele now realises that in his own quest for belonging in the late '60s, he went along with a blackness he did not really believe in, 'searching for authenticity and legitimacy as a black'. He believes that the same quest for authenticity explains Obama's years in community work and his long-term association with his mentor, Pastor Jeremiah Wright.

Steele develops the theory that oppressed groups are forced to use masking strategies to 'offset the power differential that so favours those born to the mainstream'. In the openly racist and oppressive America before the civil-rights struggles, masking was blacks' only means of securing concessions. Steele cites Louis Armstrong: his beaming smile and reflexive bowing, the great musician's way of signalling black inferiority, was the price he paid for a career in segregated America. Armstrong's contract with the white audience was that he would entertain them but not breach the protocol of segregation, and not expose their racism as a matter of prejudice rather than truth.

Today, when blacks have equal rights but much less power than whites, African-Americans employ two main masking strategies: bargaining and challenging. A bargainer makes this deal with whites: I will not use America's history of racism against you, if you promise not to use my race against me. Shelby Steele relates how his first encounters with white people who do not know his beliefs always follow the same script: as soon as it becomes apparent to them that he does not give off coolness or ambient hostility, he senses their relief and gratitude that he is not an angry black.

Challengers, in contrast to bargainers, do not magnanimously give whites the benefit of the doubt. They stigmatise whites as racist until the whites prove themselves innocent. However, both the bargaining and the challenging strategies are premised on white guilt: white innocence is traded for black power. Bargainers grant whites innocence upfront; challengers make whites earn it.

The most successful bargainers, such as Oprah Winfrey, Steele calls iconic Negroes. Iconic Negroes offer absolution for whites, who can experience themselves shorn of racism by identifying completely with an African-American. Obama is, Steele observes, the first to test the special charisma of the iconic Negro in national politics. After decades of racial challenging, white America longs for a bargaining relationship with black America. Obama appears born to answer the call.

A Bound Man purports to explain why Barack Obama, the apparently perfect bargainer, cannot win the presidency; at the time of writing the book, Steele did not even believe Obama had much hope of winning the Democratic nomination. The resulting work is an intriguing failure: the reader is left to deduce why Obama cannot win, because the subtitle is somewhat misleading and the argument to this effect that can be extracted from the book is not convincing.

The Achilles heel of both bargainers and challengers, Steele contends, is that they can 'never concede that only black responsibility can truly lift blacks into parity with whites'. If blacks made this concession, there would be no market for white innocence. Steele believes that Obama has become 'the kind of man who can close down the best part of himself' by internalising 'the first discipline of both bargainers and challengers', which is to deny that 'black responsibility is the greatest – if not the only – transformative power available to blacks.'

According to Steele, Obama works within the current paradigm of race relations – bargaining and challenging – 'to move himself ahead', when he should instead be advancing a new kind of relationship between whites and blacks, or working to end race as a significant issue altogether. Steele exhorts him to go the way of Bill Cosby: to voluntarily give up his status as an iconic Negro and make an argument for black responsibility – and white responsibility. White guilt, Steele has argued in the past, is really the mirror image of white supremacy, not its opposite: it allows whites to regain their moral authority without addressing society's unequal power relations. Steele concedes that Cosby has today lost much of his influence with whites as well as with blacks, and predicts that if Obama made such a move he would lose political capital.

Obama is the first plausible black candidate, Steele says, because white voters recognise in him a bargainer who will afford them the racial innocence they long for. Yet, in order to carry the black vote, Obama sometimes speaks to black audiences employing a rhetoric that would be perceived as racially challenging if the audience were white. Sooner or later, Steele predicts, it will become impossible for Obama to satisfy the needs and aspirations of both his two key constituencies, liberal whites and African-Americans.

Steele's mistake is to assume that the potential tension within Obama's support base is necessarily a fatal contradiction, a dilemma.

All electoral support bases are coalitions of constituencies. It is normal to have fundamental tensions between the policies necessary to build a majority; political winners manage, transcend or resolve such tensions. Steele does not show why Obama would be unable to do that. Obama has, in fact, defied all predictions ever since – as a junior senator with only two terms' experience and the most liberal voting record of any national politician – he put himself forward for the world's highest office. He usurped Hillary Clinton's position as the Democratic front-runner. The Clintons' fundraising acumen among big donors has been dwarfed by Obama's fundraising among ordinary Americans. And Obama, the outsider, has neutralised the Clintons' advantages within the Democratic establishment.

However, in March and April 2008 two so-called firestorms struck in succession: first, Jeremiah Wright and second, his 'bitter' analysis of small-town America. On their own, the events in March constituted a formidable test of Steele's hypothesis: first came news of Jeremiah Wright's extraordinarily vitriolic (for those who are unfamiliar with the traditions of America's black churches, as most white Americans certainly are) sermons; then Obama's 'A More Perfect Union' speech in Philadelphia, given on 18 March in response to the furore; and then the public reaction to that speech. Whilst immediately following the revelations the polls showed a steady flow of Democratic voters to Hillary Clinton, Obama's Philadelphia speech reversed it, and he maintained the lead from then on. Talk about being the pull-the-money-out-of-the-fire kid.

But then Bitter-gate broke on 11 April, when Obama was caught out offering the following analysis of why he was not faring well in the small towns of Pennsylvania to an audience in San Francisco:

> You go into some of these small towns in Pennsylvania, and like a lot of small towns in the Midwest, the jobs have been gone now for twenty-five years and nothing's replaced them. And they fell through the Clinton administration, and the Bush administration, and each successive administration has said that somehow these communities are gonna regenerate and they have not. And it's not surprising then they get bitter, they cling to guns or religion or antipathy to people

who aren't like them or anti-immigrant sentiment or anti-trade sentiment as a way to explain their frustrations.

I believe Obama's problem here is faulty analysis, rather than faulty articulation. The real value of *A Bound Man* stems from the questions Shelby Steele implicitly asks: Would an Obama presidency be worthwhile from the perspective of race relations? Does Obama have the ideas and the policies to oversee a transformative period in which the American republic becomes a more perfect union where race does not define people?

Obama's writings, speeches and previous policies give reason for doubt. His Philadelphia speech was very well received, but it also confirmed weaknesses in his philosophical outlook. He vowed to 'continue the long march' of the 'successive generations who were willing to do their part – through protests and struggle, on the streets and in the courts, through a civil war and civil disobedience' to narrow the gap between the republican ideal of equality and the reality of oppression and discrimination. The main shortcoming of Obama's philosophy is that he does not recognise, as Steele has, that the nature of black Americans' struggle changed fundamentally after the civil-rights victories of the '60s.

I believe that the racial question in countries with oppressed racial and ethnic minorities cannot be settled until the constitutional issue of the minority's rights is properly settled and honoured. In America, the constitutional issues have long been settled. After 1965, when discriminatory voting practices were outlawed, none remained outstanding. Socio-economic parity remained, and remains, a problem; but this must be separated from the issue of constitutional inclusion. The practical effects of racism must also be separated from the formal guarantee of rights.

Shelby Steele's great insight is that America faced a fork in the road after guaranteeing equality in 1965, and the country took the wrong turn. Whites could have said to blacks: You have long taken responsibility, but we failed to respect your rights. You now have rights and you need to continue to take responsibility. And blacks could have said in turn: We will take our rights and we will continue to take responsibility for ourselves, as we did during the days of discrimination. Instead, whites said to blacks: We failed to respect your rights in the past and now you are entitled to them. We now also undertake to take up our responsibilities to you, so that you can overcome the legacy of inequality. And blacks said: We are entitled to our rights and yes, you have a responsibility towards us.

The basic principle informing policies for black advancement should have been: after 1965, black responsibility should and will pay off. Whereas black responsibility before civil rights was mostly a burden, now there arose a chance for black responsibility to yield rewards, because it was accompanied by rights and opportunities. But the post-civil-rights trajectory of race relations in America (as in Australia) took the nation's people down the wrong road, because the wrong deal was made.

Barack Obama understands many things about black responsibility, but on balance his analysis is structural and primarily concerned with the legacy of oppression. While there is now a broad-based group of people – including Obama – who accept that human prospects are affected by both structure and behaviour, people generally fall into one camp or the other. In Obama's philosophy, as in that of his liberal fellow-travellers and those who see themselves as part of the 'long march' for social justice, structural and historical factors are more important than behaviour and responsibility.

Obama's Philadelphia speech failed to speak to black responsibility. (His galvanising keynote address at the 2004 Democratic Convention, which launched the Obama phenomenon, was powerful precisely because he spoke to responsibility as well as to unity.) When he did speak of responsibility in Philadelphia, he did so in a paragraph which the audience would likely interpret as a discussion of class and gender injustices:

> For the African-American community, that path means embracing the burdens of our past without becoming victims of our past. It means continuing to insist on a full measure of justice in every aspect of American life. But it also means binding our particular grievances – for better health care, and better schools, and better jobs – to the

larger aspirations of all Americans: the white woman struggling to break the glass ceiling, the white man who's been laid off, the immigrant trying to feed his family. And it means taking full responsibility for our own lives – by demanding more from our fathers, and spending more time with our children, and reading to them, and teaching them that while they may face challenges and discrimination in their own lives, they must never succumb to despair or cynicism; they must always believe that they can write their own destiny.

I maintain that Obama's Bitter-gate crisis betrayed a fundamental analytical problem rather than one of articulation. Another part of his speech to the San Francisco audience, one which was over-shadowed by the controversy, is telling:

> We've gotta give people a stake in this new economy, because if they don't have it they are going to be angry about it ... and obviously that is true in places like Oakland and ... South Side Chicago ... we've got a whole generation of kids, they don't need to be discriminated against because they're already redundant, they're already forgotten ... and then we are surprised when ... kids are not stupid, they understand when they have been rendered irrelevant and redundant ... and then we are surprised when they resort to the drug trade or violence as a way of shouting out 'I am relevant, I am here!'

This is the kind of (standard leftist) structural sociological thinking that underpinned his analysis of the reasons why small-town Americans cling to guns, religion *et cetera*. Irresponsible behaviour is interpreted as a symptom of, and a protest against, economic restructuring. Obama's worldview is fundamentally structural. In his Philadelphia speech, Obama explained the history of the collapse of black families, also in structural terms:

> A lack of economic opportunity among black men, and the shame and frustration that came from not being able to provide for one's family, contributed to the erosion of black families – a problem that welfare policies for many years may have worsened.

Despite the long debate about welfare reform and the clear benefits, a decade after it was enacted, of President Clinton's *Personal Responsibility and Work Opportunity Reconciliation Act 1996*, Obama still hesitates to accept a social-policy truth that sticks out as plainly as canine testes. My objection is not that a structural analysis and a focus on structural solutions is wrong, but rather that the role of personal responsibility and choice should not be forgotten. Otherwise, you end up with a kind of shallow determinism. Instead, Obama should be working out how to match the commitment to 'work opportunity' represented by Clinton's 1996 act with a complimentary commitment to personal responsibility. A truly radical leadership would be equally committed to expanding the structural opportunities available to American citizens (particularly those in the lower classes) and to equipping citizens to seize these opportunities through individual effort.

A further example of Obama's erroneous analysis is in the explanation he gave in his Philadelphia speech for black educational underachievement. He said: 'Segregated schools were, and are, inferior schools; we still haven't fixed them, fifty years after *Brown v. Board of Education*, and the inferior education they provided, then and now, helps explain the pervasive achievement gap between today's black and white students.' But the achievement gap in black education – as Abigail and Stephan Thernstrom make clear in their 2003 book *No Excuses: Closing the Racial Gap in Learning* – extends beyond segregated schools; it is widespread among the black, college-educated middle class, whose members live in good neighbourhoods and send their children to desegregated schools. To construe the crisis in black education as a legacy of ongoing segregation is to be simplistic about a critical policy challenge for Americans.

Like Steele, I firmly believe that 'black responsibility is the greatest – if not the only – transformative power available to blacks.' And the same goes for the white underclass. The conservative emphasis on personal responsibility and the liberal emphasis on individual choice and self-interest are as important as – nay, more important than – opening up opportunities for social progress. Access and opportunity are necessary but not sufficient for uplift, while personal responsibility and self-interest are indispensable.

Underclass and black uplift: this is perhaps the most intractable of all policy challenges. Lyndon Johnson's Great Society did not materialise. Bill Clinton presided over a strong economy and implemented sensible welfare-reform policies, and yet he made no major inroads into lifting up the lower classes. For me, perhaps the most hapless image of his final six months in power was his attempt to do something belatedly for poor whites in the Appalachians. It was too little, too late; there were no credible initiatives.

Tony Blair, in Britain, was the most active and committed recent political leader in this regard. He understood the problems and seemed to grasp what was needed, but his Labour government's policies for 'social inclusion' were still based on the 'co-ordinated service delivery' paradigm, and they have not produced very impressive outcomes. Andrew Mawson's recent account of the English experience, *The Social Entrepreneur: Making Communities Work*, does not bode well for Kevin Rudd and Julia Gillard's adoption of a social-inclusion agenda in this country. The proposed establishment of a Social Inclusion Board (presumably comprising the usual suspects, such as the Brotherhood of St Laurence and the Smith Family) indicates *prima facie* that the Australian attempt will fare no better.

In 2007 I wrote that Kevin Rudd did the debate about social uplift a great service by returning to first principles and to Adam Smith. Rudd argued that members of the political Right distort Smith's liberalism when they selectively 'speak of the self-regarding values of security, liberty and property'. Social democrats, he contended, are truer to Smith's original philosophy because they do not omit 'the other-regarding values of equity, solidarity and sustainability'.

Yet social-democratic solidarity has its limits: the fate of the disadvantaged can be seen to depend too much on the altruism of the economically and socially integrated mainstream. To put it crassly: poor people need to become at least as greedy as those who are not poor. Until we crank up the engine of self-interest among the underprivileged, we won't get individual, and therefore social, uplift.

Those who are well off and who devise other-regarding policies for the disadvantaged forget that they themselves are well off because of their own self-regard. Politicians of the Centre-Left are particularly prone to this kind of patronising double standard: Mate, I do well with my own self-regard, thank you very much, but self-regard isn't for you; you need everyone else's other-regard, and I'm in government to organise the very other-regarding policies you need.

Barack Obama's response to black and white disenfranchisement has, so far, been to summon up the twin spectres of evil corporate America and special interests in Washington. His challenge is to find a policy framework that indeed seeks to perfect the union and to create the Great Society, but to do this he needs to understand the reasons for the failure of previous attempts – the principal lesson being that government cannot plan and deliver a Great Society. Rather, the sole aim of government should be to allow, indeed to mandate, individuals to take responsibility for bettering their lives, and to provide them with the maximum opportunity to do so.

Shelby Steele writes in *A Bound Man*: 'Despite the fact that [Obama] clearly seems to accept the importance of individual responsibility in social reform … he offers no thinking on how to build incentives to responsibility into actual social policy.' Obama needs to correct his analysis and to move beyond the critical shortcomings of his Philadelphia speech. If that speech gave expression to the dialectical turbulence of America's racial inheritance, then it must be superseded by an analysis which locates and articulates its radical centre. Without learning from the keen analysis of black conservatives like Steele, this centre will elude Obama. I wondered if Obama was referring to Steele in his Philadelphia speech: 'On one end of the spectrum, we've heard the implication that my candidacy is somehow an exercise in affirmative action; that it's based solely on the desire of wide-eyed liberals to purchase racial reconciliation on the cheap.' If he was, Obama simply does not get Steele's critique, which is more substantial and complex than this caricature. He needs to grapple with Steele if he is to break through his intellectual shortcomings.

Obama's candidacy, Steele observes, 'asks the American democracy to virtually complete itself'. If Obama came to grips with Steele's critique he could immunise himself against the full-blown Republican campaign targeting his association with Wright, and the idea that he condescends to white Americans of the heartland. The occasion for a radically revised analysis of the fundamental issues he attempted to address formally in Philadelphia and informally in San Francisco should come in August, when the Democratic National Convention ordains Barack Obama as its candidate for president.

2008

THE CAPE YORK AGENDA

Speech to the National Press Club

My talk today will be about how Indigenous people in Cape York Peninsula can overcome disadvantage.

Our agenda is framed in the language of economist Amartya Sen. Sen considers freedom to be the critical measure of individual well-being. However, his concept of substantive freedom is not simply about the exercise of choice. He incorporates the idea that freedom may be constrained by the range of choices available to people. This range of choices is dependent on our capabilities, or the personal and social resources that we can bring to bear on improving our lives. The end goal of the Cape York agenda can thus be expressed as seeking to ensure that Cape York people have the capabilities to choose a life they have reason to value. Importantly, this agenda does not entail making choices for people, but is rather about expanding the range of choices people have available to them.

This framework exposes the failures of the previous policy paradigm. In the 1970s, it was accepted that Indigenous people in remote areas should be able to choose between a traditionally oriented life and a life integrated with the mainstream. Policymakers with the best of intentions sought to facilitate this choice, but the only capability they seriously invested in was that of income. The policy of the last thirty years sought to create choice by simply providing income through welfare and quasi-welfare systems such as communal housing.

Thus, over the last thirty years, Indigenous people were not supported to develop basic capabilities in important areas such as education, health, housing and employment. Consequently, our people were ill-equipped to take advantage of opportunities in the real economy. The so-called 'decision' to remain in their community was therefore made by default, without any real choice. Our task today is to ensure that remaining in one's own community is the result of choosing between real options.

Without education and a whole set of other capabilities, successive generations of young people, at ages when they would ordinarily seek work, were led away from engaging in the real economy by the poisonous disincentives of the welfare system. Traditional skills were eventually traded for the free stream of welfare, and the communities of Cape York descended into a state of passive dysfunction. Bureaucrats stepped in to arrest this descent and effectively propped up communities. In doing so, they shifted responsibility away from the people in the communities and towards government. Thus began the vicious cycle of dependence that led to the complete disintegration of Indigenous society and culture – the very thing the policies had first sought to protect.

What needs to be done? As a fundamental precondition, we must restore social order, attack passive welfare and tackle substance abuse. But we must also build a range of capabilities to enable real engagement. We must focus on building health, education and community life and on supporting people's efforts to build their lives. And we must get the incentives right, so that people see greater benefit in working and investing in themselves (in their education, health and so on) than in staying on welfare. It is only by doing all of this that we can enrich the choices available to people in a sustainable manner.

To illustrate how these different elements of the agenda fit together, I use a metaphor of building a staircase for Cape York people – a staircase that will give them the chance to climb out of their current deprivation. The construction of the staircase requires three things: a strong foundation of social values and norms; a generous investment in building people's capabilities; and – the steps themselves – a reformed set of incentives. Let me take these in turn.

A strong foundation of social values and norms

The foundation of the stairs of social uplift must be the re-establishment of some basic rules and responsibilities. These include society's expectations of its members in such areas as public order and safety and the care and upbringing of children.

Mainstream Australia has social order. This has a visible component, for example, in law enforcement, neighbourhood-watch groups and so on. But it also has an invisible component in the social norms that influence individual behaviour. These ensure that in mainstream Australia, bad behaviour has consequences.

In contrast, Cape York is operating at a social-order deficit, largely due to a breakdown of social norms. We need to be clear that this deficit is the legacy of our history, of dispossession, trauma, discrimination and the undermining of indigenous leadership and authority. Our people have been immensely scarred by this history: it was what made us vulnerable to substance abuse in the first place. We fell into passivity because in the years following our attainment of citizenship we were alienated from the real economy.

The past is strongly with us in the present. But while we must never forget history, we must also look to the future. Although our inequality and dysfunction have larger structural causes, they are ultimately realised in the behaviour of real human beings – who have the potential for insight, organisation and agency. If you don't confront behaviour – or if you choose to absolve people from their behaviour because you do not wish to 'blame the victim', or because you wish to demonstrate your understanding of the 'structural causes of dysfunction' – then you deny the importance of human agency in confronting disadvantage and inequality and you thereby perpetuate both disadvantage and dysfunction.

Dysfunction has ceased to be just a symptom or consequence of poverty: it has also become a causal factor. A worsening culture of dysfunction has become a major hurdle to marginalised groups' re-entry into the real economy. Most Australians underestimate the importance of social norms simply because they assume that they must exist in any society. But in the absence of social order, leadership and authority, societies cannot prosper. As a prerequisite to accessing the opportunities of the real economy in Cape York, social order needs to be restored – a basic, stable, functioning base must be established as a platform for building opportunity.

A generous investment in capabilities

On top of the foundation of social norms, we need to build the capabilities of Cape York people so that they are in a position to exercise meaningful choices. To combat the lack of capabilities in Indigenous communities, policy has traditionally targeted the most obvious source of incapability, namely the lack of income. This has been done primarily by providing welfare payments to individuals who are unable to work or who cannot find employment. However, over time, as material conditions have improved to some extent in remote Cape York Indigenous communities, wellbeing has actually declined.

Sen's concept of capabilities helps to explain this apparent paradox. First, as Sen notes, poverty needs to be understood to be a broader issue than simply lack of income. It is, more fundamentally, a lack of opportunity to exercise meaningful choices. An approach that relies primarily on redressing a lack of income will never be wholly successful if other constraints on opportunities remain unchanged.

The solution is clearly not to cut support altogether, but instead to redesign support so that it builds capabilities rather than reinforcing passivity. Let me be clear: the Cape York agenda will require more external expenditure, not less, at least in the short- to medium-term. But we can commit that this additional expenditure will be more effective in the future – because we will commit to increasing our responsibilities at the same time.

A reformed set of incentives

Together with a strong foundation of social norms and investment in capabilities, we need to make sure that people have the right incentives to ascend the staircase. If these incentives are rational, people will make choices that build their lives. This is why I have been so critical of the passive welfare state. It creates perverse incentives that tell sixteen-year-olds that it is better to go on the dole than to finish school, or that tell parents they will receive money irrespective of their child's wellbeing and educational participation. The structure of income-support payments in Cape York has set up a poverty trap; these perverse incentives actually encourage people towards welfare and away from real employment.

Apart from depriving people of a real income, unemployment has other, more serious, effects that cannot be ameliorated, and indeed may be exacerbated, by long-term income support. These effects include psychological harm, loss of motivation, skills and self-confidence, an increase in sickness and the disruption of family and social life. Welfare payments should instead be structured to support and encourage earning or learning. Where they do not, other obligations must be attached to payments so that they benefit the community.

Again, let me emphasise that this is not about cutting overall support for communities. I am acutely aware that Indigenous people in Cape York are amongst the most disadvantaged in the country. I come from such a community, and the people whom I love and care for the most suffer from disadvantage. But we must investigate innovative ways to ensure that support is not inducing passivity. We must ensure that it is really going to support the children for whom it is meant. Unless we ensure that policy is targeted at economic development and capability building, we will simply condemn Indigenous Australians to remain in the poverty trap of welfare dependency.

The metaphor of the staircase may provide some fresh insight into why our agenda has so often proven to be so difficult to categorise in conventional political terms. Our focus on social norms has an inherently conservative flavour. But we also emphasise the critical importance of supporting capabilities – and this has a distinctly social-democratic flavour. Then we talk about incentives, the steps that allow people to choose to build their own lives; this has a distinctly liberal flavour. So our agenda has elements of the three great traditions of political philosophy that underpin contemporary Australian public-policy debate.

This is not an attempt to be all things to all people. Instead, it is simply a matter of basic necessity. These themes – norms, capabilities and choice – are the basic foundations of any functioning society. The idea that everyone should have the capabilities to choose a life they have reason to value is part of the basic political fabric of mainstream Australia. This is evident in the Australian Labor Party's platform, which talks about the 'ability to exercise and enjoy the fundamental human rights to which all Australians should be entitled.' And it is evident in the prime minister's stated desire for 'an Australia where an Aboriginal child – whether born in a remote community or in one of our cities or in regional centres – can grow up and reach their full potential in life.'

This basic capacity to exercise substantive freedom should be common to all Australians. It should be truly sad to all of us, in a country as prosperous, as free and as full of opportunities as Australia, that any group of its citizens should have such little real choice as do Indigenous Australians. Nevertheless, it is the reality. We need to recreate the basic fabric of society and let Indigenous Australians enjoy that freedom. We need to be as educated as you, live as long as you, have the same access to real jobs as you.

Despite its seeming simplicity, this pursuit of basic freedom for Indigenous Australia is a radical change from the past. We characterise it as being in the radical centre because it challenges the vested political interests of both Left and Right. We ask both sides of politics to concentrate first on building the basic fabric of economic and social life – reserving the right to disagree on how policies should be framed once that basic fabric is established.

For communities, the path to rebuilding this basic fabric will require them to take a long hard look at how their community functions at a basic social level. We will have to look beyond our traditional homelands to engage in the mainstream Australian economy, all the while not forgetting who we are and where we are from. Communities will have to examine and reconcile some of the tensions that inevitably arise when a change in the economic base occurs. Ultimately, to be viable, these communities will have to be clear about their attitudes to work, to mobility, to outside investment and to mainstream Australia. Communities will have to commit to do things differently – radically differently.

At the same time, mainstream Australia will need to examine its attitudes. State and Commonwealth governments will have to seek out boldly the right policies and incentives to encourage our communities to develop. Getting those new policies right will require some radical thinking and a radical re-assessment of current policies. Government will be challenged to transfer some responsibilities to the individual and to the community. We recognise that there are risks both for government and for communities in this.

We propose to the federal government that communities such as those in Cape York ought to be able to volunteer for a 'New Deal' on welfare. Communities that want to fundamentally restructure the incentives in their communities, that want to build enabling institutions and invest in infrastructure, and that want to develop new social norms that will underpin social order should be given the space and responsibility to do this.

We believe the 'New Deal' could have the following elements. First, it would be a trial and would apply only to those communities that 'opt in'.

Second, communities would be able to go beyond conventional welfare reforms and determine new criteria for receiving welfare payments, including CDEP (Community Development Employment Projects), Newstart, Abstudy, the Family Tax Benefit and the parenting payment. These criteria would be designed to avoid the poverty traps that currently exist and to create more incentives to take up work.

Third, monies paid to families must go towards the wellbeing of the family, and there must be mechanisms to ensure this happens.

Fourth, CDEP must be designed to add value to the community while never becoming an unemployment trap, or a trap for community organisations who derive most of their funding from the program. In this trial, we cannot ignore the current funding and administrative arrangements between government and communities. These raise issues which must be resolved.

Fifth, we must look at the prerequisites to economic development, including land tenure, telecommunication, infrastructure and so on, and make changes and investments that will promote economic growth.

Sixth, we must consider legislative change to allow for increased responsibility and decision-making at the community level. Recently,

Halls Creek in Western Australia made national news by making welfare conditional on whether children attended school. Despite bipartisan and community support, and encouraging school-attendance results, the program was halted because its legality was called into question. We will have to confront laws and programs and, where necessary, secure changes so that responsibility can be held where it is due.

I believe that if we commit to these steps, we will see positive change in short order. Our belief is that the direction is clear – we are now looking for support to carry it out. We want a radical new deal, and we want the rules to be different because we need the rules to be different. We want the ability to opt in, and once in, we want the freedom – the responsibility – to make the hard changes.

If, at the end of the day, all that is offered to us is tinkering, we will see failure, and, what's worse, we will see the perpetuation of the Aboriginal 'problem' for as long as we avoid dealing with it.

2008

THE WELFARE PEDESTAL

Welfare reform is justified on various grounds. One aim is to increase Australia's prosperity by alleviating the cost of welfare, widening the revenue base and facing up to labour shortages. Another is the moral mutual-obligation argument: the idea that welfare recipients are indebted to taxpayers.

I don't much care for these two motivations. The argument that animates my insistence on welfare reform is that it is in the best interests of disadvantaged people. My advice to the federal government on welfare reform is simple: we need maximum pressure on people to work and the fairest reward for working.

Australian debate is too much focused on where to draw the poverty line. Disadvantage is not the same as poverty. I would like to define disadvantage as a high likelihood that dependency will become permanent and intergenerational. There are many households where no-one is working. Eight hundred thousand children are growing up in such households. For many of these families, welfare dependency becomes permanent and intergenerational. No amount of income support will get these families out of their disadvantage. The only way out is through participation in the economy; plainly, work.

Some people of working age have medical and other valid reasons why they are not in the workforce. Able-bodied people who are not working fall into three general categories. In the first are those who have a work ethic but have lost their jobs – or have never had a job – for reasons beyond their control. In the second are those who choose to remain on welfare, or to move on to welfare when they come of age, because the rules make it a rational choice to do so. A third category includes those whose outlook and behaviour have been severely affected by their experience of the widespread welfare-dependency in our society.

The first aim of welfare reform must be to facilitate the return to work of those in the first category. Second, welfare reform must involve creating incentives for the people in the second category to go to work. Third, welfare reform must effect cultural and behavioural change among the second and especially the third category.

There should be consensus on these aims of welfare reform. There is not. Why? The reason is that society is divided between those who believe that unemployment and disadvantage are principally structural problems and those who believe these problems, to a significant extent, are behavioural.

The welfare lobby and those left of centre have a predominantly structural view and dismiss any explanation based on personal behaviour as 'blaming the victim'. Their general view is that almost all able-bodied people who are not working – including single parents – fall within the first category I discussed above. They argue that non-working people do not have a behavioural problem, and that government is responsible for ensuring that there are jobs available. They do not think that my second and third categories, or the question of incentives and entrenched dependency, are serious issues. On the other side is the anti-welfare lobby, which has a predominantly behavioural view. While it supports government compelling people to work, it believes that opportunity-creation must be left to the market.

I believe that most ordinary Australians intuitively take the middle ground in this. They understand the structural dimension of unemployment and disadvantage and that these powerful influences can often overwhelm individuals, families, entire communities and even governments (that is, in the case of retrenchment, family breakdown, the collapse of traditional industries and recession, respectively). They understand that we need a safety net to assist those individuals who are overwhelmed by structural effects beyond their control.

But they also understand that there is a behavioural dimension to work and disadvantage. They understand that welfare support can turn into welfare dependency over time. They understand that dependency affects people's outlook. They understand that personal responsibility and obligation are key elements, and that these are corroded by long-term dependency. They understand the relationship between dependency and social problems.

Those committed to welfare reform, from the Centre-Left and Right, know that in our country not everyone falls into the first category of people ready and willing to work if only there were opportunity. Michael Raper, from the National Welfare Rights Network, argues that the egregious problems of family breakdown and substance abuse that afflict my people in Cape York Peninsula may justify implementing the policies that I advocate in my home region, but they do not justify such policies for mainstream welfare. It is up to those who care for the disadvantaged in places such as Macquarie Fields in Sydney to decide whether Raper is right or not.

I say he is wrong. It is true that in my community, most of the unemployed fall within the second and third categories that I have discussed; the incentives need to change fundamentally and there must be high pressure for people to work because we now have a significant, entrenched behavioural problem. While places such as Macquarie Fields may have significant numbers of people who fall within the first category – people who will readily work if they have the opportunity – I would think that they also have many people who are unemployed because the rules make welfare a rational economic choice. The truth is that this amounts to a choice to accept disadvantage as a permanent condition, which one can look forward to passing on to one's children.

When my people were shifted out of the cattle and other rural industries in the 1960s, our resulting unemployment was caused by lack of opportunity. The government's response – passive welfare – was wrong. Three decades later we have an entrenched behavioural problem. The difference between my region and the most disadvantaged mainstream communities across Australia is not race; it is time.

2005

*

As part of the process of developing our ideas for reforming the way the welfare system works in Indigenous communities, I have been having discussions with members from some communities in Cape York Peninsula about what motivates the life choices our people make. A central conviction in our thinking about welfare reform is that economic incentives are very important, because they motivate many of the choices individuals make about their lives and those of their families. Incentives matter. Incentives matter more than has been acknowledged in the history of Indigenous policy-making.

But what about culture? It is true that culture matters: Indigenous people's cultural traditions and values and their social relationships and obligations strongly influence the choices they make. For example, what the anthropologists call 'demand sharing' – where sharing with certain people is not an individual choice but an obligation – is a compelling institution in Indigenous societies that I know. Individual choice is a powerful engine for social progress, because it is when individuals choose to improve their lives that change happens. Collectives cannot motivate in the same way that individual choice can: this is the great contribution of liberal thought to the understanding of human behaviour.

However, in addition to the freedom to choose, development also requires that people have the capabilities to choose. Young people living in remote communities in Cape York Peninsula who are victims of a criminally disastrous education are not truly in a position to choose. The apparent decision to live a more traditionally oriented life in their remote community without benefiting from participating in the real economy is not the product of true choice. It is the product of no choice.

There is a longstanding policy assumption in this country that Aboriginal people are primarily motivated by culture; that our people are somehow different from other Australians in that we are immune to economic incentives and are instead creatures of culture. Because of the predominance of this 'cultural man' assumption, I approach discussions with community members about economic incentives with some trepidation. It seems crass to talk about how individuals are motivated by material gain or, to put it more bluntly, money.

In my search for a means to explain the role that economic incentives play in motivating the choices our people make, my most effective metaphor is an ascending staircase of ever-increasing material gain. Yes, the dollar signs I put on each step of the staircase of opportunity do look crass. But I am struck by how immediately understandable this concept is to community members. They say 'Of course' when I ask whether individuals in their lives are making calculations about prices. They have never heard of, but they get what I mean by, 'price signals'. They know that individuals are making calculations and making choices, and that where the money goes, there goes the man.

I explain that the increasing prices (representing personal income) as you ascend the staircase are not set by government, but by the marketplace. I explain that the only prices that are not set by the market are those at the bottom of the staircase. These prices are welfare prices, set by government. The price on welfare is higher than the starting price of real work in the real economy.

Immediately upon my illustration of this metaphor on the whiteboard at a public meeting in my hometown, a grandmother at the meeting referred to 'that pedestal that our young people are sitting on'. She dubbed what we have come to call 'the welfare pedestal'. The pedestal acts as a disincentive for people to progress upwards, as they must first take a step down before the process of climbing the staircase can begin. There is a bundle of payments that act together to form the welfare pedestal. One of these income-support programs is CDEP. CDEP was intended to be a stepping stone to a real job. In reality it has become a permanent destination.

In remote communities everyone is guaranteed easy, relatively well-paid part-time work on CDEP. Young people on CDEP face several disincentives against taking up an entry-level real job or traineeship. Their hourly pay rate would initially fall. They would have to conform to the discipline and discomforts of mainstream work and training: they would need to triple their work hours, and perhaps relocate. Most people who have spent many years on CDEP are no more ready for real work than when they started.

At the Cape York Institute, we are analysing the relative attractiveness of the welfare and work options open to people in remote areas. We are paying close attention to the incentives of youth and young parents at key junctures in their lives. We have found that the incentives for remote students to commit themselves to study, training or work are weak or negative. The first problem is that remote school students have limited knowledge about the choices available in the modern economy. When asked what they want to do in the future, too often a child in Cape York Peninsula will answer: 'I want to work on CDEP.'

2007

*

In an article about the Aurukun rape case, academic Marcia Langton wrote, 'It would be a fair bet that each of the adults who pleaded guilty to raping this child was receiving a government social security or Community Development Employment Program payment. It is difficult not to draw the conclusion that dysfunctional Aboriginal behaviour is financially supported by government funding.' Langton identified the nub of the problem in remote communities: government funds dysfunctional behaviour and there is no connection between what a person or a community does and the income they receive. Money for nothing – passive welfare – is in the long term corrosive.

The other explanation that has been offered for the social breakdown in remote communities is government under-investment. Anthropologist David Martin said this week that Aurukun has been 'abandoned and neglected'. 'By any measure,' Martin said, 'Aurukun is hugely under-invested in by government in terms of all the things we know are essential to civil society: decent health, decent education, decent housing, decent food, law enforcement.'

I agree that government investment should have been greater and must increase. However, those who attribute dysfunction in remote communities mainly to government under-funding must answer this question: For people who live in a welfare economy, can increased government service-delivery compensate for the total absence of the kind of incentives and signals that in the mainstream economy inform people's behaviour and form their personalities into functional citizens?

I maintain that it cannot. Mainstream Australians – with jobs and mortgages – can hardly imagine what is like to live in a community where personal behaviour carries no rational consequences. In remote communities, people's behaviour makes no difference to their circumstances; irresponsibility elicits almost no reaction from government or community. The situation in Aurukun is the direct opposite of mainstream Australians' experience. In the mainstream, people's efforts directly determine their circumstances; this is what enables them to become functional, affluent people. They take this for granted to such an extent that it has taken them many years to understand what is missing in places such as Aurukun.

I and other Cape York people have advocated a fundamental change from unconditional to conditional welfare. There are many more dimensions to our reform agenda, but putting in place some basic, universal obligations for adults who receive income support through the social security system is key. When everything in a person's life is provided by someone else and nothing is expected in return, you set in place an economic and social system of taking and no giving. Then you add alcohol to the mix and, later on, drugs. And you keep giving them money for free. So that recipients can pay for food, shelter and necessities, but increasingly, as addictions grow, the money is allocated to grog, drugs and gambling. And you do this in a society where what the anthropologists call 'demand sharing' is a strong part of the cultural system: people in kin relationships cannot resist sharing their consideration and possessions. But it's not barramundi or wild honey that is shared; it is money for drinking, drug taking and gambling. Unconditional welfare plus addiction plus demand sharing: you have all the ingredients for social disintegration and the abandonment of responsibility.

For this analysis we have been accused of blaming the victim. But, as Langton pointed out, remote Indigenous people are victims of dehumanising government policies. The worst of these policy failures is the total disconnect between income support (including CDEP), which is mainly federal, and government service-delivery, which is mainly provided by the state government.

The Family Responsibilities Commission, which is the centrepiece of the social reforms that the Cape York Institute has suggested to the Australian and Queensland governments, is intended to remedy this fatal systemic flaw. The FRC will be charged with making decisions about whether welfare recipients are fulfilling their obligations. We have recommended that four obligations be attached to welfare payments. In short:

1. Each adult who receives welfare payments and is the parent or legal guardian of a child should be required to ensure that the child maintains a 100 per cent school attendance record (other than explained absences).
2. All adults must not cause or allow children to be neglected or abused.
3. All adults must not commit drug, alcohol, gambling or family-violence offences.
4. All adults must abide by conditions related to their tenancy in public housing.

Our plan provides for a retired magistrate to chair a panel in each community. The panel would including two senior elders from the community and would hold individuals accountable to their families and especially to their children.

We proposed that the Queensland government create the FRC (the Howard government allocated funding for its operation) because this body would need to work closely with state government agencies such as the departments of education and child safety.

Let me illustrate how the FRC is intended to work by explaining how it could have intervened in the dysfunction that led to the rape of the ten-year-old Wik girl. If the FRC had been in place before the girl returned to Aurukun from Cairns, it is possible the gang rape would not have occurred. The mother of the girl might have been referred to the FRC for failing to meet one or more of the obligations outlined above. If the girl did not have a 100 per cent school attendance rate (a reasonable assumption), or if she was unsupervised by her mother and not kept safe, then the mother would have been referred to the FRC. The issuance of a child-protection order and the subsequent removal of the girl from Aurukun would also have triggered a referral of the mother to the FRC.

Assuming the mother was referred to the FRC, the two local elders and the retired magistrate would then have been able to refer her to support services to address her and her family's challenges. Such services might include as a program to improve her parenting skills, alcohol rehabilitation, or assistance with money management. A case manager would also have been appointed to provide support and advice to the mother, and to assist the FRC. The FRC could also have referred the girl (reportedly intellectually impaired) to appropriate mental-health services.

The FRC could also have redirected the mother's welfare payments to a responsible adult who would care for the girl. Alternatively, the FRC could have redirected the mother's welfare payments to our proposed conditional income-management regime, whereby the family does not lose the benefit of its income. Rather, the FRC would determine that the welfare payments must be spent on essential expenses such as food, rent, bills, medicine and education.

The FRC would also have been able to intervene in the cases of the alleged perpetrators. The parents of the younger perpetrators would have been referred to the FRC if their boys did not have a 100 per cent school attendance rate or if they were left unsupervised and not kept safe. Likewise, the adult perpetrators would have come to the attention of the FRC if they had breached alcohol or violence laws. The FRC could have referred these parents and adults to support services.

We anticipate that the introduction of the FRC would result in local Indigenous authority being rebuilt, the essential expenses of children being met, welfare payments not being spent on grog and gambling, parents taking increased responsibility for their children, and positive social norms being restored with regard to issues such as education, child neglect and alcohol abuse.

The first thing we need the Queensland premier, Anna Bligh, and Prime Minister Rudd to decide on at next week's Council of Australian Governments meeting is which of their governments will legislate to establish the FRC at the first parliamentary session of the new year. There should also be a decision to prepare legislation for introduction at the first session of whichever parliament is going to have carriage of this legislation. The Aurukun Shire Council is committed to these reforms. I look forward to the ending of the intergovernmental blame-game at next week's COAG meeting so we can start tackling the problems at Aurukun.

2007

ORBITS

Two of my maternal grandfathers, each of whom I would call *Ngaji* in our Kuku Yalanji language, and great-uncle in English, served in the battlefields of Europe and the Middle East in the First World War.

Brothers Norman (1888–1970) and Charlie (1890–1966) Baird were fathered by a Scotsman, Robert Baird, a tin miner, pastoralist and one-time mayor of Cooktown. Unlike most white men who fathered Aboriginal children, Robert looked after his two sons, who grew up at China Camp on the Bloomfield River, north of the Daintree. The brothers therefore received an English education as well as a Kuku Yalanji education in the bush.

Charlie enlisted and left for Egypt in 1915. Norman enlisted in 1917 and served in France. He returned to Bloomfield and is probably the most illustrious Yalanji person in the colonial history of this people. The brothers were two of an estimated 300 Indigenous servicemen during the First World War.

The Anzac tradition has gained an increased devotion among contemporary Australians, but it is a tradition from which the country's Indigenous people feel estranged. I do not know of any of Norman Baird's descendants who have attended an Anzac Day memorial. Norman's two elderly daughters, Polly Fisher, seventy-six, and Annie Kulka, seventy-eight, still live at Mossman and have numerous children and grandchildren. At this week's launch of Kathleen Denigan's biography of Norman Baird, *A Spark Within*, my brother Gerhardt, as chief executive of Balkanu Cape York Development Corporation, presented replicas of Norman's war-service medals to his daughters. Norman's descendants are proud of him.

However, there is an inconsistency between non-indigenous Australians urging Aboriginal Australians to 'put history behind you' and that famous lapidary reminder: Lest We Forget. Reconciliation raises the challenge of how this country deals with its histories and accommodates its traditions. One sign that reconciliation has begun will be the inclusion of Norman's descendants in the Anzac rituals.

Despite his national service, like other Indigenous servicemen, Norman returned to a country that did not accord him the same rights as his fellows. Although as a young man he had remained outside the purview of the Queensland legislation that provided for the removal of Aborigines from their families and their homelands and their confinement to missions and settlements, in his post-war life he was under constant threat of removal to that notorious destination, Palm Island.

Norman resisted the removal of Yalanji people from their homelands. He was considered a troublemaker and vigorous efforts were made to remove him. He often had to elude the authorities when attempts were made to force his family's removal from Bloomfield. One of his sons, Joseph, was removed to Yarrabah Mission near Cairns at the age of ten. Norman was not to see him again for another ten years, when he applied to the authorities to allow Joseph to visit him. Despite this treatment, Joseph later served his country in the Second World War, as his father did.

In 1935 the deputy chief protector of Aborigines in Queensland sent an 'Order for the removal from Cooktown to Yarrabah of a half-caste aboriginal named Norman Baird' to the minister for signature. In the removal order, the deputy chief protector mentioned allegations that Baird had threatened other Aborigines. But the first and main reason given in the order was that Baird 'exercises a considerable amount of control over the natives in the district. His control, however, is not conducive to the other natives [sic] welfare as he compels them to support him and also to give warning of the approach of the Police at any time in order that any native sought by the Police can be allowed to escape. He has also interfered with the employment of aboriginals on fishing vessels'. The removal order included a caution that 'this half-caste is particularly intelligent'.

Especially surreal is the Yarrabah superintendent's contribution to the exchange of letters concerning Norman's removal. On the one hand, the superintendent wrote that 'Norman is a returned soldier with a wife and several children, and I have always heard him very well spoken of.' On the other hand, the superintendent wrote that 'it would be better if he were removed to some place very much further off [than Yarrabah], for I am sure that he would not settle here so near to his own country.'

It is clear from his long struggle with the authorities that Norman felt his war service entitled him to respect as a citizen and he felt his people were treated unjustly. Despite this, during the Second World War he again enlisted to serve the country, a country in which his son had been taken from him against his wishes.

Norman's agitation of the authorities through the course of his life caused me to reflect on this fact: it is not possible for people who serve in national wars not to develop a sense of entitlement to proper citizenship. No greater commitment can people show to their nation than service in the armed forces. I am at one with Samuel Johnson, who famously averred: 'Every man thinks meanly of himself for not having been a soldier.'

As well as his steadfast advocacy for the needs of his people and his resistance to their maltreatment, Norman Baird was concerned about the survival of the language and culture of his Yalanji people. He compiled the first word list of Kuku Yalanji and translated many hymns and Bible stories. A linguist who worked with Norman, Lynette Oates, remarked that he was 'the only Aborigine I have spoken with who was fully bicultural and fully bilingual'.

Oates's formulation – 'fully bicultural and fully bilingual' – is precisely the vision that we have as the objective of our Cape York reform agenda. It is about the ability to walk in two worlds. To prosper, Aboriginal Australians will have to be integrated into the national and global economies. But we also want to remain distinctly Aboriginal and to retain our connection with ancestral lands. How we can avoid economic integration becoming a one-way ticket taking the young away from their origins, a prospect many parents and community elders dread? As a solution to this problem, I have introduced the concept of 'orbits'.

Even though Norman travelled and worked in other areas, he retained a strong link with Kuku Yalanji country and spent much of his life there. His example shows that it is possible to choose to maintain an Aboriginal identity and, at the same time, to be completely able to interact with modern society. His published writings and letters reveal a high level of education, and non-Aborigines said he 'conversed as an equal'. He was a person who would have been able to travel in orbits of the kind I envisage.

But his knowledge and patriotism – on behalf of his Aboriginal as well as his British-Australian heritage – did not save him from the oppression my people endured when we lived under the protection legislation. The fate that almost befell Norman was eerily similar to the fate being suffered by Stalin's victims at the same time as Norman's removal order was signed in 1935. Loyal service to one's country counted for nothing, the reason for the persecution was ridiculous and it was impossible for the victim to counter the charge. And as the descendants of some of Stalin's victims still live in Siberia, Norman's descendants might still have lived on Palm Island had he not used his knowledge of Kuku Yalanji country to avoid the authorities. Norman steered clear of the police until a decision was made that the removal order be 'held in abeyance'. His descendants therefore live in relative happiness in Kuku Yalanji and Guugu Yimithirr country instead of in dysfunctional exile.

At the launch of Norman's biography, one of his descendants and a young leader of the Yalanji community at Mossman, Matthew Gibson, said he had read the book and felt that 'there was a lot to learn from in the life of Norman Baird'. Matthew is dead right. Norman Baird was the first modern Kuku Yalanji and should be a model for our people's future.

2006

*

296   NOEL PEARSON

As Australians have confronted the depth of the social and cultural breakdown in remote Indigenous communities, there has been a growing discussion about their very viability, and whether these communities should continue to exist.

The previous government, especially under former senator Amanda Vanstone's Indigenous ministry, started to articulate and implement a policy that sought to grapple with the question of the viability of remote communities. Measures were introduced that discouraged decentralised settlements, otherwise known as outstations or homelands.

The viability of remote communities is an important discussion, but it is not one that can properly be led by senior bureaucrats and politicians. We must never forget that the congregation of Aboriginal people into settlements such as those on Cape York Peninsula was not by the choice of the people themselves. These missions and settlements were created in the wake of the dispossession and dispersal of Aboriginal people from their traditional lands. They were often repositories for the tens of thousands of children removed (yes, stolen and rescued and every imaginable permutation in between) from their families, and many thousands of adults who were forcibly removed to places like Palm Island.

Then there was the mass relocation of Aboriginal families from cattle stations following the equal wages case in 1965, when the actual result was not a better industrial outcome for Aboriginal station workers but their near entire removal from the industry. Removed from the only work they had (and loved) and from their traditional lands to live life on unemployment benefits in the settlements and on the fringes of country towns.

There is an ahistorical tendency in contemporary policy discussions about Indigenous communities. As if the problems of these communities are not themselves the product of earlier 'in the best interests' policies devised by bureaucrats and politicians. It is far too late in the day for arbitrary decisions to be taken to (once again) forcibly relocate Aboriginal people to where the latest policy now says is best.

While Aboriginal people are right to insist that they make the decisions about the future of their communities, the policy questions involved are of legitimate concern to the rest of the country and therefore to governments. The plight of children and families in these communities – ravaged by the perfect storm of grog, drugs and gambling addictions meeting passive welfare and cultural demand sharing – is the business of all Australians. No longer can human suffering continue behind the veil of closed communities, and no longer can real action be deterred by appeals to self-determination, if self-determination actually means not facing up honestly to the problems and taking urgent action where it is needed.

There is an increasing suggestion in the contemporary debate that remote communities are not viable, and that Indigenous people should relocate to the centres of economic growth. I have two responses to this view. First, pushing remote people into urban areas wouldn't work. Indigenous people in Cape York are in large part behaviourally disengaged from the real economy, and live in families and communities that are dysfunctional to varying degrees. Passivity is a major reason for this disengagement. If our people were pressured into relocating to urban centres, then they would just end up joining our counterparts in the dysfunctional (white, black and migrant) underclasses in the cities and regional centres.

Second, the answer to the question 'Is this community viable?' depends, I suggest, on whether, after improving education and mobility, people choose to maintain their community by maximising local development opportunities and removing passive welfare. There is uncertainty as to the choice that community members will ultimately make. There is no guarantee that young people from my hometown, after receiving an education and gaining the capabilities to be mobile, will choose to return home. They may do so later in life. They may never return at all.

There is no absolute answer to the viability question. It is entirely possible that highly educated consultants could live in remote communities and provide their services to the outside world, linked through information and communications technology. No matter how economically marginal the location might be, a high degree of education and skill could still make living in such areas viable. While this example is the extreme possibility, it just underlines how conditional viability is. The fewer local development opportunities there are, the more important education and mobility become to the viability of the remote communities concerned. This is completely counter-intuitive to the prevailing policy thinking.

In any case, it is hard to see how any remote communities will be able to realise their local development opportunities without education and mobility. After all, there are many other communities on the planet that are located in very hard places: as hard as any remote community in Australia.

2008

*

Last Sunday night I drove the five hours from my hometown in Hope Vale to Cairns, unaware that there was a debate raging about whether I was proposing to revive the stolen generations policy by sending children packing to boarding schools down south. I had spent the weekend camping with my mother and family, hunting a species of migratory fish called *gaalnggaan*. At this time of the year, the men and boys of Hope Vale are out with their spears, hunting *gaalnggaan* as they run along the beaches or shelter on the side of the mangroves at high tide.

I have done this routine every year since I was old enough to be on the tiller for my father as he stood at the front of the boat with his spears. After primary school in Hope Vale, I was a boarder at St Peters College in Brisbane, to which I had been sent by decision of my parents and by opportunity provided by the Lutheran Church and the federal government. I looked forward to the school holidays.

Almost all of the Indigenous people from remote Australia who have succeeded in education and gone on to make leading contributions on behalf of their people were educated at boarding schools – often a long way from their homes, most often at church schools. In Cape York Peninsula, no Aboriginal tertiary graduates have come from local public secondary schools.

Boarding schools are an old and well-established idea, going back to the 1960s for the people of our region. It is on this past practice – its successes as well as its failures – that we base our policy in Cape York Peninsula: scholarships to high-quality, high-expectation secondary schools down south. The allegation that Indigenous children attending boarding schools represents a repetition of the stolen generations is just silly.

A more serious fallacy is that you can provide quality secondary education in remote communities. Attendance at high-expectation boarding schools has declined in the past twenty years in favour of attempts by governments to provide secondary schooling in our communities. This experiment has failed profoundly and the remnant secondary facilities should be closed down. It is a matter of scale: with small student populations, it is impossible to provide the teachers and specialisations required to deliver a proper secondary education. Only in regional centres, such as Cooktown and Weipa in Cape York Peninsula, can a credible case be made for providing secondary education facilities. However, schools in these regional centres would need to be fundamentally reformed if they are to produce Indigenous tertiary graduates. Thursday Island State High School is testament to the fact that this can happen.

Another fallacy – expressed by Peter Holt from the Hollows Foundation – is that boarding should be rejected because students risk suffering cultural loss. First, I have as good a knowledge of the history and languages of my communities as any of my peers who never left Cape York – because of education. My advantage is that I can enjoy the best of both worlds. I can speak the Queen's English and Guugu Yimithirr. Second, Aboriginal communities are disintegrating socially and culturally because of passive welfare and substance abuse. Unlike all other government policies that are being implemented in remote communities, high-expectation education offers opportunities. A life in which you are stuck with limited opportunities in remote communities is not conducive to cultural maintenance.

A more substantial objection to increased boarding concerns racial and class prejudice. But Indigenous students will face these problems wherever they are – whether at high school in a regional centre or at a private boarding school in a capital city. This underscores the need for schools to understand the reality of this problem and to support their

Indigenous students. This is what Clayfield College in Brisbane has done so well.

Another real concern is the high drop-out rate of Indigenous students from boarding schools. However, white and Asian youngsters suffer from homesickness as much as black children. If students do not find a place in the school community where they can gain a sense of achievement and recognition, then homesickness will be a fatal problem rather than the normal kind of feeling one has for hometown and family. The principal driver of the low retention rate in boarding schools (and secondary schools generally) is the fact that the students entering secondary school at Year 8 are not up to standard. While they have nominally completed Year 7, their literacy levels are around Year 3 or Year 5 at best. If you are in a Year 8 classroom and you are really at Year 5 level, then you are going to struggle to fit in and your chances of ultimate success are poor. There is a fundamental and widespread underachievement problem in primary-school education in remote communities. That is why another of our policies in Cape York Peninsula is closing the gap between Year 7 in Cape York and Year 8 at secondary schools down south.

There is no practical alternative to primary schooling being provided in our own communities. We have to fix up primary schooling if we are to fix up the retention of Indigenous students in secondary school. This is the greatest challenge we face, to which we are now turning our attention.

2004

THE INTERVENTION

Indigenous Affairs Minister Mal Brough telephoned me fifteen minutes before he and Prime Minister John Howard made their announcement of a national emergency response to protect Aboriginal children in the Northern Territory. He took me through the measures the federal government would be taking.

I thought to myself: 'Well, mate, if you think you had your work cut out for you in Cape York, then this is going to place you in the national firing line.' While the plan is a necessary development, there are risks associated with the bold line of attack announced by Brough and Howard. My assessment is as follows.

The focus on grog and policing is correct, but as well as policing there must be a strategy for building Indigenous social and cultural ownership.

Making welfare payments conditional is correct, but the Howard–Brough plan needs to be amended so that responsible behaviour is encouraged. Responsible people shouldn't just be lumped in with irresponsible people.

The land-related measures are clumsy and ideological, but they are not an attempt at a land grab, and the problems with them are nowhere near as high a priority as action for the welfare of children.

There is a huge implementation challenge. Based on the performance of the federal and provincial bureaucracies up to now, I am not confident they are up to it. The Council of Australian Governments' trials in the past five years have not delivered meaningful results.

This is not my plan. It is the federal government's plan. If it were up to me I would do some things differently. But I am not the government and, like everyone, I have to deal with the realities as they are, not how I would prefer them to be.

A few simple questions lead me to the view that decisive action is needed. First, is the situation of children's welfare in Indigenous communities in the Northern Territory and the states a situation of national priority? We have just had the Anderson–Wild report on the Northern Territory. Similar reports have come down in recent years in Queensland, New South Wales, South Australia and Western Australia. No-one denies the situation is a national priority.

Second, is the situation with children's welfare one of national emergency? Child protection is not like poverty or educational under-achievement or general socio-economic disadvantage. Time and deliberation can be taken when considering solutions to these large structural problems. But what do you do when a child is being subjected to abuse this very day? What do you do when a child is likely to be abused next week? What do you do when the abuse is going to happen the week after next? What do you do when there are scores of children involved across the communities, the states and territories? If it were your child at risk of this suffering, would you think this a matter of emergency? This is not a moral panic. The abuse is real. This is not a media or political beat-up. Something has to be done to relieve the suffering now, not in six months, not in two years. Now.

We can't rehabilitate people from alcohol or drug dependence immediately. We can't fix the poor education immediately. We can't fix up the poor health immediately. But we must stop the suffering straightaway. Everyone, from the prime minister to his bitterest opponents, focuses on the fate of the children. No-one can escape this fact: the fate of the children is the bottom line.

Whatever one thinks of Howard and Brough, their strategy is justified on these grounds. If not Brough and Howard's plan to stop the suffering, then what alternative plan should be pursued? Here most of the critics fall into a deafening silence. They have vociferous views about what will not work, but they are silent about what will work. So the sum total of their response – 'we don't need missionary paternalism again', 'prohibition doesn't work', 'Indigenous people must consent to the changes', 'we need more government services', 'we have to provide rehabilitation', 'we have to deal with intergenerational trauma', 'we have to deal with things in a holistic way' – is inaction and procrastination while children's lives continue to be ruined. It is not that the points made by the critics are wrong – they are often correct – but their criticism does not translate and often cannot be translated into action.

I believe the government's proposal will make a difference in the short term. If one accepts that the proposed measures will save women and children this year, then the bottom line is this: rejecting the government's emergency measures equates with giving priority to some other issue before rescuing the children.

Even where extremely concerted responses have been implemented, such as the new child-safety regime in Queensland, which has made significant improvements to the child-protection system, we are a long way from stopping the abuse. All we have now is a new system to respond to abuse: we don't have a system to prevent the abuse. There are still about eighty child-welfare notifications a month across the communities of Cape York. About thirty of these are substantiated. Of the remaining fifty, there is a lot of doubt as to whether the assessment bar is too high. Officials (such as school principals and health workers) who are obliged to report cases of suspected abuse or neglect are often perplexed as to why particular cases are not able to be substantiated.

One leading principal from a school in Cape York told me: 'I fill out these reports in as objective and straightforward a manner as I can. I have a statutory duty to report accurately what I see. Unless a child is bleeding, it's very hard. There is a delay in time before the child-safety people arrive. They don't see what the teachers see.' A retired principal from my hometown who served at the primary school in the 1980s, having read my account of the problems at Hope Vale, wrote to me recently: 'You have spoken, Noel, of the sexual assault and unlawful intercourse with minors. It concerned me back in the '80s, when a Year 1 boy was playing truant through fear. He was being sexually assaulted on his way home from school by his Year 8 uncle.

'Painful as it was for me and for the mothers of these kids, I had to bring it to their notice. There was great shame and unwillingness to accept, and a wish to sweep it under the mat (through fear of community reaction, I presume, and especially that the occurrence was known to a white person). I left the matter for them to clean up, as I saw my brief was to keep the children safe, not to stir up trouble in dominating the community.'

I think about this fearful boy. I don't know who he was. I would doubtless know him if his identity were revealed. If he is still alive he is probably between twenty-six and twenty-nine. What has he become since Year 1? Has he turned into an abuser? What has his uncle, who must be between thirty-three and thirty-six, done since Year 8? Did he continue to abuse this nephew or other children? Did something in his own childhood lead to his behaviour?

Queensland may have the most concerted governmental response to child protection anywhere in Australia, but we are still talking about a system that deals with abuse and neglect after it has become a problem. We are not talking about a system that prevents the abuse or neglect before it becomes a problem.

Does the fact that Howard and Brough's plan is politically motivated make it unsupportable? Does the fact that there are electoral calculations underpinning this manoeuvre make their proposed intervention wrong? Of course not. I could not care less if the plan is accompanied by political motivations. If the plan is aimed at providing relief from suffering then this has priority over everything. Whether Howard or Kevin Rudd ends up being the prime minister of the next parliament is not worth two cents in my calculation compared with whether we have a plan that can cut through immediately.

Grog and policing are the most urgent priorities. The Anderson–Wild report makes clear, as if we did not already know, that there is a direct connection between the epidemic of grog and drug abuse and the neglect and abuse of children. It was the hapless mother in a small community called Grassy Narrows in Ontario, Canada, who told a social scientist who wrote about parallel problems in indigenous communities there more than twenty years ago that these addictions are 'a poison stronger than love'.

We have always known grog is a problem for our people. But to know that grog is a problem is not enough. Because we have plenty of problems. We have plenty of explanations for our problems. We have plenty of proposed solutions. The question is: what emphasis, what strategic priority, what urgency, what focus do we give to grog? If you acknowledge that grog is a problem but you don't make it a priority, then it is likely you will do nothing about it. This is the story of Aboriginal policy and Aboriginal leadership in this country. We have all said that grog is a problem, but we have not given it the emphasis or priority or focus it needs for us to get on top of it.

Take the Royal Commission into Aboriginal Deaths in Custody. It mentioned grog as a significant problem in the story of over-representation of Indigenous people in custody. But it did not bring grog into relief. It did not make a confrontation with grog a principal target of policy and action. Grog was just one of a long list of underlying factors. But there are factors and there are factors. Some factors are primary and need to be tackled as such. Grog and drugs must be seen as primary factors.

We are paying the price for the intellectual and policy failure of those royal commissioners of seventeen years ago. The only worthwhile outcome was a report compiled by Marcia Langton, of the commission's Aboriginal issues unit, chaired by Patrick Dodson, called *Too Much Sorry Business*. This was the only intellectually worthwhile output from that entire wasteful enterprise. Its discussion of grog as a primary problem is as fresh as the Anderson–Wild report just handed down, but it did not play a central role in the royal commission's final report and recommendations. So seventeen years of the connection between grog and child abuse goes by unrecognised by policy. How much of today's problem could have been avoided had we got the thinking and the policy right back then?

The Howard–Brough plan to tackle grog and to provide policing is correct. However, the plan needs to be amended so that there is a concerted strategy to build Indigenous social and cultural ownership. Howard and Brough need to understand that the challenge is this: we must restore Aboriginal law in these communities. We must restore Aboriginal values and Aboriginal morality in our communities. Aboriginal law, properly understood, is not the problem; it is the solution. When I say Aboriginal law, I do not just mean the laws that prevailed in our pre-colonial classical culture. I mean our contemporary values and expectations about behaviour. The old law did not deal with grog, drugs, gambling, money and private property. These new things have represented a fundamental challenge for Aboriginal culture. Many communities have struggled to apply the values that underpinned their traditional law to these new challenges. We have not met this challenge successfully. We desperately need to.

Some communities have articulated an Aboriginal law that deals with the new challenges as well as the old. Many communities have strong social and cultural norms dealing with the old challenges, but they are hapless in the face of the new challenges. What does Aboriginal law have to say when relatives want money for binge drinking?

Howard and Brough will make a historic mistake if they are contemptuous of the role that a proper and modern articulation of Aboriginal law must play in the social reconstruction of Indigenous societies. I support their determination to end the suffering.

2007

*

Paul Keating's most lethal ability was being able to identify the essential vulnerability of his political opponent, to needle and manoeuvre, and to drive the dagger into the opponent's heart. In public life, people necessarily accumulate armour, and the essence of a person's weakness can lie hidden under protective layers of real strength and bravado.

The carnivorous nose for the chink is what set Keating apart as a political killer. It was a key weapon in a vivid repertoire, more impressive because it was all employed toward that most noble of ends: the public good. It enabled Keating to achieve a politics-to-policy conversion rate unequalled in Australian public life.

Keating's destruction of John Hewson in the lead-up to the 1993 election is Australian folklore. Less known is that the Kim Beazley essential weakness – that he lacked the ticker for the top job – was identified by Keating long before John Howard delivered his fatal analysis.

Don Watson invited me to launch his biography of Keating, *Recollections of a Bleeding Heart*, at a Sydney Town Hall packed with acolytes, Labor luminaries and the media. After my long and probably tedious lecture, which Mark Latham would later complain in his diary was inappropriate for a book launch, Keating rose to take the microphone in darkest and barely restrained dudgeon. It had been uncertain whether the subject of the biography would appear at all. I stood beside my mate Don while the man we truly adored gave a variously erudite, humorous, vicious and thoroughly mesmerising black performance. I could feel the biographer's flesh being surgically pinned to the wall, with no room even to squirm in protest. It was like watching a sea hawk pin its kill with its talons, slicing a live fish into still-quivering sashimi. Don's biography is an Australian masterpiece, but I have never asked him whether it was worth those fifteen minutes.

To be on the receiving end of a scarifying Keating vivisection was to truly know political combat. I experienced that same gasping, involuntary compression of the solar plexus when the team of Indigenous negotiators led by Mick Dodson and Lowitja O'Donoghue told the nation that negotiations with the Commonwealth government on the Native Title Bill had broken down. That day, 8 October, 1993, was dubbed Black Friday. It was the acuity of Keating's riposte that cut to the quick.

Keating reached for the essence of our collective weakness when he said, at a press conference responding to our own: 'I am not sure whether Indigenous leaders can ever psychologically make the change to decide to come into a process, be part of it and take the burden of responsibility which goes with it. That is, whether they believe they can ever summon the authority of their own community to negotiate for and on their behalf. I am not sure whether we would ever reach the stage where the Aboriginal community would have said that this bill is fine. In fact I don't think that it was ever possible and I have never looked forward to it; even though I would like to see it, I don't think it was even likely.'

My first reaction to the scalding observation was to grasp for that perennial Indigenous charge: he can't say that, that's racist. But it was the truth that burned.

Two weeks ago, the Cape York Institute hosted a conference with Australian and international guest speakers on the theme 'Strong Foundations: Rebuilding Social Norms in Indigenous Communities'. This followed the completion of our report to the federal government on proposed welfare reforms for Cape York Peninsula.

Treasury secretary Ken Henry declined to patronise us when he made the following remarks: 'If you want to be involved in the development of policy, you really are going to have to get a lot better at the job of policy advocacy. Of course you are a minority group in Australia. There are extraordinarily effective political minority groups in Australia. The most effective minority group I know in Australia is the pharmacy guild. Much more effective as a group than Indigenous people.

'It's your responsibility to actively engage yourselves in the development of policy: to come up with policy ideas and articulate them in such a way that the case is absolutely compelling, so that every politician feels under pressure to implement your idea. And if you don't, you should not be at all surprised to see governments coming with their own ideas, and implementing those ideas where they perceive a crisis situation to have emerged.' The conference coincided with the federal government's intervention in the Northern Territory.

The most momentous presentation did not attract the attention it deserved. In a similar vein to Henry, Marcia Langton challenged the audience with an analysis of the dramatic political events that were unfolding hourly, but her comments distinguished themselves from the statements of other Indigenous leaders and non-indigenous champions of reconciliation.

Many people have expressed some or all of these objections to the government's intervention policy:

The government's primary motivation is the next federal election, not concern for Aboriginal children's welfare.

The government has a hidden agenda of taking control of Aboriginal land.

Strategic intervention should build on approaches that are already working, instead of draconian measures that will fail if there is no community ownership of the policies.

Some of the interventions will do more harm than good.

Langton did not need to dwell on these issues in her speech. She has struggled against all forms of racism for decades. It is well known where she stands on land issues, in particular the acquisition of and defence of communal land.

She cut to the chase: the non-conservative Indigenous and non-indigenous peoples' failure to take sufficient political and practical responsibility for social order in Indigenous communities made the recent intervention by conservative leaders inevitable. Of course the conservative leaders would ultimately intervene, Langton explained, and it is hardly surprising that their plan is shaped by their conservative ideology.

I have supported the federal government's intervention in the Northern Territory. If Queensland Premier Peter Beattie had not already tackled the supply of grog (legislation requiring alcohol-management plans was enacted in 2003), had not radically overhauled and reformed its child-protection system (Queensland's new child-safety system was introduced in 2005), and had not increased its policing effort in Indigenous communities (before the Northern Territory emergency, the Beattie government had allocated twenty-nine additional police in its 2007 budget), then I would be supporting federal intervention in Cape York Peninsula as well.

This is my two-step reasoning for supporting intervention. The first step is that you have to know what happens in these communities week in, week out. Urban-based critics simply do not know the realities. Neither did 90 per cent of Australia until recently. There is now no excuse because there has been a major exposé and official reports in almost every jurisdiction. The second step in my reasoning is that once you have knowledge of the realities, you must find its continuation unacceptable. Therefore, you support intervention. By all means, we can argue about the kind of interventions that should be undertaken, but two things are not negotiable in this discussion.

The first non-negotiable point is timing: action had to be taken immediately. There is no time to waste when children and adults are not living in safe environments. Clare Martin's Northern Territory government had already wasted six weeks before making the Anderson–Wild report public. And they didn't even have a plan at the end of their procrastination. The second non-negotiable point is that there had to be a primary focus on safety and the restoration of social order by increasing police services and controlling the 'rivers of grog'.

I have been accused of being unfair to those whom I accused of naysaying intervention to assure the protection of children. My most cogent criticism has come from someone whose record on questions of Indigenous social dysfunction and courage in devising practical solutions is unquestionable: Marion Scrymgour, a senior minister in the Martin government. In its first term, the Martin government was leading Indigenous policy reform in this country. John Ah Kit, Peter Toyne and Scrymgour were pushing fundamentally important agendas aimed at the restoration of social order in Indigenous communities. The laws relating to petrol sniffing were far ahead of Queensland's and I wrote to Beattie urging him to pass similar laws. I hoped they would lead the way with measures such as compulsory treatment for addicts, so that Queensland would follow for the benefit of our people in Cape York. I do not follow politics in the Northern Territory closely, but it seems that the reform momentum was not carried through into the second term. In relation to the Alice Springs town camps, Martin put more energy and political angst into combating *Lateline* and the federal Indigenous-affairs minister, Mal Brough, than into addressing the problems that had been exposed.

While I admire Scrymgour, it is disingenuous to characterise the coalition of anti-intervention spokespeople and organisations as being involved in anything other than naysaying. The fact is, the Canberra press conference they held in response to the government's announcement must be seen in its political context. Whatever the nuances of the individual participants' various positions on the intervention, the political reality of the moment was that they represented the following view: the federal government was wrong to intervene on child abuse in the way it had.

Scrymgour and I both support social order and land rights. Both of us would prefer there to be no need to prioritise one over the other. But if political circumstances became such that one was forced to prioritise, I would place social order ahead of land rights. That others see the dilemma as a stark choice between the two is evident in the statement by the South Australian aboriginal-affairs minister, Jay Weatherill, on 5 July: 'The communities have consistently said they will not sacrifice land rights for human rights; they will not sacrifice hard-won land rights to get something they should be entitled to, that is, a basic level of shelter and housing.' But has it really come down to such an intense dilemma? Or are Pat Turner's 'Trojan Horse for land grab' claim, and Greg Phillips's allegation that it is all an alibi for seizing uranium, overstatements?

Of course the land problem is being overstated. I have constantly asserted that the Howard government's one failing in Indigenous policy is that it has Tourette's syndrome on some ideological questions. I find the land provisions clumsy and ill-conceived; the problems with them have more to do with workability than with undermining land rights. If there is a 'land grab', then land is principally being grabbed to enable Aboriginal families to obtain private leasehold title for housing and businesses. We are waiting for the Beattie government to provide the same for communities in Queensland.

The problem with the naysayers in relation to child welfare is that they want to delay decisive action. And the actions that they propose are not decisive at all. Our mob may be steeped in the politics of Indigenous communities, but we are not so practised in politics. A psychological incapacity to step up to politics in mainstream Australia is one of the reasons why our people continue to lose in this country.

For a range of reasons, Keating's pinpointing of the psychological constraints on our leadership is still true. A few years ago, Keating gave wise counsel to a group of young Indigenous people aspiring to leadership when he told them that our mob have to get past the politics of moral indignation. In my darkest hour, consumed with febrile hatred for the Howard government in the lead-up to the 1998 election, following our harrowing battles in defence of native title during the ten-point plan, Keating gave me wise counsel: 'Don't get mad. Get even.' He also told me: 'Don't hold on to shit that doesn't work, or is in the past. Move on.'

The principal psychological problem of Indigenous leaders is their bitterness about the Howard government and its history over the past decade. Our progressive non-indigenous supporters can afford to devote all of their energies to willing the New Jerusalem – after all, even a conservative government looks after them, notwithstanding their contempt – but our people cannot afford this indulgence. We have to deal with the government and the politics of the day and devote our maximum energies and talents towards making good of things that otherwise seem bad.

2007

JOBS AND HOMES

Are inadequate housing and overcrowding the cause of the social chaos and abuse in my hometown? I may placate my critics if I say yes, but there is no necessary causal connection between overcrowded housing and under-investment in infrastructure, and abuse. There are many places in the Third World where large extended families live cheek to jowl in cramped and miserably poor housing, and there is no violence, incest and chaos. Many of the world's poorest people are strong in family life and socially rich, even if they are materially poor.

Poor and overcrowded housing do relate to many health problems and many social tensions. But it is to engage in denial to say that sexual and other violence against one's own people is the consequence of governmental neglect of housing and infrastructure needs.

The honest answer is that the source of the abuse I described is grog and drugs. The epidemics of grog and drugs, and the chaos and breakdown of social and cultural norms that they have occasioned, have resulted in people abusing their own kith and kin. Does this mean that overcrowding and insufficient governmental investment in housing and infrastructure are not major problems? Of course not. There is massive need and government investment needs to be vastly increased. But if we invested the $2.3 billion that has been estimated as the shortfall in Indigenous housing provision tomorrow, we would make little progress with social problems. Without fundamental policy changes, this investment would be wasted and follow the previous decades of investment.

The reform agenda we propose for Cape York Peninsula proceeds from a different analysis of housing from that of people who see over-crowding and under-funding as the principal problems. Whilst we agree that these and other issues such as poor construction and inappropriate design are relevant, we believe that the poor state of housing is also attributable to the behaviour of the householders. Good houses are too rapidly turned into bad houses. Public housing on Aboriginal land lasts between ten and twenty years, compared to fifty years in the mainstream. The short lifespan of houses reduces the number of habitable dwellings. The causes of the destruction of Indigenous homes include passivity (people don't value what has been delivered as passive welfare) and the collapse of responsibility.

Indigenous families must have skin in the game if we are to move from passivity to responsibility. This means home ownership. The welfare housing model introduced into Aboriginal communities thirty years ago was a poor and inappropriate model. It has been characterised by: perpetual tenancy; a mixed record of tenancy management by Community Council landlords, who lose nothing because there is always the next government grant; insufficient rental rates; poor rental collection; and poor maintenance of stock. This model has deteriorated to the point that we see today. Houses that cost a bomb to repair. Houses that have a short life. Families who expect to be provided with a replacement house after the present one disintegrates.

Before we turn to housing on Aboriginal lands, we should first acknowledge that home ownership off Aboriginal land – in the mainstream – is an outstanding success. The Indigenous home-loans program previously administered by ATSIC and now administered by Indigenous Business Australia has resulted in over 12,000 homes being owned by Indigenous families across the country.

You compare these privately owned homes to the houses rented by families, black and white, from welfare housing organisations. The contrast is profound. Privately owned homes are well maintained, the owners do not allow large numbers of people to create over-crowding problems, there is pride and all of the benefits that flow from owning one's own home. Furthermore, you compare these privately owned homes to the housing rented on Aboriginal land, and the contrast is even more marked. Welfare housing on Aboriginal land is an irrational disaster.

Mal Brough should work with Indigenous housing organisations on programs to privatise their housing stock for the benefit of Indigenous families, and to vastly increase the home-loans program and push the revolution forwards. There should not be waiting lists of people seeking loans. By all means get away from welfare housing and move people into home ownership, but don't be miserable about funding.

As for housing on Aboriginal land, let me make two things clear about my views. Firstly, community members should obtain long-term leases, for example ninety-nine years, from communal land trusts, on which they can own their own homes. There is no question of Swiss-cheese holes appearing on Aboriginal land as a result of foreclosure, because the land would remain inalienable outside of the community.

Secondly, this limitation on alienation outside of the community would mean that no real property market can be created in relation to housing on Aboriginal land. Houses will be largely unrealisable assets, more valuable as homes than as real estate.

A home-ownership program must therefore take into account the affordability of homes in a situation where construction costs are high and incomes are low. It must also not promote economically irrational decisions; families may be better off investing their capital into realisable assets off Aboriginal land, whilst understanding that the decision to live on Aboriginal land is not a costless choice.

2007

*

Speech on the signing of an agreement between the Commonwealth minister for Indigenous affairs, Mal Brough, and the Hopevale Community Council, 12 May 2007.

Three weeks ago I drove down the streets of my hometown. The community had transformed the place. The streets were clean, the lawns manicured, the buildings painted. It was a stark contrast to the Hope

Vale I described in my piece in the *Weekend Australian* earlier this year. I had been torn up by my article – written in a state of visceral emotion – because whilst there was no denying the reality it described, I felt strongly for the shame and distress it caused my people. I know that it would have been easier and preferable for my family had I not written what I did. It placed people under tremendous pressure. It placed my relationship with my own people in the crucible, and I didn't know what would become of my relationship with my home-town. I am a patriot of my community, and many would read contempt rather than love into my words.

I came to attend a ceremony for the signing of a new agreement on welfare reform initiatives, focusing on home ownership, between the Commonwealth government, represented by Mal Brough, and the Hope Vale Community, represented by Mayor Greg McLean. Several hundred Hope Vale residents were present. There was a protest by some community members. Particular reference was made to my description of the community as a 'ghetto', a 'war zone' and a 'hellhole'. An explanation was demanded of me. This is what I said:

'Thank you very much to the traditional owners for welcoming us here. I am in the controversy business, unfortunately. It would be so much easier not to be in the controversy business. I could only take on those things and say those things and only argue those things that people readily support, and I have done that in my time. If I were here to say that Aboriginal people should be free from discrimination, we would all support that, there would be no controversy. If I were here to say that Aboriginal people should have their land and be respected in relation to their land, there would be little controversy. If I were here to say that Aboriginal people should recover the wages stolen from them by government, there would be no controversy. If I were here to say that Aboriginal people's rights and entitlements should be respected by government, there'd be no argument. I'd be a hero. People would pat me on the back, and I've had many pats on the back for doing those very things.

'But my hard message is one that angers, that distresses, that annoys, that upsets. But I can't apologise for it, because I have some messages about the very Hope Vale that I'm proud of too. I'm proud of this place and I love this place, and I love the people. There're no people on the face of this planet whom I love more dearly than the people of my hometown. But I can't say things that are going to make everybody happy, because there're some things that we all have to challenge each other about. There are some things we all have to challenge each other about. And I don't retreat while kids are suffering. And I'm not going to let the carpet be swept over kids not getting the right treatment from their parents.

'You know *nganhthanun* [our] people here in Hope Vale, our people here in Hope Vale were a forthright people. We were a forthright people. You didn't have to be the father of someone to tell somebody they were doing the wrong thing. You didn't have to be the grandfather of someone to hold them to account. You didn't have to be a relative of someone to tell kids to go home. The Hope Vale of yesteryear and the Hope Vale that we at a later time grew up in does not resemble the Hope Vale of today.

'Driving into town this morning, seeing the beautiful streets, I've not had a feeling like this for a long time. I've not had a feeling like this for a long time. But I can tell you that you have within your reach here in this community the potential to be great again, the potential to live up to the achievement of your grandfathers. Because at the moment we are an embarrassment to their heritage. We are a pale moral shadow of their original achievement. We are a pale shadow of their achievement. They didn't have two cents to their name, but they never neglected their children. They never had ten cents to rub together and they brought up their children and sent them to school.

'Everybody knows the seething undercurrent. Why do you think the government is taking eighty children per month to the child safety department from across Cape York Peninsula, including from this community? And you think I am going to sit back? Sorry, I am not yielding to anybody, because this is as much my home as yours. I am not going to allow my grandfather's and godfather's achievements to just be washed down the toilet. There's got to be some leadership. There's got to be community leadership. We can't all be gutless. We can't all agree that there are these problems, and not have the courage to deal with them.

'Yes there are issues to do with traditional ownership and there has to be respect for the *Thuubi Warra* [traditional owners], there has to be respect for the *Gamaay Warra*, there has to be respect for the *Dingaal Warra*, and we historical people who benefited from being hosted by the *Thiithaarr Warra*, we have got to show respect to them. Yet at the same time all of us have got to take responsibility as well. And I won't be yielding to anyone about the definition of Hope Vale's future. This is my place. Half of those kids there are my grandchildren. And if there's nobody willing to stand up and speak for them, I'm sure as hell not sitting down.

'I have absolutely no animus for those people who feel uncertain, who've got lots of legitimate questions, who feel that they have not been apprised of all of the necessary information. But there's got to be leadership. There has to be leadership and Gregory, I want to say that you have shown a leadership in these recent months and years the like of which we have seen too little of in recent decades, the like of which we have not seen enough of. I didn't think much of your rabble-rousing before you became mayor, down the street. But when you became mayor, Gregory – you're my younger brother – your father's spirit rose in you. You're not perfect, but I can see the spirit of your father, who has a generous concern, a tender concern for the future of this community. And I don't say this to suggest that we all don't share this concern. But we can't just have the concern and not have the guts and stand up for it. We can't just say we're concerned about that last kid that was taken off to Cairns to be placed in foster care when we're too gutless to do anything about it. I'm here for a confrontation with our problems. I'm here for a confrontation with our problems, and I will yield to nobody. You can have your say to the media and to Mal Brough and to the government, you can put your point of view and I will put mine, with no apologies.

'I think there are fantastic opportunities with this agreement that Gregory has spent so much of this energy in bringing about. We've got to have home ownership, we have to increase the number of homes available. I've got nephews, nieces in this place who are about to start young families in this place. They need homes, they need to set a foundation for their kids here to have more opportunities than I've had, and I tell you the opportunities available to me: I don't have to come here and stress myself in front of my community and get nailed to the cross. I could be living large somewhere else, because of the opportunities that come from education and from your parents' concern to send you to school and teach you obedience – amazing things can come out of that. We've got to lift our expectations, we've got to stop being low class in our outlook for our kids.

'So I'm going to say, Greg, you've shown a leadership against a strong wind, and Godspeed to you for your efforts. You're not a perfect leader and neither am I, there are many legitimate things to criticise about yourself and me. But I can tell you, with today's agreement, there is the real potential to solve the housing problem for the people of Hope Vale. But it's going to involve new rules. The new rules, the new rules are no more handouts. No more handouts for nothing. And if you think that's just my rule – sorry! It's the way Mal Brough thinks, it's the way John Howard thinks, it's the way people are thinking about these things all over the planet. In France, in Britain, in America, in New Zealand, everybody is moving from handouts to a helping hand up.

'And the one thing that has destroyed our heritage has been the handout. Our elders, when we came into our citizenship forty years ago, they wanted a hand up. Imagine if the government had given them a hand up instead of a handout! We would have sailed, because we had people with moral standing, with a hard work ethic, and responsibility in their veins. But the big mistake that was made was that we got a handout instead of a hand up. So the new availability of housing and business opportunities for this community, for the traditional owners, for the rest of the communities, these new opportunities are not going to be available on a basis of a handout, they are available on the basis of a hand up. You do your bit, you'll get the support of the government and the council.

'So I want to say once again, I have absolutely no animosity, I have no animosity for anybody who has legitimate and febrile concerns about rapidly changing circumstances. But I'm afraid there are some issues that we all agree can't be swept under the carpet. I'm here to tackle grog, I'm here to tackle drugs, I'm here to tackle gambling, I'm here to tackle neglect of children. That's my policy. I'm against those things. I'm against abuse of grog, drug use, abusive gambling and neglect of children. And I will argue till Kingdom Come about the correctness of those positions and the need for action. Thank you.'

2007

*

First question: who most needs to be encouraged, whether pushed by obligation or pulled by incentives, to take jobs when they're available? Answer: society's most disadvantaged and needy people.

Second question: who would benefit most from taking jobs when they're available? Answer: society's most disadvantaged and needy people.

Third question: who are government leaders and policy makers least willing to encourage into jobs? Answer: society's most disadvantaged and needy people.

It is this senseless contradiction between the answers to the first two questions and the answer to the third that explains why Indigenous Australians represent such a disproportionate number of those who languish in poverty. It also explains why this situation will continue as long as the contradiction is not resolved.

When the issue is laid out like this, the proper policy is a no-brainer: it is the most disadvantaged and needy who most need to take available jobs. The problem with the commonsense notion that jobs – not welfare – are the only way out of poverty is that it is counter-intuitive to our notions of social compassion and empathy. It is intuitive for us to excuse the most disadvantaged from the need, let alone the obligation, to take jobs. But it requires little commonsense to expose the problems with our social intuition. We just end up allowing the most disadvantaged and needy to remain in poverty – courtesy of our gracious compassion.

You want to talk about social injustice? The unemployment rate of Indigenous Australians is a gross injustice, especially in a prosperous country. The welfare reforms of the Howard era were not sufficient to bring the benefits of jobs to the most disadvantaged and needy families. And I see no appetite in the Rudd government for anything more than fiddling with the issue. If anything, the Rudd government's approach is to ameliorate the 'harsh' aspects of the Howard-era reforms. I have seen no desire to succeed where the former government failed.

Enter Andrew Forrest. One of the country's most successful industrialists, Forrest has initiated an idea without parallel. The extraordinary feature of the Australian Employment Covenant is that Forrest and his private-sector colleagues are setting the goal of guaranteeing 50,000 jobs for Indigenous Australians. It cannot be overstated how fundamentally this opportunity changes the landscape.

Governments and other organisations have tried to support Indigenous people, in manifold ways, into a life of training and work. Many organisations have pushed to connect Aboriginal jobseekers and employers. Some organisations have moved hundreds or thousands of Indigenous people into the real economy. But the promise of 50,000 private-sector jobs may make a strategic difference to the socioeconomic status of all Indigenous people, remote as well as urban.

Including dependents, this offer corresponds to a normalised life, at least in economic terms, for 200,000 people – a bit less than half the Indigenous population. If successful, the covenant would solve the most urgent problem: namely, that vast regions of Indigenous Australia are dominated by passivity and exclusion. There is much more to reconciliation: land issues, symbols, culture, language, business development, fighting substance abuse, housing, health and education. But the comprehensive transfer of working-age people into the real economy is the key to closing the gap. Without this change, other gains will not last.

In effect, the covenant offers to do most of the governments' work for them. It is therefore the duty of governments, especially the federal government, not to squander this opportunity. However, the opportunity will be squandered unless the government takes stronger – and ultimately more compassionate – measures to encourage people off welfare and into the jobs that will become available.

It would be possible to proceed with the 50,000 jobs initiative without legislation, and on the basis of policy commitments alone, but I believe the initiative would not then penetrate deep enough into the unemployment problem in Indigenous Australia. An Australian Employment Covenant Bill is needed to give legislative structure to this initiative. Legislation would provide a single reference point for employers, workers and potential workers, and give people confidence that such an opportunity is reliable and protected.

Three sets of measures are required to ensure a broad-scale take-up of the covenant. First, we need to make a job opportunity a very attractive thing for an unemployed person or family. A 'work opportunity package' for individuals who sign up to the covenant would provide support and incentives to move into work, and a pathway to home ownership if that is what the individual chooses.

Second, we need to introduce stronger measures to push a person off welfare and into a job opportunity. Specifically the 'ninety-minute rule' needs to be amended. This rule says that a person is only obliged to take a job within a ninety-minute commute, which renders the rule virtually meaningless for remote residents. The government should legislate to exclude people aged under twenty-one from this rule. The effect would be the meaningful introduction of the 'earn or learn' policy Kevin Rudd promised before last year's election.

Third, the government should introduce measures that safeguard against welfare reversion. There is a real risk that an individual will take up a job opportunity only to drop out after a few weeks or months. Participant drop-out would not only be bad for the individual participant, but would cause a drop in employer confidence in taking on Indigenous people in the future.

The Rudd government is to be commended for its reconciliation policies. In two areas – symbolic reconciliation and addressing social dysfunction – the government is showing its mettle, most recently by staying the course on the radical Northern Territory intervention program. In a third area, an opportunity has now appeared that no government could have created. Will the government do what only a government can do to allow the Australian Employment Covenant to shift the centre of gravity of Indigenous Australia from the welfare zone to the real economy? The Rudd administration will ultimately be judged on this.

2008

OUR PLACE IN THE NATION

PEOPLEHOOD

Judith Wright Memorial Lecture

We live in the age of peoplehood. We usually do not reflect on the fact that it is quite remarkable that large collectives, such as the Australian settler culture with its Anglo-Celtic origins, exist. Individuals know only a few dozen or a few hundred members of their own culture well, but they nonetheless strongly identify with millions of people who share their ethnicity, most of whom they will never meet. My ancestors quite recently lived under circumstances where the people they strongly identified with numbered not more than hundreds. Each individual knew or had met most other individuals who spoke the same language. Such was life in all parts of the world in ancient times.

The British evolutionary anthropologist Robin Dunbar developed a theory that has been influential in business management, anthropology and other disciplines that aim to understand human group behaviour. 'Dunbar's number' is the maximum size of a group of people in which every individual has a social relationship with all other members of the group and – importantly – understands every social relationship within the community. This number is thought to be in the hundreds. These ideas are speculative, but is seems reasonable that tribal social units have a biological foundation.

On the other end of the spectrum of social organisation, the idea of a universal human community has existed for a long time. Philosophically, this ideal appears to be the natural destination of human development, once our original tribal way of life breaks down. Globalisation is perhaps currently increasing the number of people who act and feel like world citizens. However, it is remarkable that peoplehood, the intermediate level between close-knit social units and universalism, is so resilient. My thoughts are not original and I will not discuss the academic hypotheses that attempt to explain the phenomenon of peoplehood. However, peoplehood is a fact. It is the most important factor in modern history and contemporary politics.

Peoplehood is older than the modern concept of the nation-state. Kingdoms and realms were originally not the expression of a people's quest for independence. The political units could comprise any number of subject peoples; the force behind the continued existence of a political unit was a central people strong enough to hold the multiethnic realm together.

The idea of 'one people, one state' revolutionised the map of Europe in the nineteenth and twentieth centuries. The ideal is however unattainable, much more so outside Europe because of the lesser role of national movements and the greater role of colonialism in shaping the borders of the current sovereign states.

Almost every sovereign state is a shared state; almost every sovereign state faces domestic political questions about the relationship between the peoples within its borders. Ethnically homogenous nation-states such as Iceland are exceptions. The prolonged insistence that the Commonwealth of Australia was a monocultural nation has caused us great grief.

The monocultural outlook of conservative Australians has some roots in racial and nationalist thinking, but the conservatives are essentially loyalist rather than nationalist. Loyal, nowadays, not to the sovereign but to the sovereign nation-state with its insufficient recognition of national minorities. This is where the discussion between Indigenous people and the political Right in Australia must be had.

The Right has generally been reluctant to try to modify the often-unfair outcomes of the process of formation of nation-states, which has placed a large number of ethnic minorities in a precarious situation in terms of the long-term survival of their distinct identities. The argument usually put forward is that a sovereign state must not risk instability and division, and that nationwide economic progress is in the best interest of minorities. Collective rights for national minorities are criticised by the Right because of the potential socially and economically marginalising effects of identity politics.

The best way to take this discussion forward is, I think, to make clear that an advancement program for Indigenous Australia cannot be based on a cultural relativism that denies the obvious fact that Indigenous Australians must fully engage with the English language, the European social and political institutions, science, modern economic behaviour, national and global economic integration and geographic mobility.

Australia is a country shared by two peoples. People often refer to the Aboriginal Australians as several nations, reflecting the smaller pre-contact social units I mentioned before, but it is obvious that colonisation has had a unifying effect on Aboriginal people and that it is justified to regard us as one national minority with distinct subgroups. I also recognise the distinctness of the Torres Strait Islanders, but for simplicity I will in most of this speech refer to non-indigenous and Indigenous Australians as the two Australian peoples.

What policies will achieve equality for Australia's peoples and unite Indigenous and non-indigenous Australians? My main thought on this question is this: we should think about the Indigenous Australians as a First World minority, or more precisely a First World indigenous minority, instead of simply as an indigenous minority.

Our policies in Cape York Peninsula take as their starting point the ultimate context in which Indigenous people in Australia are situated: the economic context. In much of the discussion and thinking about 'indigenous peoples' there is an assumption that the Indigenous people of Australia are in a similar position to indigenous peoples elsewhere in First World countries (Maoris in New Zealand, Native Americans in the United States, Aboriginal peoples of Canada *et cetera*) as well as indigenous peoples living in the Third World (Latin America, Sarawak, West Papua *et cetera*).

Whilst there are no doubt many commonalities between indigenous peoples living in these various circumstances, I am seeking to focus on the fundamental difference between indigenous peoples living in a First World country, in our case Australia, and in the Third

World, whether they may now, after decolonisation, govern their own nation-state (as in Papua New Guinea), or are minorities within a nation-state which they do not govern (as are the people of Western Papua).

The fundamental difference is the economic context: it is a completely different thing for indigenous people to live within a welfare state provided by a First World country or in the absence of one in a Third World country. The economic context in which the Aboriginal and Torres Strait Islanders of Australia live is completely different to that of our indigenous friends over the border in PNG. This difference between the Melanesians who are Australian Torres Strait Islanders and the Melanesians of Papua New Guinea is most starkly apparent on the northernmost islands of the Torres Strait, where both groups meet. PNG does not have a welfare state and is unlikely to develop one in the foreseeable future. Australia is a welfare state and is unlikely to cease being one in the foreseeable future.

The crucial thing about a First World welfare state is this: it can completely replace the traditional or post-colonial economies of indigenous communities with income support through the government transfer system. The safety-net guarantee of sustenance for all citizens means that indigenous peoples in a First World situation can cease their traditional economic activities – because their livelihood can be obtained from the government.

Whilst this complete replacement has not occurred and Indigenous communities in remote Australia live in 'hybrid economies' – with some real traditional economic activity and some real modern economic activity – it must be admitted that what I have called 'passive welfare' is today the predominant component of Indigenous economies in Australia. And the important point is that the welfare state could go on to become the sole source of sustenance for Indigenous people and their traditional economy could stop altogether – and my people would still have a livelihood. This is the power of the First World welfare state: it can completely replace an indigenous real economy.

In my view this distinction – between indigenous peoples who live in a First World welfare state and those who do not – is decisive, and is not properly comprehended when people think about 'the survival of indigenous cultures and societies in a globalised world'.

When I have observed the cultural vibrancy and diversity of Papua New Guinea in spite of its severe problems, two thoughts have returned to me. The first is that across the world, cultural and linguistic diversity is being maintained because the lifestyles around which these cultures exist still continue, and traditional economic life still continues. It continues not just by the choice of the people of these societies, but by virtue of necessity. The sustenance and livelihoods of these societies are intimately connected to their lifestyles and their traditional cultural forms. Traditional culture and traditional economy are integrated. In some cases, it may be that the economy is not 'traditional' (in the sense of classical) but the current economy supports and is suited to the maintenance of traditional cultural forms. There was probably a time when the pastoral economy in which Aboriginal people were involved in northern Australia was conducive to the maintenance of traditional cultural forms, because it gave stockworkers and their families access to their traditional country and economy.

The problem which indigenous peoples living in a First World welfare state face is this: there is now no longer any necessity to maintain the traditional economy or lifestyle. Now that the dominant economic base is passive welfare, there has been a break between the economic base of Aboriginal society and Aboriginal cultural forms. There is no longer the necessary integration between economy and culture. The retention of traditional cultural forms then becomes a matter of choice rather than of necessity.

My second thought is that passive welfare and traditional economy and lifestyle are not compatible. Indeed, passive welfare undermines and ultimately unravels traditional relationships and values – and gives rise to social problems and, ultimately, social breakdown. You cannot live a traditional lifestyle underwritten by passive welfare. It may seem possible in the short term, but in the long run passive welfare is socially and culturally corrosive.

I undertake this discussion of economic context so that we can clearly understand the choices we face as an indigenous people living in a First World welfare state. There are in theory three choices that I can think of.

One is to remain where we are: attempting to retain our traditions and cultures while depending on passive welfare for our predominant livelihood. For the reasons advanced earlier, I would say this is not a choice at all. If we do this, the social and cultural pauperisation of Indigenous society in Australia will continue unabated, and we will not establish the foundations necessary for cultural vitality and transmission to future generations. We therefore need to confront and demolish the mistaken policy that passive welfare can subsidise the pursuit of traditional lifestyles in remote communities.

The second choice is to go back: to maintain our cultural and linguistic diversity in the way the peoples of PNG, and other indigenous peoples throughout the Third World, are able to. But this is hardly possible. Indigenous Australians are now engulfed by the Australian economy and society, and it is impossible to see how territories could be established where the welfare state no longer reached and traditional economies could be revived (this is not to say we cannot reform the welfare state within Indigenous regions). For one thing, my people would simply refuse this course in practice.

The third choice is to go forward and find a way to achieve a bicultural and multilingual future. That is, Indigenous Australians must face the challenges that come when culture and traditions are no longer linked with our economy by necessity, but rather by conscious choice. This is what I have in mind when I suggest that we are a First World indigenous people, rather than a Fourth World people.

The program I propose is not a separatist program. I advocate restoration of social order and a real economy in Indigenous communities, education and proficiency in English in order to make my people completely socially and economically integrated, national unity and geographic mobility. There should be much common ground here for Indigenous people who agree with me and for conservatives and liberals.

I was invited to discuss these questions in this lecture: 'What, if anything, might Aboriginal people wish to take from the various settler cultures? What might they wish to keep and define as their own?'

I understand that these questions express a will to extend to Indigenous Australians the right to self-determination. This is right in principle, but the answer must be: 'Everything that enables our younger generations in Cape York Peninsula to achieve their fullest potential, talent and creativity, so that they have the confidence and capacity to orbit between two worlds and enjoy the best of both.'

2004

LAYERED IDENTITIES AND PEACE

Speech to the Brisbane Festival

Now is the winter of our discontent
Made glorious summer by this sun of York;
And all the clouds that lour'd upon our house
In the deep bosom of the ocean buried.

Now are our brows bound with victorious wreaths;
Our bruised arms hung up for monuments;
Our stern alarums chang'd to merry meetings,
Our dreadful marches to delightful measures.
Grim-visag'd war hath smooth'd his wrinkled front,

And now, instead of mounting barbed steeds
To fright the souls of fearful adversaries,
He capers nimbly in a lady's chamber
To the lascivious pleasing of a lute.
                    —Shakespeare, *Richard III*

Nhilaaygu nganhthanun guli muganh
Yumurr York-nganh ngalanda bayjarrin
Wulbu nguulbaan bayan nganhthanun jiinbaanbiga
Thalun bathaalbay duugamani

Nganhthanun ngaabaay ngan-ganda yuurrbay
Mangal malathirr than-gamanaathi
Guli dubiithi, nganhthaan nhila garrbunthirr
Warra wunay, nhila dabaar
Guli Muguulbay buthiil walu-yindu manaathi

Nhila yarraman naaybuthirr-bay ganbanbarr
Bama ngarrbalngay wawu yiniilgurranhu
Guli nyulu gabiirrthirr wawuway duugaathi
Guuruthirr manaathinhu gunbu dabaarthirr.

I wish to speak today on the matter of identity.

I have long considered that we labour under impoverished conceptions of identity, and have long believed that we need a better metaphor for popular comprehension of how peoples with varied identities come together to form a united nation.

The American metaphor of the 'melting pot' is the most famous of the identity metaphors. But for people concerned that the melting pot implies an utter assimilation of all the diverse ingredients into a muddy soup, the melting pot does not adequately capture the diversity of identities within a nation.

Other attempts, such as the 'patchwork quilt' or the 'rainbow' or the 'salad bowl', have not succeeded in becoming the defining metaphor for a multicultural society. But people convinced of the value of diversity are likely to subscribe to some kind of metaphor such as the patchwork quilt, implying as it does that society is composed of diverse and interesting parts that make up a united whole.

There are two great problems with the dominant popular understanding of identity. Firstly, the identity of a group in society is assumed to be singular, arising from some salient characteristic such as ethnicity or religion. Secondly, the identity of an individual within such a group is also assumed to be singular – again arising from some salient feature of the group of which she is taken to be a member. This reductive approach to identity assumes that the individual or group has a single affiliation, or a principal affiliation that overrides all else.

I have long considered that individuals and groups both possess 'layers of identity'. These layers include identification with cultural and linguistic groups; religions; places of birth, upbringing, residency and death; local and regional geographic communities; regional, provincial and national polities; and professional, literary, recreational, philosophical and other sub-cultural groups. Each individual has many layers of identity. She shares many of these layers with her closest kin, but there are some layers that she does not share with them. She shares these other layers of identity with other members of society, sometimes distant from and unknown to her. In the same way, other members of her family share layers of identity with other strangers in society, which she does not share.

It is the same with groups. Groups may be formed around a dominant characteristic such as ethnicity or religion – but the individuals or subgroups that make up the group will also harbour layers of identity. Each member of the group will share layers of identity with people outside of the group. Some of the layers shared with non-members of the group will be shared with some members of one's group, but not with others.

I first thought about layered identities when I considered my own Aboriginal identity. I am patrilineally descended from a group whose language – called Guugu Warra by its eastern neighbours – is now extinct. My great-grandfather Arrimi spoke this language and his patrilineally inherited estate was called Bagaarrmugu in the language of the neighbouring nation, the Guugu Yimithirr.

Arrimi spoke his own language as well as Guugu Yimithirr and many other languages of neighbouring groups. Multilingualism was a necessary feature of life in classical times. With the colonial destruction of the Guugu Warra speakers, my grandfather, who was removed to the Cape Bedford Lutheran mission in the early part of the twentieth century, became a Guugu Yimithirr speaker: a language his people spoke, but did not own in classical times. My great-grandfather, who continued to live a traditional life, remained in contact with my grandfather, who lived on the mission; my family's connection with our ancestral lands was therefore not broken. My father and myself therefore grew up on the mission as Guugu Yimithirr people, which we are in terms of the history of the past century, but not in classical terms.

My mother was born in Kuku Yalanji country, Guugu Yimithirr's neighbours to the south. From her I learned the Kuku Yalanji language. Furthermore, as well as local clan affiliations, there are larger group affiliations around language, cross-clan kinship and land-tenure systems. It is simply not possible to understand traditional Aboriginal identity in a singular, reductive way: there are layers of identity. The identity of individuals is context-dependent – and there are no absolute boundaries that can be drawn around solidary groups. On top of the complexity of traditional identities, there are the identities that have arisen out of my history. I am a member of a community that was gathered together by governmental fiat into a mission, where my paternal grandfather and grandmother rebuilt what would become the Pearson clan out of the ruins of traditional society. We live in and are intimately connected with a place called Hope Vale; we know its place-names, the events that have taken place there, and we know its contours: its sand dunes, rivers, rainforests, mountains, swamps and reefs. We have camped and fished and hunted and walked around this place which we love dearly and which we would not hesitate to call 'home', even though our traditional country is not at Hope Vale.

We also identify as Christians and specifically as Lutherans. We connect with the members of another Lutheran mission nearby at Wujal Wujal, on the basis of our traditional, marital (my mother is from there) and Lutheran connections. We also feel a connection with our fellow Aboriginal Lutherans at Hermannsburg in central Australia and Yalata in South Australia – though we do not know them. Stranger still, we feel a connection with Lutherans of German and Scandinavian descent in Australia – Lutheranism being one of the more culturally insular denominations, it must be admitted – with whom we share a common conviction in Martin Luther's theological proposition that we are saved by the grace of God, not by our own straps. Even stranger still, we feel some remnant connection with Neuendettelsau in Bavaria, from which the Lutheran mission to Cape Bedford was launched in 1886. It is, in the striking words of one of our Indigenous pastors, a spiritual wellspring for the people of my village. We also identify as

Bama. Variants of the word 'Bama' mean 'Aboriginal person' in the languages across Cape York Peninsula. Of course, we also identify as Murri – Aboriginal people from Queensland, as distinct from Kooris down south and Noongars out west. We also identify as Aborigines of Australia, who share a common layer of identity from Tasmania to Cape York, from Brisbane to Perth. The Aboriginal flag, one of the world's greatest flags if I may say so, is also a potent symbol of our identification.

The point of my biography of identity is that I have long understood that it was not possible to answer the question 'What is your Aboriginal identity?' in a simple, reductive way. I, and the members of my community, possess layers of identity, some of which are shared with each other, some of which are distinct.

And more layers of identity come to bear when we consider our wider geographic, political, social and sub-cultural affiliations. We are North Queenslanders, but we are also specifically people of Cape York Peninsula. We are Queenslanders when the Origin of the Species is running, though some of us are overcome by some kind of Oedipal compulsion to barrack for the Blues. I must say I am a less fervent participant in the tribal passions of Rugby League, preferring instead The Game They Play in Heaven. I well understand that my private schooling inculcated this finer appreciation of the merits of Rugby Union, though the class dimension of this particular passion is not at all attractive to me. In respect of Rugby, I part ways with the passions of most of the members of my community, and indeed my own history.

But I probably share with most of my community members a complete perplexity about the point of Australian Rules Football. Where many Indigenous Australian friends from western and southern Australia find excitement, I find boredom. I am indeed reaching such a stage of intolerance that if soccer is going to take over as the national sport of Australia – and every four years I am persuaded of this – then I think Australian Rules should be folded up.

When it comes to patriotism, my feelings about identity are more volatile. Of course I am an Australian, but I am not necessarily a proud one. I feel too troubled about the place of my Indigenous Australian people in this, their own country, to just simply say 'I am a proud Australian'. And the 'Oi, oi, oi' is just embarrassing. I have a strong intellectual appreciation for all those who serve in our country's armed forces. I consider few things more honourable in citizens than service in the armed forces. But on Anzac Day, that 'one day of the year' which is the subject of a growing patriotic identification on the part of younger generations of Australians, I feel a faint nausea. Two of my maternal Aboriginal grandparents served in France in the First World War, but still I feel alienated about Anzac Day. I suspect I feel alienated because my grandparents' service to their country did not make them citizens when they returned to Australia. I feel alienated because I find it hard to stomach the sight of white Australians saying 'Lest We Forget' at the shrines of Anzac whilst vigorously seeking to forget what happened to the country's Indigenous peoples. I feel alienated because Anzac Day just feels too white to me.

Amartya Sen has supplied us with a theory of what I have called layered identities in his most recent book, *Identity and Violence*. Before turning to Sen, let me first turn to the expatriate intellectual Robert Hughes, who is I think indispensable to understanding the debates about multiculturalism and its relationship to the 'culture wars' which emerged in the United States and which later became the grist for Australian mills. We live today in the age of anti-'political correctness'. True it is that the intramural cultural Left of the '80s and '90s constructed the more ridiculous and easily mocked aspects of what became known as political correctness. True it is that many of the excesses of leftist political correctitude were anti-intellectual and part of a political and cultural agenda against the Right.

However, leftist political correctness based on anti-intellectual premises has been replaced by a rightist PC: patriotic correctness. In the same way as the Left on campus used PC as a club with which to beat the so-called Neanderthals of the Right, the Right is now in the ascendancy in the cultural wars, and they now wear Neanderthal insensitivity and anti-intellectualism with pride. And this has yielded much fruit for the parties of the Right in their electoral successes of the past decade.

Most of the intellectual and cultural surf in our country originates in currents emanating from the United States. The cultural wars in

Australia are usually a shallow reproduction of whatever themes are raging Stateside, albeit time-delayed, like an international phone call. The antipodean version usually lacks the depth, insight, wit and interest of the original – but as long as these polemics advance an emotional argument, they serve their purpose.

It is ironic that it was an Australian who first properly elucidated the problem of political correctness in the United States, in a lecture series at the New York Public Library in 1992, subsequently published as *Culture of Complaint: The Fraying of America*. Robert Hughes did not just attack 'political correctness', 'Afrocentrism' and 'postmodernism' – he also attacked the populist demagogy of Reagan and the American Right, with its appeal to monocultural nativism and its disingenuous attack on elites.

In a chapter titled 'Multi-Culti and Its Discontents' Hughes makes the following defence of multiculturalism: Multiculturalism asserts that people with different roots can co-exist, that they can learn to read the image-banks of others, that they can and should look across the frontiers of race, language, gender and age without prejudice or illusion, and learn to think against the background of a hybridised society. It proposes – modestly enough – that some of the most interesting things in history and culture happen at the interface between cultures. It wants to study border situations, not only because they are fascinating in themselves, but because understanding them may bring with it a little hope for the world. Hughes tackles the two tribes of PCs: the politically correct on the Left and the patriotically correct of the Right. He writes:

> It is too simple to say that America is, or ever was, a melting pot. But it is also too simple to say none of its contents actually melted. No single metaphor can do justice to the complexity of cultural crossing and perfusion in America. American mutuality has no choice but to live in recognition of difference. But it is destroyed when those differences get raised into cultural ramparts. People once used a dead metaphor – 'balkanisation' – to evoke the splitting of a field into sects, groups, little nodes of power. Now, on the dismembered corpse of Yugoslavia, whose 'cultural differences' (or, to put it plainly, archaic religious and racial lunacies) have been set free by the death of Communism,

we see what that stale figure of speech once meant and now means again. A Hobbesian world: the war of all on all, locked in blood-feud and theocratic hatred, the *reductio ad insanitatem* of America's mild and milky multiculturalism. What imperial rule, what Hapsburg tyranny or slothful dominion of Muscovite apparatchiks, would not be preferable to this? Against this ghastly background, so remote from American experience since the Civil War, we now have our own conservatives promising a 'cultural war', while ignorant radicals orate about 'separatism'. They cannot know what demons they are frivolously invoking. If they did, they would fall silent in shame.

As I said earlier, identities and the layers of identities within each individual are issues which I have been thinking about for more than a decade. During this period, the general Australian public has associated my name with two different political campaigns. Firstly: land rights and native title. Secondly: Indigenous Australian economic development and education. I believe that many people do not see any relationship between those two policy areas. Native title is seen to be an issue about Indigenous Australian identity, and about preservation of identity. Economic development and education, on the other hand, are perceived as issues that automatically pose challenges for the preservation of identity. Some people have probably concluded that I have fundamentally changed direction during the last decade, and that I no longer prioritise the survival of a distinct Indigenous Australian identity. Others have perhaps concluded that I strive for the emergence of a distinct Indigenous Australian identity incorporating elements of European learning and economic behaviour.

The assumption underpinning this latter interpretation is that some human affiliations, such as economic affiliations, can be instrumental rather than essential. That is, that peoples and nations have essential cultural identities, and that human activities such as economic development can be the means by which cultural identity is preserved. For example, the lives of the people of Japan have changed enormously during the last century and a half. This fundamental transformation of Japan is not interpreted as evidence that the Japanese cultural identity has disappeared.

Indigenous Australian identity, on the other hand, is often said to be so intimately connected with the organisation of our traditional society that it will cease to exist if we embrace modernity. The widespread inability to understand my political goal highlights the fact that in the modern world, people are far too eager to categorise all other people according to a system of singular, exclusive identities. Amartya Sen calls this tendency in contemporary thinking 'the illusion of singular identity'. As is obvious from the title of his recent book – *Identity and Violence* – Sen is trying to find solutions to much more severe conflicts than we will ever face in Australia. However, his general argument is, I believe, useful for us Indigenous Australians and for non-indigenous Australians when we try to find answers to questions about my people's place in this country. Sen's main thought is that we should recognise 'competing affiliations' or 'competing identities'. Taken out of context, these expressions may sound alarming. But Sen is not referring to 'competing loyalties' or to lack of loyalty to the sovereign state where one lives. On the contrary, Sen's thought is that globally, we could reduce what are usually labelled 'sectarian' or 'ethnic' or 'religious' conflicts by recognising the plurality of our identities and the implications of this diversity.

In Australia, we do not have and will not have open conflicts between groups of people. But Sen's thinking is still relevant for the resolution of the issues we are facing. I am convinced that the correct policy for Australia is recognition of Indigenous Australian identity, of Indigenous Australian peoplehood within the Australian nation. This idea will meet instinctive opposition: it may be perceived by some as a separatist agenda. Agendas that can be labelled separatist are rejected on three grounds. First, they are seen as threats to the unity of the country. Second, Aboriginal unity and peoplehood are said to be modern, artificial constructs. Third, in terms of practical policies, separatism is seen as the main reason why the last forty years of Indigenous policies have had such disappointing results.

However, I do not think that recognition of Indigenous Australians' identities must lead to disunity and isolation. The goal of Indigenous policy should be, simultaneously, the successful integration of our people and recognition of Indigenous Australian peoplehood.

Rather than being mutually exclusive, I believe that successful integration is a precondition for the survival of distinctness and vice versa.

I have started a translation of Shakespeare's *Richard III* into Guugu Yimithirr. I do this because my own cultural heritage is steeped in the literature of England, because the play also resonates deeply with the politics and kin-conflicts of my own hometown (I have several cousins who could play the part of Richard to perfection), and because I want the body of texts in Guugu Yimithirr to grow.

The question is, am I driven by my affiliation with English literature or my affiliation with the Guugu Yimithirr nation? This simple example shows why Sen is correct in rejecting the notion that every individual has one single dominant identity. Sen does not ignore the fact that what I have called the layers of identity often compete with each other. Reasoning and individual choice must guide the resolution of these competing affiliations – not fundamentalism or an illusion of singular identity. Individuals and groups are assisted in this reasoning process by having a more mature theory of identity and a model for unity and diversity which is not reductive or essentialist.

I wish also to add another dimension to the concept of layered identities, one borrowed from the literature on social capital. Professor Robert Putnam, in his now well-known writings on social capital, identified two forms of social capital within societies: 'bridging' social capital and 'bonding' social capital. Bonding social capital refers to relations within a relatively homogenous group (such as an ethnic, religious or socio-economic group); it strengthens the social ties within the group. Bridging social capital, on the other hand, refers to relations between groups, and strengthens ties between groups. Examples of bridging social capital include the civil-rights movement and ecumenical religious organisations.

I propose that we should think of some identity affiliations as 'bonding' identities; these are the ties that bind us to those closest to us. Other identity affiliations are 'bridging' identities; these are the ties that unite us with other less proximate members of society, with whom we nevertheless share commonalities. Our policy must be to support bonds and, importantly, strengthen and draw attention to bridges between the diverse individuals and groups within our society. The unity of the nation depends on the strength of its bonds and its bridges. This is a matter of both quality and quantity. A country that relies on the bare patriotic devotion of individuals and groups to the nation does not gain the strength that comes from overlapping connections between citizens. Bonding ties are important because they give expression to primary and proximate relationships. Bridging ties are important because they increase our recognition of the wider affiliations between individuals right across society – even between cultural strangers.

Australia is generally committed to the concept of multiculturalism (and it has been a real achievement in Australia), although there has been a gathering conservative critique of this model. Prime Minister John Howard's misgivings about the word reflect a widespread ambivalence about whether multiculturalism is the optimal model. I get the sense that Howard is not entirely happy with the concept of multiculturalism, but does not have an adequate analysis of its shortcomings, and does not have a persuasive alternative model. He knows that it is far too late in the day for Australia to be monocultural.

Sen puts his finger on the main problem with multiculturalism, and this crucial insight flows from an analysis of what I have called layered identities and Sen has called 'affiliations'. 'Culture', implying ethnicity and religion, is not the only layer of identity. There are many other layers with which individuals in a particular ethnic or religious group will affiliate. Societies that sponsor 'cultural' diversity to the exclusion of other affiliations reinforce the problem of ethnicity or religion being seen as the single dominant affiliation. Cultures become identity blocs.

Sen's insight is that there is not a simple duality between two policies: 'monoculturalism' and 'multiculturalism'. There is a third condition: 'plural monoculturalism'. Plural monoculturalism occurs where a policy of multiculturalism promotes culture as the dominant singular affiliation and ends up in a situation where there is a plurality of monocultures. This is the potential problem with multiculturalism.

The problem of plural monoculturalism must be understood if the mostly successful achievement of multiculturalism in Australia is to be improved upon. As Sen points out, it is not a matter of multiculturalism having gone 'too far', as many conservative critics tend to think.

Rather, the problem – on the part of both conservatives and progressives – lies in viewing ethnicity or religion as the only sources of identity. The diversity of identity, of both groups and individuals, is overlooked. A mature society will be one in which individuals prioritise their competing affiliations with an understanding of the complexity of identity. The challenge for policy is to supply this understanding of layered affiliations, and to show that this can be consistent with diversity and national unity.

That competing affiliations are not always settled in the breasts of individuals, and that people will often be torn both intellectually and emotionally, was best illustrated to me when I heard a speech by the Reverend David Passi at a conference in Townsville some years ago. Reverend Passi is an elder from the Murray Islands in the eastern Torres Strait. He was, along with Eddie Mabo, one the plaintiffs in the *Mabo* case. His address discussed the annexation of the Murray Islands in the second half of the nineteenth century, and how sovereignty had been acquired without the consent of the Meriam people. He spoke of how the Meriam people had not agreed to become Queenslanders and Australians, and he challenged the moral and legal claims of the Crown in respect of his people and his homeland. Then, in the midst of his electrifying denunciation of this constitutional history, he recalled that he had once been to Bible college in one of the southern states and was flying to Brisbane on his way back to the Torres Strait. He said that when he put his feet on the tarmac, he said to himself (thousands of kilometres from his island homeland and in the capital of the very Crown that had usurped his sovereignty): 'I'm home!' And his next words, as he gently thrust his fist into the air, were: 'Go the Broncos!'

2006

NATIVE TONGUES IMPERILLED

In 1973, a linguist doing field work on Aboriginal Australian languages realised he had met the last speaker of Yaygir, a language once spoken in what is now north-eastern New South Wales. The custodian of this invaluable piece of Australian culture, Sandy Cameron, was living in obscurity and had naturally not spoken Yaygir for several years. He was, however, eager to work with his university-educated guest to record and preserve his ancestral language. The linguist decided to return to Cameron's home in a couple of months to finish the recording of this national treasure. But Sandy Cameron died before the linguist returned. A region of Australia lost its heritage.

Such tragedies happened in many parts of Australia in our lifetime, and are still happening. A few years ago my old friend Urwunhthin died as the last speaker of his people's language from Barrow Point on the south-eastern coast of Cape York Peninsula. Urwunhthin's knowledge was at least recorded to a large extent. In the late 1960s and into the '70s an organised effort was made by many young anthropologists and linguists, urged on by an indefatigable sponsor, Dr Peter Ucko, then director of the Australian Institute of Aboriginal and Torres Strait Islander Studies (AIATSIS) in Canberra, to describe the country's cultures and languages. Their salvage operation was dubbed 'Before It Is Too Late' or BIITL. Many of today's senior Australian ethnographers were involved in this push.

The original BIITL preserved a large amount of information, now archived in Canberra. Much of this record is, however, inaccessible to laymen. When I was a boy starting primary school in my hometown of

Hope Vale, an American linguist, John Haviland, came to live with a local family two doors away from us, and in the following years he compiled a grammar and dictionary of Guugu Yimithirr – the language that Captain Cook encountered in 1770 and which gave the world the name kangaroo, after the Guugu Yimithirr word for a species of wallaby called *gangurru*.

Haviland mastered classical Guugu Yimithirr. His Guugu Yimithirr grammar is a necessary, but by itself insufficient, foundation for the maintenance of our language long into the future. It is hard enough for privileged people to learn languages. It is near impossible for dysfunctional people. Few of my people can learn anything from Haviland's published grammar. The scientific work has not been complemented by effective language-transmission efforts such as have occurred in New Zealand. The multitude of Australian languages means that our challenge is much more complex than in New Zealand, but we should learn from the strategies adopted across the Tasman.

A new BIITL operation is needed in Australia, because we risk losing our country's languages as spoken tongues. Intergenerational transmission of a large number of Australia's languages is declining or has ceased. This is not the result of Aboriginal Australians choosing to abandon our culture. Like almost every other problem in our communities, it is a result of our disadvantage. Social dysfunction disables cultural and linguistic transmission.

Our country must understand that a new BIITL effort is an indispensable part of reconciliation. It will be difficult to save our languages if the gap in transmission becomes much wider than it already is. Other than the work undertaken by AIATSIS in Canberra, the most important (and more promising in terms of providing a solution to the challenge of intergenerational transmission) effort has been undertaken through the translations of the international subsidiary of the Wycliffe Bible Society, the Summer Institute of Linguistics (SIL). Two languages of Cape York Peninsula, Wik Mungkan and Kuku Yalanji, have been the media for magisterial translations of the New Testament by SIL, along with a number of other languages across the country. SIL has made an estimation of the vitality of each of Australia's remaining Indigenous languages, and the number of languages that are on the brink of extinction should be cause for national consternation and urgent response. But, notwithstanding the richness of this country's linguistic heritage, there is almost no public recognition of this national priority. To find an eloquent expression of the preciousness of this heritage you would need to go back to the late W.E.H. Stanner's Boyer Lectures of 1968.

Let me make some points about language policy. As a first step, Australia must recognise its languages. It is ridiculous that Australia is behind Europe in this respect. The European states have signed the European Charter for Regional or Minority Languages. The status of minority languages varies greatly, but a large number of European minority languages are now official in the provinces where they are spoken. Australia has not even adopted an official listing of her languages.

Second, the purpose of preserving and maintaining Australia's Indigenous languages is not just that these languages serve a communication purpose within Indigenous societies (for many communities, they do not), but because they are inherently valuable as part of the country's rich heritage. These languages constitute the identity of its custodians, and these are the primary words with which the Australian land and seascape have been named and described. These languages are intimately related to the nature and spirit of the country that all Australians now call home.

Third, Indigenous people must understand that Indigenous language transmission must move from an oral culture to a written (and digitised) one if there is to be long-term maintenance. This means that Indigenous children must be fully literate in the language of learning – English – in order to be literate in their own languages. Reliance upon oral transmission alone will not work in the long term.

Fourth, there must be a separate domain within Indigenous communities for cultural and linguistic education – that is, separate from the domain of Western education. Schools are not the place for cultural and linguistic transmission, and we must stop looking to schools to save our languages. The primary purpose of schools is to provide our children with a mainstream Western education, including full fluency in English. Schools will never be adequately equipped to transmit our language and culture, and all we end up doing is compromising our children's mainstream educational achievement. Indeed, without full English literacy our children will not have the tools to become literate at an advanced level in their traditional languages.

Fifth, language learning must start in earliest childhood, and this means both English and traditional languages. Children must have access to both domains from the start if they are going to become properly bilingual. Communities that delay the learning of English until late primary school in favour of traditional languages in the early years might end up disadvantaging their children if they remain far behind in the language they need to obtain a mainstream education.

Sixth, a new generation BIITL must integrate the newest technology. Information technologies can provide a bridge between academic linguistics and language transmission. There are many examples of how information technology can enable cultural transmission, and these need to be brought together as part of a concerted program.

Finally, the basic infrastructure for this national project needs to be developed at the national level. There should be room for a lot of regional and local adaptation, but there must be a range of off-the-shelf technical solutions developed by people with the necessary expertise at a national government agency such as AIATSIS. There needs to be a generous government-funded campaign for the maintenance of each Indigenous language, employing full-time linguists and other expert staff. Private, not-for-profit and public organisations should work together, but language policy and adequate funding must be provided by the national government.

2007

A PECULIAR PATH THAT LEADS ASTRAY

During the past decade we have been told that some myths pertaining to the Aboriginal people of Australia have been debunked. The myth of frontier massacres is said to have been debunked by Keith Windschuttle. The myth of the stolen generations is said to have been debunked by *Quadrant* magazine. The myth of the noble savage is said to have been debunked by Roger Sandall. The myth of *terra nullius* is said to have been debunked by Michael Connor.

Now an environmentalist, William Lines, has stepped up to debunk the myth of 'the ecological Aborigine' in an article taken from his book *Patriots: Defending Australia's Natural Heritage*. Oh, my poor people! You have been subjected to a relentless and seemingly endless cultural cleansing. And you appear to be utterly defeated in a cultural war in which you have shown a declining and eventually feeble resistance. All that remains is to smooth the dying pillow of our remnant dignity as a people. There is a breathtaking vehemence to this neo-conservatism. What could be next?

The perennial complaint of both sides in the culture wars between Left and Right is that their opponents dominate public debate. Each side claims that the other exerts a disproportionate influence over policy and culture. Both the Right and the Left believe they speak for a majority of ordinary people who have to put up with follies and injustices imposed by ideologues or interest groups. Who is right? The answer is that both sides establish and maintain stifling orthodoxies, often at the same time and in the same policy areas. Indigenous affairs is a prime example of a policy area severely affected by the tribalism of Australian political and cultural life.

Before we started our reform work in Indigenous affairs in Cape York Peninsula, my colleagues and I realised that our political theory and practical policies would be controversial and that we could not escape the dynamics of the culture wars. This was a choice I had to make, because there were progressive orthodoxies that had to be challenged and overturned if it was going to be possible to make progress.

My Indigenous friend and colleague Professor Marcia Langton understood my argument about what was wrong with progressive policy. But she was hesitant about new policies that could be construed as concessions to the Right, even if those policies were correct. She thought the Right would not meet us halfway; instead, they were intent on waging total war.

Progressive nostrums had to be confronted, but Langton's concern was prescient. A set of conservative interpretations of history, together with established perceptions about the shortcomings of Indigenous leaders, dominate public opinion. By association, my people's rights in our own country have disappeared from the agenda. The progress towards recognition of the Indigenous Australian peoples as national minority peoples with certain rights has been indefinitely stalled.

The worst effect of the neo-conservative ascendancy is that opinions that normally would be seen as mean and ungracious in a generous, democratic country become acceptable and indeed *de rigueur*. An example is Gary Johns's view that government does not have any obligation to support the cultures of national minorities as well as the culture of the majority. In a government-endorsed paper, Johns argued that Aboriginal Australians have no right to government-funded education about their culture and languages. His irrational argument was that a modern Western education system by definition cannot maintain a preliterate, nomadic culture.

Of course it cannot. But we have a right to government support for a modern, literate, prosperous version of our culture. This right to cultural continuity is exactly the same right the non-indigenous conservatives demand for their people when they fight to prevent postmodern gobbledygook from pushing knowledge about old Western culture out of the curriculum, and when they suggest that school chaplains maintain our pre-modern Christian heritage.

The difference between Australia and most other shared Western states is that the Australian minority peoples until recently had a pre-modern culture and no connection with the world economy. To secure Aboriginal economic development, it might be necessary for us to make far-reaching concessions to the dominant culture. For example, English should perhaps be the regular language in schools and government-funded teaching of our languages should be an extracurricular complement. Aboriginal Australian culture and economy have changed and must change. But it seems that conservatives increasingly believe that the difficulties of this transformation justify or necessitate a complete denial of Aboriginal Australians' national rights as minority peoples.

I am very concerned about the damage conservative Australians are doing to the prospects of reconciliation through their uncritical endorsement of people like Keith Windschuttle and Johns. The influence of Windschuttle and Johns has been such as to diminish public empathy with Aboriginal Australians. Windschuttle and Johns would probably reply that it is their critics who lack empathy, because the Left defends flawed policies that ruin Aboriginal Australians' lives. However, the lack of empathy that Johns and Windschuttle exude is more insidious than indifference to humanitarian disasters. Their coldness reveals an inexplicable antagonism to Aboriginal Australians' wish to remain distinct.

Windschuttle's defence against the charge of lack of empathy is that 'the responsibility of the historian is not to be compassionate, it is to be dispassionate … to try and get at the truth'. But Windschuttle and Johns's antagonism to Aboriginal Australians means that they are unable to remain dispassionately objective. For example, Windschuttle's generalisation that the early stages of dispossession were 'not against [the] will of … most Aborigines' is not a correction of leftist distortion of history; it is distortion in the opposite direction.

There has been nothing more dispiriting for me than the prominence of Windschuttle's and Johns's ideas in conservative political and cultural circles. Windschuttle's thesis about the absence of a notion of land ownership in Aboriginal Australia, and Johns's notion that our culture is unable to change and must therefore be left to die, are threatening the prospects of successful co-operation between Aboriginal Australians and conservatives.

Another example of the extreme thinking that can pass for mainstream debate in Australia can be found in the article by William Lines. Lines criticises romantic notions about Aboriginal people and argues that some contemporary Aboriginal practices pose problems for conservation. It is no problem to have a debate about these issues. It is a huge generalisation to say that Aboriginal Australians are more concerned with conservation and that non-Aboriginal Australians are more concerned with consumption and the accumulation of wealth. For one thing, this generalisation ignores the strong ideological commitment to conservation that has developed among Westerners. It also ignores evidence of environmentally destructive practices in contemporary Aboriginal communities.

Yet Lines is partly wrong in his criticism of the figure of 'the ecological Aborigine', because this generalisation is largely accurate. In his Menzies Lecture in 2000, John Howard acknowledged that 'inconsistencies between Indigenous and non-indigenous approaches remain at the root of much of the current difficulty', including the gap 'between exploiting land and living with it'. The environmental affinity of hunter-gatherers arises from their economy: nature is the source of their sustenance and it is no wonder religion and culture are intimately concerned with the natural world. These traditions are still strong and relevant today.

There are threads of valid insight in Lines's criticism of non-indigenous people's romanticisation of native culture and denigration of their own. The problem is that these legitimate insights are interwoven with a farrago of polemic, usually aimed at discrediting Indigenous rights to land and recognition as a people. The core of Lines's article is his contention that the land-rights movement is to a large extent based on 'racial thinking'. Lines writes: 'Land-rights activists couched their arguments in terms of them and us.' He continues: 'Race thinkers, however, insisted on discrimination. The 1991 Queensland land-rights

Bill allowed Aborigines to claim land rights over all the state's national parks.'

Lines regrets that the Queensland government did not exempt national parks from claims. He believes the government should have arbitrarily stopped recognition of our ownership of some of that Crown land in national parks. This is symptomatic of a political and cultural climate in which Indigenous people's rights can be attacked in an unprincipled way: how could Burkeian conservatives and Hayekian liberals countenance government arbitrarily taking away land that is the lawful inheritance of citizens?

It is depressing to have to explain that Aboriginal people are traditional owners of land who are belatedly having their ownership recognised. This ownership is based on the original, traditional occupation and possession of the land (which is recognised by the common law of England as a basis for title to land), not on race. Race is incidental to the fact that Aborigines occupied the land at the advent of the common law. Native title, as the law has developed in Australia, is extremely favourable for non-indigenous people. All non-indigenous rights are automatically protected; Indigenous people have to go through a difficult process to get what is left over, including some Crown land.

In typical fashion, Lines turns words such as 'race thinking' and 'discrimination' against my people, who until recently lived in absolute discrimination and oppression because of their race.

I am not arguing that there is a hegemony of extreme conservative ideas today. The problem is that in many cases, what passes for mainstream debate is in fact a debate between the real mainstream and quite extreme ideas. Such a debate is bound to confer legitimacy on extreme thinking. The question is what we should do about this situation. The first thing is to speak clearly about the fact that Australia is treading a *Sonderweg*, as the Germans say: a peculiar path that will lead a nation astray. Compared with other democratic countries with national minorities, Australia is developing abnormally. We Aboriginal Australians are being reduced to beggars in our own home.

The tragedy is that even as many progressives cling to destructive policies, many people of the Right are focused on a cultural war that attempts to reverse the good things that did happen during the progressive reconciliation era, namely the recognition of our rights and our rightful place in this country.

2006

OVER 200 YEARS WITHOUT A PLACE

Australia has never been clear about the place of Aborigines and Torres Strait Islanders in the nation. It was not clear at the time of the founding of the colonies in Australia. There has been long and unresolved debate about the terms on which the British Crown instructed the colonists to make sovereign claims to territories that had been, for up to 60,000 years, the home of its indigenes. If the colonists disobeyed their instructions then, the meaning of such infidelity is now moot. Only in respect of the acknowledgment of native title to land have the terms of Australia's settlement been revisited and made clear: the common law imported from England included recognition of indigenous entitlement to traditional lands.

It was not clear at the time of the formation of the Commonwealth in 1901. What was clear was that under the new Constitution, the new federal parliament would have no power to legislate in relation to members of the Aboriginal race, and Aboriginal people were not to be counted in the census. In other words, Indigenous people were not citizens of the new nation.

At the time of the sesquicentenary of European colonisation in 1938, the place of Indigenous people in Australia remained unsettled. While white Australians celebrated, the famous pioneers of the Aboriginal political struggle, William Cooper, Jack Patten and William Ferguson, organised a congress attended by 1000 people that passed the following resolution: 'We, representing the Aborigines of Australia, assembled in conference at the Australian Hall, Sydney, on the 26th day of January 1938, this being the 150th anniversary of the white men's seizure of our country, hereby make protest against the callous treatment of our people by the white men in the past 150 years, and we appeal to the Australian nation to make new laws for the education and care of Aborigines, and for a new policy which will raise our people to full citizen status and equality within the community.'

The day before, Prime Minister Joseph Lyons had met a delegation of Aboriginal representatives. Nothing came from it. It is said that Lyons's main motivation was to take the opportunity to meet pastor Doug Nicholls, later governor of South Australia and the first Aborigine to be knighted, who was then a footballer with the Fitzroy Australian Rules football club. No Commonwealth legislation would be enacted. Indeed, no legislation could be enacted without a change to the Constitution. The change to the Constitution would not be made for another thirty years, and the 1967 constitutional referendum, which removed the barriers to Indigenous citizenship, required a heroic, decade-long campaign by Faith Bandler and the next generation of Aboriginal campaigners for Indigenous recognition.

The questions at issue in the 1960s – questions about the place of Indigenous people within the nation – had arisen during that earlier period of Indigenous policy consternation in the '30s. From 1938, against the mainstream assumption that Aborigines were a doomed race and that all that remained was to 'smooth the dying pillow', a burgeoning political movement emerged. It insisted that Aborigines had survived and would continue to survive, and sought recognition for Aboriginal people as the indigenous people of the country.

The 1967 referendum was only a negation of discrimination. It got rid of the original discrimination in the Constitution. It left unresolved the positive question about the place of Indigenous people in the nation. Legislation during the past forty years – not least the *Native Title Act* in the '90s – would provide recognition of Aboriginal rights to land, heritage, health and education (with varying degrees of success), but the question about the place and future of Indigenous people within the nation remained unresolved.

There was no clear resolution of the consternation of Aboriginal policy in the '30s and there was no resolution of the moral quandary of the '60s. Out of the '30s came a general commitment to the concepts of advancement and assimilation: the white Australian emphasis on assimilation met with an Aboriginal desire for equality and advancement. But while policies at the state level aimed at assimilation, there was little concerted policy supporting equality and precious little investment in advancement.

Out of the '60s came the general commitment to the concepts of self-determination and advancement, and a banishing of assimilation. The idea that Aborigines, particularly in remote areas, should be able to choose to pursue a more or less traditional lifestyle became dominant, but the basic capabilities necessary for true choice (such as good health and a good education) were neglected. Consequently, life in remote communities was in no sense a matter of choice: it was the only option.

The same policy confusion dogged the desire for advancement. Advancement, both social and economic, requires an acceptance of integration even if one is opposed to assimilation. But all too often the integration baby was thrown out with the assimilation bathwater. So little advancement ensued.

So, forty years on, we end up with a full-blown Indigenous policy crisis in the first decade of the twenty-first century. This is no longer a matter of consternation, it is no longer a matter of moral quandary: it is a matter of crisis. The extremity of the issue is demonstrated by the fact that those who most bear the consequences of the irresolution of this question are the innocents: Aboriginal children. It is always the case that it is the innocent children who suffer. But I would argue that the suffering today is more egregious than the suffering of the past.

In the '30s, the children overwhelmingly suffered at the hands of white society and governments, who removed them from their families (and who created and allowed to continue the conditions that often made removal to missions a better option than leaving them where they were). The debate about whether these were 'stolen generations' or 'rescued generations' is unnecessary and anachronistic. The options available to Aborigines at the time too often made removal a lesser evil. The greater evil was to leave children, young girls in particular, vulnerable to predation by whites, who had unlimited prerogatives over Aborigines, especially on the frontiers. Australia was a cruel society back then.

In the '60s, the children overwhelmingly suffered at the hands of poverty and lack of opportunity in a discriminatory society.

Today, as is plainly obvious, the children overwhelmingly suffer at the hands of their own people, often their own loved ones. The profound change in the nature of this innocent suffering tells us about the depth of the crisis. And at the heart of the matter lies the still-unclear answer to that old question: what is the place of Aboriginal and Torres Strait Islander people in the Australian nation?

In 1981, Prime Minister Malcolm Fraser sought an answer to this question when he instructed the Senate Standing Committee on Legal and Constitutional Affairs to examine 'the feasibility of a compact or *makarrata* between the Commonwealth and Aboriginal people'. The committee's report, *Two Hundred Years Later*, was tabled in 1983. Nothing has yet come of it. In 1988, Prime Minister Bob Hawke's impulsive commitment to a treaty, subsequently called a compact, at the Barunga Festival in the Northern Territory, soon came to naught.

During the past forty years, the question of the place of Aborigines within the Australian nation has surfaced momentarily in public life, only to return to the troubled subterrain of the Australian consciousness. This consciousness includes an enormous goodwill on the part of the great majority of Australians for the country's Indigenous people. The problem is that the answer to the unresolved question is tied up in a long, fraught history of advocacy, polemic, debate and policy implementation, some of which has succeeded and much of which has failed. This murky territory is intellectually and politically polarised and confused. There is often furious disagreement over language rather than substance.

We will never solve 'the Aboriginal problem' until we answer this fundamental question: what is the place of Aboriginal and Torres Strait Islander people in the Australian nation – its past and its future?

2007

A NATIONAL SETTLEMENT

Mabo Oration

When I suggest that Indigenous Australians have the right to retain a link to their ancestral lands and their culture, and that this should be accomplished not just through their own efforts but also with the legislative and administrative support of government, then I do suggest that Indigenous Australians should be treated differently to non-indigenous Australians. Non-indigenous Australians have no recognised right to retain a link to a certain area or a certain culture. Whether or not a family of non-indigenous Australians continues to own, say, land that their ancestors have cultivated for five generations, or whether or not they continue to speak, say, German, are questions determined by market forces and personal choice.

Therefore, the answer to the question of what constitutes the national rights of the Indigenous Australian people is:

1. The right to take responsibility for achieving economic equality with other First World peoples; and
2. The right to retain a link with ancestral lands and culture, and to have this right guaranteed by agreements and legislation, and by the enduring goodwill of the non-indigenous majority.

There is one sense in which the concept of sovereignty has been discussed which in my view most aptly describes the special relationship between indigenous peoples and their homelands. It is in a passage in

Judge Amoun's ruling in the International Court of Justice's advisory opinion in the *Western Sahara* case, which was quoted by Justice Brennan in the *Mabo* case:

> Mr Bayona-Ba-Meya goes on to dismiss the materialistic concept of *terra nullius*, which led to this dismemberment of Africa following the Berlin Conference of 1885. Mr Bayona-Ba-Meya substitutes for this a spiritual notion: the ancestral tie between the land, or 'mother nature', and the man who was born therefrom, remains attached thereto, and must one day return thither to be united with his ancestors. This link is the basis of the ownership of the soil, or better, of sovereignty.

This passage captures the essence of the traditional relationship with land, not just in Australia, but in my view right across the world. It captures a universal concept of indigenous people's relationship with the soil of their ancestors – known to Japanese and Amazonian Indian cultures, I expect, as much as to the cultures of Australia's two indigenous peoples. This is the very meaning of 'ancestral homeland'.

Some Indigenous and non-indigenous leaders and commentators have proposed that reconciliation can be secured through what some have called a 'treaty' and others a 'national settlement', recognising Australia's Torres Strait Islanders and Aboriginal people as distinct peoples within the nation.

The Aboriginal Treaty Committee was established in 1979 and chaired by H.C. 'Nugget' Coombs. Together with Coombs, Stewart Harris and others, Judith Wright led a vigorous advocacy between 1979 and 1983. She published a book, *We Call for a Treaty*, in 1985. The work of the treaty committee precipitated an inquiry by the Senate Standing Committee on Legal and Constitutional Affairs, commissioned by the Fraser government and concluded after the election of the Hawke government in 1983. This inquiry looked into 'the feasibility of a compact or *makarrata* between the Commonwealth and Aboriginal people'. The committee's report, *Two Hundred Years Later*, recommended that there be an amendment to the Australian Constitution authorising the Commonwealth government to negotiate and settle an agreement between the Commonwealth and Indigenous peoples covering an unspecified range of issues.

Whatever consistency there may have been between this recommendation and the position of the Indigenous leaders of the National Aboriginal Conference, the work of the Aboriginal Treaty Committee was superseded by an alternative view of a treaty, which became the 'Treaty '88' campaign. One of this campaign's most energetic advocates was the late Wiradjuri intellectual Kevin Gilbert. Gilbert had published blistering criticisms of the concept of the *makarrata*, describing it in 1980, 'in Aboriginal way', as 'a dog deal, a Jacky Jacky deal, a pact with the devil on the devil's terms' and 'the kiss of Judas'.

The differences between those who pushed for a compact or *makarrata* and those who pushed for a treaty were profound, but perhaps not substantial. The first difference was whether what was being sought was going to be called a treaty or something else, such as a compact or *makarrata*. The second difference was whether the proposed agreement should be premised on the assumption of Aboriginal sovereignty, and whether it would be an agreement between two sovereign nations – the Australian nation and an Indigenous nation or nations.

One option – the *makarrata* – was not proposed as a treaty as defined by international law – that is, a treaty between two sovereign nation-states. The other approach, which became the approach of the Aboriginal Provisional Government in the 1980s, of which Michael Mansell was the most well-known proponent, was proposed as such a treaty. It was premised on the recognition that the Indigenous peoples of Australia were sovereign, and that their sovereignty had not been lawfully extinguished.

As to the substance of the terms of the agreement, the differences between those advocating a treaty and those advocating a *makarrata* were less obvious. Both approaches suggested that issues to do with land rights, jurisdictional rights and economic and political rights would form the subject of any agreement. So, putting aside the profound differences in nomenclature and in the international legal status of the parties to the agreement and the agreement itself, the substantial issues the proposed agreements would cover were similar.

Of course, notwithstanding Bob Hawke's commitment to a treaty (later called a compact) at the Barunga Festival in 1987, the Bicentenary deadline of 1988 was missed. The 1990s was the 'reconciliation' decade and talk of treaties, *makarratas* and compacts was replaced by talk of 'unfinished business', 'a document of reconciliation' and 'a national settlement'. The High Court's *Mabo* decision in 1992 gave hope that there would be substantive reconciliation. However, the new target, the centenary of Federation in 2001, came and went and this hope remained unfulfilled.

Now is not the time for me to say whether or not a treaty, *makarrata* or national settlement should be pursued and what purpose such an agreement might serve. Too much confusion surrounds these questions; little will be gained from supporting or rejecting the concept of a national agreement until we get much more clarity in the discussion. Confusion surrounds the following questions: the necessity and purpose of a settlement; the fundamental legal premise of a settlement; the nomenclature of a settlement; and the strategy for the achievement of a settlement. Let me make some brief comments about each of these.

The necessity and purpose of a settlement

Advocates have often assumed that the achievement of a treaty is a precondition of Indigenous social and economic recovery. I do not accept this. We must and we can act now to confront the problems afflicting our people. We cannot allow the uncertain goal of achieving a national agreement to leave us sitting on our hands. Secondly, I do not accept the assumption that the achievement of a legal or political settlement will automatically guarantee solutions to social and economic problems. Legal and political settlements can only be a part of any solution. The other part involves responsibility and hard work.

Much more rigorous thinking is needed about the case for a settlement. There is far too much scepticism – often justified – in the Australian community about what substantive gains will result from what is currently seen as a 'symbolic' gain. The case must be made for how and why Indigenous and non-indigenous Australians will gain from a national settlement.

The fundamental legal premise of a settlement

A national agreement would be a domestic legal agreement between the Indigenous peoples of Australia and the Commonwealth government on behalf of the Australian nation. Treaties in the United States, Canada and New Zealand have not had the character of international-law agreements between nation-states. This does not deny the fact that Indigenous peoples possessed sovereignty before colonisation, and it does not deny the fact that Indigenous peoples did not consent to colonisation and to the extinguishment of their original sovereignty. It also does not deny the possibility of sovereignty or jurisdiction in a domestic sense. It is an acceptance of the fact that talking about a treaty as an agreement between two sovereign nation-states is fantasy.

The nomenclature of a settlement

The implication that a treaty involves an agreement between sovereign nation-states is the reason for much of the resistance to the proposal. Only if it is clear that the proposed agreement is a domestic treaty will the term 'treaty' be widely accepted. The nomenclature represents a longstanding and as yet unresolved obstacle to the identification of common ground. For many opponents, the word 'treaty' represents a threat to the Australian nation. For many supporters, any word less than treaty is not good enough (ever since I saw the Alan Moir cartoon in the *Sydney Morning Herald* depicting an Aboriginal sitting in front of a mirror applying Bob Hawke's new 'compact', the word has not done a great deal for me either).

These opposing positions ignore three facts: firstly, that the word treaty has been used in its domestic meaning in North America and New Zealand; secondly, that most of the supporters of a treaty are in fact talking about a domestic agreement; and thirdly, that many of the opponents of a treaty would support a domestic agreement.

The strategy for the achievement of a settlement

This is where I believe proponents of a treaty have been the weakest: they have failed to articulate the necessary strategies to achieve their desired goal. Indeed, they have not even faced up to basic considerations.

Almost all of the proponents of a national agreement – including both the Aboriginal Treaty Committee and the Senate Standing Committee that reported on the *makarrata* – have concluded that a treaty would require an amendment to the Australian Constitution. During the 1990s, much of the discussion (facilitated by the Council for Aboriginal Reconciliation) about a 'document of reconciliation' was based on the hope that it would lead to a national agreement underpinned by constitutional amendment. Even the proposals put forward by Kevin Gilbert included amendment of the Constitution, including a Bill of Aboriginal Rights.

Well, the basic consideration in relation to any proposal to amend the Australian Constitution is this: you need a majority of voters in a majority of the states to support a referendum. That is, you need the support of 80 to 90 per cent of the Australian people. In order to have any chance of securing this, you will need bipartisan political support – and furthermore, in the case of an amendment concerning Indigenous peoples, it will have to be championed by the conservative political parties if it is to have any chance of succeeding.

It is as plain as day that unless a national agreement has the support of the most conservative (but decent) end of the Australian political spectrum – regional and rural Australia – and its political leaders, no form of national settlement stands any chance at all.

Conclusion

The political truism that only Nixon could go to China is pertinent here. Only a highly conservative leader, one who enjoys the confidence of the most conservative sections of the national community, will be able to lead the country to an appropriate resolution of these issues. It will take a prime minister in the mould of Tony Abbott to lead the Australian nation to settle the 'unfinished business' between settler Australians and the other people who are members of this nation: the Indigenous people.

2005

A TWO-WAY STREET

Democratic participation in the existing judicial, legislative and executive institutions of governance in Australia is the only means available to Indigenous Australians to achieve and exercise power. But do the existing mechanisms of democratic participation by such a small minority, who are unique in that they are Indigenous to the country, and whose socio-economic circumstances are so egregiously out of step with the rest of the country, work to ensure my people enjoy the same expectations of life as their fellow citizens?

No, they do not. Indigenous people are too small a minority to make government work for them. The breakdowns in communication between government and Indigenous communities are not caused only by shortcomings of government representatives and Indigenous leaders; there is a fundamental power imbalance that distorts even the best intentions.

When it comes to the judicial institutions, apart from making provision for Indigenous mechanisms of justice at the local level, it is not possible to see how there could be a more level playing field so far as the needs of Indigenous people are concerned. And when it comes to representation in legislatures, it is not possible to see how there could be a more level playing field in this arena, too.

Apart from the Northern Territory and the odd seat in other parliaments, the small numbers of Indigenous people can only minimally affect power through political representation in parliaments. When it comes to Indigenous dealings with the executive of government, again,

Indigenous people – as a result of our small numbers – are not in a position to make government work for us.

First, there will never be a sufficient number of Indigenous people working for the governments (even if the longstanding under-representation is addressed). Second, there are too few Indigenous leaders with the necessary expertise to deal with all the programs, policies and procedures of government that affect Indigenous people; there is a problem of sheer scale. This is not just a result of lack of education; it is also a function of the numbers. Even if we had a disproportionate number of qualified people, we do not and will not have enough people to work across the full range of institutions and issues that affect our people if the only means to do this are the existing mechanisms.

Third, the administrative arms of government work because there is always democratic demand from the mainstream. Government works for the mainstream because citizens are able to exercise electoral power; voters can force political leaders to ensure government delivers. Indigenous people do not have this leverage.

Fourth, the issues that are essential to Indigenous wellbeing are not all similar to those affecting the mainstream, who do not have the same socio-economic problems. Government is frequently incapable of properly addressing Indigenous issues, as it is used to servicing the needs of the mainstream.

Finally, the existence of an institutional bias against Indigenous people, sometimes referred to as institutional racism, also makes it hard for Indigenous people to get government to work for them.

There are three ways to think about how to address this lack of structural power on the part of a small minority within an otherwise functioning democracy that serves its mainstream well.

First, one could seek to increase representation and participation of Indigenous people in the institutions of power and in administration. This is the usual response and this aim should continue to be pursued. But even if aggressive affirmative action were adopted, the comparative weight of numbers means an increase in representation and participation would not fix the structural power deficit. Affirmative action is likely to be strongly resisted. Although proposals for special provisioning of parliamentary representation have been put on the agenda in Australia, the fight for such an outcome is likely to be far greater than the benefit of the outcome. Getting a small minority of political representatives into legislatures will not fix the nub of the problem.

Second, one could establish separate institutions of governance for the Indigenous community. The creation of the Aboriginal and Torres Strait Islander Commission and other national, regional and local institutions have been supported by federal and state governments from time to time for this purpose. Indigenous governance institutions are important; however, it is their interface with government that is the key question. How do these Indigenous institutions relate to the real sources of power in Australia, namely its governments? Is the relationship based on negotiation, and is there mutual accountability in the relationship?

It is one thing for governments to delegate to Indigenous institutions certain space for governance of their own affairs (as was done with ATSIC), but the crucial question remains: what is the nature of the interface between the Indigenous institution and government? This was particularly important in the case of ATSIC, because its jurisdiction did not cover the whole field of Indigenous affairs. The Commonwealth continued to be responsible for important components of Indigenous affairs (such as education, health and income support), and state and territory governments also held a jurisdiction unconnected to ATSIC.

ATSIC's purview was not comprehensive and in any case its relationship with the Commonwealth was in the nature of a client commission, subject to direction by a Commonwealth minister and accountable through various mechanisms to the federal government. This accountability was not mutual; it did not impose return obligations on the federal government, and no attempt was made to establish equality between ATSIC and the government. The point of ATSIC was not to establish an interface with government; rather, it established an Indigenous-affairs ghetto away from the main game.

Third, one could focus on the interface between Indigenous people and governments, state and federal, and construct mechanisms that ensured equality between them. Partnerships between grossly unequal partners are not real partnerships; rather, they are master–servant, boss–client relationships. If consultation and not negotiation is the principal official means of transaction between the parties, then there is not a true partnership. Rather, one party has the power to act unilaterally and the other is subject to that power.

There has never been a serious attempt to focus on the institutional interface between Indigenous people and governments in Australia. To construct an interface that creates greater parity and mutual accountability (and true shared responsibility) would require governments to agree to limitations on their existing powers and prerogatives and to make accountability a two-way street. It would also require governments to be bound not just by policy commitment but by law.

2007

BOOM AND DUST LIFESTYLE

Mammon led them on
Mammon, the least erected spirit that fell
From Heaven, for even in Heaven his looks and thoughts
Were always downward bent, admiring more
The riches of Heaven's pavement, trodden gold,
Than aught divine or holy else enjoyed
In vision beatific. By him first,
Men also, and by his suggestion taught,
Ransacked the centre, and with impious hands
Rifled the bowels of their mother earth
For treasures better hid. Soon had his crew
Opened into the hill a spacious wound
And digged out ribs of gold. Let none admire
That riches grow in hell; that soil may best
Deserve the precious bane.
                        —John Milton, *Paradise Lost*

Over the course of the Howard decade, each and every Australian has been reminded that the country's wealth is still very much dependent on its minerals. If we had come to believe since the economic reforms of the 1980s that our prosperity no longer rode the sheep's back, the extraordinary balance sheets presented by Treasurer Peter Costello at successive budget nights have driven home the fact that, make no mistake, we are China's quarry.

There is not an Australian who has not benefited from this astonishing boom. For shareholders watching their stocks it has been far from all ordinary; it has been a vision beatific. From the high wages caused by the insatiate demand for skilled tradespeople and professionals and the provision of services and infrastructure in support of the resource industries, to the welfare payments to Indigenous people living (and mostly dying) in the shadows of this efflorescence of development, mining revenues pay a large share of the bill. Not since paradise was lost has rifling the bowels of Mother Earth been more lucrative.

This boom was preceded by the contentious changes to land titles across the continent resulting from the *Mabo* decision and the passage of the *Native Title Act*. In theory Australia's Indigenous peoples should therefore have been prime beneficiaries of the minerals boom of the past decade.

They have not been.

Last Tuesday, the *Australian* reported research by Ciaran O'Faircheallaigh, a minerals economist at Griffith University. O'Faircheallaigh has analysed forty-five agreements negotiated in the past ten years, and he concludes that half of the Indigenous land-use agreements 'were either basket cases that should never have been entered into' or had delivered few cultural and monetary benefits to Aborigines. Many Aboriginal groups were no better off, or even worse off, than in the absence of any agreement with the companies concerned.

O'Faircheallaigh said this week: 'We found that a small number of the agreements, about a quarter, are delivering very substantial outcomes to Aboriginal people. However, at the other extreme, we found that about half of the agreements have little by way of substantial benefits. They're either doing very well in a minority of cases, or, in a majority of cases, they're not getting substantial benefits.'

There is no doubting that O'Faircheallaigh is right. While there are more or less honourable agreements, such as those made by Rio Tinto with Indigenous communities in the Kimberley (regarding the Argyle diamond mine) and on western Cape York Peninsula (regarding the Comalco bauxite mine), the great majority have involved mining companies, in American parlance, taking candies from Indigenous babies. The sheer shonkiness of many of the deals mirrors the process by which Indigenous peoples have had their traditional lands deforested by Asian logging companies throughout Melanesia, with very little to show for it at the end of the day. The only difference between Papua New Guinea and the Solomons, and, say, the Western Australian goldfields, the New South Wales Hunter Valley or central Queensland's coalfields is that the Australian deals take place within a clear legal framework.

O'Faircheallaigh cites cases of big projects, which will deliver billions in returns to shareholders and the coffers of governments, where companies have agreed to provide local Indigenous communities with $100,000 for the life of the project. If you want to see the starkest contrast of benefit and burden, no place is as egregious as the Pilbara, where two of the world's largest companies – BHP Billiton and Rio Tinto – are digging out ribs of gold, and the blackfellas live in the miserable shadows of the capacious wounds. Yes, Rio Tinto, under former chief executive Leon Davis, took steps to ameliorate this unjust situation, but the company has since tended to bank more on presentation and less on substance. BHP Billiton does not even try.

There is no doubt that Indigenous communities are not engaged in and enjoying the benefits of the mining boom in their backyards; there will, however, be disputes as to the reasons for this astounding situation. My views on the reasons for this failure are as follows.

First, the legal framework that applies to mining and native title severely disadvantages Indigenous landowners. Section 38 of the *Native Title Act* explicitly says that in arbitrating an application for mining, the National Native Title Tribunal 'must not determine a condition ... that has the effect that native title parties are to be entitled to payments worked out by reference to: (a) the amount of profits made; or (b) any income derived; or (c) any things produced.'

The law might as well say that the tribunal can only determine beads and mirrors as acceptable payment, because that is in effect what it has been doing. The mining lobby has been quiet on land rights for the past decade. Having secured an advantageous legal framework through the bitter conflicts over the *Native Title Act* in the '90s, they have learned that ideological opposition to land rights is unproductive for its members. As long as member companies are winning hands down through the so-called agreement-making process, they have had no interest in conflict. The federal government has continued to legislate to weaken the Indigenous position, both in terms of the procedural rights of landowners and the institutional support they receive from land councils. They are now proposing another round of amendments that further threaten the capacity of Indigenous people to deal with developers.

Second, we have yet to work out how best to deal with the clash between communal land title and the demands of modern development, of which mining is the most obvious kind. There is often conflict and contradiction.

Mining royalties pose fundamental challenges to Aboriginal culture, and can end up being indistinguishable from passive welfare in their effect. But this is not just a culturally specific problem; the problems posed by rentals and windfalls are well known to economic theory. Some of the most dysfunctional nations in Africa are those richest in resources, leaving beleaguered peoples to reflect that riches do indeed grow in hell and some treasures are better hid. I will leave for another day a discussion of the problems involved in reconciling resource development and Aboriginal culture, including communal land title.

Third, and related to this last point, is the 'fistful of dollars' mentality that predominates, both in the minds of Indigenous individuals and groups and in those of developers who exploit febrile expectations of short-term gain. The idea that royalty agreements should automatically result in cash distributions to individuals is a powerful animator of disputes and conflicts, within landowner groups and between them. Land councils seeking good outcomes invariably face an enormous cat-herding challenge: fragmentation and overlapping claims are the order of the day, with unscrupulous lawyers picking off individual cats like marauding dingoes.

Fourth, there is limited commercial and financial capacity within the land councils charged with supporting landowners. The typical lawyer acting for Indigenous groups is a master of pedantic, Geoff

Boycottish back-and-front-foot defence, but the drive or the pull or the hook is simply not in his repertoire. Meanwhile, the mining companies have Adam Gilchrist flashing the blade for them. There is no contest.

By way of solution, I put forward two thoughts.

First, I think that Indigenous people, governments and industry need to decide whether Indigenous groups should benefit from procedure or through guaranteed benefits. At the moment, the law provides for Indigenous people to seek benefits through negotiation and arbitration procedures. I would venture that the transaction costs involved in these procedures are more often than not higher than the benefits to Indigenous people. A statutory scheme for royalty payments could guarantee benefits to Indigenous landowners and free the negotiation and arbitration procedures from arguments about financial compensation. Those few groups who have done well or will potentially do well from arbitration procedures may oppose a guaranteed benefits scheme, but for the vast majority who are losing out, guaranteed benefits would be an enormous improvement on the present situation.

Second, we need to get away from the fistful of dollars paradigm to an integrated economic development paradigm. Resource development should be seen as an opportunity for economic development for Indigenous communities – and distributing cash to individuals is never the best way to achieve economic development. Education, employment and business development are the principal means by which Indigenous people can benefit from mining without incurring the real problems that resource rentals too often entail for people who hold communal title to land.

John Milton was a radical republican. I doubt that his glorious epic, and particularly the incendiary passage quoted at the beginning of this article, is proudly framed in the boardroom of the Minerals Council of Australia or in Rio's palatial headquarters at St James's Square in London. I am not an opponent of mining and in fact firmly believe that sustainable resource development is reconcilable with Indigenous social and cultural sustainability in remote Australia. Indeed, it is imperative that this reconciliation is achieved, because without the opportunity for economic development Indigenous people have no future in remote

Australia. Currently, however, the terms upon which mining takes place in Australia wreak more harm than benefit to Indigenous peoples, most of whom live in the dust of development.

If these issues seem too far removed from the average Australian in Sydney or Melbourne, or indeed Brisbane or Perth, then we should consider that we all benefit from mining: the billions of dollars of tax cuts enjoyed by Australia's middle and high income earners come in no small part from the ransacking, by the impious hands of Mammon's most primary industry, of the bowels of mother earth.

2007

KEVIN RUDD

Amigos para siempre. Friends for life. The theme song of the Barcelona Olympics was the ironic caption we had printed on the bottom of a commemorative photograph of myself and elders in front of a large ant-hill in the middle of Cape York Peninsula, together with the then Queensland premier Wayne Goss and his *wunderkind* head of the cabinet office, Kevin Rudd, in 1991. At the time, Rudd was leading the development of Queensland's land-rights legislation and, at Goss's invitation, I had taken time off from my law studies at the University of Sydney to join the taskforce. I was later to fall out with the Goss government over the miserable legislation that resulted.

Rudd was my first boss in my first official job. Notwithstanding the acrimony of our parting – which developed into a febrile conflict when Goss and Rudd attempted to sabotage Paul Keating's commitment to a principled outcome in the 1993 negotiations on the *Native Title Act* by conspiring with the states then ruled by the conservatives – it was not possible to work with Rudd without being impressed by him. I detested what I considered to be his mealy political trimming when dealing with issues that had been on Labor's policy platform during the long winter of National rule in Queensland. But even in the depths of my detestation, I have never been able to deny a grudging regard for Rudd. After all the expletives and bile would come: 'Yes, but this man is formidable.'

Rudd has the intellectual power of Keating, but he probably lacks the breadth of imagination that drove Keating's policy brain. He will need to find his muse. The federal Labor caucus would be mad not to elect Rudd as its leader at Monday's secret ballot. Beazley should be put out there in the long yard, as Slim Dusty used to sing, with those other frontbenchers who are to resign at the next election. It is trite but nevertheless true to say that Beazley's problem is that of the dynastic son: he has been waiting for the crown to be offered to him on a plate. People who don't come from royal lines have only their hunger and their grasping hands with which to seize power. The fact that Beazley had to tell Australia that he was 'hungry for the job' was very telling. When you have to tell people you're salivating, you're already behind. They should be able to see from your spittle that you're hungry.

Mark Latham was an outsider and he reminded us of this *ad nauseam*. But Rudd is also a true outsider; the difference is that he has never used this as a political credential. His chief credential for Labor leadership is that he knows power and has exercised it at the highest levels of government. He ran the government of Queensland for six years as the director-general of the cabinet office. In this sense, he has more experience and knowledge of the workings of government than most ministers accumulate in a lifetime. No other member of federal parliament is as qualified as Rudd in this respect.

Thanks to his diplomatic background, there are few harder and more inscrutable negotiators than Rudd. I recall witnessing a 33-year-old Rudd deal with industry and civic leaders and lobbyists with breathtaking verve and skill. His arrogance, however, was equal to his abilities. In meetings with mining-industry leaders, Rudd would hold court with his feet on his desk in front of his supplicants. Rudd is now forty-nine and much wiser, but he still gives the impression that he is mightily impressed with himself; he has done the hard yards and come a cropper often enough.

I don't fear his lack of ministerial experience; everybody who comes to the prime minister's job for the first time is inexperienced. In those areas where John Howard has been so comprehensively ascendant over Labor – security and economic management – Rudd is strong and not at all flaky. It is in relation to security issues that ordinary Australians have come to know him and be impressed by him. It remains to be seen whether he will keep pushing his recent polemical crusade for what I could call a more Christian capitalism, with its consequent risks to his economic-policy credibility. I think Queensland MP Craig Emerson has a much better feel for the interface between economic and social policy.

My reservations about Rudd concern his attitude to welfare reform and social policy. I fear he is mostly an unreconstructed defender of the traditional welfare state. This, I think, is a product of his experience. He and his family were assisted by the welfare state to rebuild their lives following the death of their father, so Rudd, correctly enough, will never repudiate the safety net. But my view is that welfare worked in the way it was intended to in relation to the Rudds. Passive welfare is a different problem, and Rudd must take seriously the problems of dependency and passivity that now sustain disadvantage, not just in Indigenous communities but in the Australian mainstream.

For Rudd to succeed on Monday and for Labor to a have a real chance next year, two things have to take place within the ALP. First, Rudd's frontbench colleagues must concede that he is now the first among equals. Rudd's fellow Queenslander and fellow Nambour State High School alumnus Wayne Swan and Western Australian Stephen Smith must jettison the alliances and prejudices born of the manoeu-vrings of their own aspirations. They must acknowledge the higher imperative. Swan, in particular, is key. He knows Rudd intimately and Monday's ballot will be a measure of his capacity to see things from the commanding heights rather than from the trenches of competitive brotherhood.

Second, the Australian Workers' Union supremo Bill Ludwig must end the fatwa against Craig Emerson. He is the most economically lit-erate member of the caucus and it is ridiculous that he sits on the back-bench. He must be brought into a senior economic portfolio, if not as shadow treasurer.

These are, of course, not the only things that need to change within the ALP. But they will be the bellwethers that determine whether the grand old party is serious about seizing government at the federal level next year.

2006

*

Paul Kelly and Dennis Shanahan reported on the front page of the *Australian* yesterday that Kevin Rudd will not be pursuing a constitutional referendum on reconciliation if he wins government. Such a referendum was the first pledge of the 2007 federal election campaign, made by Prime Minister John Howard at the Sydney Institute on 11 October, on the eve of the campaign.

That very evening, Rudd and the Opposition spokeswoman on Indigenous affairs and reconciliation, Jenny Macklin, issued a statement as follows:

> Federal Labor notes the Prime Minister's announcement tonight on constitutional recognition of indigenous Australians. Constitutional recognition of indigenous Australians has been long-held federal Labor policy, and this was affirmed at the ALP national conference in Sydney earlier this year. Obviously, we will need to examine the detail of Howard's proposal with particular regard to its legal and constitutional implications. Nevertheless, federal Labor offers bipartisan support to a commitment for constitutional recognition, regardless of the outcomes of the federal election. A referendum will succeed if it has strong public support, and bipartisan leadership and, in the spirit of the 1967 referendum, federal Labor offers this support.

Rudd's very first 'me-too' policy pledge of the campaign has now been thrown into the dustbin two days before the election. This is a disgraceful and heartless abandonment of a policy promise that has had bipartisan commitment for the past six weeks. I was pleased that such an ambitious commitment to reconciliation had secured both parties' support. Rudd has now reneged on that commitment. This shows a flagrant contempt for Indigenous policy.

There are those who might think that Rudd needs to secure the foundations for a second term in office by not championing unpopular issues such as those concerning Indigenous people. Some may hope that reconciliation will be the subject of a second- or third-term agenda under the ALP.

There are two problems that make this hope forlorn for those who desire a proper settlement of the Indigenous question. First, we will end up with the Bob Hawke scenario. Hawke came from a less conservative position than Rudd and had greater ambitions for Indigenous people – including a treaty – but at the end of four terms as prime minister all he had to show were tears of regret at not having done more. Are we supposed to wait another couple of terms before Rudd has the guts to deal with this issue? Second, we have a unique opportunity at this point in history, because Australia's most conservative political leader, John Winston Howard, has finally taken a step towards reconciliation. Now is the time for Australians interested in progress to capitalise on the opportunity to get this issue right for all time. When you've got conservative Australia in the cart, you need to act.

In Rudd and Macklin's joint statement, issued a few hours after Howard's reconciliation speech, they offered 'bipartisan support to a commitment for constitutional recognition, regardless of the outcomes of the federal election'. According to Kelly and Shanahan, Rudd said this week that he is 'unlikely to pursue Mr Howard's plan for a reconciliation preamble to the Constitution if he were elected' and that 'a referendum on Aboriginal reconciliation [and] a separate Aboriginal treaty … would not occur in the first term of a Rudd Labor government, if at all'.

This statement directly contradicts Rudd and Macklin's promise. It is not possible to argue that Labor retains a commitment to Indigenous constitutional recognition, and that Rudd has merely rejected the prime minister's time frame – a bill in parliament within 100 days and a referendum within eighteen months – as unrealistic. If you are not committed to pursue a policy in your first term, you are not committed at all. As Rudd pointed out when Shanahan asked whether we would see action from Labor on the republic during the second term of a Rudd government: 'You have to get elected to have a second term.'

What has transpired is surely a first for Australia: a party leader who is highly likely to become prime minister breaks his first election promise just before the polling booths open. It comes as no surprise that Indigenous Australians are the victims of this disrespect. I have had long experience with Rudd's political cynicism and opportunism when we argued bitterly over the Goss government's Aboriginal land legislation in 1991 and over Paul Keating's *Native Title Act* in 1993.

I regret that Rudd has not changed what I have long considered to be his innately contemptuous view of Indigenous people and Indigenous policy.

I am conscious that my criticism of Rudd on the eve of the election will result in an acrimonious relationship with an incoming Labor federal government, but I will not stand silent while an election contender reneges so flagrantly on a commitment he made on day one of the campaign. To me this issue is more important than Rudd's ambitions. For this betrayal, I dread a Rudd prime ministership.

2007

WHEN WORDS AREN'T ENOUGH

There is no one simple angle to take on this week's apology by Prime Minister Kevin Rudd to members of the stolen generations and their descendants and families on behalf of the parliament of Australia. There are different angles, some of which are at odds with each other. On the eve of its delivery I remain convulsed by these contradictions, but the majority of Australians – black and white, progressive and conservative, Labor and Coalition, young and old – believe that the apology is the right thing to do. Before I yield to this overwhelming view, I will discuss the various fraught angles from which this week's apology might be assessed.

Firstly, one can analyse the apology through the prism of cultural war. Let us first admit that the imperative to apologise is a product of Australia's culture wars of the past decade. The political and cultural Right's motivations for making Aboriginal history and policy the battleground for the culture wars predated the conservative ascendancy of the past eleven years. The Right's culture wars were themselves an accumulated reaction to the Left's own vociferous cultural crusades of the '60s and '70s. The Right launched a relentless blitz on an intellectually hapless Left, vulnerably bloated by the excesses of political correctness. The Right returned the contumely to which they had been subjected, with interest.

John Howard's refusal to apologise to the stolen generations was used by those who opposed his prime ministership as a moral and political bludgeon with which to beat him. Their chief motivation was not policy or spirit or moral philosophy; it was cultural war. The progressives wished for Howard either to humiliate himself by saying sorry or to show, by refusing to apologise, how much of a heartless bastard he was. To the end, Howard refused to prostrate himself in the way his cultural opponents demanded, and in retrospect they can say that he was out of step with the feeling of decent Australians. But this was not the case for four consecutive parliamentary terms.

Howard himself was equally engaged in cultural war. He understood that the excesses of leftist political correctness had yielded the Right a huge cultural advantage, which meant that his refusal to apologise was an electoral plus. As with so many of the other cultural battles of that decade, the progressive contempt for Howard in respect of Aboriginal history and policy only increased his standing with voters. I always think of this (somewhat unsavoury) image: the teflon with which Howard for so long was coated was made from the spit of his opponents. The more spit, the more teflon.

So let's not get too caught up with the 'this is an act of decency whose time has come' line. The imperative for the apology was a product of cultural war. Even if that was not what was originally intended, it immediately became a weapon in this war.

A second way to consider the apology is from a philosophical angle, and my argument here has been pre-empted by, of all people, Keith Windschuttle, writing in last weekend's *Australian*. Which is the more sincere of the two following positions? To say, 'We will not apologise to the stolen generations – and we won't pay compensation' or, 'We will apologise – but we won't pay compensation'?

It is not possible to say that there is no money with which to compensate those who have been wronged. If this issue is of such importance to the majority of Australians, then surely an appropriate fraction of the $30 billion tax cuts could be committed to compensation?

It is not possible to say that there are no legal grounds for compensation, because the Trevorrow case has established that the wrongs done against stolen-generations member Bruce Trevorrow gave rise to a legal entitlement to compensation. It may be argued that the liability falls upon the states rather than the Commonwealth, but if the Commonwealth is this week going to assume moral responsibility on behalf of the country, then why not assume the responsibility for redress?

It is not possible to say that those who are entitled to legal redress can chase their claims through the courts. What if this position were taken towards the asbestosis victims of James Hardie? Those who are likely to be entitled to similar claims as Bruce Treverrow are soon going to die. The greater number already have. Talk about Bernie Banton: there are thousands of Bernie Bantons involved here. How sincere is it to say sorry and then to leave them to the pain, cost, inconvenience and uncertainty of interminable court proceedings?

A third way is to look at the psychological angle. There is no doubt that the majority of political leaders and ordinary white Australians hope that the country will be able to, to use the prime minister's own words, 'move on'. There are two ways to interpret this hope. The first is ominous: that it represents a hope to dispose of the apology in as decent (and politically and financially costless) a way as possible, and to put the whole subject into the 'that box is ticked' category. The second is optimistic: that it represents a necessary starting-point for a genuinely hopeful era in Indigenous affairs.

But who will be able to 'move on' after this Wednesday's apology? The majority of white Australians will be able to move on (particularly with the warm inner glow that will come with having said sorry), but I doubt that Indigenous Australians will. Those people stolen from their families who feel entitled to compensation will never be able to move on. Indeed, too many of them will be condemned to harbour a sense of injustice for the rest of their lives. Far from moving on, these people – whose lives have been much consumed by this issue – will die with a sense of unresolved justice.

One of my misgivings about the apology has been my belief that nothing good will ever come from our people viewing ourselves as victims and making our case to the wider community on the basis of our status as victims. We have been – and the people who lost their families certainly were – victimised in history, but we must now stop the politics of victimhood. Because we lose power in ourselves when we adopt the psychology of victimhood. Whatever moral power we might gain over white Australia by presenting ourselves as victims, we lose in ourselves. Our people have survived two harsh centuries because of the agency of our ancestors – not because of the charity of the wider society. Indeed, our ancestors underwrote our survival as a people not-withstanding gross and widespread un-charity. My worry is that this apology will sanction a view of history that cements a detrimental psychology of victimhood, rather than a stronger psychology of defiance, survival and agency.

Then there is the historical angle on the apology. The 1997 report by the late Sir Ronald Wilson and Mick Dodson is not a rigorous history of the removal of Aboriginal children and the breaking up of families. It is a report advocating justice according to the authors' judgment. As a report advocating justice the report is fine. But it does not represent a defensible history – and, given its shortcomings as a work of history, the report was open to the conservative critique that followed. Indigenous activists' decision to adopt historian Peter Read's now famous nomenclature – the stolen generations – inspired *Quadrant* magazine's riposte: the rescued generations.

There is always danger when historical phenomena are characterised with such simple titles. Such titles are necessarily reductive generalisations and complexity is susceptible to being lost. The truth is that the removal of Aboriginal children and the breaking up of Aboriginal families is a history of complexity and great variety. People were stolen – people were rescued; people were brought in chains – people were brought by their parents; mixed-blood children were in danger from their tribal step-fathers – others were loved and treated as their own; people were in danger from whites – and people were protected by whites. The motivations and actions of those whites involved in this history – governments and missions – ranged from cruel to caring, malign to loving, well-intentioned to evil.

The nineteen-year-old Bavarian missionary who came to the year-old Lutheran mission at Cape Bedford in Cape York Peninsula in 1887, and who would spend more than fifty years of his life underwriting the future of the Guugu Yimithirr people, cannot but be a hero to me and to my people. We owe an unrepayable debt to Georg Heinrich Schwarz and to the white people who supported my grandparents and countless others to rebuild their lives after they arrived at the mission as young children in 1910. My grandfather Ngulunhthul came in from the local bush to the Aboriginal reserve that was created to facilitate the mission. My great-grandfather Arrimi would remain in the bush in the Cooktown district, constantly evading police attempts to incarcerate him at Palm Island and remaining in contact with his son, Ngulunhthul, and later his grandson, my father. My grandmother was torn away from her family near Chillagoe, to the west of Cairns, and she would lose her own language and culture in favour of the local Guugu Yimithirr language and culture of her new home. Indeed, it was the creation of reserves and the establishment of missions that enabled Aboriginal cultures and languages to survive throughout Cape York Peninsula. Today, those two young children who met at the mission have scores of descendants who owe their existence to their determination to survive in the teeth of hardship and loss. Schwarz embodied all of the strengths, weaknesses and contradictions that one would expect of a man who placed himself in the crucible of history. Would that we were judged by history in the way we might be tempted to judge Schwarz – we are not a bootlace on the courage and achievement of such people.

The past is a complex place, and no amount of what Robert Hughes called 'anachronistic moralising' can assist us in its appreciation or understanding. My own view is that Aboriginal people's lives were stolen by history. It wasn't just that children were stolen in a literal sense; it was that the prospects of Aboriginal people being able to pursue any form of sustainable and decent life were stolen from them. Yes, there was grog, there was prostitution, there was untold misery in Aboriginal camps – but if an Aboriginal mother brought her child to the gates of the mission for protection, nevertheless were not these lives stolen from them? And even where Aboriginal people managed to carve out some form of life for themselves in the midst of an unforgiving and unrelenting white society, they were still vulnerable to the arbitrary removal powers of the state.

This history cannot be understood solely by considering the specific policy intentions of the governments and the missions. It must be understood with reference to the severe choices that were available to Aboriginal people in the wake of European occupation and Indigenous dispossession. The life choices available to the Guugu Yimithirr on the frontiers of Cooktown in the 1880s had nearly collapsed and were diminishing fast. Without the Cape Bedford mission, the Guugu Yim-ithirr had no good survival options. Yes, like missions throughout colonial history, the Cape Bedford mission both provided a haven from the hell of life on the Australian frontier and facilitated the process of colonisation. It was Schwarz's possible role in bringing about the end of the traditional life at Barrow Point, north of Cape Bedford, through his influence on government policy, which troubled my late old friend, Urwunhthin Roger Hart – last native speaker of the Barrow Point language – to his dying day. On many counts, this old man had reasons to respect and thank Schwarz, but history is never simple.

There is a political angle to this week's apology. For the Rudd government the apology will work politically, provided that there is no issue of compensation. If compensation had been part of the deal, the electoral support for the gesture this week would have unravelled. For this reason there is no conceivable way that Rudd will revisit the issue of compensation, no matter what hopes Indigenous leaders might have for this. The tide of support in the Australian community has no doubt influenced the federal Coalition to change its opposition to the apology, but the fact that this bipartisan support has been secured by Rudd makes it even more certain that the issue of compensation will never be revisited.

Which brings me to the main political point about the strategy of Aboriginal leaders. Mick Dodson said recently, 'I think this is monumental. It is something people have waited for, for a very long time … It's hugely important to us as a nation and to members of the stolen generations.' He then went on to say that the case for compensation would be pursued in the future. Lowitja O'Donoghue said last December that an apology without a compensation fund 'won't settle anything'. But it would appear that she also is prepared to take the apology now and defer compensation for a later campaign. The National Aboriginal Alliance spokesman, Les Malezer, said last weekend that the apology was 'not enough'. But even the Alliance is prepared to defer compensation to a later campaign: 'Once the apology has been issued, and providing the apology is not qualified, we will then go on to ask the government to now consider how it will pay compensation.'

From a strategic angle, these Indigenous leaders are fooling themselves or their constituents. If they were serious about compensation, then the time to address it is at the same time as the apology. It was never going to be easy to insist on the link between the apology and compensation, but Michael Mansell calling for the creation of a billion-dollar fund is exactly what one must not do if one were serious about securing compensation. Blackfellas will get the words; the whitefellas will keep the money. And by Thursday the stolen generations and their apology will be over as a political issue.

Then there is the emotional angle. Empathy is a necessary part of the teaching of history. There is a more advanced discussion in Canada about what teachers of history call 'historical empathy'. However, this discussion has drawn an important distinction between 'historical empathy', which is said to be legitimate history, and 'emotional empathy', which can be shallow and simplistic. Hollywood films, for example, present history through emotional empathy.

It is not possible to discuss fully here the problems with empathy in history, but it is one of the most basic mistakes to think that we can understand past epochs and events simply by imagining ourselves in the past. Without first having a thorough understanding of the political economy of that past, any act of imagination based on contemporary feelings, values and moral convictions will be teleologically silly and misleading. This is the problem that arises when history as a discipline meets history as popular culture.

The case for the apology put by Indigenous leader and businessman John Moriarty, and this last weekend by Cathy Freeman, is compelling to me. They urge me to accept that this week's apology is of value, notwithstanding the strong arguments to the contrary which I have traversed in this article.

The final angle is spiritual, and I will tell of my own view. There is a remote place on the lands of the Guugu Yimithirr of striking magnificence, which I visit about a half dozen times a year. To the south of this place, from the top of a massive parabolic dune which constantly changes shape with the winds, you can see south across the distant bay the two mountains of Cape Bedford, the place to which Missionary Schwarz dedicated his life's work. Down near the water is an ancient

Aboriginal campsite with evidence of Aboriginal occupation going back hundreds, possibly thousands, of years. The fresh water, fresh breezes, clean sand, shelter from insects and a clear view of any approaching strangers made this place a good place to camp. People could hunt and fish along the river and in the surrounding swamps and rainforests during the day and return to this camp in the afternoon.

The last time camps like this were occupied by Aboriginal people who still lived traditional lives outside of the mission was in the years leading up to the Second World War. This place in particular was a good place to hide from the police. It was not just children who were liable to be removed, but adults and old people were also removed to Palm Island. My constant thought when I return to this place is the history of this camp, when children laughed and played in the sand dunes and in the lake. Children would have loved this camp especially. I can see and hear them and I know why this camp was favoured since ancient times.

But then I think of the camps when they were occupied only by the last of the old people living in the bush. People like my great-grandfather Arrimi. Depleted of their children and their young people, these camps must have become increasingly sad and lonely. The old people who escaped being removed to Palm Island ended their days in loneliness.

Every time I visit this place I have cause to think about these old people. And the mission. And their children, gone.

2008

PUBLICATION DETAILS

Many of the pieces reprinted here have been edited or abridged, in particular when they summarise or repeat material found elsewhere in the volume. Titles have often been changed, and in all but one case footnotes or sources have been omitted.

The Mission

'Forebears' was delivered to the Australian Reconciliation Conference, organised by the Council for Aboriginal Reconciliation and held in Melbourne in May 1997.

'Family' was delivered to the Queen's Trust Indigenous Future Leaders Program, Brisbane, April 2000.

'Old Man Urwunhthin' was first published as the foreword to *Old Man Fog and the Last Aborigines of Barrow Point* by John B. Haviland and Roger Hart (Bathurst, Crawford House Publishing, 1998).

'Peoples of the North: Anthropology and Tradition' was written with Mervyn Gibson, who delivered it to the Australia and New Zealand Association for the Advancement of Science Conference, Townsville, August 1987.

Fighting Old Enemies

'*Mabo*: Towards Respecting Equality and Difference', a 1993 Boyer Lecture, was first published in *Voices from the Land* (Sydney, ABC Books, 1993).

'The Concept of Native Title' was first published in *Our Land Is Our Life: Land Rights, Past Present and Future*, edited by Galarrwuy Yunupingu (St Lucia, University of Queensland Press, 1996).

'After *Mabo*', the Lionel Murphy Memorial Lecture, was delivered in Sydney in December 1994.

'For All of Us (But Not For Them): *Mabo* and the 1996 Federal Election' was delivered to the Sydney Institute in February 1996.

'Shifting Ground Indeed' was delivered to the ACT Council of Social Services Conference, Canberra, April 1997.

'The *Wik* Decision and Howard's Ten-Point Plan': These three pieces appeared in the *Courier Mail* on 29 March, 12 April and 9 September 1997.

'The Coalition Government, *Mabo* and *Wik*' was delivered to a function organised by the Australian Jewish Democratic Society, Melbourne, September 1997.

'Talking to the Right' was delivered to the Castan Centre for Human Rights Law, Monash University, Melbourne, June 2004.

'Land Is Susceptible of Ownership' was delivered to the High Court Centenary Conference, Canberra, October 2003.

'A Mighty Moral Victory' was first published in the *Weekend Australian*, 23–24 September 2006.

Challenging Old Friends

'Hope Vale Lost' was first published in the *Weekend Australian*, 17–18 February 2006.

'Our Right To Take Responsibility' is an edited extract from a book first published by Noel Pearson & Associates in 2000.

'On the Human Right to Misery, Mass Incarceration and Early Death', the Charles Perkins Memorial Oration, is an edited extract from a speech delivered in Sydney in October 2001 and published in *Quadrant* and *Arena* in December 2001.

'The Light on the Hill', the Ben Chifley Memorial Lecture, was delivered in Bathurst in August 2000.

'Addiction Epidemics', the Australian Medical Association Oration, was delivered at the Australian Medical Association National Conference in May 2004.

'After Keating' was delivered at the launch of Don Watson's memoir *Recollections of a Bleeding Heart: A Portrait of Paul Keating PM* in Sydney in May 2002.

'Land Rights and Progressive Wrongs' was first published in *Griffith Review 2: Dreams of Land*, ABC Books, Summer 2003/2004.

The Quest for a Radical Centre

'White Guilt, Victimhood and the Quest for a Radical Centre' was first published in *Griffith Review 16: Unintended Consequences*, ABC Books, Winter 2007.

'Barack Obama' was first published in the *Monthly*, May 2008.

'The Cape York Agenda' was delivered to the National Press Club, Canberra, in November 2008.

'The Welfare Pedestal': These three pieces were first published in the *Australian* on 17 May 2005 and in the *Weekend Australian* on 10–11 February 2007 and 15–16 December 2007.

'Orbits': These three pieces were first published in the *Weekend Australian* on 28–29 October 2006 and 5–6 January 2008, and in the *Australian* on 5 November 2004.

'The Intervention': These two pieces were first published in the *Weekend Australian* on 23–24 June and 7–8 July 2007.

'Jobs and Homes': The first of these pieces was first published in the *Weekend Australian* on 3 March 2007. The second was delivered in Hope Vale on 12 May 2007. The third was first published in the *Weekend Australian* on 25–26 October 2008.

Our Place in the Nation

'Peoplehood', the Judith Wright Memorial Lecture, was delivered in Sydney in September 2004.

'Layered Identities and Peace' was delivered at the Brisbane Festival in July 2006.

'A Peculiar Path That Leads Astray' was first published in the *Weekend Australian*, 21–22 October 2006.

'Native Tongues Imperilled' was first published in the *Weekend Australian*, 10–11 March 2007.

'Over 200 Years without a Place' was first published in the *Weekend Australian*, 25–26 August 2007.

'A National Settlement', the Mabo Oration, was delivered in Brisbane in June 2005.'

'A Two-Way Street' was first published in the *Weekend Australian*, 16–17 June 2007.

'Boom and Dust Lifestyle' was first published in the *Weekend Australian*, 3–4 February 2007.

'Kevin Rudd': These two pieces were first published in the *Weekend Australian* on 2–3 December 2006 and 24–25 November 2007.

'When Words Aren't Enough' was first published in the *Australian* on 13 February 2008.

INDEX